CONTRIBUTORS TO THE QUARTERLY REVIEW:
A HISTORY, 1809–25

The History of the Book

Series Editor: *Ann R. Hawkins*

Titles in this Series

Conservatism and the Quarterly Review: A Critical Analysis
Jonathan Cutmore (ed.)

Forthcoming Titles

Wilkie Collins's American Tour, 1873–1874
Susan R Hanes

William Blake and the Art of Engraving
Mei-Ying Sung

CONTRIBUTORS TO THE QUARTERLY REVIEW: A HISTORY, 1809–25

BY
Jonathan Cutmore

Routledge
Taylor & Francis Group
LONDON AND NEW YORK

First published 2008 by Pickering & Chatto (Publishers) Limited

Published 2016 by Routledge
2 Park Square, Milton Park, Abingdon, Oxfordshire OX14 4RN
711 Third Avenue, New York, NY 10017, USA

First issued in paperback 2015

Routledge is an imprint of the Taylor & Francis Group, an informa business

BRITISH LIBRARY CATALOGUING IN PUBLICATION DATA
Cutmore, Jonathan
Contributors to The Quarterly Review : a history, 1809–1825. – (The history of the book)
1. Quarterly review 2. English periodicals – History – 19th century 3. Romanticism – Great Britain 4. Politics and literature – Great Britain – History – 19th century
I. Title
052'.09034

ISBN-13: 978-1-138-66367-1 (pbk)
ISBN-13: 978-1-85196-952-4 (hbk)

Typeset by Pickering & Chatto (Publishers) Limited

CONTENTS

ACKNOWLEDGEMENTS

Some years ago I wrote that the John Murray Archive is 'a national treasure worth whatever many millions of pounds it will take to keep it intact and in the United Kingdom'. To the great convenience of future researchers into the history of the *Quarterly Review*, that archive is now at the National Library of Scotland alongside the Sir Walter Scott papers. The move has had one unfortunate consequence, however: no longer will students of John Murray's flagship journal enjoy the giddy pleasure of consulting William Gifford manuscripts in the first floor drawing room of 50 Albemarle Street. Lamentably, I am therefore one of the last students to express my gratitude to Virginia Murray, John R. Murray, and the late 'Jock' Murray for kindly welcoming me over the course of many visits.

Would that I could list all of the persons and institutions whose efforts are reflected in this book. Archives and libraries gave me access and, where applicable, generously permitted me to quote from material; these institutions are cited in the key to abbreviations, in footnotes, and in the bibliography. I especially wish to acknowledge with gratitude the assistance of Dr Christopher Stray. I also happily thank David McClay and Rachel Thomas, John Murray Archive Curator and Assistant Curator at the National Library of Scotland, and, once again, Dr Iain Brown, Principal Manuscripts Curator at the NLS. I must state that I alone am responsible for errors of fact or format.

I dedicate this book to my wife, Sylvia Jones Cutmore, who at an early stage provided valuable advice on the history and who, as I stated in *Conservatism and the Quarterly Review*, over the course of many years has given so much of her time and treasure to 'the books'.

JC
June 2007

LIST OF ABBREVIATIONS

Article #	*QR* article serial number assigned in Appendix A
Barrow	J. Barrow, *An Auto-biographical Memoir of Sir John Barrow* (London, 1847)
BC	*British Critic* (London)
Beinecke	Beinecke Rare Book and Manuscript Library, Yale University Library, James and Marie-Louise Osborn Collection
BL Add. MSS	British Library, Additional Manuscripts
Bodl. Lib.	Bodleian Library, Oxford, Western Manuscripts
Cambridge Lib. vols	Bound vols of Croker's *QR* articles presented to him by John Murray, now at the Cambridge University Library (shelf-mark Lib.6.81.30)
Clements Lib. lists	Croker's holograph lists of his *QR* articles preserved at the Clements Library, University of Michigan, Ann Arbor
Courier	*Courier* newspaper (London)
Derbyshire	Derbyshire Record Office, Wilmot Horton Collection
Devon	Devon Public Record Office
ER	*Edinburgh Review* (Edinburgh)
ER #	*Edinburgh Review* article serial number, derived from the *Wellesley Index* (see *WI* below)
GM	*Gentleman's Magazine* (London)
Houghton	Houghton Library, Harvard University
Iowa	University of Iowa Libraries, Special Collections, Leigh Hunt, Series 2, Murray-Croker
JM Archive	John Murray Archive, London (now at the National Library of Scotland, Edinburgh)

JM II's office copy	John Murray II's notes in his office copies of the *Quarterly Review*
JM III's Register	Notes taken by John Murray III on *Quarterly Review* author identifications
JM MS	John Murray Archive manuscript
Leeds	West Yorkshire Archive Service, Leeds District Archives, Sheepscar, Earl and Lady Harewood deposit
Liverpool	Liverpool City Libraries, Hornby Library, Autograph Letter Collection
Millgate	Millgate Union Catalogue of Walter Scott Correspondence: <www.nls.uk>
Morgan	The Pierpont Morgan Library, New York, Literary and Historical Manuscripts
M. Ch.	*Morning Chronicle* newspaper (London)
NL	*New Letters of Robert Southey*, ed. K. Curry, 2 vols (New York: Columbia University Press, 1965)
NLS	National Library of Scotland, Sir Walter Scott Collection and John Murray Archive
NLW	Llyfrgell Genedlaethol Cymru / The National Library of Wales
No.	*Quarterly Review* issue number
Northumberland	Northumberland Record Office, Society of Antiquaries of Newcastle upon Tyne deposit
ODNB	*Oxford Dictionary of National Biography*: <www.oxforddnb.com>
OED	*The Oxford English Dictionary*: <http://dictionary.oed.com>
Perkins	Perkins Library, Duke University, Rare Book, Manuscript, and Special Collections Library
p/mark	postmark
PRO	Public Record Office, Kew, London (now the National Archives)
QR	*Quarterly Review* (London)
QR Archive	J. Cutmore (ed.), *The Quarterly Review Archive*: <www.rc.umd.edu>

QR Letters	The present author's unpublished edition of *QR*-related letters
SL	*The Letters of Sir Walter Scott*, ed. H. Grierson, 12 vols (London: Constable, 1932–7)
Smiles, *Memoir*	S. Smiles, *A Publisher and His Friends: Memoir and Correspondence of the Late John Murray*, 2nd edn, 2 vols (London: John Murray, 1891)
Thorne	R. G. Thorne (ed.), *The History of the House of Commons 1790–1820 (The History of Parliament)*, 5 vols (London, 1986)
Trinity	Monk-Sanford Papers, Trinity College Library, Cambridge University
Wellcome	The Wellcome Library, The Wellcome Trust, London, Western Manuscripts
Westminster	Westminster School Library, Westminster School, London
WI	W. E. Houghton (ed.), *The Wellesley Index to Victorian Periodicals 1824–1900*, 5 vols (Toronto: University of Toronto Press, 1966–87)
w/mark	watermark
Young's list	Thomas Young's definitive MS. list of his *QR* articles transcribed in [Hudson Gurney], *Memoir of the Life of Thomas Young, M.D., F.R.S.* (London: John and Arthur Arch, 1831), pp. 56–60

LIST OF TABLES

For Sylvia

INTRODUCTION

In 1809, at the time of the first appearance of the *Quarterly Review*, each British political-literary journal was as a bell, some mighty, some minor, ringing out from the particular edifice to which it belonged – the church party, the university clique, the parliamentary interest. Supported as the *Quarterly Review* was by a set of liberal-conservative politicians and literary men, every article in it was as the tap of a bell sounding out to all who heard it the unmistakeable chords of the Canningite faction and its sympathizers.[1] Whether finely or harshly struck depended upon the talent and intention of its writer, the hammer muted or the sound amplified by editor or publisher, in accordance with their temper or purpose.

Each reader of political-literary periodicals in the period of coverage was as acutely tuned to his or her prejudices as each reader of the present volume is today and could pick out from the intellectual cacophony nuances of ideological colour. At this distant point in time, because we lack the detail of experience and received impressions that constituted John Murray's and William Gifford's mental landscape, we hear only faint echoes of what were once clear tones and can therefore pick out only the grosser sounds of party propaganda. The historian's task, however, is to detect shades of pitch finer than the often puerile designations of 'right' and 'left', 'progressive' and 'reactionary', a task that is made easier when the source is amplified by voluminous and various evidence. A purpose of this volume, then, is to aid historians in interpreting the *Quarterly*'s ideological colour by presenting fresh evidentiary detail.

The student of early periodicals who turns his or her attention to the *Quarterly Review* is richly rewarded by the fortunate preservation of thousands of letters and other documents. The *Quarterly* is the paper equivalent of a finely grained stratigraphic horizon; by it, the literary archaeologist can more surely interpret the past. As Donald Reiman pointed out some years ago, the student of the *Quarterly Review*, however, is rewarded by too much detail.[2] A reason why after the passage of almost two hundred years the history of this important journal had not yet been written was because there was too much information, unpublished and otherwise, to be tackled by any researcher with an eye on the health of his or her academic career. Besides locating and digesting hundreds, indeed thousands, of unpublished letters scattered across dozens of repositories around the world, the scholar who wished to get close to the material would have to become familiar with yards of *Quarterly Review* volumes, over 15,000 pages published under the editorship of William Gifford alone. As the journal's articles were published unsigned, a necessary first step would be the application of bibliographical rigour to the identification of the *Quarterly*'s authors. From there it would be necessary to trace the history of each writer's association with the journal, in most cases largely uninvestigated. With this preliminary work out of the way, the next step would be interpretation, then the writing of history itself, and then, lastly, the sharing of materials and opinions with a scholarly community. The reader who has followed me thus far will recognize that the present volume is the record of the process of historical investigation and interpretation just described. This book makes available to scholarship some of the primary materials I have collected over the years and expresses my views on the origins and early development of a significant historical artefact, the *Quarterly Review*.

A Note on Appendix A

In the early nineteenth century it was customary for articles in literary-political journals to be published unsigned. Preliminary to writing a history of the *Quarterly Review*, it was therefore necessary to uncover authors' hidden identities. Discovering who wrote for the *Quarterly* has involved four major efforts. In the mid-nineteenth century, John Murray III, researching his company's archives in preparation for Samuel Smiles's *Memoir*, recorded author attributions in a bound manuscript Walter Graham dubbed the 'Register'. Hill Shine and Helen Chadwick Shine in the late 1940s used the 'Register' as the basis for *The Quarterly Review under Gifford: Identification of Contributors 1809–1824*. In extending coverage of the *Quarterly* into Coleridge's and Lockhart's years, and beyond, the editors of *The Wellesley Index to Victorian Periodicals* Volume 1 (1966) also depended largely on Murray's 'Register'. Unfortunately, John Murray III did not, for the most part, document his author attributions. While the Shines made a start on compensating for Murray's lack of system, their results were uneven. The Shines' enduring contribution is their digest of secondary source references. I repeat several of their citations to works published before 1949.

Appendix A is a permanent record of my effort, begun some fifteen years ago, to employ scholarly rigour in the identification of writers for the *Quarterly Review* under Gifford and Coleridge. It is a revised edition of results first published in a series of articles in *Victorian Periodicals Review* and in the *QR Index* section of the *Quarterly Review Archive*, a 'Scholarly Resource' on the University of Maryland's *Romantic Circles* (www.rc.umd.edu).[3] The material corrects a number of author attributions, expands coverage to include articles published under Coleridge, and is presented in what I hope is a convenient and useful format.

Identifying anonymous authors is an analytical exercise fraught with pitfalls. Only a rigorous and methodical procedure can ensure reliable results. On the question of assigning authorship, I hold views similar to those of P. N. Furbank and W. R. Owens, Defoe scholars. Furbank and Owens state that 'there is something unsatisfactory in works being attributed to an author ... on internal evidence alone. It is not till there is some scrap of external evidence present that internal evidence comes into its own'.[4] The editors of the *Wellesley Index to Victorian Periodicals* thought so, too, until they discovered that stylistic or internal evidence, when used by knowledgeable investigators, can yield excellent results. Still, in the absence of external evidence, regardless of how certain the individual scholar may be that he or she recognizes the mark of an author in a work, others have a right to be less than certain. Consequently, I agree with Furbank and Owens that, with rare exceptions, attributions based on internal evidence can at best be considered 'probable'. In the early *Quarterly* the exception, to my mind, is Sir John Barrow, who by design left clear signs of his authorship.

Regarding format, for each number (issue) of the *Quarterly Review* published between the years 1809 and 1825, the following information is supplied:

- Volume, issue number, and title page date.
- Publication date as indicated on the title page.
- The number's real publication date.[5]
- The article's serial number.[6]
- The article number within the issue.
- The last name of the author under review. Multiple authors are indicated.
- The short title of the book under review. Multiple volumes are indicated.
- The article's inclusive page numbers.
- The article's author, his collaborators, sub-editors, and suppliers of information. Where the attribution is less than certain, I have indicated if it is 'probable' or merely 'possible', depending upon the strength of the evidence.
- Evidence of authorship. Keys to abbreviations employed in the evidence section appear at the head of the appendix and at the front of this book.

1 ORIGINS

The *Quarterly Review* was launched, on the first day of March 1809, under the imprint of the young London publisher John Murray by a consortium of powerful conservative politicians and literary men, George Canning and Walter Scott foremost among them.[1] Their avowed purpose in setting up a new periodical was to combat the 'radically bad principles' of Archibald Constable's flagship journal, the *Edinburgh Review*.[2] Repelled though they were by the *Edinburgh*'s politics, they were at the same time attracted by its wit, its verve, and, not least, by its success with the public. In response, they created a contending journal similar to its northern rival in outward appearances but opposed to the *Edinburgh* in its critical, religious, and above all its political principles.[3] With conservatives' objections to the 'Northern blast'[4] involved in the origins of the *Quarterly Review*, it is therefore to the *Edinburgh* that we briefly turn.

The *Quarterly*'s doppelganger and nemesis was started in October 1802 by three young Edinburgh University graduates, Sydney Smith, Francis Jeffrey, and Francis Horner. As it was first constituted, the *Edinburgh Review* was not a Whig party journal. Instead, it reflected philosophic Whiggism: it was egalitarian, materialist, and anti-dogmatic.[5] By 1808 it had as many as 8,000 subscribers, in that day a substantial number for a weighty political-literary journal. The *Edinburgh*'s influence extended beyond these few thousand readers, however; to judge from contemporary correspondence, the nation's elites habitually took account of its opinions.

A reason for the *Edinburgh*'s extensive reputation and reach was its innovative approach to book criticism. Reviewing before the *Edinburgh* was conducted in journals that contained numerous brief articles top-heavy with quotations.[6] In contrast, the *Edinburgh*'s writers used books as launching pads for lengthy opinionated dissertations. The editor Francis Jeffrey's reviews in particular were regarded as 'witty, saucy, and eloquent' and under his direction the periodical was generally acknowledged to be 'superior in genius and vivacity'.[7] Even conservatives admired the *Edinburgh* reviewers' 'unquestionable talent' and considered the journal 'essential to the library of a literary man'.[8]

Some readers, though, found the *Edinburgh*'s long articles 'egotistical'. Criticism also arose because Jeffrey settled into a standard approach to reviewing – 'hard words and hanging' – that was, if sometimes playful, often harshly dismissive. Yet the journal's impact was so great that contemporaries struggled to understand its attraction and the motive behind Jeffrey's method.[9] Typical of many commentators, Robert Southey's friend the civil servant Grosvenor Bedford recognized scientific rigour and disinterestedness in the *Edinburgh*'s criticism, but also professional preening: 'The Scotchmen', he wrote, 'are like those philosophical anatomists who care not whether the dog they cut up be dead or alive, so they cut deep enough and flourish their instruments with the air of a flugelman'.[10] Applying eighteenth-century standards of critical decorum, Bedford thought some of the *Edinburgh*'s articles 'most unworthy of literature, and derogatory to the character of a scholar and a gentleman'.[11] In December 1807, Southey, the *Quarterly*'s future 'sheet anchor', declined Jeffrey's invitation to become an *Edinburgh* reviewer because, reflecting a common complaint, he saw corruption of character in the *Edinburgh*'s approach to criticism. He wanted no part in a journal that could wound a man 'in his feelings and injure him in his fame and fortune'. 'Its morals and its politics', he later declared in his usual blunt manner, 'are equally base – its principles of taste, absolutely below contempt'.[12]

If the *Edinburgh* gave offence with some of its literary reviews, many of its readers were scandalized by the journal's anti-religious tone. Jeffrey's reviews of the evangelical poets Cowper and Montgomery especially caused wide-spread consternation among subscribers. Between 1802 and 1808, religious readers were also angered by a series of articles Sydney Smith contributed on Methodism and on Christian foreign missions, by a review of the sermons of the leader of the Scottish evangelical party, Sir Henry Moncreiff, by an article on Hoyle's poem 'Exodus', by Sir William Drummond's review of the evangelical matriarch Hannah More's *Hints to a Princess*, and by Smith's sarcastic article on a bill before Parliament to increase the salaries of Church of England curates.[13]

Jeffrey's slashing criticism and the *Edinburgh Review*'s materialist ethos, however, did not alone inspire the creation of a rival that might 'exhibit the Ability without the Acrimony of the Northern Lights',[14] for it was the appearance in the *Edinburgh* of proto-radical sentiments on foreign and domestic policy that ultimately led 'many ingenious men' to support the creation of a journal that might counter its 'dangerous tendency'.[15] Jeffrey and his chief political writer, Henry Brougham, published reviews that hinted at alternative constitutional arrangements, they trenchantly criticized the Continental war effort in a period when British policy was going awry, and they impudently celebrated the 1808 Spanish insurrection against French occupation as a populist uprising of the 'lower orders ... a warning to all oligarchies'.

Three political articles in the *Edinburgh* are way points in the formation of the *Quarterly Review*. Jeffrey's July 1807 review of Cobbett's *Political Register* was the first article in the *Edinburgh* to contain political sentiments liberal enough to raise the ire even of the Whig denizens of Holland House.[16] In the *Edinburgh's* July 1808 number, in a review of Whitbread's anti-war pamphlet *Letter on Spain*, Brougham challenged the British government's optimism that the Spaniards could succeed in their rebellion.[17] Most offensive, though, was Brougham's October 1808 review 'Don Pedro Cevallos on the French Usurpation of Spain', in which he interpreted the Spanish uprising as a rebellion against oligarchic oppression that held lessons for aristocrats and reformers closer to home.[18] A writer in the *Courier* for 2 December 1808 speculated that the *Edinburgh* reviewers dared utter such sentiments because their 'uncontrolled power [had] led to a degree of insolence, tyranny, and caprice ... to respect no objects, and fear no punishments'. 'Thomas Paine', the writer concluded, had 'never published any thing more seditious than the last number of the Edinburgh Review'.

Although these political articles, notably 'Don Pedro Cevallos', galvanized opposition to the *Edinburgh* and were used by the *Quarterly Review's* projectors in late 1808 and early 1809 to consolidate support for a new journal that might curb the *Edinburgh's* 'uncontrolled power', it is telling that the initial effort to set up a rival publication was started *before* they appeared. Even in the absence of transparently liberal political articles in the *Edinburgh Review*, some of that periodical's *quondam* admirers, offended by its attacks on the nation's religious and literary 'establishments', set the starting blocks for a new conservative journal.[19]

As is often the case with revolutions, a group of young people were in the vanguard. In about mid-June, during a walk together along Pall Mall, Stratford Canning, then only twenty years old, with two of his Eton and Cambridge friends, Gally Knight and Richard Wellesley, originated the idea of the *Quarterly Review*.[20] One of the students proposed the publication of 'a counter review here'. The friends came up with the name the journal was later known by, further serious discussion followed and they drew up 'the sketch of a prospectus'. Sometime that summer Stratford Canning walked the prospectus over to the Foreign Affairs office in Downing Street to present it to his powerful cousin George Canning, then the Foreign Secretary and the dominant personality in Cabinet.[21] Canning then introduced his cousin to William Gifford, 'the first Satirist of the day',[22] the man who in 1797–8 had, with Canning, conducted a brilliant Pittite political newspaper, the *Anti-Jacobin; or, Weekly Examiner*. Gifford 'in his turn approved the proposal'.[23]

A scant few weeks later, John Murray sent a letter, dated 27 September 1807, to the Foreign Secretary in which he suggested a plan remarkably similar to that of Stratford Canning's.[24] The statesman did not reply but instead opened a back channel to Murray through his cousin.[25] Given John Murray's and Stratford

Canning's identical intentions, designating Murray as the projected journal's publisher was an obvious move, one no doubt seconded by the younger Canning as he owed Murray a debt of gratitude. In April–October 1805 the publisher had rescued Canning, Knight, Wellesley, and one of their friends, Thomas Rennell, from complications that had arisen over their Etonian publication, 'The Miniature'. As Murray had come to know Stratford Canning through the agency of his neighbour the elder Thomas Rennell, and as every effect has a cause, Murray almost certainly learned via Rennell about the friends' project of setting up a counter review; he then wrote to Canning in the expectation that the Foreign Secretary would suggest him as the project's publisher. Intervening to take over 'The Miniature' from the publisher Charles Knight was a watershed event in Murray's history: it led to his introduction to George Canning, indirectly to the formation of the *Quarterly*, and thus to his becoming the 'Prince of Booksellers'. Years later, in comments to Knight's son Murray epitomized its importance. 'Your father helped to make my fortune', Murray wrote:

> When I kept a little trumpery shop in Fleet St., Dr Rennell, the Master of the Temple, told me one day that his son and young Canning owed an account for printing the 'Miniature', to their publisher, who held a good many unsold copies. I took the stock; paid the account, made waste paper of the numbers; brought out a smart edition which had few buyers; got the reputation of being a clever publisher; was introduced to George Canning, in consequence of the service I had rendered to his cousin; and in a few years set up the Quarterly Review.[26]

Progress toward the formation of the journal was brought to a temporary halt in October 1807 when Stratford Canning was sent to Europe on a diplomatic mission. Shortly after he returned, at the end of the year, he introduced John Murray to William Gifford, no doubt on the suggestion of the Foreign Secretary. The two men who fourteen months later would become the *Quarterly*'s publisher and editor first met in Westminster at Gifford's residence, 6 James Street, Buckingham Gate, on Friday, 8 January 1808.[27] In the first months of that year, Murray occasionally consulted Gifford on the best course to take in setting up a new journal.[28] Meanwhile, Stratford Canning attempted to arrange additional political sponsorship and to identify a body of potential contributors.

In the late winter or early spring of 1808, probably under George Canning's auspices, Murray met the old *Anti-Jacobin* clique at the Spring Gardens home of the Canningite diplomat George Hammond. Given the *Quarterly*'s future association with government and the civil service, it was a fitting location as Spring Gardens, between Pall Mall and Whitehall, is at the geographical heart of British political and administrative power. No record has emerged of the meeting's attendees beyond a statement that Gifford and Hammond were present and that Murray was introduced there to the diplomat John Hookham Frere. It is likely, though, that some of the following men were also present: Stratford Canning, Charles Long, George Ellis, Charles Bagot, John Charles Herries, Charles Paget, Henry William Paget, George Rose, William Huskisson, and Lords Aberdeen, Hawkesbury, and Palmerston. Along with George Canning, Robert Dundas, and Archibald Campbell-Colquhoun, these Pittite-Canningite politicians and diplomats were the journal's charter political sponsors.[29]

In the span of a year there had been introductions, much discussion, mutual lamentation, and readily proffered advice, but, except on Murray's part, no commitments. When in early May 1808 Canning was again sent to Europe on a diplomatic mission, progress appeared to stall. With liberals characterizing the Spanish uprising as democratic resistance, on 19 October 1808 Canning, who like other conservatives saw the insurrection as nationalist support for the *ancien régime*, wrote in frustration to Wellesley, 'If I were in England I think I should set to scribbling in *mere despair* ... I doubt whether you will find a better opportunity ... for putting our old designs into execution. Surely Gifford would lend a hand'.[30] Despite the fortuitous convergence of obvious need and ready resources, young Canning's efforts appeared to have been nugatory. Unbeknownst to the junior diplomat, however, in the meantime Murray had picked up the baton and was racing toward the finish line.

Stratford Canning's early efforts to set up a new conservative journal had been inspired by his and his friends' belief that in certain of its articles the *Edinburgh Review* had attacked bulwarks of British identity: the nation's aristocratic underpinnings and its literary and religious 'establishments'.[31] The idea of the *Quarterly Review* therefore first emerged as a conservative nationalist project in defence of the social, cultural, and constitutional status quo. Canning's efforts misfired, not because there was insufficient support for such a defence, but because he failed to recruit the right mix of personnel. It was not until John Murray co-opted Walter Scott that a set of English and Scottish conservatives managed to start the *Quarterly Review*. Following Scott's lead, the group then used the *Edinburgh*'s objectionable literary and religious articles and its reviews of Cobbett, Whitbread and Don Pedro Cevallos to marshal political support and inspire contributors.

As early as April 1808, Murray recognized that despite Canning's enthusiastic labours essential elements were still missing – literary sponsorship and a willing capable editor and, because these were absent, serious political commitment. To fill these gaps, the publisher prepared to insinuate himself more deeply into the affairs of a prominent literary man, Walter Scott, than he had hitherto managed. Murray believed Scott could accomplish what William Gifford had proved unwilling or unable to do, build on Canning's efforts to energize a set of political patrons, organize and motivate contributors, and act as or identify an editor. As Murray put it sometime later, 'without the generalship of Scott it would have been difficult to have drawn them [politicians and contributors] into action at this time'.[32]

To get Scott involved, he wisely calculated that a flanking move via James Ballantyne, Scott's printer, business partner, and friend, would be more effective than a direct assault. By 1808 Murray's relationship with the Scottish magus was slight; his association with Ballantyne, however, was well advanced. Ballantyne and Murray first met in 1805 when the printer was in London to drum up commissions. Because he saw in Ballantyne an opportunity to advance his connections to the Scottish trade, and because he knew about the printer's friendship with Scott, Murray took pains to impress Ballantyne with his 'friendly zeal, and solicitous regard'.[33] So successful was he that by the time Ballantyne returned to Edinburgh following his two or three-month visit, he already regarded Murray as someone he could turn to for advice. Over the coming months, the two men shared confidences, including as a point of pride on Ballantyne's part, information about Scott.

The somewhat desultory partnership the two young businessmen formed in 1806 was complicated by their contrasting personalities and business styles. Ballantyne, emotive and guileless, tried to place the arrangement on a footing of affection as well as commerce. He declared himself to Murray as 'a man who loves you' and he openly expressed the hope that the publisher and he 'should run the race of life together'.[34] Murray, rational and calculating, weighed the benefit of the relationship by its strategic value to his firm and periodically crushed Ballantyne's enthusiasm by reminding him that he was the printer's employer. In a July 1807 letter to Murray, Ballantyne nicely caught the symbiotic nature of their association and, perhaps without realizing it, its superstructure of dominance and dependence: 'Friendship so efficient as yours demands gratitude of the most substantial kind and mine shall be shown by my earnest endeavours to promote your interest, while I am advancing my own'.[35]

This friendship, which was of great significance to the early history of the *Quarterly Review*, led in the spring of 1806 to the commencement of Murray and Scott's correspondence. The occasion was Murray and the Whig poet Thomas Campbell's effort to set up a literary magazine.[36] Campbell, who in the previous year had with Ballantyne and Scott projected a volume of selected British poets, advised Murray to involve them in the magazine project. The result was that in early April the publisher asked Ballantyne for an introduction to Scott. In his 16 April reply to Murray's letter, Scott offered to assist; what was more, he issued an open invitation to Murray to visit him when he was next in Scotland.[37] Because Ballantyne cautioned Murray that Scott had 'some fears of C's steadiness',[38] the publisher set the project aside, but the experience was important to Murray, for in certain respects it was a dry run for setting up the *Quarterly Review*. In both the Campbell episode and in the lead up to the Ashiestiel conference, Ballantyne functioned as Murray's page, scheduling introductions, flattering, facilitating.[39]

Building on the entrée Campbell had supplied, Murray insinuated himself by degrees into Ballantyne's and Scott's affairs. Murray and Ballantyne together published editions of Cicero, Pliny, and Thomson's *The Seasons*. Murray and Scott cooperated in the publication of a number of volumes, Slingsby's *Memoirs*, Jamieson's *Popular Ballads*, Scott's edition of Strutt's *Queenhoo Hall* and his translation of Bürger's *The Chase* and *William and Helen*. Murray had a share as well in Scott's 1808 poem *Marmion*. In the meantime, Murray had become Constable's London agent, the metropolitan distributor of the *Edinburgh Review*, a contract he took over from Longman in 1806. As Scott was at this time still involved in the *Edinburgh* as a contributor, subeditor, and recruiter, Murray's role helped keep him in Scott's mind's eye.

The various strands of Murray's business career that contributed to the founding of the *Quarterly Review* – his contacts with the Cannings, his arrangements with Ballantyne and Scott, his meetings with Gifford – came together in 1808 during Ballantyne's long-contemplated follow-up to his 1805 visit to the metropolis.[40] The timing of his 1808 visit, April through June, was propitious because it meant he was in London just when Murray took the initiative from Stratford Canning in setting up the *Quarterly*.[41] It was not by coincidence that Ballantyne was proximate when the publisher heard that Scott wished to ease himself out of his arrangements with Constable or that the printer was close by when it occurred to Murray to use the journal as a hook to catch Scott.[42]

Other developments in early to mid-1808 reinforced Murray's sense that now was the time to attempt to break Constable's hold on bookselling north of the Tweed, to thwart the great Edinburgh publisher's growing presence in London, to win Scott from Constable, and to obtain a greater share of the Scottish trade. In April a negative review of *Marmion* appeared in the *Edinburgh Review*. There were also liberal political articles in the April and July numbers that Murray speculated would set Scott's conservative teeth on edge. Lockhart, who in after years spoke to the publisher about the *Quarterly*'s origins, told the story this way: Murray considered that 'Walter Scott has feelings, both as a gentleman and a Tory, which these people [Constable and Jeffrey] have wounded; the alliance between him and the whole clique of the *Edinburgh Review* is now shaken.'[43]

To take advantage of these developments, following overtures to Scott via the grocer-scholar Octavius Gilchrist in which he manoeuvred to bring Scott and Gifford together,[44] in September 1808 Murray travelled to Edinburgh ostensibly to return the favour of Ballantyne's London visit. In mid-June, Murray had discovered, undoubtedly from Ballantyne, that Scott intended to support James's younger brother John in setting up a bookselling and publishing business; it was knowledge that gave him an additional reason to travel north.[45] When he arrived at Edinburgh, he was confident, he told his wife, 'Annie', that he had 'every prospect of placing in a most decided train certain unmentioned ~~secretive~~ projects', the 'chief objects' of his coming north, namely, contracting a formal alliance with the Ballantynes and, with James Ballantyne, an exclusive partnership with Scott.[46] On the evening of 20 September, after a dinner in Edinburgh with Constable and other local publishers and their wives, he and Ballantyne went for a long walk together. Murray recorded the essence of their conversation a few days later in a letter to his wife. He and Ballantyne had 'entered into mutual explanations and discussions and discovered' that they had had 'for nearly six months past the same views respecting the connexion which [they] might form with each other'.[47]

With obtaining Scott's business as their alpha and omega, the two men agreed upon a fourfold strategy to pull Scott away from Constable. They would offer him favourable publishing arrangements for his works in Edinburgh and London; they would involve him in the scheme Murray long had in mind to issue a uniform set of standard English novels;[48] Murray would support Scott in his desire to promote the Ballantyne brothers' business interests; and together they would challenge Constable's prestige by setting up a London rival to the *Edinburgh Review*. The first step was to see Scott in person, so to that end Ballantyne arranged an interview for Sunday 2 October 1808 at Scott's country residence, Ashiestiel.[49]

Meanwhile, Scott himself had been scheming. In the autumn of 1808, in responding to and creating conditions that made possible the formation of the *Quarterly Review*, he managed events and persons more than he was managed by them. Sometime before Murray arrived at Ashiestiel, Scott had considered breaking his relationship with the house of Constable; because its politics had become 'so warm', he had already ceased contributing to the *Edinburgh Review*.[50] He was embarrassed by the *Edinburgh*'s stance on the Spanish rebellion. He was upset by its 'degrading the Sovereign, exalting the power of the French armies and the wisdom of their counsels, [and] holding forth that peace ... is indispensable to the very existence of our country'.[51] He later told William Gifford and their mutual friend the diplomatist and man of letters George Ellis that for two years he had noted the increasingly violent tone and radical content of the *Edinburgh*'s political articles.[52] Jeffrey and his reviewers, he thought, were trying their utmost to hasten Napoleon's triumph, to defeat Britain's war policy, and to encourage the rise of popular disaffection.[53] Even before the October 1808 publication of Brougham's 'Don Pedro Cevallos' article, then, Scott's connection with the *Edinburgh Review* had become untenable. The time had arrived, he later recorded, 'to attempt to divide the public with the Edinburgh Reviewers, and try if it be not possible by a little learning and fun upon the other side of the question to balance the extensive and extending influence which that periodical publication [had] acquired'.[54]

By an accident of history conservative journalism's support for the government's war policy and its suppression of rebellious forces at home came to be mixed up in no minor way with Scott's personal and business affairs. The *Quarterly Review* was founded in 1808–9 when Scott was driven out of the *Edinburgh's* fold because of his grievances with Constable and Company who, for political reasons so it appeared to Scott, were thwarting his and some of his friends' nationalist literary projects. In July 1808 Scott signed a contract with Archibald Constable and Constable's partner Alexander Hunter to produce an edition of Swift.[55] During contract negotiations, Hunter deeply offended Scott by questioning his business acumen and by referring disparagingly to the volumes of Romance literature he wanted to publish.[56] Constable and Hunter had repeatedly refused to help Scott advance his various schemes. In March 1807 Scott had attempted without success to pique Constable's interest in an 'antiquarian miscellany called either *Rhadamanthus* or the *British Librarian*'.[57] In May 1808 he tried again with a similar proposal, and again Constable and Hunter turned him down. In late September of that same year, Ellis blamed Jeffrey for inculcating the 'anti-romantic taste' that had taken hold among the reading public and that had thus discouraged Constable from supporting Scott's projects. Ellis thereby gave Scott an additional reason to want to take the fight to the 'rogues of Cowgate', the *Edinburgh* reviewers.[58] That the Romance projects were important to Scott is clear from the number of friendships he formed around them. In May 1808 he had, with William Stewart Rose, considered setting up what he called 'a society in which an *esprit de corps* may be generated' for the republication of old romances. Pursuing these projects, over the period 1801–8 he sustained a voluminous correspondence with many of the men with whom he later conspired in the *Quarterly Review*. Scott's interest gave Murray an opening in October 1808 to involve him in his plan to publish a uniform set of English novels.[59]

In severing his connection with Constable and the *Edinburgh*, Scott was driven by feelings of resentment and betrayal, then, and by his increasing political alienation from the journal and its publisher. He told his friend John Bacon Sawrey Morritt that he plotted to 'counterbalance the predominating influence of Constable and Co/ who at present have it in their power and inclination to forward or suppress any book as they approve or dislike its *political* tendency'. Emphasizing political motives, he wanted to avenge, he said, 'certain impertinences which in the vehemence of their *Whiggery* they [Hunter and Constable] have dared to indulge towards me'.[60] If he was upset at the *Edinburgh's* April 1808 review of *Marmion*, it was because he believed Jeffrey's motive in criticising the poem was wholly political.

It is commonly assumed that Scott avenged himself on Jeffrey for the *Marmion* review, and on Constable and Hunter for their offensive behaviour toward him, by setting up a rival periodical. Though Scott himself appealed to both these causes to explain his actions of late 1808, really his primary motive was political and the *Quarterly Review* was a windfall. Some weeks before Murray arrived at Ashiestiel, Scott had already matured a set of arrangements to counterbalance Constable and Jeffrey's political influence, to which arrangements he now added the *Quarterly*.[61] As it turned out, the main branch of Scott's 'grand plan' to 'turn the flank of Messrs. Constable and Co.',[62] the one he pursued last but realized first, was the establishment of a 'new Review in London to be called the Quarterly, William Gifford to be Editor Geo: Ellis, Rose, Mr. Canning, if possible, Frere and all the ancient Anti Jacobins to be concerned'.[63] Two other branches of his plan occurred to him earlier, however, the *Edinburgh Annual Register* and setting John Ballantyne up in business as an Edinburgh bookseller. He and James Ballantyne commenced the *Register* project in September 1808 to circumvent Constable's 'arranging one on the footing', the politics, 'of the Edinburgh Review'.[64] By distracting Scott, by diluting his appeal to Scottish writers for contributions, and by costing Murray bundles of cash and good will, the *Edinburgh Annual Register* retarded the *Quarterly*'s progress. But in late 1808 it appeared to be a sensible element in Scott's multifaceted scheme.

The other 'corollary' to Scott's 'grand plan' was his effort to set John Ballantyne up as a bookseller 'in direct opposition to those misproud stationers Constable & Hunter'.[65] Scott had a deep regard for his friend James Ballantyne and so to help James's brother he pledged to give him what assistance he could, thus to make a 'start against Constable and the Reviewers'.[66] Though the younger Ballantyne had, according to Scott, 'a long purse and a sound political creed', he was known to be impetuous and he was certainly untried in business. He could therefore use a level-headed, savvy partner. Murray's Scottish connections appealed to Scott and the Ballantynes. He was a McMurray by origin (his father, John McMurray, had emigrated from Scotland in 1768); and, too, Murray's wife, Anne Elliot, was a daughter of the head of one of Edinburgh's oldest publishing concerns. With his reputation in the London market, because he was a 'bookseller of capital and enterprise' who had, Scott said, 'more good sense and propriety of sentiment than fall to the share of most of his brethren', Murray was the ideal candidate to partner with John Ballantyne.[67] James Ballantyne's request for an audience to introduce Murray in person and discuss business therefore found Scott receptive because he saw opportunity falling into his lap. When Murray arrived at Ashiestiel, on Sunday 2 October 1808, while he thought he was piloting events, really he was small fry in the sea of Scott's intentions.

By a fortuitous coincidence Richard Heber, the wealthy 'bibliomaniac' and William Gifford's Westminster neighbour, then on a 'flying visit from Craven', his West Yorkshire country seat, was already at Ashiestiel.[68] A mutual friend of Scott and Canning's, Heber was – effectively, if not by design – a surrogate for the Foreign Secretary. These, then, were the men who were present at the creation: Scott, Murray, Heber, and Ballantyne. Scott's plans for Murray were important enough to him that he desired to spend time with the young man, to test his soundness and develop a relationship, and so he pressed Murray to extend his visit by a few days. Murray naturally 'was too happy in the opportunity of improving [his] acquaintance with him not to remain'.[69]

On Monday, Scott took his three guests 'on a truly delightful walk' around the countryside to the Braes of Yarrow and to Newark Tower. The group returned at five o'clock and then in the evening Murray revelled in Scott and Heber's 'charming conversation', in which both men excelled. On Tuesday, with Murray and Heber in the main part of the carriage and Ballantyne 'on the Dickey' (the jump seat) this brilliant company set out for Melrose Abbey where Scott again acted as tour guide. At 'Holy Melrose' Murray and Ballantyne took leave of Scott and Heber and set out for Ballantyne's home town, Kelso, where they spent the balance of the day with Mrs Ballantyne. On Wednesday at six in the evening Murray commenced a letter to Annie that he finished on Thursday. Having recounted the events of the previous three days, he concluded ecstatically, 'I am truly happy in being able to assure you of the most complete satisfaction which I derive from my visit to Mr Scott and it has now realized or [is] likely to do so, all that had been agitating in my mind for this last Twelve months'.[70] At six the next morning, Murray and Ballantyne departed for Edinburgh. On Friday, having said goodbye to Ballantyne, Murray set out for Bridgenorth via Preston where he intended to meet up with Annie and with her return to London.

Would that we had a verbatim transcription of the Ashiestiel conference, for its participants' conversations greatly determined the shape of the *Quarterly Review*. From evidence supplied in the correspondence we can however with some confidence outline what happened and what was said. At the commencement of their three days' meeting, Scott, acting as host and moderator, appears to have listened patiently and noncommittally as Murray made observations and retailed news. The publisher explained that the thought of establishing a journal to rival the *Edinburgh Review* had been 'revolving in [his] mind for nearly two years'.[71] When Murray mentioned that he had made 'indirect' contact with George Canning on the subject and that he had conversed with William Gifford about the idea, Scott grew enthusiastic. If the *Quarterly* can be said to have had a single starting point, it was at that moment. As Scott later told the antiquary Charles Kirkpatrick Sharpe, this bit of news meant that Murray was involved in a plan championed by one of the nation's most powerful politicians, the statesman who had launched the *Anti-Jacobin*. As such it was 'likely to be a very well managed business'. Scott told Sharpe that if he was to take on the *Edinburgh*

Review he would be 'engaged with "no foot land-rakers, no long-staff sixpenny strikers, but with nobility and tranquillity, burgomasters, and great oneyers"'.[72] That Canning backed the scheme was just what Scott needed to hear.

Scott now shared with the little group his own evidently well-evolved analysis of why the *Edinburgh* was successful and the shape a counter periodical must therefore take. No doubt with his eye on Murray, he especially drew a circle around the rights and duties of the journal's publisher. The *Edinburgh* was popular with writers and readers first because it was independent of bookselling influence – Constable did not insist upon favourable coverage for his books – a dimension of the journal that inspired confidence in its independence, that gave the *Edinburgh*'s editor greater freedom in selecting books and subjects for review, and greater control over their treatment. The *Edinburgh Review* was also popular because Constable paid his contributors well.[73] A new journal should adopt these policies. It should also differentiate itself and gain credibility and utility by being a repository of inside government knowledge; it should employ a temperate, rational tone in its book reviews; it should calmly demonstrate conservative arguments on political questions; and it should avoid party politics, 'unless in cases of great national import'.[74]

At this point in the conversation, Heber injected a note of caution and exposed a possible weakness in the scheme. It would be difficult, he said, to attract capable regular contributors. Where would they come from? The *Edinburgh* had corralled the best reviewing talent. Scott's passionate reply to Heber's prescient objection shows that his thoughts were guided by emotion as well as by reason. He saw no such difficulty. Asserting his authority as a seasoned contributor and sometime subeditor of the *Edinburgh Review*, with too much assurance he declared he understood the mechanics of serial production. With a modicum of assistance from a few fellow northern scribblers, following the publication of one or two powerful numbers writers would rush to become contributors and then the journal's editor would be encumbered with help. Catching Scott's enthusiasm, the little group now shared the names of possible coadjutors, Mathias, Malthus, Moore, the Roses, Ireland, Frere, Canning, and Gifford, among others.

During the conference it appears that Murray tried to settle both the editorship and his own role in the journal. Apparently he proposed that Scott 'undertake the office of Editor' and someone, logically it must have been Murray, held out 'great prospects of emolument' to Scott if he accepted.[75] Scott deferred that decision. Although Murray did not at this point state how much he was willing to pay the editor or contributors, probably Scott proposed and Murray agreed that the *Quarterly*'s terms should if possible match those at the *Edinburgh Review*. When Murray offered to underwrite the project, he cleared away a large impediment to the nascent journal's future success. He also by this means staked his claim to be the *Quarterly*'s publisher and moral and legal owner. The principals therefore had *in posse* more essentials than many a similar project at such an early stage: the promise of political sponsorship from the highest authorities; in Scott a leading man of letters whose participation would encourage others to contribute; and, through their angel Murray, a bank roll and guaranteed distribution in London.

Despite Scott's laudatory statements about him, during the conference Murray was not uniformly impressive. Some of his suggestions show he was out of his depth, such as his enthusiastic emphasis on the journal's name. He thought the geographically specific *London Review* would nicely compete with *Edinburgh Review*. When Scott later made it clear that, while he was willing to indulge Murray, he thought any simple name would do, the publisher realized he had spoken with too much passion about a triviality and adopted Scott's more reserved view. Of much greater importance was Murray's suggestion that the journal's first number should be prepared in the deepest secrecy, an idea even Murray's official biographer, Samuel Smiles, usually his apologist, thought incomprehensible.[76] Unfortunately, the curious plan inspired Scott's imagination, and so they agreed no prospectus would be issued; there would be no 'other annunciation than the dispersing [of] a certain number of gratis copies'.[77] As Scott explained it to Gifford, the intention was to avoid setting unreasonable expectations or giving the enemy an opportunity to prejudice their case. Fancifully, Scott anticipated that following this plan the journal would burst among the Whigs 'like a bomb'.[78] Well before publication, by early December, Francis Douce, Archibald Constable, Francis Jeffrey and many others learned that a new journal was in progress.[79] But despite the difficulties Murray's strategy caused – cramping the planners' communication, restricting their recruiting pool, obviating any chance of marketing the journal – up to the day of publication the principals enjoined each other to keep their activities secret.

When the Ashiestiel conference broke up, Murray and Scott took away substantially different impressions of who had persuaded whom. Sorting out the truth of these impressions is of interest because Murray's sense in the meeting's aftermath that he was being sidelined inspired him to campaign for moral ownership of the *Quarterly Review* and it later helped unsettle his relations with Gifford. Too, Scott never acknowledged what most historians have since assumed, that there was a cause and effect relationship between Murray's arrival at Ashiestiel and his, Scott's, part in the formation of the *Quarterly Review*, that Scott agreed to participate in *Murray's* plan. In letters to friends in which he set out his first, fresh interpretation of recent events, while Scott described the two developments – Murray's visit and the establishment of the journal – as having occurred at about the same time, he denied the one event led directly to the other.[80] He regarded the *Quarterly Review* project and his 'alliance offensive and defensive with John Murray' as distinct if related branches of *his* 'grand plan'.

In Lockhart's and Smiles's telling, the *Quarterly Review* originated in the publisher's waging a successful Scottish campaign, in his careful management of James Ballantyne, and in his persuasive powers with Walter Scott. Their interpretation was greatly influenced, indeed to some extent it was directed, by Murray. They tell Murray's story and, as such, their version is subject to the usual limitations of a first person master narrative. By reading with care the difficult syntax of Scott's letters, however, we shift our point of view and discover that Scott recognized in the publisher's news the validation of an idea he had independently conceived.[81]

Scott's communicating this interpretation to his friends explains why in letters of 25 October, 2 November and 14 January to Gifford, Ellis, and Morritt, respectively (and in Bedford's and Gifford's letters that reflect the same information received through a third person), Scott portrays himself as the project's instigator, it explains why Southey believed 'the idea [of the *Quarterly Review*] originated with Walter Scott' who had suggested it 'to some of the men in power',[82] why Ellis characterized 'the plan' as Scott's, why he called Scott the journal's 'father', and why he named him as the 'first instigator of our enterprize'.[83]

And yet, and yet. Despite Scott's interpretation and the claim Murray later made, regarding himself, that 'by his own sagacity and by his own means alone' he had 'given birth to' the *Quarterly Review*,[84] the involvement of no single person – George or Stratford Canning, Murray, Scott, Gifford, Heber, or Ballantyne – was sufficient to launch this 'New Literary Journal'.[85] Instead, the periodical originated in a confluence of events and personalities: Murray's taking over 'The Miniature' from the publisher Charles Knight; Ballantyne's pursuing a personal and business relationship with Scott and Murray; Campbell's suggesting that Murray involve Scott and Ballantyne in setting up a literary magazine; Stratford Canning's bringing the *Quarterly*'s future principals together over the idea of a periodical that might counter the *Edinburgh Review*; Murray's successfully negotiating an alliance with Ballantyne and Ballantyne's introducing Murray to Scott; Scott's estrangement from Constable and Company, his displeasure with the *Edinburgh* over its attitude toward the insurrection in Spain, and his unhappy desire to promote the fortunes of James and John Ballantyne;[86] George Canning's and other high English and Scottish officials' providing political sponsorship for a conservative nationalist project in defence of the constitutional status quo; Murray's committing capital to the venture; and Gifford's agreeing to undertake the editorship. Equally important, 'the detestation of' the *Edinburgh Review* 'long rumbling in the breasts of many ingenious men'[87] created a body of potential contributors and primed the reading public for a journal opposed to the 'great *Northern* Light' on political, religious, and moral grounds.

2 LAUNCHING THE *QUARTERLY REVIEW*

Launching a new political-literary journal was a tactical component in each of Scott's and Murray's independently conceived if remarkably compatible business and personal strategies. Over the coming months the two men's conflicting perceptions of who originated the plan conditioned their relationship with Gifford and with each other. Because Murray placed the Ashiestiel conference in a continuum that stretched back to September 1807 and beyond, he regarded himself as the prime mover of events. Scott considered the Ashiestiel meeting as a commencement, his post-Ashiestiel activities as first steps, and therefore himself as the *primum mobile*.

Scott knew that Murray's design in coming north was to obtain his business and he understood that the publisher was using the *Quarterly Review* project as his calling card, yet he saw himself as having been given a commission not by Murray but by high politicos who looked to him for decisive action. In the following weeks he conducted himself accordingly, mostly without reference to the publisher. Murray, on the other hand, saw himself as a benign Svengali cleverly manipulating Scott; consequently, he became alarmed when the journal's principals acted without regard to his opinions or interests. Though Murray was sensible enough not to mention most of them, he had a long list of duties he expected Scott to fulfil: that he would take the editorship, contribute articles, suggest a marketing strategy, recruit contributors from among his scribbling friends, secure Scottish political sponsorship, inspire confidence that the game was worth the risk, sever his relationship with Constable, strike a crippling blow to the *Edinburgh* by withdrawing his subscription, and act as the journal's head of state. For a season, Scott eventually undertook all of these tasks, even the first, as he essentially co-edited the journal's inaugural number. While Murray was therefore happy to use Scott and was willing to be used by him in turn, he wished not to be taken for granted by his co-projectors.

As Murray's Ashiestiel visit drew to a close, the conspirators agreed that a practical step toward establishing the *Quarterly* would be for Scott to travel to London. There he would meet the journal's political patrons, Canning in particular, and 'urge some very formidable plan into activity'.[1] Despite Stratford

Canning's efforts of the previous year, Scott's pledge to undertake the London trip suggests that in the absence of plausible literary sponsorship George Canning and his old *Anti-Jacobin* peers had yet to make a serious commitment; in that respect the post-Ashiestiel activities were indeed a beginning. Murray's use of the phrase '*some* very formidable plan' in his 26 October letter to Scott also suggests that discussions during the Ashiestiel conference were polite, restrained, and incomplete, an impression reinforced in Ballantyne's 28 October letter to Murray in which he reported on 'the progress of the other Great Plan'.[2] The printer expressed the hope that Scott's 'present feelings, excited by the Review of Marmion', would be intensified and his will to set up a counter journal solidified by the appearance of 'a tickler' by Jeffrey of Scott's *Life of Dryden* in the *Edinburgh*'s twenty-fifth number. That Ballantyne and Murray believed they had to wait until Scott read the review to gain Scott's full commitment and participation implies that while the little group agreed a journal was necessary and were verbally committed to the objective, whether Scott would follow through was, so they thought, still in doubt; too, how the plan would be realized and who would be the editor were up in the air.

In his enthusiasm to counter the political influence of the house of Constable, Scott had instead taken ownership of the project, so much so that rather than wait for an opportunity to visit London or for Murray to return home, within days of the Ashiestiel meeting he unilaterally moved the plan forward. The nationalist dimension of the project is illustrated in his decision to seek as his first step Scottish-English political cooperation. He 'strongly recommended to [the] Lord Advocate' – his best friend William Erskine's brother-in-law Archibald Campbell-Colquhoun – that he 'think of some counter-measures against the Edinburgh Review which politically speaking', Scott wrote, 'is doing incalculable damage'.[3] It appears he also asked Campbell-Colquhoun to contact George Canning. Sometime between 6 October and 10 October, the Lord Advocate filled his commission by writing a letter to the Foreign Secretary. In his letter he told Canning about the plan (he referred to it as Scott's plan), and about Murray's willingness to be involved, which of course Canning already knew.[4] As Ballantyne put it, Canning bit 'at the hook eagerly'.[5] Gifford, to whom Canning showed the Lord Advocate's letter, confirmed these details when he later told Edward Copleston, '[t]he idea of this Review was not started by me'. 'The Lord Advocate of Scotland, who had witnessed the pernicious effects of the Edinburgh Review first, I believe', Gifford wrote, 'mentioned it to the Government, by whom it was taken up; and, as I happened to be known to some of them, the conduct of it was warmly pressed upon me'.[6]

The Lord Advocate appears to have told Canning he would encourage Scott to accept the editorship. Canning, knowing that until a pilot was identified the vessel would never leave port and anxious to see it under canvas without delay, risked offending Gifford by making him wait upon Scott to exercise his right of first refusal. Only a week after Murray's Ashiestiel visit, on 12 October Gifford acceded to Canning's request that, contingent upon Scott's decision, he commit himself to the editorship. Gifford later said he owed the post to Scott's 'partial judgement', by which he meant only that he was grateful Scott raised no objection, not that Scott recommended Gifford to the Lord Advocate or that he was otherwise involved in the appointment.[7] To the contrary, as we learn from Scott's letters to Ellis and Murray, he doubted Gifford was the right man for the job.

Canning's appointment of Gifford to the editorship and Scott and Murray's response to it expose the *Quarterly Review* as lock, stock and barrel a political engine. Whatever literary, commercial, or career imperatives came into play, by accepting Gifford, with whom they were not at all happy, as the cost of securing political sponsorship, Scott and Murray proved that in founding the *Quarterly* they were driven first and foremost by concerns about politics and politicians. Scott did not object to Gifford's appointment and Murray later did not try to remove him only partly because they respected Gifford for his acknowledged taste and his native genius, but more so because they wished to retain Canning as the journal's chief political sponsor. Neither man wanted to risk losing the Foreign Secretary's good will by questioning his judgement.

While the nuances of Murray's political commitment have to be teased out of the record, Gifford explicitly stated that his involvement was an expression of political fealty. 'I do this', he told Canning, 'because I know of no other whom you could securely trust – with me, you are perfectly safe'. Demonstrating, like Scott, the essentially political nature of his commitment, rather than immediately beat the bushes for potential contributors or arrange a meeting with Murray, Gifford's inaugural act as editor-elect was to sound out high political men, Hawkesbury, Long, and Huskisson. Gifford was circumspect by nature, so regardless of his and Canning's long and close association with these men, he kept the details of the plan to himself while he secured their assent in principle.

Shortly after Gifford agreed to be editor, the Foreign Secretary informed the Lord Advocate he anxiously supported the plan and he mentioned Gifford's willingness to serve. Campbell-Colquhoun now placed Canning's letter in William Erskine's hands, probably with the idea that Erskine might convince Scott to accept the editorship. Erskine held onto Canning's letter for a few days until he 'had an opportunity of conversing with Walter Scott', whom he saw on the evening of 22 October 1808. The following day he submitted the results of his interview.[8]

Erskine's report to the Lord Advocate is illuminating. Evidently, Campbell-Colquhoun had given Erskine limited information about the events to date, for it was Scott who told him about Murray's visit to Ashiestiel and that 'the plan alluded to' by the Lord Advocate was 'already in some measure begun'. Erskine

related that Murray had asked Scott 'to undertake the office of Editor'. Scott
had thought about it, he said, but he wished now to inform the Lord Advocate
through Erskine that he irrevocably declined. His reasons, Erskine recorded,
were that 'his hands [were] already too full for such an undertaking' and he
believed 'if any assistance or countenance [were] to be given by Government,
the Editor ought to reside in London'. Unbeknownst to Erskine, prior to their
meeting Scott had almost certainly received a separate communication from
Campbell-Colquhoun in which the Lord Advocate informed him that, should
he decline it, the editorial department was to be offered to Gifford and that Gifford would probably accept.[9] Knowing he had an understudy perhaps made it
easier for Scott to refuse the Lord Advocate's overtures.

Having firmly and finally declined the editorship, on 25 October 1808
Scott wrote to Gifford to confirm arrangements and outline his understanding
of the editor's duties and prerogatives. Scott claimed, as a gesture of *politesse*,
that he wrote the letter on the order of their 'distinguished friends' who, recog-
nizing Scott as the project's instigator, wished him to tutor Gifford as the man
who would implement Scott's vision. Again confirming the journal's status as a
nationalist political instrument, he showed the 'letter of policy' to Erskine and
then to Campbell-Colquhoun; the Lord Advocate was to ask Canning to read it
before handing it on to Gifford.[10]

Gifford's reply of 9 November was delayed, he said, because he wanted to
consult Canning, which may have been true, though peevish self-assertion was
also involved. While he appeared to take in stride being schooled in the editorial arts by a tyro fifteen years his junior, his letter to Scott is studiously written
in *le langage des hommes raisonnables*, so much so that between the lines one
can read resentment and irony. 'Every word that you have written', he states as
if humbly, 'convinces me that you have declined (I know not for what reason) a
department for which you are so much better qualified than the person whom
your partial judgment has recommended to it, that I wonder at my own temerity
… in retaining it a moment; which, after all, I can only do, by your kindly condescension to be "viceroy over me"'.[11] Evidently, it was humiliating to Gifford to
be cast as Scott's subaltern. Earlier in the year his political sponsors had failed to
rally to his standard; now they hearkened to Scott's war cry and positioned Scott
as Gifford's superior. Gifford later called 'preposterous' the mode by which he
obtained the editorship, 'a publisher being appointed, and some progress made,
before an Editor was fixed on'.[12] Muted resentment will out, as well it did for in
the coming months, as we shall see, Gifford punished Scott by thwarting the
friends and colleagues he put forward as contributors to the *Quarterly Review*.

In the meantime, confident he was making excellent progress, Scott continued to manoeuvre. At the end of October 1808 he gained the support of Robert
Dundas, the powerful President of the Board of Control for India.[13] A few days

later, on 2 November, he enlisted George Ellis, who had already heard about the project from George Canning.[14] In the weeks after the Ashiestiel conference, Scott, Canning, Erskine, Campbell-Colquhoun, Gifford, and Ellis busily discussed the budding journal. Notably missing from this circle was Murray who, aside from correspondence with his wife, composed his first letter on the subject, to Scott, on 26 October. At this time the other principals regarded Murray as a functionary and referred to him reductively as 'our publisher'. It did not occur to them to involve him in executive decisions, such as the appointment of an editor, an event he learned about weeks after the fact, when Scott wrote to him on 30 October.[15] In his letter of 26 October that crossed Scott's in transit Murray demonstrated he had no inkling Gifford was editor-elect.[16] Murray told Scott that shortly after he returned to London, on 16 October, he paid Gifford a visit. Gifford 'admitted the most imperious necessity for' a new journal, hinted 'distantly at a Review', and led Murray to understand he had had some 'very important communications upon the subject'. He did not, however, let on that he knew about the conference at Ashiestiel or that he had been offered the editorship.[17] In late October the other conspirators clearly regarded Murray, if they thought about him at all, as a contingent member of the planning group.

Besides contributing to the practical requirements of identifying contributors, writing copy, and formulating an editorial policy – duties the planners in various combinations shared in November and December – Scott meanwhile made some bold strategic moves. He took advantage of the publication in the October *Edinburgh Review* of Brougham's 'Don Pedro Cevallos' article to explain his break with Constable and Constable's journal. In his private correspondence he constructed an informal prospectus to guide perceptions of his motives and to mobilize support for a new periodical. On 19 November, he wrote to his brother to describe the plan and justify his participation in it. Emphasizing political reasons above all, he mentioned that the Whigs had been displeased with *Marmion* and that their displeasure was reflected in Jeffrey's review. He drew attention to the 'late articles on Spain [that had] given general disgust'. He admitted he had grown cold toward Constable and even more so toward 'that Bear his partner', Alexander Hunter, who, he complained, had 'behaved to [him] of late not very civilly'.[18]

In a 20 December 1808 letter to John Murray, James Ballantyne conveys the impression that Scott's actions toward Constable and Company were finely calibrated, that his public manipulation of the 'Don Pedro Cevallos' article initiated a well-plotted campaign of shock and awe. 'Ever since the journey we made together to Ashiestiel', Ballantyne told Murray, 'I have witnessed a growing coldness on the part of Constable's House to the literary fame of Mr Scott. ... At length, the publication of the last No. of the Edinburgh Review, arrived to hasten the catastrophe. Mr Scott gave up the Review, and Hunter's rash folly led him to the use of some expressions which reached Mr Scott's ears'. On 28 December, Ballantyne informed Murray that Scott 'shewed [him] a letter bidding a final farewell to the house of Constable'.[19]

Many commentators ascribe Scott's break with the *Edinburgh* to his disgust over 'Don Pedro Cevallos' and they explain that Brougham's essay pushed other conservatives as well to act against Constable's journal. In the month of October, however, the article played no recorded role in the principals' deliberations or decisions. Smiles states that the October number of the *Edinburgh Review* arrived during Murray's visit to Ashiestiel and that it sealed the principals' determination to act. Whether the number arrived that week or the next,[20] it was as a *casus belli*, not as a goad, that 'Don Pedro Cevallos' was important to the *Quarterly*'s history. Murray, Ballantyne, and Scott do not mention the article in their letters of October and early November. It was not until mid-November that Scott began to act upon 'Don Pedro Cevallos'. He then took advantage of it to set up his personal break with Constable and Constable's flagship journal and to encourage other subscribers to run from the *Edinburgh*.[21]

In a 21 November letter to Murray, Ballantyne recorded how Scott used 'Don Pedro Cevallos' to advance the components of his 'grand plan':

> You have no doubt heard ere this time of the universal indignation and disgust which the last No. of the Edin. Rev. has given. Many people have given it up, and, if I may judge from what I hear, the general dissatisfaction is increasing. W. Scott was, I believe, the first who discontinued it. Constable was greatly affected by the annunciation; and I tell you *in entire confidence*,[22] that from the aid which W Scott determines to give your glorious work, and other causes, he anticipates an entire rupture with that house. He further told me, that if that event took place, you, if you chose it, should have the first offer of his future works. Indeed, he on every occasion expresses himself respecting you in the most flattering terms of approbation and respect. What an incentive to Gifford *jr* this last No. of the Edinburgh Review will be! The *mansion* deserves to fall.[23]

Like a one-man creeping barrage, Scott emboldened the troops and scattered the enemy. The community of outrage he created through his calculated reaction to 'Don Pedro Cevallos' for a brief moment caused Jeffrey to lose his equilibrium. For a few weeks it even appeared that Scott had mortally wounded the *Edinburgh Review*. Although Sydney Smith downplayed the defections and was flippant about public reaction to 'Don Pedro Cevallos', clearly he was concerned. 'You have no idea', he told a correspondent, 'of the consternation which the Sieur Brougham's attack upon the titled orders has produced: the Review not only discontinued by many people but returned to the Bookseller from the very first volume: the library shelves fumigated, &c'. Teasingly, he accused Brougham of having 'behaved in an unwhiglike manner' and humorously complained that his coltish *Edinburgh* colleague had been 'bolting out of the course again ... It is extremely difficult to keep him right.' Yet to protect his own reputation and career, he considered withdrawing from the journal and he more or less advised Jeffrey to do likewise.[24]

The bare suggestion of a general rout caused Jeffrey to overreact. In a 6 December letter to Horner he spoke of a 'Cevallos crisis' and apologized to his coadjutor for publishing an essay that put the whole enterprise at risk.[25] He rushed to Scott to assure him, 'there should be no more politics in the review, – *party* politics'.[26] Scott now showed that his actions at the end of 1808 were the result of a settled conviction, that the plan he followed had enjoyed a long gestation. He gave the same answer to both Jeffrey and Constable: the time for explanations, assurances, and apologies had passed; the van was on the march and nothing could now turn it from its course.[27] With Scott's letter of 25 October, Gifford's delayed response of 9 November, and Ellis's reply to Scott of 11 November, the determination of this 'little band' to take on the *Edinburgh Review* was sealed.[28]

The *Quarterly Review*'s troops soon discovered, however, that the war would not be over by Christmas. The rout was not general; they were in for a long campaign. Of the *Edinburgh*'s thousands of readers, only a few dozen had cancelled their subscriptions. Indeed the 'Don Pedro Cevallos' article, a *succès des scandale*, pushed the journal's trade sale to record numbers. As the *Edinburgh*'s London distributor, on December 2nd Murray reported to Constable that the journal was 'selling much faster than usual'. Three days later he wrote, 'The Edin. Review has sold as well and indeed better than it did any number before'.[29] Clearly, the threat to the *Edinburgh* was political, not financial. By the end of the year, Jeffrey and Constable had heard about Scott's effort to set up a rival periodical, and yet they were not afraid. They believed only the opening number would be published in London. After that it would be 'a Scotch job' with limited reach and they supposed its impact would therefore not be formidable.[30]

Against this backdrop of encouraging and discouraging events in Scotland, the English component of the *Quarterly*'s cabal got off to a good start. Scott's 25 October letter in hand, Canning, Ellis and Gifford made rapid progress on settling the journal's editorial policy and in acquiring additions to the roster of contributors. The Scottish-English nexus produced results as well with Ellis and Scott doing the intellectual heavy lifting. Even Canning was involved in the planning, to an impressive extent given his responsibilities at Foreign Affairs. Canning, Gifford, and Ellis met to discuss strategy on 27–29 November at Claremont, the country residence of Ellis's cousin Charles Rose Ellis. In early December, Gifford arranged a pro forma interview between Canning and Murray to permit the publisher to pay fealty to the great man.

Scott's and Ellis's letters of October and November, supplemented by letters of Gifford, Murray, and Ballantyne, are our best stand-in for a prospectus. From his close observation of the reasons for the *Edinburgh*'s success, Scott, as we noticed, determined that the *Quarterly* should establish credibility by resisting booksellers' influence. Its principles would not be those of any party but rather, as he later told Sharpe, they would be 'English and Constitutional'.[31] The journal should generally support the Cabinet, but he thought it would be a 'dereliction of duty' and they would lose the public's trust if the editorial group were to provide the Ministry 'indiscriminate support'. The *Quarterly* would nevertheless differentiate itself in the marketplace by becoming a journal of record. Gifford enjoyed the confidence of high government men and, as such, he had access to official information. Besides his friendship with Canning, they saw access as his chief asset and it is what Southey and Murray pointed to when, years later, they said it would be difficult to replace him. The *Quarterly*'s projectors thereby designed a paradox. They wanted Gifford, at 'the Headquarters of intelligence',[32] to obtain government information and by that means establish the journal's credibility and authority. At the same time, they wished to preserve their credibility and authority with the public by having Gifford maintain an arm's-length relationship with the Treasury. In the coming years, Gifford's difficulty in reconciling this paradox caused problems for the journal that its principals did not anticipate in November–December 1808.

For the *Quarterly* to function as an effective mouthpiece for conservative constitutional principles, Scott, Murray, and Ellis agreed it should not appear to be exclusively political but should be 'complete as to scholarship, literature and science'. Articles 'upon science and miscellaneous literature' would lend the journal intellectual weight, 'challenge comparison with the best of contemporary reviews', and present a plausible rejoinder to the dismissive accusation that the journal was ministerial propaganda, which, Scott believed, was 'the only ground from which it can be assaild [*sic*]'. An 'open and express declaration of political tenets or of opposition to works of a contrary tendency' would be avoided, Scott decreed. Murray posited that by using the 'merely literary' articles as a screen, 'honnied [*sic*] drops of party sentiment may be delicately insinuated into the unsuspecting ear'.[33]

To answer the requirement, agreed by all but insisted upon by Southey, that the *Quarterly* represent a model of 'moral reviewing', Scott recommended that works not be treated harshly or prejudged by politics. Even 'a weak brother', Scott explained, should he put his hand forth unadvisedly 'to support the ark of the constitution', would be treated impartially. Though he might 'approve of his intention and of his conclusions', the reviewer in such a case would disinterestedly 'expose his arguments'.[34] The projectors went back and forth on the tone the journal should adopt, rigorously disinterested or occasionally satirical.[35] Scott's view was that it should 'be of a liberal and enlarged nature, resting upon principles – indulgent and conciliatory as far as possible upon mere party questions, but stern in detecting and exposing all attempts to sap our constitutional fabric'.[36] He believed a politically independent journal would convince the reading public 'by the accuracy of its facts and the stile of its execution', not by coming out with all guns blazing in a direct assault on the *Edinburgh Review*; indeed, he advised, their enemy should not be named.[37]

Ellis was concerned that in contrast to the *Edinburgh* the journal should establish its integrity as an arbiter of taste by disinterestedly reviewing the best books of the day. He particularly objected to the *Edinburgh* reviewers' practice of producing 'a premeditated essay of their own on some popular subject, selected, as an excuse for the introduction of that subject, any paltry pamphlet that without their notice might have been lost or misplaced at the printer's warehouse'.[38] To achieve their political purposes, though, he admitted the *Quarterly*'s conductors might sometimes have to engage in a similar practice. Ellis later reflected: the *Edinburgh* was 'seriously formidable ... as a political engine'; therefore, politics was the chief ground upon which it must be opposed.[39]

When Scott determined in mid-November 1808 that he could not be in London any time soon, Gifford set aside his initial resolution to wait for Scott's arrival before starting. He and his coadjutors then set to work in earnest.[40] The principals' primary effort in mid to late November was to decide which books to review and to recruit writers beyond the inner circle. We know from Murray's notes, serendipitously preserved in a now frail memorandum book, that the planning group engaged in much preliminary thought about who might write for the journal. Murray recorded a pool of over one hundred candidates, of whom only thirty-five eventually wrote for the *Quarterly Review*.[41] Murray's lists cohere remarkably well: almost all the nominees are from the liberal conservative end of the ideological spectrum. The exceptions – notably, James Mill, William Shipley, Leigh Hunt, and Thomas Moore – are testimony to Murray's desire to mute the *Quarterly*'s political character and thereby attain as broad an audience as possible.[42]

Setting the pattern for the first few years, it was not Gifford alone who made assignments. Nominally subject to Gifford's approval, the principal writers, Scott, Ellis, and Southey selected their own books for review and assigned books to others. Southey brought in a friend of his, Barré Charles Roberts. Canning enlisted Ellis who in turn convinced his physician Thomas Young to contribute.[43] Young recruited an Etonian usher, James Pillans. Murray commissioned articles from Sharon Turner[44] and Isaac D'Israeli.[45] For his part, Richard Heber tackled relatives and friends, his half-brother Reginald Heber, Edward Copleston of Oriel College, and Thomas Gaisford of Christ Church.

Scott tried to bring in 'as many blue bonnets' as he could.[46] He approached his brother and a number of his friends, including Sharpe, Erskine, Douglas, Morritt, and Walker, to each of whom he pledged that Gifford would kindly receive their submissions.[47] For reasons of propriety, none of the principals commented that a chief reason for Scott's failure to attract more and better talent was that in his recruiting drive he adopted a flawed strategy. In soliciting contributions for the *Quarterly*, he invariably requested support for the *Edinburgh Annual Register* as well. Simultaneously working on the *Register* and the *Quarterly* divided his energy and drew off contributors who might otherwise have offered their wares to the London journal.

William Gifford recruited his two best friends, the Reverend John Ireland, at the time subdean (later dean) of Westminster Abbey,[48] and the Whig society portrait artist John Hoppner.[49] Hoppner in turn identified the Oxford chemist John Kidd as a reviewer; Copleston later convinced Kidd to participate. Gifford also approached Robert Southey, via their mutual friend Grosvenor Bedford. Through Lord Teignmouth, Gifford was in contact with the 'Saints', a powerful group of evangelicals under the leadership of William Wilberforce. The Saints were active supporters of the *Edinburgh* until Sydney Smith turned on them in a series of articles on evangelical missions he published in 1807 and 1808. Thus betrayed by their former propaganda partners in the slave trade abolition campaign, they too had been contemplating a counter journal. They now pledged to support the *Quarterly*. When he learned about this, Scott, who distrusted the Saints' reformist political and social agenda as much as he did their religiosity, warned Murray not to allow Gifford to grant them any preponderance in the journal.[50]

Now and throughout Gifford's tenure, the *Quarterly*'s editorial group mostly drew upon a network of conservative writers who were well known to one another through personal, family, educational, professional, and social linkages.[51] Scott, Murray, and their co-conspirators had in the course of these initial efforts especially solicited contributions from men whose reputations Jeffrey had 'murdered, and who [were] rising to cry wo upon him, like the ghosts in King Richard',[52] Young, Gregory, Rogers, Moore, Douce, Sotheby, Wordsworth, Coleridge, Southey, and various Saints. Under Gifford and Coleridge, no women wrote for the *Quarterly*, although Murray approached Elizabeth Inchbald, Scott asked Joanna Baillie to contribute and Ballantyne apparently contacted Elizabeth Hamilton. Partly because he wished to broaden the journal's appeal by obscuring its political signature, later Murray encouraged liberals and even radicals to contribute.[53]

In early November, when Gifford recruited Southey through Bedford's agency he misunderstood Scott and Canning's intentions and proposed that Southey write the *Quarterly*'s reply to 'Don Pedro Cevallos'. On 9 November 1808, he advised Canning that he considered Southey to be an 'honourable man' and that on 'this particular point', the insurrection in Spain, his 'heart [was] as it should be'. When Murray, who in his 1808 *Quarterly Review* planning notes indicated that Gifford would take responsibility for inviting Southey to become a reviewer, found that the editor had asked Southey to contribute the article on Spain, he was appalled. 'It is true' Murray wrote to Scott, 'that Mr S— knows a great deal about Spain, and upon another occasion would have given a good article upon this subject – but at present – *his* is not the kind of knowledge which we want, and it is, moreover, trusting our secret to a stranger who has, by the way, a directly opposite bias in politics'. Murray was right, for while Southey regarded 'Don Pedro Cevallos' as shamefully defeatist, he sympathized with its representation of the Spanish revolt as a democratic uprising. Much to Murray's relief, instead of writing on Spain, Southey wished to answer Sydney Smith on evangelical missions. On 29 November, Gifford, having seen Canning, reported to Murray 'Ellis has readily undertaken the Spanish article'. By mid-December, however, Ellis still had not set pen to paper. To get his friend started, on 18 December Canning brought 'down little Gifford' to Claremont. There he and Ellis, overseen by the editor, worked on the *Quarterly*'s response to 'Don Pedro Cevallos'.[54]

In his letter to Gifford of 25 October, Scott had recommended that the *Quarterly*'s inaugural issue come out in January, thus to answer 'Don Pedro Cevallos' before a further number of the *Edinburgh Review* appeared. To meet Scott's expectations, Murray set an aggressive publication deadline of early January; he stipulated that all articles should be in Gifford's hands by the end of December. Scott so dominated the group at this point that when the impossibility of meeting the January publication target became clear, neither Murray nor Gifford would contradict him. It took someone from outside the editorial group, one of the journal's political sponsors, Charles Long, to point out the unreasonableness of a December submission date. Thus emboldened, in early December the publisher revised the target for submissions to 10 January. Even that date proved unrealistic. Scott wrote on 4 January to say that legal duties would cause him to delay his articles. On 11 January, Ballantyne further alarmed Murray with news that Scott was having 'difficulty in getting others to write'. Adding to the stress, by inserting a notice in the 5 January *Morning Chronicle*, Murray publicly committed the planners to a specific date: 'On Monday the 23rd of January will be published, The FIRST NUMBER of the QUARTERLY REVIEW'. In the coming years the publisher continued to use tactics of this sort in a vain, indeed often counterproductive, effort to motivate Gifford and his writers.[55]

Meanwhile, in early January 1809, amidst a terrible snowstorm that had commenced on 3 January, Ballantyne and Murray attempted to meet in Yorkshire. Ballantyne set out from Edinburgh on 4 January, Murray at about the same time from London. 'It is blowing the devil's weather here', Ballantyne told Murray, 'but no matter – if the mail goes, I go'. The London *Courier* reported on 5 January that the 'fall of snow within these last two days has been so great that the roads have become in many places impassable'. Yet both men pressed forward, driven by the need to discuss arrangements upon which, they believed, their fortunes depended. Murray made his way north via the six-horse mail coach, the *Royal Charlotte*, ironically in the company of a 'Mr McDougall, a lawyer, employed about the *Edinburgh Review* by Constable'.[56] Murray arrived several hours ahead of his business partner late on Friday 6 January at a seventeenth-century coaching inn, *The Crown*, at Boroughbridge, in North Yorkshire, 'shriveled with the cold like an autumn leaf'. Late that evening, in the tap room the two men enjoyed an 'imperial dinner'. Believing that their hopes warranted 'this stretch', they drank each other's health over a bottle of the inn's finest claret, and then, on Saturday, settled down to business. The two men reviewed the commitments they made to each other in Edinburgh and at Ashiestiel and Murray asked Ballantyne to convey to Scott how important it was that the troops exert themselves for the first number of the *Quarterly Review*.[57]

In January and February Murray was in a state of anxiety over the journal, with good reason for he was bedeviled by problems. Upon his return to Edinburgh, Ballantyne wrote that he was 'excessively grieved at the luck' the publisher was having with contributors. Murray also had to absorb an increase in paper and printing costs scheduled for the beginning of February, just when he would incur the expense of printing 3,000 copies of the *Quarterly Review*. Another worry was the competition for attention the *Quarterly* faced in the advertising columns of London's main daily newspapers, the *Courier, The Times*, and the *Morning Chronicle*: the inaugural issues of Richard Cumberland's *London Review* and Samuel Taylor Coleridge's *The Friend* were announced as forthcoming in February and June, respectively. Coleridge's journal, Murray knew, would appeal to a minority taste and was therefore no threat. Cumberland's periodical, however, was a problem, not because it would be a worthy competitor, but because it would dilute the *Quarterly*'s novelty. There was more. John Murray's heart must have sunk when on top of all this he learned in late January that Archibald Constable had initiated a counterattack. Beginning in February, he planned to compete directly against Murray in the London market by setting up a 'general bookselling business' at 10 Ludgate Street under the sign of 'Archibald Constable, Alexander G. Hunter, John Parker, and Charles Hunter'.[58]

With the January deadlines missed, with no definite February deadline announced, and in the shadow of this set of bad news, the publisher was frantic. Heartened by the arrival, in mid-January, of one of Scott's articles, Murray's elation was soon deflated when Scott, upon receiving the proofs from Gifford, found them 'horribly incorrect'. To Murray's chagrin, Scott now made 'large additions' to his article that occasioned more delays and more expense. In mid-February, the editorial group was in despair at the failure of a number of reviews to appear, including Sharpe's and Douglas's.[59]

Ballantyne tried to buoy Murray's spirits by relating a conversation he over-heard in which Scott stated, 'there are difficulties attending the commencement of every work, which time and habit smooth away. But I think the first Number will be a good one; and in the course of three or four, I think we'll sweat them'. A few days later he commiserated with Murray on the publisher's 'greatest cause of anxiety – the editor'.[60] Except in the sense that he bore executive responsibility, however, Gifford was no more to blame for the journal's teething pains than were other members of the journal's inner circle. Murray's policy of maintaining secrecy caused difficulties, for example, as did Scott's canvassing for the *Edinburgh Annual Register.* If identifying willing and able writers within a restricted set – liberal con-servatives – proved troublesome throughout Gifford's tenure, how much more so during the start-up period when Murray's policy of maintaining deep secrecy made it difficult for Scott to nurture and for Gifford to take advantage of the enthusiasm for a new project that might have attracted a larger pool of contributors. Scott and Murray blamed Gifford for their problems nonetheless.

From the outset, the two men spent much anxious energy worrying about Gif-ford. The relationship between publisher and editor perhaps got off to a bad start when in early 1808 Murray and Gifford met to discuss the need for a journal to combat the *Edinburgh Review.* At the time, keen to dissuade Murray from thinking of him as a possible editor, Gifford may have characterized himself in disparaging terms that conditioned the publisher to expect the worst. There is evidence from Murray's early November 1808 communications with Scott that this was so. In writing to Scott, Murray described Gifford in words the prospective editor himself used in letters to the journal's other principals at about this time: 'Our friend Mr G whose writings shew him to be both a man of learning and wit – has lived too little in the world lately – to have obtained that delicacy of tact whereby he can feel at one instant, and habitually, what ever may gratify public desire or excite public attention and curiosity'. Similarly, in his response to Canning's invitation to take up the editorship, and in his reply to Scott's letter of policy, Gifford highlighted his own inadequacies: 'I am, like Othello, declined into the vale of years, and from nature and habit, very inert'. To Canning, Scott, and Murray, Gifford advertised his isolation and indolence. He wrote to Scott on 9 November 1808:

> So far there is nothing to discourage, but I have many and serious fears of myself. From habit, feebleness of constitution ... and, perhaps, from years, there is come upon me, in the language of Bottom such an *exposition* of dullness, that, if my friends did not sometimes stick pins in my cushion, and set me in motion, you would certainly read among the casualties of this or the following year, 'Died, of an elbow chair. Wm Gifford'. The natural and unfortunate consequence of this, is a dread of society, and an estrangement from many valuable acquaintants, who might ᶰᵒʷ, do 'yeoman's service'.

In the hope that he might dampen his coadjutors' expectations for the amount of work he could undertake and to encourage them to prop him up, in the coming months the editor continued to retail this negative self-assessment. Gifford himself was thereby partly to blame for the weakness of Scott and Murray's confidence in him and in the *Quarterly*'s prospects under his tutelage.[61]

From Ellis's letters we obtain a catalogue of 'all the inconveniences' the principals feared from Gifford's superintendence. Lamenting that the editor's 'fondness for the most poignant and even caustic spices [was] the distinguishing characteristic of his taste', Ellis agreed that Gifford must 'sacrifice his pepper-box'. 'Our supervisor will require the most attentive supervision', he advised, though he could not say who among them would dare edit the editor. The little band also fretted over his refusal regularly to supply copy from his own pen. In his 12 October letter to Canning, Gifford stipulated that if 'an Editor be wanted to take a leading part in the composition, I must then reluctantly decline ... on the score of inability. The business of revising, altering, occasionally adding, and finally carrying a work of this kind through the press will occupy fully as much time as I can ever promise myself'. When Scott learned about Gifford's stipulation, he saw intractable difficulties. In his 25 October letter, he used words of obligation and compulsion – 'responsible', 'duty', 'compelled' – to convince Gifford to change his mind. The editor was 'responsible to the Public and to the Bookseller' to meet the quarterly deadline, so if a given issue came up short in the number of required articles, to fulfil his obligations the editor would have 'to appear ... (occasionally at least) in the field'. Having pushed, Scott now pulled. 'At the same time if you think my services worth acceptance', he wrote, 'I will do all in my power to assist in this troublesome department of Editorial duty'. It was a promise he would soon renege on.[62]

At the end of November, Ellis and Canning succeeded where Scott had failed, inasmuch as they inspired Gifford to take up his quill. Consequently, he supplied two brief articles for Number 1, but, minimal though his effort was, it was one of the few times he produced more than a single article for a given number. True to his prediction, ill health prevented him from becoming a regular contributor. Besides corresponding with the journal's writers, he managed to 'arrange and overlook the various articles, and carry them through the press', but he only infrequently wrote reviews. Scott, too, had been prophetic, for the *Quarterly Review* under Gifford seldom came out on schedule. The editor's careful attention to articles' rhetoric and their stylistic purity often led to delays; so did his difficulty in obtaining sufficient copy. This was 'the Original Sin of our undertaking', he told Copleston. '[W]e began without materials, and when I printed the first Article, I did not know what the fourth would be'.[63]

Murray multiplied the complaints. Gifford's self-described isolation was a particular worry. His 'seclusion render[ed] him ignorant' and incapable of supplying the 'skilful management and judicious instructions' without which the conductors, Murray feared, would 'totally mistake the road to the accomplishment of the arduous task ... and involve the cause and every individual in not merely a defeat, but also disgrace'. With these exceptionally damning words, Murray started a drum beat he kept up incessantly over the next two years and opened topics that recur in his correspondence to the end of Gifford's tenure. He allowed Gifford was 'a man of learning and wit', but he thought he lacked what Jeffrey had in abundance, the ability to choose engaging subjects and 'treat them well'. By early December, convinced Gifford was not actively pressing the journal's political sponsors for information, Murray attended him 'almost every day' and 'impressed upon [him] so very strongly the urgent necessity for the immediate exertion of the higher powers'. Surveying the number and seriousness of these many defects – some of them self-confessed – begs the question whether the success the *Quarterly* eventually achieved under Gifford was because of him or in spite of him.[64]

3 COMPETITION FOR EDITORIAL CONTROL

The first number of the *Quarterly Review* was finally ready for publication at the end of February 1809. Murray hoped to have it appear at the same time in London and Edinburgh, but it was a forlorn hope. On 28 February, Ballantyne received printed sheets for Scott and himself. That same day, Murray sent 200 copies to his Edinburgh partners by coach, far fewer than the 650 he had promised. With unspecified problems in the printer's shop continuing to delay the production of Ballantyne's quota, Murray reluctantly decided to proceed with his London sale ahead of the journal's appearance in Scotland.

Printed by Charles Roworth of Bell-yard, Temple Bar, the number, eventually a run of 3,000, was published in London on Tuesday 1 March 1809; it was not sold in Scotland until 6 March, and then only in limited numbers. (By some unidentified agency, Constable and Jeffrey obtained a copy on 3 March.) The journal was expensive, 5 shillings, the equivalent of about £10 in today's values. Scott was ecstatic when he saw his advance copy. 'I have just one second to say', John Ballantyne reported to Murray, 'that I supped with Mr Scott last night. He is *transported* with the Review. "Capital – *most* capital!" burst from him again and again.' In Scotland, the journal sold rapidly. Only two hours after he opened his shop, John Ballantyne had cleared away all but twenty-eight of the 200 copies he had on hand. By 8 March, he had sold his whole supply and he had orders for fifty more.[1]

James Ballantyne thought well of most of the articles in the number, but – Scott's initial enthusiasm aside – his was a sycophantic and minority view.[2] The other co-founders considered the issue serviceable at best and all were dissatisfied with how ploddingly it had come together under Gifford's putative supervision. Bedford reflected an opinion generally held, that Ellis's important article on Spain beat Brougham's 'Don Pedro Cevallos' on points but that its prose was uninspiring. 'Against such attacks as that', he told Southey, 'the Edinburghers need not put on mail'.[3] Two days after the commencement of the London sale, Scott, now in a more considered mood, told Sharpe the 'whole [bore] marks of precipitate and hurried composition'.[4] In its first ever 231 pages, the *Quarterly*

Review was far from what Murray had hoped it would be, 'most brilliant ... in every respect'.[5]

In addition to content, Scott complained about process. With the last minute rush having prevented his seeing the final proofs of his articles, he directed Murray 'to have the goodness to attend to this'.[6] He looked to Murray and Gifford so to arrange matters that the little band would 'never again feel the pressure [they had] had for this Number'. The events of the summer and autumn of 1809 would prove that, although he may not have realized it, Scott had thus set a mark for the publisher and his editor. Each number, he declared, must produce 'one or two powerfully commanding articles, upon subjects of national interest exhibiting compleat [*sic*] possession of *knowledge* as well as talents, and grappling with the *Edinburgh* in extent and depth of research'.[7] Should their performance fall short of his expectations, his continued commitment would be at risk. Beyond the journal's inner circle, Scott admitted he had 'reasons for not being very sanguine' in his 'hopes of success'. With Number 1 the harvest had been meagre and the labourers few; he saw no sign matters were about to improve.[8]

In his analysis of the *Review*'s distemper, Scott was remarkably un-self-critical. He for instance drew no connection between the fulfilment of Heber's prophecy – that the great difficulty would be to identify and motivate worthy contributors – and the part the *Edinburgh Annual Register* played in drawing off potential writers from the *Quarterly Review*. Blaming human nature in general, he rationalised, aphoristically, that 'the energy of folks in a right cause is always greatly inferior to that of their adversaries. They trust, good souls, to the intrinsic merit of their cause'. Blaming Gifford in particular and himself not at all, he told Sharpe he wished he 'had some part of the influence' over the journal that rumour ascribed to him, for if he had 'he would most certainly have pushed the work much faster forward'. In saying this, he failed to recall his own tardiness in submitting his articles.[9]

Murray too was unwarrantedly despondent and readily blamed everyone but himself for a bad first result. In early March in an elaborate epistle, he outlined for Scott and Ballantyne what had gone wrong and how matters might be set right;[10] he lamented the journal's poor reviews and its sluggish sale; he complained government had not fulfilled its promise to supply striking information that would catch public attention and establish the journal's authority. No article had shown the depth of research that would render it permanently interesting, he thought. Continuing the theme he began in early November 1808, he also complained about Gifford's disorganization and indolence. He even faulted Scott. The journal's fate hung in the balance, he believed, and so, given the pressing need, he chastised Scott for failing to come to town to motivate the troops. In itemizing the perceived or real failings of others, he left his own decisions unanalyzed: his insistence upon secrecy; his seeing no need for a prospectus; his precipitously advertising publication for the end of January; his mismanaging production and his printing too few copies to recoup his investment.[11]

Scott imperiously delegated to James Ballantyne the initial reply to Murray's elaborate letter of complaint. Perhaps reflecting Scott's impatience, Ballantyne assured the publisher, '*he* [Scott] sits not down in vain and spiritless despondency but has ... tasked *himself* to produce more, and better, than he did in the first Number'. Scott took Murray's concerns seriously enough, though, that upon receiving the letter he immediately arranged a conference between James Ballantyne, William Erskine, and himself. Scott and Ballantyne elicited from Erskine a commitment to produce a political article for Number 2 that, supposing government supplied him with information, might be weighty and impressive. He also wrote 'a long and most pressing letter' to Gifford and one to Canning. When on 19 March he wrote to Murray, he suggested that because he was proximate to Gifford the publisher bore primary responsibility for motivating and organizing him. As for his coming to town, he wished not to come at his own expense but looked to Murray to convince government to finance the trip. By drawing a connection between the opening of John Ballantyne's shop and his hopes for the *Quarterly Review*'s success, he also demonstrated that he continued to be distracted by the Ballantynes and to mistake his involvement with them as a benefit to the *Review*. 'His making a stand', Scott insisted, 'is most essential to the Review and all our other plans for every other bookseller here has sunk under the predominating influence of Constables house and they literally dare not call their souls their own'.[12]

Spurred by Scott's admonitions (not to say his ultimatums), in the lead up to the publication of the second number, at the end of May 1809, Murray urged Gifford to act with greater energy and alacrity:

> I begin to suspect that you are not aware of the complete misery which is occasioned to me, and the certain ruin which must attend the Review, by our unfortunate procrastination. Long before this, every line of copy for the present Number ought to have been in the hands of the printer. Yet the whole of the Review is yet to print. I know not what to do to facilitate your labour, for the articles which you have long had lie scattered without attention, and those which I ventured to send to the printer undergo such retarding corrections, that even by this mode we do not advance. I entreat the favour of your exertion.

During the preparation of Number 2, Scott appeared to grow more hopeful – 'The Quarterly has taken root and will thrive', he told Southey – but he was merely encouraging an important contributor. Really, he had reason to doubt the *Quarterly Review*'s crew could make headway.[13]

In bringing out Numbers 1 and 2, to protect the journal's quality and its political ethos, the editor thwarted Murray and Scott. To avoid publishing articles they thought would strike the wrong tone in politics and religion, Scott and

Murray, with less success, tried to thwart their editor. Upon hearing that Gifford had proposed his hyper-orthodox friend Ireland as a reviewer of Sydney Smith's sermons, Scott, concerned that Ireland would be too strident, told Murray 'the thing must not be' and instructed Gifford to give the task to Erskine. Regardless, Ireland, assisted by Gifford, went ahead with the review. Murray, who was dissatisfied with Ellis's foray into high politics in the first number and who wished to influence even this aspect of the journal, put forward his solicitor Sharon Turner as a writer on foreign affairs. Gifford was pulled up short by the resulting article, a piece on Austria. 'Surely S. T. must be out of his senses', Gifford wailed. 'Part of his Article ... is aimed at us'. Consequently, in mid-May the editor placed Turner's draft in Canning's hands. The Foreign Secretary substantially rewrote the article, Gifford and Ellis assisting.[14]

Besides Gifford's magnificent indifference to the business side of reviewing and his, as Scott and Murray thought, lack of judgement in the selection of reviewers and of books to review, they had other reasons to be unhappy with their editor. For one thing he seemed to be willy-nilly rejecting their nominees. He declined to publish Charles Kirkpatrick Sharpe's review, prepared for Number 1, unless Sharpe allowed him to trim the tail of the already brief article. He had turned away a piece John Murray had solicited from James Mill, and when one of the publisher's favourite early contributors, James Pillans, prepared a review in time for its inclusion in Number 2, Gifford, insisting a complete rewrite was necessary, turned it aside as well. Too, the editor was the cause of missed opportunities. A promising man of letters, Barron Field, stepped forward in February to offer his services, but Gifford could suggest nothing for him to review.

While Scott and Murray had reason to complain about this or that decision of Gifford's, they exaggerated the editor's faults. During the *Quarterly's* first months, they repeatedly accused him of failing to bring out the journal on time when really his record was unassailable. In May, as we have seen, Murray feared that by Gifford's 'unfortunate procrastination' the enterprise faced 'certain ruin'.[15] Work on the first number, however, had taken three months, from the end of November 1808 to the end of February 1809; work on the second number had also taken three months, from the beginning of March to the end of May; in both cases, this was the exact period required for a quarterly publication. Yet Gifford was blamed when he failed to satisfy his coadjutors' arbitrary expectations.

Murray and Scott's negative attitude appears to have stemmed from their sanguine expectations of early success. Though Murray initially said it would take two years for the *Quarterly* to make a profit, within months he was crying that the journal was not paying its way. He dreamed the *Quarterly* would bring him fame and fortune, but after months of unrelenting work and worry he had gained nothing but heavy bills and taunts from his peers, such as that of a respectable old publisher, Edward Harding, who came into his shop to abuse the *Quarterly* as 'very dull if not stupid'. Measured by sales, the first two numbers were not failures. As both numbers had sold out, the sale could only have been better if Murray had printed more copies. In a July 1809 letter, Murray admitted to his wife that the journal was doing as well as possible, but that was not the impression he gave his coadjutors. Because he was impatient for success, in a misguided effort to drive his men forward Murray stirred up trouble by overemphasizing Gifford's faults and by obscuring the truth about the journal's sale.[16]

Scott hoped to see the *Quarterly* cut the *Edinburgh*'s subscription list in half. That did not happen; indeed, Constable's journal sold in greater numbers than before. He also anticipated the *Quarterly* would force the *Edinburgh* reviewers out into the open where their 'champions who having been long accustomed to push [had] lost the art of parrying' and might be vanquished in a fair fight.[17] Jeffrey and Horner were too savvy to fall into Scott's trap.

An atmosphere of discontent and recrimination therefore hovered over the *Quarterly Review*'s editorial machine when Scott – the publisher having agreed to bear the cost – made his way to London in early April 1809. Ostensibly he came to oversee the publication of Number 2 and to 'rally and review [the] forces'; it appears he spent much of his time fussing over William Gifford. How different now was Scott and Murray's conception of the purpose of the London visit from what they planned in October 1808 during the conference at Ashiestiel. Then Scott was to come to London to consolidate political support and plot a winning course. Now Scott and Murray saw his mission as preventing the ship from being run upon the sands. The emphasis during Scott's London visit might have been on setting realistic financial goals, establishing a sensible publication schedule, and attracting more and better talent. Undoubtedly these themes were covered in his discussions with John Murray and his gentlemen, but Scott and Murray's obsession in this period was with Gifford's performance. Predictably, during his three-month visit, Scott heard little to encourage him; to the contrary, his confidence in the journal's prospects for a time all but collapsed. While he was in London he wrote to his friend Morritt, 'a good deal happened ... to show me that Gifford wants much of that tact which is necessary to conduct with spirit the work he has undertaken'. When he wrote to Southey in July he called Gifford 'the laziest of editors'. In August he told Morritt he 'tremble[d] for the fate of the Quarterly'.[18]

We see in his reading of events that Scott was predisposed to judge Gifford harshly. Scott faulted Gifford for his rejection of Morritt's 'excellent article' on Warburton, yet Gifford rejected it because it was top to bottom a diatribe against the *Edinburgh Review*. In setting it aside, he therefore exercised Scott's own advice that the *Quarterly* would come before the public with better grace if it adopted a temperate tone and refrained from naming its northern rival.

Taunted by Morritt, who thought the *Quarterly*'s editor was afraid to engage the enemy, Scott accused Gifford of exercising 'a tame and cowardly caution'. Blusteringly, he assured Morritt that were he the editor, once having drawn the sword he 'would have hurled the scabbard into the Thames'. He claimed he advised such a course but was not 'listened to upon that topic'. It was with some difficulty, he informed Morritt, that he and Ellis 'prevailed for the admission of the Austrian article that saved the last number'. This was a surprising interpretation as it discounted Gifford and Canning having pulled into presentable shape what had originated from Turner's pen in a much inferior form.[19]

In a hand-wringing letter to Morritt, in July 1809 Scott stated his intention to abandon the *Quarterly Review* unless Gifford became a 'more determined' and active editor. He would 'write once more and very fully to Gifford', he told Morritt darkly, 'but it shall be for the last time. ... All Gifford's excellent talent and no less excellent principle will do little to save the Review unless he will adopt a more decisive tone of warfare and greater energy in his mode of conducting it'. A few weeks later in a letter to the same correspondent, he continued in this ominous vein. He pictured the *Quarterly Review* as a vessel piloted by an editor who had wrecked it on the rocks. He was not, he wrote, about to 'take to the [life] boat ... while the ship holds together', but he would no longer impose upon his friends. Despite assurances that he for one would courageously abide, Scott contributed nothing to Number 3. Nor did he, despite telling Morritt he thought the best way forward was to consult Ellis, manage more than a cryptic line in his next letter to him: 'We must think what is to be done about the Review'.[20]

If Murray and Scott were anxious about their editor's lack of application and sagacity, Gifford, too, was concerned – about Scott and Murray. He was worried about Scott's intentions and his confidence in Murray's judgement and transparency had been sorely tried. One particular incident occurred during the preparation of Number 3 that opened Gifford's eyes to Murray's character. His publisher, he found, could be vacillating, rash, and even duplicitous. In August 1809, an Oxford scientist, John Kidd, who appeared set to be a steady and valuable contributor, abruptly withdrew his services. He did so because a harsh assessment of his *Outlines of Mineralogy* had appeared in the *Quarterly Review*.[21]

Murray was to blame for one of the journal's own reviewers having been attacked. Earlier in the year he had solicited a review of Kidd's *Outlines* from an author he was just then courting, Thomas Thomson, an illustrious Edinburgh chemist. With no article from Thomson promised, Gifford commissioned a review from John Kidd's colleague, the Oxford professor of Anglo-Saxon, John Josias Conybeare, who dutifully supplied a friendly assessment. Meanwhile, Thomson finally came through, but the review he sent to Murray was condemnatory, and harshly so. Without informing Gifford, Murray now did something extraordinary. He wrote to Conybeare to tell him, falsely, the editor had declined his review because he thought it too flattering. Through Conybeare, that story got back to Kidd who, naturally, was deeply offended. Gifford later told Copleston, 'With respect to Dr Kidd, I am perfectly innocent. I entertain a sincere regard for him, and have profited by his talents'. He had liked Conybeare's article, he said, well enough to send it to the printer. Only then did he learn about Murray's machinations. When he wrote to Scott about the incident, because Scott and Thomson were friends, he covered up the true circumstances and his real opinion of Thomson's article. Although he lamented that Thomson's review was 'severe against our poor friend', he nevertheless claimed he was 'pleased with the critique'. For years thereafter, Gifford tried through Heber and other agents to bring Kidd back onboard, but to no avail. To observers it appeared Gifford had tactlessly risked Oxford's support for the *Quarterly Review*, a potentially important source of contributors. Really, the editor was blameless; indeed, he had even gone out of his way to protect the reputation of his publisher, a man who by his unconscionable actions had impugned his editor's character. As in this instance, so in others, Gifford took blows for an associate. Such rectitude and loyalty won the admiration of men like Canning and Ellis, but, especially early on, his virtues were often lost on Scott and Murray.[22]

In August 1809, the publisher challenged his editor by again insisting Sharon Turner be permitted to write on domestic politics and foreign policy. Clearly, Murray was trying to wrest control of the *Quarterly*'s political direction from Canning and Ellis, or at least obtain a share of it, but this the journal's political supporters could not permit. When Ellis, through Gifford, objected, Murray attributed the statesman's motives to jealousy and he threatened to appeal to Canning. Fortunately for the fate of the *Review*, he remembered he dare not risk annoying the journal's key political sponsor, so he backed away. For the most part, Murray seems not to have consciously conspired against Gifford. Instead he acted impulsively or instinctively, but his behaving as 'lord paramount' Gifford found offensive nonetheless.[23]

By the close of summer 1809, Scott was on the verge of deserting, Gifford was close to resigning, and Murray was in a frenzy. Complaining to his wife about the 'manner in which the Review *zig zags* my time', at the end of August the publisher showed how impetuous and arbitrary he could be when he was ill or otherwise under stress. He offered Gifford a rope by which he might hang himself:

> I have been exceedingly harassed today by Mr G[ifford]. who was excessively hurt that I had not printed the article on Porter's Travels in Russia written by Mr R Heber although I have already exceeded the Quantity of Sheets by a whole one. ... Mr G. talked very seriously of resigning – of my want of confidence and friendship &c &c – I have made the printer – who when I took the article to him to print, looked as

> if he were shot, send me a letter explaining the impossibility of the thing – which I intend to inclose to Mr G – with a note telling him if he will only let me have my way in this number he shall have his in the next. ... This is I think worth the trial of one Number.

With a reticence that bordered on cowardice, Murray told Gifford nothing about his manipulative and fractious plan. Instead, in the midst of preparations for Number 4 he simply disappeared for a few weeks, leaving Gifford bewildered by his publisher's 'unaccountable silence'.[24]

In his *Memoir*, Smiles interpreted Murray's behaviour as a by-product of his anxious pursuit of contributors. Gifford, though, saw the publisher's interventions as an unwarranted and destructive encroachment upon his editorial duties and prerogatives. He believed Murray to be 'flippant, presuming, and very troublesome and even offensive in his zeal' to make the journal a success, and that by placing onerous demands and restrictions on his editor he bore part of the responsibility for delays and confusion. Problems in the handling of authors, texts, and production arose, Gifford felt, by Murray's having 'too many advisers, and I too many masters'. Gifford was left to wonder why he bore the title of editor at all. In August 1809 he told a correspondent, more or less seriously, his influence on the journal was 'little more than nominal'.[25]

If in this early period we attend only to the noisy discontentedness we find in Murray and Scott's letters, we can easily mistake Gifford's character and contribution. There is every reason to conclude he needed assistance, as he said he would, in performing the mechanical duties of book production and in generating sufficient copy to fill each number. But in addition to lamenting Gifford's disorganization and lack of energy, Murray and Scott also disliked his selection of books for review, especially his insistence upon publishing articles on theology and classics. Here, however, their objections were mostly misplaced for Gifford proved to have a keen sense of the journal's purposes and how best to win the attention and loyalty of some of its natural constituents, notably conservative clerics and academics. He alone among the *Quarterly*'s primary collaborators recognized, for instance, that a principal purpose of the journal was to defend the idea of Britain as a Christian nation buttressed by great 'establishments': 'I had long seen', he wrote, 'with thousands besides, that the Government was calumniated, the great literary Establishment of the country depreciated, the Church insulted, and even Religion itself attacked with the unfairest and most odious weapons: and I flattered myself that when a fair opportunity was afforded, the friends of Order, Morality and rational Piety, would muster in their defence'. When Murray complained to Erskine, Scott, Heber, and Ellis that religious articles could be ponderously dull and were of little interest to the public, Gifford countered that religious conservatives' displeasure over the *Edinburgh Review*'s impiety had helped start the *Quarterly Review*. The *Quarterly*'s religious readers,

Gifford understood, looked to the journal to supplement and improve upon the leading pro-Church periodical the *British Critic*.[26]

Gifford was demonstrably in tune with the principles the *Quarterly Review* was set up to promote. The decisions he took, the books he chose to notice, the publishers who fell under his critical eye, the authors he selected for review, the contributors to whom he gave assignments, were part and parcel of his editorial practice. Murray's interfering with the 'œconomy of the work'[27] not only humiliated his editor and made the smooth running of the enterprise impossible, it made it difficult for Gifford to achieve the journal's ideological *raison d'être*.

When the *Quarterly* finally achieved success, it did so in large part because of Gifford's excellence in the one duty he shared with no one: his wielding of the editor's blue pencil. At the outset he declared that 'for the sake of consistency and many other urgent causes, I must be endowed with a sort of Dictatorial power over what comes before me'. 'I will', he told Canning in mid-October 1808, 'use it with lenity, but with the strictest vigilance'. Indeed, a few weeks later Scott used remarkably similar terms to describe the editor's prerogatives: 'he must be invested', Scott wrote to Gifford, 'with the unlimited power of controul [*sic*] for the purpose of selecting curtailing and correcting the contributions'.[28] It was by policy, therefore, as well as by personal inclination that every draft review that arrived on Gifford's desk became the property of the *Quarterly* to be shaped to the journal's purposes. Partly through Southey's crowing, Gifford unfairly gained the reputation of wielding his power broadly and insensitively. So it was that tyros in the art of reviewing, such as John Keble and Thomas Arnold, were afraid and resentful of Gifford even before they dealt with him. Despite his reputation, his editorial practice generally was sensible and reasonable.

In describing Gifford's editing of their subjects' *Quarterly Review* articles, *ODNB* contributors and other biographers have strained the resources of the English language to discover negative epithets. But in many cases their criticism is exaggerated or unwarranted. In more than one instance, men who saw both a writer's manuscript and his published review wondered at the author's loud complaints, as for instance Keble commenting on an article by Southey: 'I do not see that Gifford's alteration in the passages you speak of was enough to alter the sense, or to put the writer in a passion'. The *Quarterly*'s first editor made it clear that he understood, even if he did not sympathize with, his writers' protectiveness of their material: 'I suppose tis as hard to be an author and wise', he told John Coleridge, 'as it is to be in love and be wise'.[29]

In shaping articles, though he often pruned, he seldom grafted. Claims that he made authors say something other than what they intended are for the most part false; the truth of his assertion to the civil servant Robert Hay that 'I never presume to alter the author's mode of thinking, so as to make him say what he never intended' is supported in the manuscript record. 'I have no capacious itch for alterations', he insisted. Mostly he trimmed articles; the additions he made generally involved the insertion of factual material that complemented the author's argument. Otherwise, he obeyed Scott's injunction in his 25 October 1808 letter to enliven dull articles by adding 'spice'. Though he sometimes took liberties with poor submissions from first-time or infrequent contributors who had yet to make their mark, in his own eyes his practice was benign: 'I view every Article with a paternal eye, and am never happier than when I can suggest any trivial improvement either from situation or incidental knowledge', he assured James Henry Monk. To Hay he wrote, 'I feel the same interest in every thing which appears in our Review, as if I were the author of it. I take as much care as if that were really the case'. The changes he did make were by no means arbitrary. He made excisions 'to preserve consistency of plan' and, as he told young Coleridge, some of the 'wounds and gashes' he inflicted on articles were to avoid repetition, some to preserve uniformity, some to serve stylistic fastidiousness or the 'eager impatience of the reader'. 'I have many tastes to conciliate, if possible', he wrote, 'and you know what a beast – belua canticeps – the public is'.[30]

To some extent, outside of his conduct of the *Quarterly Review* Gifford deserves his reputation as a dry-as-dust scholar competently manipulating the minutiae of textual apparatus and collation. But he exercised pedantry where pedantry is a virtue, in his classics translations and his careful editions of old playwrights. In his editing of articles for the *Quarterly* he was mindful of the general reader's impatience with tedious detail and ponderous learning and saw to it that articles not wear 'too forensic a cast' or 'too scholastic a form'. Articles on Greek and Latin texts were of course by definition technical and scholarly, and these he mostly did not touch. In other types of articles, he was wary of ostentatious learning and would cancel classical references and sesquipedalian Latinisms, as he did for instance in the draft of Coleridge's review of Milman's *Samor*. When he elided a classical allusion in an article of Hay's, he apologized to the author for being 'a stern hard-hearted barbarian'. 'I have learning from my soul', he wrote on that occasion, 'but I have always dreaded any thing that seemed like an untimely display of it'. Similarly, he advised Hay to remove a 'Saxon note' from a draft article because 'not three people in the world [would] read it'.[31]

There was another reason for Gifford's interventions – he received inferior material that could only be admitted if he reshaped it. As Murray colourfully put it, the roster of submissions was 'a desert the Editor has occasionally to fertilize'. Unlike Jeffrey, Gifford never managed to establish a backlog of articles or to accumulate a large stable of professional writers. For regular copy he relied primarily upon the journal's sheet anchors, Barrow, Southey, and Croker. Otherwise, he frequently accepted submissions that he then had to draw up to the *Quarterly*'s high standard. Much to Murray's chagrin, Gifford often delayed an issue for weeks while he improved a single article. Applying eighteenth-century ideas of taste and decorum, Gifford vigilantly hunted for lapses in tone, word choice, and idiom: 'Your friend', Gifford wrote to Barrow, speaking again of Hay, 'is not aware of the stile which our Review requires, and writes rather colloquially. ... We must always be careful in our language'. Gifford glossed a manuscript submitted by John Hughes, no doubt to the author's mortification, 'Is not this in very bad taste?' Given natural sensitivities, it is not surprising that some of the *Quarterly*'s authors bristled at Gifford's interventions, Southey and Lamb only most famously.[32]

Gifford also adjusted articles to ensure uniformity of opinion and to see to it that the journal did not run up against the men the *Quarterly* was, in part, set up to serve. It was mainly for these reasons that he aggressively enforced the convention of anonymous authorship, which made it easier for him than it would otherwise have been to maintain in the journal an appearance of discursive harmony. The more difficult imposition of a 'house voice' he effected in two ways, through editorial amendments and by excluding contributions he found 'unsafe'. This latter practice Murray later codified into a rule, that 'of never *contracting* for any article for the Review', the editor to keep himself 'free to accept or reject [an article] after it has been written', that there should never be 'even an implied agreement of any sort in either party'. By way of excusing a 'little omission and addition' to an article by Lord Dudley, he told Copleston that 'we must sacrifice something to our plan, and ... many things which I would gladly offer under my own name, I cannot venture to produce in a review, where I have many palates to please, and many ticklish tempers to study'.[33]

If the nature of Gifford's editorial conduct was more nuanced than is generally recognized, so too were his personality, his politics, and his published works. Gifford's reputation for acid partisanship needs to be qualified and a distinction drawn between his sometimes harshly judgemental non-*Quarterly Review* productions and the disinterested tone he generally encouraged in the journal. He wrote polemical material of the worst sort for the *Anti-Jacobin*; he was responsible for some particularly nasty notes in his editions of Elizabethan dramatists; and he issued satirical poems that stung; but for the *Quarterly*, though he wrote a small number of intemperate articles, injected vituperative passages in some submissions, and encouraged writers such as John Coleridge and Henry Taylor to produce harsh reviews, for the most part he held his worst tendencies in check.

When personally attacked, and especially in his early years when he was striving to establish his reputation as a translator and textual editor, he showed considerable weakness of character by purchasing his reputation at the expense of others'. Indeed, it was in the notes to his editions of dramatists and in some of his other writings outside the *Quarterly Review* that he had much to answer for. When Ellis said of Gifford that though he was 'the best tempered man alive' he was '*terribly* severe with his pen',[34] he mainly had in mind not Gifford's articles in the *Quarterly* (which were few), but his earlier writings and some sentences he added to other men's reviews. His textual notes on previous editors of Elizabethan dramatists show him in turns petty, boastful, spiteful, splenetic, paranoid, unforgiving, and uncharitable – a catalogue of bad behaviour. These lapses produced a blot on his character that he never managed to remove.

Consequently, when slashing criticism appeared in the *Quarterly Review* it would be imputed to him. Those articles legitimately reflect Gifford's editorial and personal principles in the sense that he bore executive responsibility for them, but also because he sometimes pushed his writers onto the attack. He did so, he claimed, to protect principles the journal stood for. He self-righteously concluded that although the *Quarterly* was sometimes as harsh as the *Edinburgh*, his own journal was superior because it spoke the truth. 'I know not what to say about the Edinburgh Reviewers', he wrote to Hay, 'and yet I cannot help thinking that we take a higher tone. They are partisans – they attack with fury, because it matters not whether they are right ... That they will find readers is true, so does, and so will the Morning Chronicle – but who can turn back with pleasure, or even patience to their political and personal articles, which are as false and foolish as they are confident, abusive, and unjust'.[35]

Robert Southey nicely caught the distinction – for distinction there was – between Gifford's sometimes brutal public polemics and his consistently mild private character: '[he] had a heart full of kindness for all living creatures, except authors; *them* he regarded as a fishmonger regards eels'.[36] We can trace the origins of Gifford *Agonistes* to the man's inner demons.[37] The early loss of his parents, his physical deformities, and his failure to establish an affirming love relationship[38] appear to have fractured his personality and made him in subtle ways an emotional predator. Seeking psychical, practical, and emotional security, he applied the golden rule in his private life in the hope that his friends and patrons would reciprocate. Living in the shadow of the early hardships he endured, he resented other writers' easy success and in his public writings punished them for it,[39] his unsophisticated origins impairing his ability to express himself, sympathetically and with self-restraint. He was especially hard on authors who attacked the establishment, the surrogate parent that had rescued him from social and intellectual degradation. And yet one detects in the particular quality of Gifford's attendance upon rich and powerful men the flinching caution of an abused child. Gifford petted the *ancien régime* as one might calm Britannia's lion, fearful of its claws.

The civil servant and sometime *Quarterly* reviewer Henry Taylor speculated that Gifford's hardscrabble upbringing deadened his sympathies and that the temper of the times occasionally pushed him to permit, encourage, or even arrange cruelly dismissive reviews:

Southey said to me of Gifford, that all his gall was in his inkstand. The same may be said of Jeffrey. But they had to fight their way in life in their youth; and they, like many others then and since ... adopted the evil habit of regarding literary life as a fair fight, of which the honour and glory belonged to him who could use weapons of offence with most skill and effect. Under cover of this view they 'corrupted their compassions', and they hardened their hearts to acts of literary cruelty and wrong, dealing death-strokes at the feelings and hopes and fortunes of this or that literary aspirant, perhaps with one or another plea or pretext of a public or a party purpose to be answered, but in reality with little other object than that of raising their own credit as journalists by the force and brilliancy of their writings. There was no malice in this. ... But there was an utter indifference to human suffering ...[40]

Gifford's lack of sympathy for writers was a weakness Hazlitt indicted him for, with some justice as the editor's own words condemn him. Writing to Scott, he thought it humorous to ask, 'Can not you find out some poor but presumptuous devil to laugh at again? Why will not blockheads be more alert, and do something to serve us?' He sometimes adopted the role of avenging angel, as when he directed Taylor to assassinate Landor in print for his political and religious sins:

Why should we spare Mr Landor? He is a hypocritical tyrant. He began life as an atheist and a Jacobin of the most rancorous kind. He has been a preacher of sedition, a sower of malignity, and a decided hater of his country. That he could be kind and charitable to his slaves and tools, and admirers, I know; – so could Caligula, and so could Robespierre – but once oppose him, and then!!!

It is possible to explain, if not excuse, such attacks. Gifford permitted or directed his writers to be censorious and sarcastic when he scented stupidity or presumption, righteous and avenging when he uncovered infidelity or heterodoxy, forensic and unforgiving when he detected disloyalty or treason.[41]

Yet far from uniformly encouraging a vituperative tone in the journal, Gifford often pulled authors back from inflated criticism of measures and men. A note he wrote to Hay about a draft article is typical: 'What have the doctors done to you that you fell upon them so fiercely? Do you wish to have them dispatch me – who am already in their hands?' When he constrained authors, it was to maintain the journal's dignity and to create an aura of imperious disinterested authority. In justifying redactions to an article, he told an author, 'We cannot say all that we wish. Names, in some cases, must be respected, and, as we are anonymous, a certain degree of decorum and forbearance must be maintained – unless against culprits of a notorious nature'. Typical was his letter to Murray of 9 August 1809 in which he gave his reasons for eliding Thomson's review of Kidd: 'It is very splenetick and very severe, indeed, much too *wantonly* so. I hope, however, it is just. Some of the opprobrious language I shall soften, for the eternal repetitions of *ignorance, absurdity, surprising*, &c are not wanted. I am sorry there is so much Nationality in it'.[42]

Gifford watched the intellectual horizon for signs of trouble, then, from 'culprits of a notorious nature', that is, authors and publishers known for their opposition to existing institutions in Church and State. In doing so, in Hazlitt's words, he turned the journal into a 'link which connected literature with the police'.[43] With programmatic consistency he promoted 'correct' views and targeted heterodox writers and their publishers. The editor instinctively chose to review books that struck a liberal conservative chord or that otherwise permitted him to pursue favourite topics. A dip into a few of the early *Quarterly*'s articles reveals patterns of editorial selection and practice that held true throughout his tenure. The examples that follow describe the theses and preoccupations typical of many articles published during Gifford's years. In them we trace the editor's pursuit of a limited number of political and religious themes and well-defined sets of enemies: radicals and Unitarians especially. In contrast, we find that while Scott and Ellis also exercised ideological choices, they did so less systematically and expressed themselves less stridently than Gifford.

As we have seen, the *Quarterly*'s projectors determined the journal would gain credibility if it were not obviously and exclusively political but 'complete as to scholarship, literature and science'. The purpose of the *Quarterly*, though, was wholly political, so it was Gifford's task, without drawing too much attention to his practice, to ensure that reviews of literature and science served the journal's editorial programme. Exasperated that the *Quarterly* had reviewed a volume on *Extraction of the Cataract* while it had ignored his own book on King Arthur, Frere asked Gifford, 'What has the Quarterly to do with cataracts, or catheters, or cataplasms, or with any subjects which are neither of a political, national, or literary interest?' As Kevin Gilmartin observes, non-political and non-literary works were noticed in conservative review journals such as the *Quarterly* 'in part to advance a claim that subversion was migrating from overt political agency to the more elusive form of mind and manners'. Gifford and his coadjutors addressed a wide range of cultural products because they regarded the arts and sciences as part and parcel of British civilization, a conservative vision of which they were determined to promote and defend. Similarly, Jeffrey and his writers reviewed science, mathematics, music and other such topics in an equally systematic effort to tilt the nation's cultural establishments leftward.[44]

It was to achieve these programmatic ends that Gifford in the *Quarterly*'s inaugural number reviewed Lady Sydney Morgan's *Woman; or, Ida of Athens*. In February 1814, he identified what it was about Morgan that upset him and why through his reviewers he returned to her time and again: 'The woman is dangerous. She is labouring to acquire notoriety; she is a professed writer for the public; and her impudent and persevering puffs cannot, I suspect, be met by gentle means. She is evidently capable, and desirous of doing mischief. It is necessary to put an extinguisher on her popularity with the ignorant and young and innocent.' Gifford's brief satirical review declares Morgan's allusive language incomprehensible and her histrionic peripatetic plot 'merely foolish'. Longman, her publisher, worried that readers might suspect her 'work of being tainted with the philosophy of the new school of French moralists, and of promulgating Deistical principles'.[45] His concerns proved warranted as Gifford disdains Morgan's preference for Nature over Revelation. Exhibiting the patriarchal condescension he often slipped into when reviewing a woman's book, Gifford suggests that Morgan would benefit from reading the Bible. Then she might become 'not indeed a good writer of novels, but a useful friend, a faithful wife, a tender mother, and a respectable and happy mistress of a family'.[46]

The next article in *Quarterly Review* Number 1, Sharon Turner's review of *Grammars of the Sanskrita Language*, commenced the journal's advocacy of Britain's expansive imperialism. The particular quality of imperialism the *Quarterly* advocated – the liberal sort exemplified in the writings of Sir John Malcolm – is reflected in the books under review, works by Carey, Colebrooke, and Wilkins. We should read the article in the light of British angst over how best to dominate the Indian subcontinent. Gifford's recourse to his friend Lord Teignmouth as Turner's subeditor reveals a subtext, the contest in the East India Company between the so-called Company and India interests. The Company interest, led by the evangelical Saints' Charles Grant, Edward Parry, and Lord Teignmouth, favoured winning the hearts and minds of Indians by inculcating Western ideological norms, including Christianity, while working through local structures and cooperating with Indians in commercial enterprises. The Company interest supported positions Sir John Malcolm and John Stuart Mill later held in a modified form. Led by Warren Hastings and his henchman John Scott-Waring, the India interest advocated dominating the subcontinent politically and commercially while, for purely pragmatic reasons, tolerating native rites and practices. Turner, Gifford, and Teignmouth selected the authors in the article's headnote, then, because they represented positions held by one or other of the Company's factions.[47]

The seventh article in Number 1, Isaac D'Israeli's review of Zouch's *Life and Writings of Sir Philip Sidney*, is of little interest until we consider why Gifford admitted notice of the book at all: the review appeared in acknowledgment of some of the journal's sponsors. Thomas Zouch, a Cambridge-educated Church of England clergyman was uncle to William Wordsworth's patron, William Lowther, the Earl of Lonsdale. Gifford and Murray counted Lonsdale among the *Quarterly*'s political sponsors.[48] It is not beside the point that Lonsdale was the friend and political patron of a man who would become one of the *Quarterly*'s most prolific contributors, John Wilson Croker.[49] Zouch's brother Henry, a prominent social and moral reform advocate, was an associate of the Saints' leader, William Wilberforce. As we have seen, Gifford also considered the Saints to be patrons of the *Quarterly Review*.

The full title of the book reviewed in the eighth article in Number 1 is worth stating for it contains the reason why Gifford noticed it, Cockburn's *The Credibility of the Jewish Exodus, Defended against Some Remarks of Edward Gibbon, Esq. and the Edinburgh Reviewers*. Along with Southey's review of Baptist missions in issue Number 1, this article opened Gifford's long campaign to counter the *Edinburgh*'s anti-Christian bias. The *Quarterly* reviewer calls upon conservatives to guard against the corrupting influence of the *Edinburgh Review*. The author under examination, Sir William Cockburn, the Dean of York, is offered as a case in point. A man of Cockburn's conservative pedigree and pious profession, the reviewer implies, ought to know better than to be an apologist for the *Edinburgh*. The author of the review (probably John Ireland) criticizes Cockburn for calling into question the historical reliability of the Mosaic text and he contemptuously dismisses Humean skepticism regarding the veracity of biblical miracles. The reviewer also chastises Cockburn for temporizing in the face of the *Edinburgh*'s infidelity. How can Cockburn sincerely believe the *Edinburgh*'s writers 'are Christians', the reviewer asks. Another reason why Gifford and his reviewer noticed Cockburn's volume was because it bears the imprint of John Hatchard, bookseller to the Queen, an evangelical publisher patronized by liberal Tories. By implication, Hatchard is criticized for publishing the book.[50]

The *Quarterly*'s nationalist agenda is clearly exemplified in article 10, a review by the eminent scientist Thomas Young of Laplace's *Théorie de l'Action Capillaire*. Pierre-Simon, Marquis de Laplace, French astronomer and mathematician extraordinaire whose *Mécanique Céleste* is one of the great books of nineteenth-century science, extended Newton's geometrical mechanics to physical astronomy and in so doing revealed the basic stability of planetary orbits. While Young rightly praises Laplace for his intellectual 'sublimity', his hostility in the article derives from British distrust of Continental methods that emphasized pure abstraction (British scientists privileged empirical experimentation). Given the scientific value of Laplace's contribution, Young's criticism of what he calls Laplace's 'rage for abstraction and prolixity' seems trivial. The review can best be explained by Young and Gifford's nationalistic chauvinism.

When *Quarterly Review* Number 1 appeared, James Ballantyne told John Murray that readers liked all of the articles but one, the review of *Public Characters*. Gifford was the butt of satire in that book, but he also noticed the volume to pester its radical publisher. An annual compendium of specially-commissioned biographical sketches, *Public Characters* was published in London between 1798 and 1810 by Sir Richard Phillips. Phillips, who originated as a bookseller and publisher in Leicester, welcomed radical and democratic agitators to his store and he distributed books and pamphlets the government considered subversive.

For his pains, in 1793 he spent a few months in prison. Two years after his parole, he set up shop in London in the St Pauls area where he soon commenced the *Monthly Magazine*. Godwin, Malthus, and Hazlitt were contributors, as was Southey in his rebellious youth.

The fourteenth article in Number 1 appeared in part because the book reviewed, *Accum on Mineralogy*, issued from the radical press and because Gifford had a bone to pick with its publisher. Friedrich Christian Accum, a Westphalian chemist who moved to London in 1793 to work in a pharmacy was an entrepreneur. In 1810 he conducted a chemistry school and he successfully promoted coal gas lighting for London's streets.[51] Accum's publisher, George Kearsley, sponsored the *North Briton*, a journal founded by a prominent radical, John Wilkes. Kearsley's most successful author was John Wolcot (pseud., Peter Pindar), the man who in August 1800 physically assaulted William Gifford because he mistook him as the author of criticism that John Gifford had published in the ultra-Tory *Antijacobin*. Kearsely, then, was certainly well known to Murray and Gifford.[52]

In the sixth article in Number 2, *The New Testament, in an Improved Version* came under scrutiny both as a Unitarian text and because it bears the imprint of the radical publisher Joseph Johnson. This was the first of many reviews Gifford commissioned from George D'Oyly, a Church of England clergyman and Cambridge academic who was preoccupied with the defence of orthodox Christianity and the Established Church against the twin threats of Unitarianism and radicalism.[53] D'Oyly attacks the book as a publication of the Unitarian Society for Promoting Christian Knowledge. The St Pauls Churchyard publisher Joseph Johnson was the primary London distributor of Unitarian books and tracts. He published the radical *Analytical Review*, and his soiree attracted leading liberal lights, Wollstonecraft, Godwin, Priestly, and Paine. For these reasons, over the course of his tenure Gifford reviewed an inordinate number of Johnson's books.

An obscure topic, Richardson's *Memoir of Fiorin Grass*, the eighth article in Number 2, was noticed in part because of its author's social, political, and religious sympathies. Fiorin grass was introduced in the seventeenth century for use as animal feed (it is now employed mainly for golf courses). An Irishman, William Richardson, prominently advocated Fiorin grass in *Gentleman's Magazine* as a cash crop that could be cultivated by the rural poor. When the Oxford scientist John Kidd proposed this unusual subject for review, Gifford admitted it because Richardson was known to him for his conservative religious and political views. A number of moral reform articles published under Gifford, such as this one, anticipate Tory Radicalism and can be seen to have contributed to the counterrevolutionary campaign conservatives engaged in during this period.[54] A writer in the *London Magazine* later noted perspicaciously that the *Quarter-*

ly's conductors awkwardly balanced their social conscience and support for the powers that be:

> The faculties of [its] writers are all enlisted on the side of what is strong in the country; but their dispositions are not hostile to those who are weak, injured, and distressed. If they could do the latter much good without seeming to bear hard on the former, they would willingly do so. According to their philosophy, whatever *is* is right; but they would have no objection to make the right a little better, if it could be done without conveying any reflection on it as imperfect ... [The journal] seems like one who, if he were not withheld, would do something: it has an air as if it would be intrepid, were it not timid.[55]

The *Quarterly*'s ambiguous moral reform agenda is further exemplified in Thomas Young's review of various works on insanity by Haslam, Pinel, Davis, Cox, and Arnold, the eighth article in Number 3. John Haslam, an Edinburgh-educated physician, in his *Observations* recommended the benign treatment of the insane. Philippe Pinel advocated moral over medical treatment. Joseph Mason Cox, a Baptist, was a Bristol physician and asylum keeper. In his influential *Practical Observations*, he criticized beatings, but he nevertheless advocated a physically invasive, degrading regimen. Thomas Arnold, the owner-operator of a Leicester asylum, was related by marriage to the evangelical Macaulay family. He recommended isolation in protected surroundings and treating the insane with gentle consideration. In his political opinions, Arnold was a radical. In his review, Young surveys definitions of insanity, efforts at classification, statistics on cures and remission, and, most interestingly, 'management'. He believes the medical practitioner needs to establish moral ascendancy over the patient and he asserts that corporal punishment is ineffective. He is enthusiastic about 'bleeding, purging, vomiting ... and narcotics'. The thrust of the article, though, favours humanitarian treatment.[56]

If Gifford habitually selected books as ideological targets, Scott branched out by seeking opportunities to apply standards of literary taste. Such is the case with his review of Carr's *Caledonian Sketches, or a Tour through Scotland in 1807*. In this book, Sir John Carr, a Londoner, supplies an early example of what is now called travel journalism. Between 1803, when he published his first travel book, on Paris, and 1811 when his marriage to a wealthy woman removed his need to write for a living, Carr churned out a series of travelogues on Holland, the Baltic, Ireland, Scotland, and Spain. In literary circles, if not among the public, with whom his works were popular, Carr was despised for the machine-like regularity and poor quality of his output. Scott bothered to review Carr because of the subject matter (Scotland), to fulfill his mandate, which was to supply what Gifford called 'fun and feeling', and to advocate 'taste' in literature.[57]

Deviating from Gifford's obviously ideological topics and themes, in his review in Number 2 of *John de Lancaster: a Novel*, Scott contemplates whether only good men can produce good books. The novel's author, Richard Cumberland, dramatist, memoirist, periodical editor and writer, 'the friend of Garrick, of Goldsmith, and of Johnson', stood too high to be quizzed. In any case, Scott was generally sympathetic to Cumberland who, like Scott himself, was a hard-working middle-class man of letters. Scott wrote elsewhere that on balance there was more to commend than criticize in Cumberland's oeuvre (*Biographical Memoirs*). Scott's plan was to offer a generally positive review, but because Gifford had heard 'a miserable account' of the book from George Hammond, he encouraged Scott to offer Cumberland no quarter. Scott describes Cumberland as an author 'never ... in the very van' but 'seldom lagged in the rear' of literature, a 'dignified and respectable mediocrity' whose 'accurate taste ... beautiful and flowing stile, and ... pleasing subjects ... compensate in some degree for want of depth of thought, or novelty of conception'. In a fine passage, he chastises Cumberland for his monomania and peevishness.[58]

When he chose to, Scott could pursue an ideological agenda, though he went about it with a more delicate touch than Gifford. In issue Number 2, for instance, he noticed Campbell's *Gertrude of Wyoming, a Pensylvanian [sic] Tale, and other Poems*. The Whig poet Thomas Campbell who, as we have seen was involved in the pre-history of the *Quarterly Review*, was popular in his day for his didactic poem *The Pleasures of Hope* (1799), the subversive democratic subtext of which was overlooked by most readers, but certainly not by Scott and Gifford who were sensitively attuned to such details. Campbell mixed with Whig members of Edinburgh's establishment and he otherwise wore his liberalism on his sleeve. Scott, however, does not hold this against him; even more notably he only mildly rebukes him for his choice of topic – an incident during the American war for independence when British loyalists massacred a group of American settlers in Pennsylvania. Scott writes: 'feeling as Englishmen [sic], we cannot suppress the hope that Mr. Campbell will in his subsequent poems chuse a theme more honourable to our national character, than one in which Britain was disgraced by the atrocities of her pretended adherents'.[59] By adopting a tone of mild reasonableness even in treating controversial subject matter, Scott hoped to model an approach to reviewing that stood in contrast to the *Edinburgh's* (and Gifford's) vitriolic prose.

As the journal's designated political reviewer, George Ellis was encouraged to select topics with an obvious application to current events. In the eighteenth article in Number 1, he reviewed Vaughan's *Siege of Zaragoza*, for two reasons: to reinforce points he made in his leading article on Spain; and to notice the work of a fellow liberal conservative, Sir Charles Richard Vaughan. A traveller and minor civil servant, Vaughan was the brother of Sir Henry Halford Vaughan, a prominent physician whose blue-blood clientele eventually included each of the sovereigns from George III to Victoria.[60] Another brother, a judge, Sir John

Vaughan, actively supported Pitt and he later prosecuted Sir Francis Burdett in the wake of the so-called 'Peterloo Massacre'. The background of Vaughan's *Narrative* is his trip through Spain in 1808, during which time he made contact with Spanish patriots and acted as an informal courier to Sir John Moore. Later in life he was private secretary to Henry Bathurst, a moderate conservative, who, like Vaughan's brother, had been one of Pitt's allies. The subjects of the article, the siege of Zaragoza (Saragossa) and its defence by the Spanish soldier Palafox, are celebrated by Wordsworth in his so-called 'Liberty poems', 'Hail, Zaragoza! If with unwet eye' and 'Ah! where is Palafox? Nor tongue nor pen'. The Liberty poems also enter the history of the *Quarterly Review* again, if indirectly, in 1817 in connection with an article for which Samuel Taylor Coleridge supplied the 'rough matter'.[61]

In contrast to Gifford's single-minded pursuit of the journal's ideological purposes, Scott's complex of personal and political strategies, and Ellis's political agenda, Murray meddled in the journal's editorial conduct because he was controlling by nature and because he wished to protect his business. To satisfy the tastes of multiple audiences, he tried to balance the selection of reviews; he saw to it that mild fare was published alongside Gifford's spicier dishes. Over the course of many years, the push and pull between the two men probably benefited the *Quarterly* by ensuring a good variety of politically charged and non-political articles.

Regardless of their positive contribution, problems between publisher and editor for a time made it seem likely the journal would fail. Number 3 was a monument to their deteriorating relationship. No doubt because he played so great a part in bringing it together, when the August 1809 issue appeared Murray declared it 'masterly and attractive beyond measure', but others who were not emotionally invested viewed it as a disaster. The issue was published on time, three months to the day from the publication of Number 2, but, again, no one article stood out; indeed some of the reviews were off-putting. It probably contained too much science, classics, and theology for a political-literary journal, which led Ellis to declare the number 'most notoriously and unequivocally *dull*'. D'Israeli damned the whole enterprise. Some of the articles were so long he expected to 'live to see a Quarterly Review composed on only one book!' Even the number's political article, written by Canning and Ellis, raised his ire. 'What have they done for you?', D'Israeli challenged Murray about the journal's much-vaunted political sponsors. Henry Stephen's sermonizing review of Maria Edgeworth was in Scott's estimation 'impertinent'. Frank Sayers's anti-Unitarian disquisition on Middleton's 'Doctrine of the Greek Article' involved the analysis of New Testament Greek and, as such, was inaccessible to most readers. Except for its subject, there was little of interest in the ninth article, a review of Pinckney's *Travels through France*.[62]

Soon after the publication of Number 3, Murray was again fretting about the journal and his editor. The tension between the two men led to another major flare up in September 1809. Gifford wrote to Murray, 'That you want openness is apparent; because you never inform me what you intend to do; but suffer me to blunder on to my own disgrace'. The publisher insisted his only concern was for the success of a work upon which his profit and reputation depended: 'If I am over-anxious it is because I have let my hopes of fame as a bookseller rest upon the establishment and celebrity of this journal'. Now and often in his conduct of the *Quarterly Review* Murray acted 'like a sick man, restless, [who] thinks that every turn will give him ease'. Yet, as Croker noted, he was soon 'as tired of lying on one side, as on the other'. Gifford complained, 'Murray cries like the horse leach incessantly, not for more men! but for novelty'.[63]

Scott, who as we have seen had become passive, did nothing to smooth the troubled waters that were threatening to swamp the *Quarterly Review*. It was left to Ellis to calm the two men down and bring Murray to his senses. In November he sent the publisher a detailed assessment of the journal's progress and problems. Concerning Gifford's management, he challenged the publisher, 'can you or I assert that he rejected what was new and lively, and selected what was old and dull?'[64] Regardless, in that same month Murray went ahead with his plan to see if his editor could mange without him. The result was the opposite of what he expected; Number 4 was the first issue to gain wide approval. The good news did not come too soon, because the future of the *Quarterly*, if it had one, depended on Murray and Gifford gaining respect for one another.

Gifford was understandably anxious about Murray; he was also concerned about Scott whose commitment was clearly in doubt. In a letter to his putative co-editor he wrote, 'If you desert us, I do not think we can stand, and my hopes, which were once pretty sanguine, begin to fail me'.[65] He was right to worry because in 1811 Scott would effectively abandon the *Quarterly Review*. Between the publication of Number 9, in April 1811, and his essay on Jane Austen's *Emma* in Number 27, published in March 1816, he contributed nothing.[66] Besides being pulled away by scholarly, literary, and legal work, Scott withdrew because he believed the journal no longer needed him, because he disliked writing reviews, and because he was unhappy with Gifford's management. One of the benefits he hoped to gain through his association with the *Quarterly* was employment for friends, relatives, and acquaintances. Yet far from providing a source of satisfaction in this regard, the *Quarterly* became to him an embarrassment. As we have seen, he promised his friends easy access to the journal. On 13 January 1809 he assured Charles Kirkpatrick Sharpe, 'Seriously, I will be most happy to transmit an article written with your usual fun to Anti-Jacobin Gifford, and will be bail for its being kindly received'.[67] In that case, as in many others when Scott's friends found Gifford unreceptive, his words turned to ashes in his mouth. In his letters to Scott, Gifford was respectful and friendly – he referred to him at one point as 'our Coryphæus'[68] – but it appears he resented having been the principals' second choice and took his revenge by thwarting Scott's nominees.

Scott also gave up the *Quarterly* because of his hatred of 'task-work'. '[P]ropose to me to do one thing', he wrote, 'and it is inconceivable the desire I have to do something else'. Similarly, Scott told Sharpe, 'writing has been so long a matter of duty with me, that it is become as utterly abominable to me as matters of duty usually are'. Following the publication of Number 1, Gifford found it difficult to get Scott to apply himself; he also noticed Scott's articles tended to be light and brief and the quality of his productions uneven.[69]

Scott understood that with the *Quarterly*'s editor, publisher, and main political support in London, the journal was primarily a metropolitan affair. He kept in contact with Gifford and Murray and he supplied copy only until he was confident they could manage the task alone and that the journal, as a London production, would flourish.

A final reason for Scott's desertion was because he began to regret that he shared accountability for a journal that so often caused offence. It made him deeply uncomfortable when, in separate episodes, Edgeworth, Berwick, and Moore approached him to complain about reviews. Scott resented being mistaken as the author of the 'very silly and impertinent review' of Edgeworth's *Tales of Fashionable Life* in Number 3. When Berwick drew attention to unmerited sarcasm in the review in Number 6 of his *Life of Apollonius*, Scott found himself agreeing with the disgruntled author. James Moore, the brother of the hero of Corunna, wrote to Scott to complain about the review in Number 3 of his book on the Spanish campaign. Scott replied that as he had nothing to do with the article it was unreasonable of Moore to ask him to apologize for it. Unlike Gifford, who for sixteen years uncomplainingly took blows for his anonymous authors, Scott, despite being a member of the journal's editorial cabal, denied his share of corporate responsibility. He insisted to Moore that the editor and the article's writers were 'individually and exclusively responsible' for their work.[70]

With Scott on the way out, with Murray irrationally pessimistic, and with Ellis well-meaning but largely on the sidelines, Gifford, 'a miserable invalid, old in years, older in constitution, without eyes, without strength, without anything, grubbing on, while the mighty men of war [were] satisfied with looking at [him]' nevertheless survived.[71] He persisted in the editorship and made it through years of struggle in part because toward the end of 1809 he found an effective ally in the brilliant Oriel College intellectual Edward Copleston. Copleston benefited the journal primarily by being an efficient recruiter, but also by confirming Gifford's self-worth. As such, he became the editor's 'man of men'.

Copleston introduced Gifford to the writing talents of his friend the fabulously wealthy Lord Dudley, a young parliamentarian. Dudley proved highly useful, not only because he wrote well, but, as importantly, because he suspended the competition between Murray and Gifford over the journal's political content. As a Whig, it was vitally important to Dudley that his identity be kept a deep secret. Copleston made Gifford and Murray go to extraordinary lengths to remain ignorant of Dudley's identity. Not knowing who their mysterious contributor was made it impossible for either man to claim him as their own or to worry that through him the other man was inordinately influencing the journal's direction. Instead, both men basked in the praise Dudley's political reviews received and in the moderately improved sale his much-admired articles helped bring about. Later, Copleston also supplied a large number of writers from Oxford and Cambridge, including members of the collection of Oriel College intellectuals known as the Noetics: Senior, Whately, and Davison. Among Copleston's other recruits were Blomfield, Elmsley, Kidd, Mitchell, Monk, Hughes, Potter, Grey, Phillpotts, and Rose.[72]

Although the editorial group had their eye on Copleston from the start – his name appears in the list of prospective reviewers Murray drew up in consultation with Scott and Gifford as early as November 1808 – it took two years before his first article appeared. Copleston, who was a fellow at Oriel during Reginald Heber's student days, was a particular friend of Reginald's half-brother Richard. Beginning in November 1808, Richard repeatedly approached Copleston to request that he contribute to the *Quarterly Review*; he succeeded only to the extent that Copleston encouraged other Oxford men of his acquaintance, Kidd and Penrose, to offer reviews.

It was not until late 1809, when Richard Heber requested he review a book by Thomas Dunham Whitaker,[73] that Edward Copleston revealed why he was reluctant to become a *Quarterly* reviewer and why he had stopped asking other men to submit articles. On 12 November 1809 he sent Heber a discouraging reply: 'I have read thro' Whitaker's History and think it a very reviewable book. But I shall not think of communicating an article to that Review, after the treatment Kidd has experienced – and the unmannerly rejection of Penrose's article'.[74] Heber assured Copleston that although he was personally unaware of the circumstances, he was sure there must have been a misunderstanding. He touted the superiority of the *Quarterly*'s politics over those of the *Edinburgh* and he tactlessly held out as incentive the high remuneration Murray paid contributors. In his reply of November 23rd, Copleston now broadened the grounds of his complaint:

> You are, I perceive, warmly interested in the success of the Quarterly Review. My Anti-Edinburgh feelings are as strong as yours can be – but I cannot say I am a great admirer of this Quarterly. It has many of its rival's faults – hasty and imperfect view of the book reviewed – political prejudices of a narrow kind continually interfering – and a morigeration to the false taste of the public in order that it may be a selling article.

> Many sheets dedicated to the review of an Austrian manifesto, as a literary work,
> are rather more than my loyalty and anti-gallicanism can swallow. Upon the whole I
> am not over-fond of their politics. As to terms, I can say without any affectation, that
> they would not have the slightest influence upon me. If I ever write it shall not be for
> profit.[75]

Except on the question of payment, about which he was undoubtedly sincere, Copleston was posturing, for he now qualified his earlier refusal: '*If* I review Whitaker's book I shall give him the highest praise – but I shall point out many errors in the Latinity', he wrote.[76]

Before Gifford stepped into the picture, one more exchange of letters took place between Heber and Copleston. In his November 28th reply to Heber's final letter of invitation, Copleston narrowed his objection to a single matter – Gifford's 'unmannerly rejection' of Penrose:

> That Penrose's treatment is very discouraging I still think – and I cannot agree with
> you that Oxford has shewn itself indifferent to the cause of the *Quarterly Review*.
> Many pens were employed, as soon as invited – Penrose in particular, at my desire....
> So indignant did I feel at this neglect, that I had determined through Ward, to send
> some communications to the Edinburgh – but the infamous libel in the last number
> restrained me – and I think I must declare open war against them.[77]

Gifford saw his opportunity. If he could give a plausible explanation for the Penrose incident, Copleston might capitulate, which is just what happened. The rhetoric of the editor's 8 December 1809 letter to Copleston is impressively nuanced.[78] Gifford personalized his appeal by contrasting his decisiveness in the face of the *Edinburgh*'s provocations with the tepid response of the men of Oxford. The letter begins with an almost liturgical survey of the high purposes of the *Quarterly Review*, its standing up for the nation's institutions, for government and the Church. Thinking the 'friends of Order, Morality and rational Piety would muster in their defence', and encouraged by the 'prospect of support from Oxford', Gifford had stepped forward. It was in particular Copleston's 'admirable little Critique', *Advice to a Young Reviewer* (1807),[79] that 'flattered' him into hoping that 'you, Sir, would view with kindness a work hazarded with similar views, and be induced at some favourable moment to befriend it', Gifford wrote. He now only had to explain the *Quarterly*'s handling of Penrose; he faulted the publisher. The appeal worked. Copleston came onboard immediately as a subeditor of a number of Oxford-related reviews, and he saw to it that some of his friends contributed, including Lord Dudley. Never a prolific writer as scholar, priest, or reviewer, sixteen more months passed, however, before he produced his first article for the journal.[80]

Copleston, Ellis, Ireland, and Canning supported Gifford well enough to make him feel the editorship was legitimately his and that he was sufficiently effective in the role. He needed their reassurance. Murray and Scott, possibly mistaking hectoring as an effective way to motivate their editor and his contributors, in the early years were twin Cassandras clamantly worrying over the fate of the *Review*. Gifford and his supporters saw them instead as bearers of false news. It was Gifford, along with his few allies, who held the journal together while Scott was poised to shake the dust off his sandals and Murray was constantly crying 'Foul!' With Ellis largely quiescent and Scott for the moment not actively involved, the close of 1809 saw the *Quarterly* in the hands of a publisher and editor whose relationship appeared to be terminal.

4 THE *QUARTERLY REVIEW* ASCENDANT

Over the course of the journal's first year, with competing captains at the helm and few men at the pumps, the *Quarterly Review* nearly foundered. The journal was buoyed by Robert Southey's contribution and it was finally set on its course by the arrival in Number 4 of a freshening wind. Though it was terribly late (it should have appeared at the end of November but it was not published until 23 December 1809), it was the best issue to date. For this number, Murray recorded some interesting extra costs, a £25 bonus for the editor perhaps for producing the journal with minimal assistance, an additional £13 10s. for Southey, one in a series of top-ups that soon led to his earning a standard £100 per article, and £2.19 to reprint the wrappers. Murray incurred the latter expense to alter the journal's price from 5 to 6 shillings, an adjustment that permitted the *Quarterly Review* to begin to pay its expenses and eventually to become highly profitable.

Number 4 was the inaugural issue for two reviewers who made a major contribution to the *Quarterly*'s future success, John Barrow, Second Secretary to the Admiralty, whose travel reviews came to be a staple and much-anticipated feature of the journal, and Robert Grant, who helped establish the *Quarterly*'s reputation for brilliant writing and authoritative information.

John Barrow was introduced to the *Quarterly* hard on the heels of the incorporation of his soon-to-be superior at the Admiralty John Wilson Croker into the journal's editorial council. Croker was present at one or more of the April–July 1809 meetings attended by Canning, Scott, Murray, Ellis, Heber, and Gifford, some of which took place in the back room of Murray's Fleet Street shop and at least one of which was held in the Westminster office of Croker's father.[1] Croker or Canning must have suggested at one of these meetings that Barrow should be approached and so it fell to Canning in July to request that Barrow call on Gifford. Barrow's inaugural review – of a Chinese work just off the press[2] –was the first of almost two hundred articles he contributed up to the end of 1824. The great popularity of Barrow's reviews and their sheer weight in numbers helped shape the journal's character. While other periodicals, the *British Review* for example, may have rivalled the *Quarterly* in the frequency and sometimes in the quality of their travel articles, the *Quarterly* had what no other journal could boast, reviews that expressed the opinions of and incorporated facts uniquely available to the executive administrator of the Admiralty and that opened, so readers believed, a window on that important department's counsels.

Number 4 also introduced the talents of an unjustly overlooked figure, Robert Grant, whose review of *Characters of the late Charles James Fox* was the issue's leading article.[3] Years later, John Murray wrote in his office copy in the margin of Grant's review, 'This was the first Article that excited general admiration'. Though Smiles states that 'it largely increased demand for the *Review*', really its positive impact on the sale was temporary at best.[4] Grant came to the *Quarterly* through the Heber brothers' good offices. In late 1809, Reginald Heber asked his best friend John Thornton to 'procure recruits for the *Quarterly Review*, in which', he said, 'several of our common friends are likely to be engaged'. Grant, who was Heber and Thornton's intimate, was the unstated target of Heber's appeal.[5] Richard Heber took the hint from Thornton and it was he who managed the insertion of Grant's inaugural contribution. After this auspicious beginning, his article on Fox, inspired by the evangelical banker and economist Henry Thornton, a fellow Saint, and by his exposure to political economy at Edinburgh University during a northern Grand Tour in 1800–1, Grant followed up with an important article on 'paper money', a review of Ricardo in Number 5.[6] In his desire to guard the Saints' independence, he required that his authorship of these productions remain a deep secret; he hid his identity even from Murray and Gifford.

For Number 7, Grant supplied a bookend to his Fox review, an article on John Gifford's *Life* of William Pitt. The importance of Grant's 'Pitt' article to the early history of the *Quarterly Review* cannot be overstated. Gifford declared it 'masterly', he thought 'some parts of the language [had] never been excelled' and he touted it to the editorial coterie as 'a sort of Manifesto of the Pitt-principles', and 'our political creed, which we must contend for'.[7] At the commencement of the article's production, Grant and Gifford thought Canning should be involved as the chief promoter of Pitt's memory. Indeed, both men preferred that Canning write the article, but Gifford could not convince the statesman to take up his pen. Grant insisted that as Pitt's political protégé Canning, at a minimum, should vet the review to keep it free of factual error and to add observations and personal anecdotes. Although Canning cast his eyes over a draft or two, he made only a few suggestions. The work was almost entirely Grant's, but many contemporary readers attributed it to Canning, confused by their expectation that Canning ought to have been the article's author and by the writing being equal to the statesman's parliamentary oratory and the brilliance he had exhibited in the *Anti-Jacobin*. Murray doubled Grant's fee for the review, a sure sign he wished to retain the services of this able young man. He did well, for Grant's next article, a review in Number 8 of Crabbe's *The Borough*, Ellis justly declared 'superb'.[8]

With Grant and Barrow onboard and the journal's mainsail to the wind, the *Quarterly* began to make headway. In Number 5, Gifford and Murray published what is now an acknowledged classic, Southey's 'most beautiful Essay on the Lives of Nelson'. Everyone recognized and most readers admired Southey's articles for their exhaustive research and carefully crafted prose. While a number of the articles he published in the *Quarterly* achieved a degree of fame among contemporaries, 'Nelson' alone entered the literary pantheon. Readers in 1810 needed no encouragement from Southey to worship Nelson, but his essay powerfully renewed what they had felt upon the arrival of the glorious 'heart-shaking news' of Trafalgar and upon the occasion of Nelson's apotheosis, his state funeral. The essay preserves a sense of the overwhelming pride and reverence contemporaries felt for the man.[9]

Incredibly, had Murray prevailed 'Nelson' might not have seen the light of day. When he read Southey's essay in its original incarnation he thought it lacked 'animation'. With some urgency, he requested on a Saturday that Sharon Turner and Isaac D'Israeli come round to his Fleet Street office so he could consult them on its content, manner, and length. At four sheets (sixty-four pages) he directed Gifford to cut it by a third. On 4 February 1810, Ellis told Murray he was glad Southey's article would now be '*animated* and inserted'. Following its publication, on 4 April, Ellis wrote to Murray to enquire how he ever 'could have thought ill of Southey's Nelson'. Though the article was certainly admired at the time ('the whole review ... rivets you to your seat'), it was when Murray published it in book form that it gained wide circulation and eventually came to be considered the iconic treatment of Britain's greatest naval hero.[10]

Despite improvements in the journal's quality and interest, in September 1810 Murray and Gifford reached the nadir in their relationship. It arrived during the production of a review by the Oxford theologian John Davison for Number 7 of Edward Copleston's *A Reply to Calumnies of the Edinburgh Review against Oxford*. Buttressed by Ellis's opinion that Davison's article was 'tedious and feeble', Murray adamantly opposed its publication. Almost a year earlier, Gifford had assured Copleston that the publisher had 'become more modest and tractable'. Evidently, that was not entirely true. Though Gifford himself did not think well of the essay (he told Ellis it was 'not altogether what he wished'), he resolved to make a stand against Murray's 'intimidation'. The editor refused to repeat the fiasco that followed Murray's rejection of Conybeare's review of Kidd. When Davison had travelled to London for the express purpose of looking over the proofs, neither Murray nor Gifford had indicated anything was amiss. Moreover, the editor had specifically and repeatedly promised Davison the article would appear. Should Davison's essay now be set aside, Gifford's reputation for trustworthiness and consistency, already damaged by the Kidd and Penrose episodes, would be irrecoverable. If he lost Davison he would lose Copleston, Davison's colleague and friend. Given Copleston's influence at the university, the *Quarterly* could well end up being shunned by Oxford, a calamity it could ill afford. In causing the article to appear, Gifford won an important battle. For much of the rest of Gifford's tenure, Murray – like the bully given his comeuppance – was more modest and tractable. By struggling to reach an accommodation with Murray in cases such as these, Gifford was casting bread upon the waters; as the publisher kept slipping back into his old patterns it appeared to be a futile exercise, but eventually the editor was rewarded for his act of faith.[11]

The two men's relationship improved in tandem with the slow but steady progress in the journal's reputation and sale. Though no other reviews in the first half of Gifford's tenure equalled 'Fox', 'Pitt', or 'Nelson', some did make an impression. Two articles by Thomas Dunham Whitaker were still being singled out as remarkable fifteen years after their publication, his review in Number 13 of Cooke's *History of the Reformation in Scotland* and his article in Number 14 on Hurd's edition of Bishop Warburton's works. The noted bibliophile Thomas Frognall Dibdin called the Warburton essay 'perhaps one of the most perfect specimens of acute analysis, and impassioned eloquence, that the pages of modern criticism record'. Likewise, Peter Elmsley's review, also in Number 14, of Markland's Euripides was highly thought of by classicists. Two other essays by Southey stood out, his inaugural piece on evangelical missions and an article in Number 12 on the Spanish Inquisition.[12]

What also helped the journal gain a reliable sale and to rise in the public's estimation were Barrow's travel reviews, its well-informed financial articles contributed by Grant, Ellis, Canning, and Huskisson, and these men's and Dudley's similarly weighty contributions on domestic and foreign affairs. Boosted by controversy that followed the publication of some of the journal's reviews, the public's interest in the *Quarterly* gradually increased, to the point where, in February 1811, Gifford could state, 'I am alarmed at our own success. We stand so high, that I feel uneasy lest we should not keep our elevation'. In late 1811, Murray presented Gifford with a generous gift, £500, partly as a sop for the grief he had caused his editor, but also to celebrate the success the journal had begun to enjoy under his tutelage.[13]

With the *Quarterly* finally having made its colours, the good news accumulated. In 1812 there were persistent rumours (they proved false of course) that 'the *Edinburgh Review* [was] about to close in consequence of the great luminaries, Jeffrey, Brougham and Horner all finding themselves too much employed in the law to spare time for conducting it'. In mid-1812, Murray, wealthy again – profits from the *Quarterly* and Byron's *Childe Harold* were filling his coffers – purchased the society publisher William Miller's copyrights and his premises, an eighteenth-century building in London's upscale West End, 50 Albemarle Street, to which the firm moved from its Fleet Street location. At the end of

1813, Murray gave Gifford another large gift, which prompted the editor to protest that his publisher was 'too kind and munificent'.[14]

Not all was now plain sailing for Gifford, however. With Copleston's attention having wandered from the *Quarterly Review* in 1814 when he became provost of Oriel College, and with Ellis's death, on 10 April 1815, the editor was left with no ally to help him control Murray. Consequently, in the latter two thirds of Gifford's editorship, Murray, conspiring with Croker, successfully influenced the journal's direction. The only departments that remained exclusively within Gifford's purview were politics, religion, and the classics. Notably, the *Quarterly*'s 'sheet anchors' – Croker, Barrow, and Southey – corresponded almost exclusively with Murray, not Gifford.[15] Between 1809 and 1824, the *Quarterly*'s triple pillar contributed over forty percent of the journal's articles, about forty-five percent of its articles up to 1816. In gauging Gifford's and Murray's share in the journal's conduct and in assessing the relative contribution of publisher and editor to the *Quarterly*'s achievements, Murray's management of the triumvirate and the preponderance of its articles should be taken into account. The publisher and his editor were involved in the production of an almost equal number of articles. Likewise, they shared responsibility for the journal's popularity in almost equal measure.

The lamentable destruction of Gifford's *Quarterly Review* papers in accordance with a stipulation in his will renders conclusions about Murray's and Gifford's relative contribution less secure than they might otherwise be. But the thousands of existing documents that mark the journal's trail point to the two men having jointly contributed to the *Quarterly*'s success: Murray because he creatively managed the business end of reviewing and kept its mainstay contributors primed with books, cash, and plaudits; Gifford because he ensured that the *Quarterly* remained true to its original principles and, by applying the genius of his pen, sustained its quality.

The *Quarterly Review* also attracted attention and improved its sale because its privileged access to the highest levels of state power loomed large in the public's imagination. So heady was the *Quarterly*'s reputation as the repository of opinions of Men of the World that its articles were read and had influence *because* they appeared in its pages. As Murray observed, 'let any one of [the *Quarterly*'s] Essays be printed as a pamphlet [and] they would not find 750 readers'. A writer in the *London Magazine* reflected that 'discussions in the Quarterly have a quality of judge-like summing up about them'. He highlighted the journal's gravitas, its imperious demeanour, and its connection with government: 'There is ... a pains-taking spirit, and a substantial construction, about the Quarterly now, which reflect credit on its management: furthermore, it carries an air of establishment with it that is imposing: it comports itself as if it constituted a fourth estate of the realm – King, Lords, Commons, and The Quarterly Review'.[16]

Largely unknown to the public, however, the *Quarterly*'s relationship with government was problematic. At the time of its formation, the *Quarterly Review* was rare among British serial publications that generally supported the Ministry: it was not a Treasury journal.[17] Boyd Hilton points out that when 'the four Pittite loyalists William Gifford, John Murray, Walter Scott, and George Ellis combined to found the *Quarterly Review*, their purpose was entirely political'.[18] The *Quarterly* did not, however, slavishly reflect ministerial policy. While the editorial coterie agreed 'to a certain extent ... to justify to support or to recommend and assist' the ministers and their measures,[19] its conductors did not receive Secret Service money or a subvention from the Treasury. To maintain its independence, the *Quarterly Review* under Gifford and Coleridge declined to be a government propaganda poster. Its purpose instead was to resist the unmooring tendency of contemporary political and intellectual developments by promoting nationalism and by supporting conservative 'principles of morality, loyalty, respect for constitutional authorities', the monarchy and the Established Church.[20] Gifford and his core contributors therefore stood not for a party, the prime minister, or the Cabinet, but for a structure of society threatened by the principles of the French Revolution, a structure they were willing to see adjusted through moderate institutional and social reforms, if only for the sake of preserving it in its essentials.

As the guardian of constitutional principles, not measures or men, the *Quarterly*'s conductors wished to maintain their independence from government; but at the same time they looked to it for information. In his apodictic 'letter of policy' of 25 October 1809, Scott posed to Gifford the challenge of thus balancing dependence and independence:

> On the one hand it is certainly not to be understood that we are to be tied down to advocate upon all occasions and as matter of course the cause of the administration. Such indiscriminate support and dereliction of independence would prejudice both ourselves and our cause in the eye of the public. On the other hand the work will obtain a decided ascendance over all competition so soon as the public shall learn (not from any vaunt of the conductors but from their own observation) that upon political subjects the new critics are possessed of early and of accurate information.[21]

Gifford was determined to carry out Scott's strictures, but following Canning's September 1809 duel with Castlereagh the government lost that statesman's 'grace and vigour'. The editor now faced a problem. His main source of information was no longer in power and most of the remaining ministers were not sympathetic to a journal they identified as the organ of a liberal conservative faction. For his part, Gifford often complained about the 'weakness of the present men'. He was no more inclined to support them than they were the *Quarterly Review*. In 1809, the Portland Ministry survived, he thought, not because it was strong or deserved power, but because the out-of-power factions were so weak and self-serving 'the country would not bear them'. While he generally thought well of Perceval and even more so of Liverpool, he cared less for many of their ministers.[22]

With each passing year the need grew, as Gifford saw it, for government to give tangible support to the *Quarterly*, yet Cabinet treated him with coy indifference. 'We are pigeon livered and lack gall', the editor cried out in the midst of increasingly desperate national circumstances, bewildered that the government did not do more to buttress the *Quarterly Review*. 'Here is our peculiar hardship', Gifford wrote to Canning in 1817,

> the Edinburgh Review may talk at random; its falsehoods affect nothing but its own character, and provided that they are rancorous enough, its friends are satisfied; but we cannot, and ought not to move without a knowledge of facts, of which government alone are possessed: and this makes assistance so much more necessary to us – yet whom have I but you? It is really astonishing that they will not take more advantage of us, and influence a great portion of the country which we have brought almost to their feet.

Gifford told the civil servant Robert Hay, 'I have no patience with the Cabinet People – When it is too late they rub their eyes and begin to see that the Review might be of the "utmost importance" to them. ... Yet who among them procures a single line? ... Croker is the only link that unites us at all with the Ministers, and the service he has done for them by his various papers is incalculable'.[23]

The *Quarterly's* editorial machine may have felt 'entitled to expect confidential communication' from government 'as to points of fact',[24] but as it did little to inspire the government's confidence, the much desired information often was not forthcoming. Government had good reason to be shy of the *Quarterly Review*, for on at least three notable occasions the editor stung the administration's senior ministers when they attempted to insert their opinions in the journal. On each of these occasions, Croker was the agent of powerful men who wished to dictate the *Quarterly's* contents. On each occasion Gifford pushed back, twice successfully. When he failed, it was towards the end of his tenure when his life's tide was on the ebb.

In December 1810, the editor turned aside an article on paper currency that Prime Minister Spencer Perceval tried to introduce through Croker's representations. In March 1813, Liverpool attempted, again through Croker, to dictate the *Quarterly's* position on the East India Company charter; again Gifford indignantly spurned a prime minister. In 1819, however, by locking arms with Murray and Barrow, Croker forced Gifford to withdraw a reference to Lord Lonsdale in an article on Brougham's education committee.[25] Gifford's capitulation in that instance marked a turning point. From then on, Murray and Croker's belief in Gifford's political untouchability began to wane.

A fourth episode explains why Gifford sometimes permitted third party influence that usually he would have labelled interference. In 1815 Croker, once more acting as the agent of a powerful man, this time the Duke of Wellington, vetted Southey's portrayal of the Iron Duke's commanding leadership in the battle of Waterloo.[26] Gifford welcomed the changes Wellington dictated through Croker and he resisted Southey's effort to reverse Croker's edits. The essential difference between this episode and the other three involves a question of control. In the former cases Gifford was imposed upon; in the latter instance it was he who invited Croker to ensure Southey's review was 'safe'.

Gifford himself described the kind of influence by government the journal required and he permitted. In an effort to convince a liberal-minded potential contributor, Charles James Blomfield, to abandon the *Edinburgh* for the *Quarterly*, he insisted that the journal's politics 'have never been party politics. I told the government, when I was persuaded by them to undertake a task for which neither my abilities, nor time of life, nor strength qualify me, that I would not be fettered, nor obliged to follow them; nor, to do them justice, did they require it'. In statements to Horace Twiss and Robert Hay, he stressed that when it came to public policy or constitutional principles the *Quarterly* perhaps represented the views of a political faction, but not directly those of government. He wrote to Twiss:

> I scarcely know how so important a work as the Quarterly [can] be safely trusted to one person's judgment. In many cases undoubtedly, I decide definitively; but in great political questions, where it is not allowed to err with impunity, it becomes expedient to consult those whose sphere of observation is large, and whose personal knowledge is deep and extensive. We are supposed to speak the language of Government – this is certainly not exactly the case; but still, a great degree of information is necessary, as we direct the opinions of a considerable party.[27]

Another of Gifford's clear pronouncements on the *Quarterly* and government is in an 1814 letter to Hay: 'The politics of the moment are not to be hazarded by us, who hope to live to future times and instruct permanently'. By not expressing an opinion on transient government policy but instead reserving the pages of the *Quarterly Review* for discussions that addressed basic political principles, he aimed to raise the status of the journal above ephemera and to avoid its being read as Treasury propaganda. Instead of writing on day-to-day matters before Parliament, 'there are always', he advised Hay, 'fixed principles which we can advocate with honour and advantage, and for which, indeed, the Review was first set up'.[28]

Sympathetic and hostile readers alike accepted that the *Quarterly's* relationship to government, however problematic and paradoxical, made it a formidable political engine. The *North American Review* observed:

> It is well known, that this Journal is *to a certain degree* semi-official, in its character. It almost without exception speaks the sense of the English government. Some persons connected with the administration of affairs, have the credit of being regular contributors to its pages. The public offices and archives of state are habitually opened, to furnish materials for articles contained in its numbers. It is also in itself a journal of circulation too wide, and influence too great, to be left uncontradicted in serious statements.[29]

Hazlitt indignantly confirmed the journal's reputation as a repository of official information, and as an arbiter of 'taste' in literature, if only to deny its legitimacy: 'The dingy cover that wraps the pages of the *Quarterly Review* does not contain a concentrated essence of taste and knowledge, but is a receptacle for all the scum and sediment of all the prejudice, bigotry, ill-will, ignorance, and rancour, afloat in the kingdom'.[30]

Sustained by its relationship to government, then, by its connection with Scott that attracted readers to its reviews of Scott's poetry, and by Murray's association with Byron that drew readers to its Byron reviews, through its first few years the journal enjoyed a respectable circulation of about 5,500 copies. As we have seen, notable articles contributed by Grant, Dudley, Whitaker, Croker, Southey, and some of Murray's other 'four o'clock visitors', including articles by Scott, Canning, and Barrow, also inspired interest. Sales were healthy, but circulation growth was relatively flat.[31] Then suddenly at the end of 1816, amid increasingly tense conditions in post-Waterloo Britain, during the 'heroic age of popular Radicalism' the *Quarterly Review's* subscription base greatly expanded.[32]

Conservative readers looked to the *Quarterly* as an intelligent voice in support of a stable and independent British nation. Consequently, the journal's sale grew with the increase in radical agitation for reform. Among conservatives there was a vast difference in mood between the journal's first seven years and the period 1816 to 1825. In 1809, British conservatives assumed existing institutions in Church and State would be preserved as long as Napoleon was kept at bay. In 1811, Church-and-King men may have worried that the Regent would return the Whigs to power and thus change the government's war policy, but only alarmists predicted the ruin of all things.[33] In 1812 Gifford pooh-poohed Southey, who saw creeping rebellion in every mob. But in the shadow of Spa Fields, the Pentridge Rebellion, Peterloo, the Cato Street Conspiracy and other challenges to the established order, despite the collapse of radical agitation in 1820 the editor himself was now deeply alarmed. Writing to Canning in 1821, Gifford evoked the spectre of Jacobinism: 'There is something terrible in our present state; for if we fall, we fall to rise no more. The radicals ... are waiting with open jaws, for our absolute and total destruction, careless of the universal annihilation which is to follow their bloody feat'. The *Quarterly* gained marked success when, as Croker later put it, the views it expressed accorded with the 'predominant opinion', at least among those who were sinecured, moneyed, propertied, or represented in Parliament.[34]

The journal also attracted attention in the period following Waterloo because it regularly contained authoritative articles on subjects the public keenly followed, Wellington, Napoleon in exile, the Elgin marbles, 'the internal state of the country', emigration, America, the Waverley novels, and world exploration. Murray's print run inched up in 1814–15 to about 7,000. In December 1815 he issued 8,000 copies of Number 26. In it was Southey's well-received article on Wellington. The sale of Number 26 cannot have been as good as Murray anticipated, because in March 1816 he dropped the print run for Number 27 back to 7,000. That number contained multiple articles on those subjects about which the reading public were greatly interested, Wellington, Waterloo, and the Elgin marbles. That each of these articles had evidently been passed by men of power and influence helped the journal gain a 'powerful hold upon the Public Confidence' and taught readers to value the *Quarterly* more than ever as a repository of inside information.[35]

The same three topics attracted readers to Number 27, but when they opened its pages they discovered Scott's wonderful essay on Austen's *Emma*. The combination of Scott's analysis and information on topics of national concern gave the *Quarterly* a piquancy it now began to enjoy more consistently. The journal's reputation as a reliable source of authoritative conservative commentary, cogently described by John Gibson Lockhart some years later, was gained in this period:

> our influence on many subjects even of the grave kind with the gravest people depends to a very great extent on the belief that the *QR* is written & edited not by recluses but by Men of the World. We must, to keep up this impression shew on all fit occasions *knowledge* of what is the tone of thought and feeling in the highest and best Society of London on subjects of all classes – light as well as grave. ... We have huge means within our reach. The vast mass of intelligence is on our side

Like its rival the *Edinburgh*, the *Quarterly* generally treated 'Subjects – not Books', a practice that helped it achieve Murray's goal to include in each number at least one article 'that will go home to Men's Business and Bosoms – one that they will read instantly from its anticipated pleasure'.[36]

At just the right moment, with public enthusiasm for the journal primed, Gifford managed to get an issue, Number 28, out on time. Appearing in May 1816, it contained another article on the Elgin marbles, a review of Hobhouse's *Letters from Paris* that brought into readers' drawing rooms fresh news of the situation in post-Napoleonic France, and an article by Hay on the Congress of Vienna, the gathering of European diplomats everyone recognized was of world-historical importance. The latter article was vetted, and obviously so, by high government and diplomatic officials. The number also contained two articles that were, in Murray's words, of 'extra ordinary Power and Interest', contributions by Scott on the Culloden papers and on Polwhele's *Fair Isabel of Cotchele*.[37] Anticipating increased demand, Murray cautiously raised the print run back up to 8,000. He should have raised it even higher. The number sold at an astonishing rate, 7,500 copies in four days, so with Number 29, published in August 1816, he bumped the print run to 8,500. Articles in Number 30 on Waterloo and France sustained these high levels. Recent numbers had sold so rapidly that in February 1817 Murray boosted the print run, for Number 31, to 10,000 copies, almost double the number he had printed only three years before. His initial sale of 8,500 inspired him to print an unprecedented 12,000 copies of Number 32.

Published in April 1817, that issue contained yet another article by Croker on Napoleon and an essay on the rise and progress of popular dissent that was unmistakeably from Southey's pen. With a review (by Scott himself!) of Scott's *Tales of My Landlord*, Number 32 also fed the public mania for the Waverley novelist, the Great Unknown. Though of course knowledge of Scott's authorship of the review was not supposed to escape the walls of 50 Albemarle Street, the novelist himself had a motive for dropping hints. He may have hoped 'rumours of his authorship of the review would ... trump rumours of [his] authorship of the novels themselves.'[38]

A solid if unremarkable issue, Number 33 was nevertheless a publishing phenomenon. On Saturday, 6 September 1817, booksellers and private individuals flocked to Albemarle Street for the initial sale to purchase 8,500 copies on that day. Buyers came in such great numbers to pass through 'Mr Murray's' green door that they disrupted traffic on Albemarle and Piccadilly and jostled each other in the narrow hallway leading to Murray's bookshop. To satisfy demand and keep civic peace, Thomas Underwood and Murray's other assistants resorted to distributing the *Quarterly Review* to customers queued on the sidewalk at the open ground floor windows. That scene was repeated over the years as the journal continued to attract eager attention and sales grew. Concerning Number 34, on the first day of December 1817 Gifford wrote to Hay, 'I am almost afraid to tell you what I should scarcely have credited myself, had I not seen it with my own eyes. The Revw was published on Saturday, & 10,000 were brought to Murray's for sale. Before the close of that day, there was hardly one remaining – this is quite unprecedented'. With the publication of Number 36, in June 1818, the periodical reached its maximum circulation under Gifford of 13,000. At a time when copies were shared through reading societies, circulating libraries, coffee houses, and clubs, the journal enjoyed perhaps as many as ten times that number of readers.[39]

The *Quarterly Review* finally had the weather-gauge and outstripped its rival, the *Edinburgh Review*.[40] It went from strength to strength. Barrow's articles on American democracy and the opening of the West fed the public's intense interest in those topics. Moreover, the year 1818 saw the commencement of voyages of Arctic exploration inspired by Sir Joseph Banks and managed by John Barrow. Barrow's impact on the nineteenth-century frame of mind is underappreciated. Indeed, what he wrote in one of his articles about a remote group of islands could equally apply to the unwarranted neglect in historical and literary studies of his works: 'This very extensive group is yet to be visited and described, and would, no doubt, afford an interesting field to the geographer, the moralist, and the natural historian'.[41] For two generations of chair-bound explorers, he was a geographical oracle, the diviner of new worlds. His *Quarterly Review* articles played a significant part in creating the nineteenth-century enthusiasm for exploration literature and, indeed, popular and official interest in world exploration itself.[42] Through his books, various articles in the *Quarterly*, and via his influence at the Admiralty, Barrow renewed the search for an Arctic Northwest Passage and he helped drive interest in African exploration. By speculating on the personalities and motivations of Bligh and Christian, he took a relatively minor naval incident, the *Bounty* mutiny, and turned it into an enduring element in the collective imagination of the West. Because of his closeness to the centre of imperial power, Barrow's geographical and exploration articles were widely believed to reflect, if not official policy, certainly policy under official consideration. His participation in the *Quarterly* therefore added weight to its reputation as a repository of authoritative government information, in the matter of exploration of course, but also whenever the journal addressed naval and colonial affairs.[43]

Barrow's reviews of official reports of the Admiralty's expeditions in search of a Northwest Passage are among the most famous in the *Quarterly*'s history. Regency readers digested news of Arctic voyages with the enthusiasm citizens in 1969 had for television broadcasts from Tranquility Base on the moon. Like the risky moon landings, the Arctic explorations involved expensive and innovative technology applied to a profitless end only a government agency would have thought to spend money on; they were therefore touted as a great national endeavour that gave evidence of Britain's superiority over France and Russia. More positively, because they involved scientific discovery, because they tested the limits of human endurance, and because their goal was a hard-to-justify abstraction, they became wrapped up in matters of spirit and imagination. The voyages inspired pleasure in shared discovery, nationalistic pride, and pride in human accomplishment. The public craved information about the voyages, but the Admiralty accounts were expensive books beyond the reach of most readers.[44] It was to the *Quarterly Review* that eager eyes therefore turned; it was Barrow's reviews that inspired the imagination of thousands.

Because the reading public generally regarded Barrow's Arctic reviews as authoritative and in some respects official, they were a lightning rod for criticism, especially from the high-quality evangelical journal the *British Review*. Apparently benefiting from the expertise of the Scoresbys, father and son, the *British* countered Barrow's articles one for one. In 'Captain Ross's Voyage of Discovery' (May 1819), for example, the *British* was scathing in its condemnation of the 'crude and unphilosophical form' of the Admiralty's official instructions (drafted by Barrow); of its rejection (by Barrow) of the younger William Scoresby's services; and of the cost of Ross's volumes (published by Murray). For his part, though Barrow called him 'a very intelligent navigator of the Greenland seas', he failed to notice the younger Scoresby's books, *Account of the Arctic Regions* (1820) and *Journal of a Voyage to the Northern Whale-Fishery* (1823). Naturally, controversies of this sort attracted attention to the *Quarterly*, sold more copies, and filled Murray's purse.[45]

Barrow's articles, reviews of Byron and Scott, and articles on France and Napoleon and on the state of the country kept the public buying the journal in large numbers, so much so that Murray made a fortune. By 1819 – the year of giant reform demonstrations across England – assuming a print run of at least 12,000, the *Quarterly* was generating around £3,600 per number, £14,400 per annum. Though the cost of producing Murray's flagship periodical was astronomical, £200 per thousand, the enterprise generated a great profit. Not taking into account miscellaneous expenses and reinvestment, the publisher cleared around £1,200 per issue, £4,800 per annum. The warehouse produced additional revenue; Murray annually harvested at least £300 through the sale of reprints.[46]

In 1821 Gifford even solved, if only temporarily, the problem that plagued him from the start, the paucity of articles held in reserve. In August he wrote to Murray words he must have thought he might never pen: he had 'enough now for two or three excellent numbers'.[47] A reason for his good fortune was that Barrow had become a preternaturally productive writer. In the last five years of Gifford's editorship, the Second Secretary published a minimum of two articles in every number, more often than not three or four; for Number 55 he churned out five of the issue's thirteen reviews.

With the journal's growing success, the editor and his publisher settled into a kind of father-son relationship, attended by mutual respect but also by the occasional disagreement. Gifford and Murray saluted each other as dear friends and they exchanged acts of kindness, but from time to time Murray acted insensitively and Gifford's illnesses and indolence continued to cause trouble. The result was that the *Quarterly*'s editor and publisher sometimes exchanged terrible blows. In March 1813, compelled by some unidentified grievance, Gifford wrote to Murray, 'I have no quarrel to [*sic*] any other part of your conduct – you are liberal, generous, and friendly – but I tell you freely that you want what I shall call a forthright mind'. Two months later Gifford warned the publisher that should matters continue in this vein he would consider resigning: 'Your letter of last night, as far as the language is concerned, appeared studiously calculated to affront me – I see no necessity for this, as we can part without further quarrelling'. In 1816 there was another flare up with Gifford uttering his by now standard threat to withdraw: 'As your man is waiting I can only say that I am neither hurt nor angry. I certainly have made several observations of late, which have given me cause to think – but I shall consult others before I speak – meanwhile I will proceed conscientiously with the Number'. Yet another serious clash occurred in early 1819, over Monk's review of Brougham's education committee, the incident, noticed above, when Murray and Croker forced Gifford to bow to the will of Lord Lonsdale by removing a reference to him. That troubles arose despite the evident success of Gifford and Murray's co-management of the journal must be laid primarily at Murray's feet. His efforts to direct his gentlemen and gain control over every aspect of his business may be excused as his way of managing risk, but his behaviour was a reflex, an extension of his controlling nature.[48]

A manifestation of Murray's need to dominate was his habit of forming alliances, not always to achieve a creative, mutually beneficial purpose, but sometimes to pit force against force. He also nurtured relationships to make use of other men's skills. As long as they benefited his firm, he was not always particular about the ends to which those skills were applied. His friendship with Croker was one such joint venture, engaged in on Murray's part to take advantage of the First Secretary of the Admiralty's hyper-productivity and with the long-term goal of setting up an alternative to Gifford and Canning in the political department. Because in proportion with the journal's deepening notoriety the *Quarterly*'s subscription list and the publisher's purse swelled, Murray who in 1808 counselled the production of even-tempered reviews ('when we must chastise ... let it be with the gentle hand of a parent rather than with the scourge of a slave master', Murray wrote) in 1818 fed Croker's taste for moral prescription. He suggested, for instance, that Croker 'give the author of the wicked Novel' (*Frankenstein*) 'the castigation which he merits'.[49]

Murray acquiescing, the First Secretary published some of the journal's most infamous reviews. Croker's treatment of Lady Morgan's *France* the *New Monthly Magazine* thought 'too notorious to dwell upon', but the two articles he published in the *Quarterly Review* that lastingly sullied the journal's reputation were his reviews of Keats's *Endymion* and Shelley's *Frankenstein*. By issuing such judgments as these articles contained, Croker's aim was to protect readers from morally and politically subversive literature. In his 1818 review of Keats, though he admired the writer's talents, he accused the young poet of member-ship in what he called, quoting Lockhart in *Blackwood's Edinburgh Magazine*, the 'Cockney School' of poetry. 'It is not that Mr. Keats ... has not powers of language, rays of fancy, and gleams of genius', Croker wrote, 'he has all these; but he is unhappily a disciple of the new school of what has been somewhere called Cockney poetry; which may be defined to consist of the most incongruous ideas in the most uncouth language'.

It was also for political, moral, and ostensibly for aesthetic reasons that Croker condemned Mary Wollstonecraft Shelley's *Frankenstein*. While he was offended by the author's dedication of the novel to the radical propagandist William Godwin (Mary Shelley's father), whose 'disciples', Croker wrote, 'are a kind of out-pensioners of Bedlam', it was as a Gothic novel *per se* that *Frankenstein* stood no chance with Croker whose 'taste and ... judgement alike', as he put it in the article, 'revolt[ed] at this kind of writing'. Croker praised the author's 'powers, both of conception and language', and he would have given *Frankenstein* unqual-ified approbation had he been able to accept it on its own terms. But he could not do so, for, he declared, 'the greater the ability with which it [the Gothic] may be executed the worse it is'. Because of its very power *Frankenstein* was morally suspect; it has passages, Croker wrote, 'which appal the mind and make the flesh creep'. Croker concluded that because the Gothic 'inculcates no lesson of con-duct, manners, or morality; it cannot mend, and will not even amuse its readers, unless their taste have been deplorably vitiated – it fatigues the feelings without interesting the understanding; it gratuitously harasses the heart'.

Croker authored some of the journal's universally condemned articles, but he was not alone guilty of destroying egos. Gifford, too, permitted or encouraged a number of his recruits to emulate the worst features of the *Edinburgh Review*. In 1818 and 1821, the Christian crusader John Taylor Coleridge and two of his friends, Eaton Stannard Barrett and Sidney Walker, produced scathing reviews of the younger Romantics, Hunt, Hazlitt, and Shelley. In 1820, Charles James Blomfield contributed a review of Stephens's *Thesaurus* that destroyed its edi-tor Edmund Henry Barker's career by accusing him of padding his work with irrelevancies. In the same year, John Barrow was inordinately critical of Thomas Bowditch's *Mission to Ashantee*. In 1824, as we have seen, the civil servant Henry Taylor, urged on by William Gifford, gave William Savage Landor a critical flog-ging so severe Taylor never forgave himself for it.

All this 'brutal insolence'[50] stigmatized the *Quarterly* as the spawn of the evil dwarf Gifford and thus played into the hands of the journal's enemies.[51] Yet to the benefit of English letters, some offended authors channelled their high dudgeon into creative effort. Barrett's accusation that Hazlitt lacked sympathy so upset the 'great hater' that in 1819 he fired off his masterpiece of invective, *A Letter to William Gifford*. In the same year, in the poem 'St Crispin to Mr. Gifford',

Charles Lamb evoked the patron saint of shoemakers to gain a 'gentle revenge' on the *Quarterly*'s editor for his perceived hostility.[52] As Lamb's father was a cobbler, by contrasting Gifford's shoemaker apprenticeship with his lofty position as a literary critic, Lamb in his sonnet created a suggestive, if unintended, ambiguity. It is ironic, too, that the doyen of the 'Cockney School', Leigh Hunt, in his poem *Ultra-Crepidarius; a Satire on William Gifford* (1823) should slight Gifford's working class origins; in the poem the editor of the *Quarterly Review* appears in the guise of a shoe.

The *Quarterly*'s 'witty malignity'[53] also inspired much doggerel, notably George Colman's *Vagaries Vindicated; or, Hypocritick Hypercriticks* (1813), a reply to Croker's treatment in Number 15 of *Poetical Vagaries*:

> Oh, heinous Sin! – from what am I exempt?
> I – '*write to bring the CLERGY in contempt!*'
> Contempt! I'll worship, next, if this be true,
> That Calf who writes the Quarterly Review.[54]

The ever-increasing number and virulence of attacks on the *Quarterly* in daily newspapers, pamphlets, and monographs is testimony to the power contemporaries believed the journal had to sway opinion and determine the sale of books. Shelley elevated the influence of the *Quarterly* so high in his imagination that he absurdly held the journal responsible for the death of John Keats.[55] As early as 1819 he yearned to see the *Quarterly* knocked down in a counter review. In that year he wrote to Thomas Love Peacock:

> I have just seen the Quarterly for September (not from my own box). I suppose there is no chance now of your organizing a review. This is a great pity. The quarterly is undoubtedly conducted with talent, great talent and affords a dreadful preponderance against the cause of improvement. If a band of staunch reformers, resolute yet skilful infidels, were united in so close and constant a league as that in which interest and fanaticism have bound the members of that literary coalition![56]

By the early 1820s, under Gifford and Murray's sometimes tempestuous management the *Quarterly Review* reached a summit of popularity, infamy, and commercial success unprecedented for a periodical journal. Praise and notoriety were its rewards in equal measure, as it now held the position its nemesis the *Edinburgh Review* had enjoyed in 1808, admired for its carefully crafted articles, vilified for its ideological stance and its occasionally intemperate criticism. The *Quarterly*'s editor and publisher were thus poised to pass steadily from triumph to triumph when in 1822 William Gifford fell gravely ill.

5 THE TRANSITION TO LOCKHART

In the lead up to Gifford's retirement, various men, singly or in combination, attempted to use the succession to gain the *Quarterly Review* for their personal or corporate cause. From mid-1822, when Murray was first confronted by the prospect of Gifford's imminent withdrawal, to September 1824, when the incumbent could no longer proceed, in his effort to wrest control of the editorship from the journal's political sponsors, Murray sometimes acted unprofessionally and, to those unaware of his intentions, at times inexplicably.

During the succession crisis, Gifford taunted Murray for his indecision, yet he himself continually set up road blocks. In his stubbornness he was venting sixteen years of sublimated resentment, but he was also trying to derail Murray's plan to hire a subservient, tractable editor. In the end, Murray and Gifford settled on John Taylor Coleridge – 'a nice young man' the editor called him – Southey's literary protégé whom they regarded as a safe candidate. In person deferential and refined, in print a self-righteous moralist, Coleridge crusaded in the *Quarterly Review* to clean up the literary neighbourhood. His campaign made Gifford, to whom his anonymously published reviews were imputed, the *bête noire* of the Cockney and Satanic Schools, but as Gifford enthusiastically shared his views, Coleridge's articles endeared him to the editor. Murray, though, had his doubts about Coleridge's commitment and perhaps was uncomfortable with his religiosity. In December 1824, when the transition took place, neither man knew they had hired a fifth columnist; Coleridge, along with Southey and a collection of High Churchmen and High Tories, in 1822 had resolved to gain the *Quarterly Review* or, if that proved impossible, to compete with it by setting up a new conservative journal.

Murray opened the contest for the succession when in September 1820 he introduced the idea at the end of a letter to Croker in which he complained that Cabinet had failed to avail itself of the *Quarterly Review*, a 'machine' that a million pounds could not suddenly create. 'The Government have such a confidential man in Gifford', Murray wrote, 'that I question if ever they will have such an opportunity again – his life is precarious now – and who is to succeed him ... who can tell – I hope you will think the subject of sufficient importance to talk to Gifford upon it – at least'.[1] In the next year and a half the question of who might succeed to the editorship came up again only in passing.

Throughout his tenure (indeed from the 1780s), Gifford suffered from asthma, but it was not until 1822 that he was so ill he felt he could no longer carry on. In March of that year the editor wrote to his friend Octavius Gilchrist, 'I have not breath enough to walk up stairs, nor strength enough to dress myself'. The time had come for Murray to look seriously for Gifford's successor. His first instinct was a good one, to identify someone upon whom he and the incumbent editor could readily agree. He had in mind the Reverend Reginald Heber, a man who was syncretic, a conservative, but not stridently so (in these respects he was much like Murray). A writer in the *London Magazine* caught, tongue-in-cheek, what made Heber ideal for the editorship of a conservative journal: 'he possesses, admirably, the tact suitable to the Quarterly Review; for he contrives to write as a gentleman and a man of honour, without once running the slightest risk of shocking a single prepossession nursed by what is "fat and full of sap" in venerable establishment'. Dr Samuel Parr observed that Heber had 'ingenuity and a good share of much worth. But he is visionary and I fear intolerant.' Parr's concern was misplaced, for Heber was a watchword for tolerance as well as exemplary piety. Though he was Erastian, he was accommodating of Dissent and he was respected by members of all the Established Church's parties. He had solid literary credentials and a wide circle of acquaintance and, through his half-brother Richard, he was well known in government circles. Especially among liberal conservatives, indeed, he commanded the confidence of powerful men. A disciplined reliable writer, Heber could have provided copy in a pinch and thus have succeeded where Gifford notably failed. Murray and Gifford regarded him as an excellent prospect, but when in June 1822 one of them asked him to accept the editorship, he 'declined the part, wisely, perhaps', Gifford told Copleston, mindful of the burden the cleric would have taken on. When, in November, Murray asked him again, again he declined. As a consolation, Heber suggested a replacement for Gifford that at the time seemed inappropriate but in the end proved prophetic: 'Among the possible conductors of the *Quarterly Review*, a name has just occurred to me likely to answer. It is that of Lockhart ... [A]s his principles are decidedly Tory he might be very useful at the present moment'.[2]

In the same 1820 letter to Croker in which Murray broached the question of Gifford's successor, the publisher mentioned Robert Grant as a man 'who thinks much on the state of the country – is a lawyer – master of style'. Indeed, Grant was Gifford's first and Murray's second choice. He was the author of two of the *Quarterly*'s most masterful articles, his essays on Fox and Pitt, he frequented the same circles as Reginald Heber, he was knowledgeable about literature, politics, and economics, and though he was a committed evangelical, his was the liberal, Clapham variety. Despite his mild demeanour, his religious bent caused Gifford pause as he thought his 'saintly propensities would render him suspected'. In any case, sometime in 1822 when Murray or Gifford offered Grant the editorship, he 'proved timid'.[3]

Following his annual six-week hiatus at Ryde on the Isle of Wight, in the summer of 1822 Gifford found the strength to edit Number 54. But as the effort sorely dragged him down, he wrote to Murray, Southey, and Heber to confirm he could not continue in the post. It was then incumbent upon Murray to make a second serious attempt to find a replacement, but he could think of no one who combined journalistic experience, editorial skills, and the proper ideological credentials.

With Heber and Grant having declined, and with no other obvious successor on the horizon, in the autumn of 1822 Murray conferred with his lawyer and sometime literary advisor Sharon Turner about what to do. Turner suggested a scheme for broadening the pool of candidates. To give the new editor time to gain experience in the position, Gifford should only gradually withdraw. Initially, the new editor would prop Gifford up by managing the correspondence, undertaking the copy editing, and seeing articles through the press. Gifford would retain the title and a portion of his salary, advise his editorial assistant, and continue to act as guardian of the journal's political ethos. Under this plan, Murray could hire a person with the basic requisite skills whose journalist résumé was brief but whose ideological pedigree was sound. There is no direct record of Gifford's response to Turner's proposal, but it appears that he thought it elaborate and certainly unnecessary if Murray found the right candidate.[4]

Over the course of two years Murray and Gifford considered a dozen men for the post, some only in passing. Unlike Gifford, who was discretion itself, Murray was unable to keep his own counsel.[5] For reasons of propriety, the publisher should have kept negotiations a tightly held secret. He did not do so, and the result was embarrassing rumours and hurt feelings. Murray's carelessness encouraged public speculation and behind-the-scenes plotting and caused some men to believe they had been singled out for consideration when the publisher had only enquired after their willingness to serve.

In late 1823 Murray contradicted a rumour that Henry Hart Milman had been appointed to the editorship. The rumour was soon revived, however, now with the caveat that Walter Scott supported Milman's supposed candidacy. Murray had indeed talked to friends and literary advisors about Milman's suitability, but he never directly approached Milman himself, who in any case was not interested.[6]

When Francis Cohen found out through William Sotheby that Murray had talked about him in connection with the editorship, he wrote to the publisher, 'there are means – to a certain degree within my ranks – of making the publication much more efficacious and *useful* than any other of the kind'. Though he was an industrious imaginative researcher and a favourite of Gifford's, and though he later showed he was more than equal to the business requirements of the position – he virtually founded the Public Record Office – it appears Murray and Gifford never seriously considered him, possibly because he was Jewish. On Cohen's letter in which he accepted a post never intended for him, the annotation 'a mistake!!!' appears in an ancient hand. In what must have been an awkward interview, Murray had to set Cohen right.[7]

After their two preferred candidates declined, Murray and Gifford cast their eyes over Oxford in search of a replacement, particularly among the set of Oriel College intellectuals known as the Noetics. As we have seen, the Noetics' leader, Edward Copleston, had supplied the *Quarterly*'s editor with a steady stream of accomplished writers. Indeed, some of the journal's most distinguished articles were produced by Noetics. Richard Whately's 1821 review of Jane Austen was seminal in Victorian interpretations of the novelist's motivation and character. Nassau William Senior, who introduced his theory of value in his 1821 article 'Report – On the State of Agriculture', in a series of essays in 1821 and 1822 gave a balanced view of Scott's accomplishment in the Waverley novels.[8]

Murray and Gifford might have expected to find a suitable candidate from among these men, but the Noetics had, at best, a tangential interest in periodical writing. Probably none of them would have considered it for a career. In deference to Copleston, Gifford had given the Noetics more or less free admission to the *Quarterly* to express their views on literature, society, and economics. They were pleased to write articles as a form of mental exercise and for the pleasure and advantage of exposing their opinions to a wide and influential audience. Perfectly satisfied as they were with Gifford's treatment of them, unlike John Coleridge and the High Churchmen the Noetics did not itch to steer the journal in another direction. It was only later when the *Quarterly* was under the tutelage of John Gibson Lockhart that the Noetics were motivated to set up a rival review. Lockhart allowed Southey to write against Roman Catholic Emancipation, he permitted ultra-Tories to gain ascendancy in the journal, and, moreover, he thought the Noetics were 'a set of d—d idiots' and locked them out.[9] Consequently, in 1829 the Noetics started the *London Review*, to some extent as an alternative to the *Quarterly*. At the time of Gifford's retirement, then, Copleston and his fellow Noetics approached the succession with a complacency that did not fire Murray and Gifford with enthusiasm.

Whately and Senior were exceptionally accomplished men, but it is an open question whether either of them would have considered accepting the editorship had it been offered to them. It is a moot point because the offer never came. In October 1822, at Reginald Heber's suggestion Copleston positioned Whately as a candidate, his former student whom he called 'by far the ablest man I have ever known during my residence at Oxford'.[10] Gifford, though, considered him 'totally out of the question', probably for the reason Thomas Arnold gave to Keble, that 'Whately would not make a good Editor; – his Knowledge of the World would be … very unequal to such an Undertaking'.[11]

Edward Copleston's final serious nominee, Nassau Senior, received the highest possible recommendation, George Canning's endorsement. It was a bad sign, however, that Murray and Gifford did not include Senior in their first tranche of candidates in 1822. It was not until 1823 that his name was brought forward. Despite having Canning and Copleston's backing, Senior's nomination fell on rocky ground because, for reasons unknown, the publisher had taken a disliking to him.[12]

Murray and Gifford had run through the list of obvious candidates. The men they wanted would not consider risking their primary careers by carrying the additional burden of the *Quarterly Review*. The men they passed over lacked experience, were politically suspect, or were otherwise disliked by Murray or Gifford. As Scott put it to Southey, a difficulty they faced was that 'of getting a person with sufficient independence of spirit, accuracy of judgement, and extent of knowledge, to exercise the profession of Aristarch'.[13] What they needed, in other words, was not a literary dilettante but a professional writer and editor. The pool of such men was exceedingly small. Outside of the newspaper industry, few men tried to earn their living through journalism, partly because it was accorded a low social standing and also because, with the notable exception of writers for the *Quarterly* and the *Edinburgh*, they could not gain enough income by it. While these two journals advanced the creation of a professional class of respected and well-remunerated reviewers and editors, in 1822–4 that category did not exist.

John Murray and William Gifford did have one highly accomplished writer in their stable who made his living solely by his pen, Robert Southey. With some hesitation, Scott nominated Southey for the editorship, but neither Murray nor Gifford took the suggestion seriously. Though Southey hoped he would be offered the post, he was realistic enough to know that Gifford and Murray saw him for what he was, 'an impracticable person' who would 'suffer nothing to appear in the journal' unless it accorded with his own out-of-the-way principles. 'I am considered by Murray too bigoted', he lamented, 'and by Gifford too liberal'. In any case, what Murray wanted in an editor, a glorified – if talented and hard working – office assistant, the intractable Southey could never be.[14]

While Murray and Gifford were mulling over the roster of likely and less likely candidates, other men were at the same time looking for an opportunity to put themselves or their favourites in front of the *Quarterly*'s editorial coterie. In particular, a set of High Church intellectuals who coveted the *Quarterly* for its reputation and its imputed power regarded the editorship 'with envious eyes, and slowly and surely drew their plans'. They were led by John Taylor Coleridge, whose yearning was not a casual longing but an infatuation; he was determined to win the *Quarterly Review* or destroy her. He loved her worldly success and her powers of attraction, but he hated what she had become in Gifford and Murray's hands. He aimed to transform her into a High Church, journal, to make her the salt of the earth and a light unto the nations.

When in the summer of 1822 rumour spread that Gifford would have to abandon the editorship, Coleridge discussed with friends his long-held conviction that something needed to be done to move the *Quarterly* in a new direction. As he had no idea he himself might have a serious chance at the editorship, his first thought was to attack the *Quarterly* at the moment of its greatest weakness by setting up a counter review. To that end, in cooperation with some friends in Oxford and London he resurrected a plan first floated in Oxford in 1816–17. The focus of this earlier scheme – which had not borne fruit – had been the *British Critic*, an earnest, dull, and, consequently, ineffective propaganda instrument for morality, orthodox Christianity, and the Established Church. By starting what they hoped would be a livelier and intellectually engaging church-oriented periodical, Coleridge, Keble, Arnold, Dyson, and an Oxford publisher, Parker, aimed to improve upon that High Church journal. In 1822 some of the same plotters now set their sights higher.[15]

Coleridge and his fellow conspirators conceived of a periodical that would succeed where the *Quarterly Review* had failed because of the 'disgraceful influence exercised by Murray over it'. It rankled with them that Murray was both Byron's and the *Quarterly*'s publisher. They believed that as the nation's premier conservative journal it was the *Quarterly*'s duty to set its readers' morals and religion to rights; therefore it should expose Byron's pernicious influence on the nation's youth. Instead, Murray was Byron's promoter and protector. 'How I wish Gifford would assign that noble peer to your correction!', Keble told Coleridge.[16] Ellis and Croker had admonished Byron in the *Quarterly* to be sure, but for his bad company and bad politics, not for immorality and irreligion. Wordsworth's 'What a Monster is a man of Genius if his heart is perverted' captures Coleridge and his friends' prejudice that Byron – talented, charismatic, famous – was damaging the souls of a generation of readers.

Coleridge viewed periodical literature as a form of preaching; Murray thought it 'ridiculous to attempt to convert a man in a Review'. What Coleridge wanted was a moral disquisition on Byron's conduct and character. What Murray wanted was to retain the public's sympathy for a blockbuster author and to sell books. What he and Gifford gave the public, therefore, was Scott's 1817 review of *Childe Harold* and the *Prisoner of Chillon* in Number 31, by which the *Quarterly Review* collective hoped to bring Byron 'back to sound politics and sound sense'. Scott's review addressed the poet's character to be sure, but so sympathetically and appreciatively that Byron was forever grateful for it. The 'many persons' behind Coleridge's scheme thought kowtowing to Lord Byron as this anonymous reviewer had done 'scandalous in such a journal' as the *Quarterly Review*.[17]

Even if the conspirators managed to set up a counter publication, there was no telling if it would be profitable, but, except for the publisher, profitability was not the goal. Instead, the strategy was to occupy the same market as the *Quarterly Review*, to grow as a vine on the *Quarterly* tree, to compete for its light – its audience and contributors – and thus destroy it or train it in a new direction. To that end, they elected as a first step to draw off the *Quarterly*'s sheet anchor, Robert Southey, John Coleridge's faithful correspondent and friend. In mid-1822, therefore, Coleridge suborned Southey by asking him to accept the editorship of the proposed journal. Echoing sentiments Coleridge, Keble, and Arnold shared when they made their plans in 1816–17, but in doing so emphasizing his own preoccupations – Murray's power over him and the role of the press to influence popular opinion – Southey told Bedford why the scheme had now emerged. Murray had 'made a great many enemies, especially in his own trade', which explained why a London publisher, Mason, was willing to take up the cudgel against him. Mason agreed to pay an editor £500 a year and to share the profits. He was also willing to move to the West End, thus to compete in Murray's back yard. Another reason to start a counter periodical was because the *Quarterly* was 'too much in the hands of the Ministers'. Southey blamed the journal's government sponsorship for its 'wretched inconsistency' upon Malthus and the Poor Law, the bullion question, Catholic Emancipation, abolition policy, and Christian missions to India.

By failing to take a firm, consistent stand in favour of protectionism, Protestantism, and paternalism, Southey concluded, the *Quarterly* had 'disgusted a great many persons who [were] by principle strongly disposed to be its friends'. When in the 1820s younger conservatives began to speak the language of rescue and renewal in their political and religious discourse, they were reflecting the Romantic Conservatism of Robert Southey and Samuel Taylor Coleridge that had left its mark on a group of men with influence in the arts, the church, politics, and the law.[18] The generation to which John Taylor Coleridge belonged, men who came to maturity in the 1810s and 1820s, were, as Donald Reiman points out, 'more vitally involved in religious and political conflicts' than their elders. They were not 'content ... in their criticism to treat as lapses in taste what might be considered moral perversions'. John Coleridge was a conservative counterpart to the third generation of liberal Romantics who (Reiman again) 'confronted the discrepancy between their ideals and the outer world ... by attempting to implement those values through symbolic actions'. In John Coleridge's case, the attempt to co-opt, or if that was not possible subvert, the *Quarterly Review* was, as we shall see, just such a symbolic act. By it, he would reinforce rather than challenge morality and preserve and perfect what others were trying to over-throw.[19]

In late 1822, Robert Southey put John Coleridge's name in nomination in letters to Gifford and Murray. He asked Murray to consider Coleridge 'as a person in whom all the necessary requisites [are] to be found, – acquirements, talents, discretion, sound judgment, and a character upon whom the most entire reliance may be placed'. Apparently Southey was oblivious to contradictions between his friend's professions and performance and to significant differences in emphases between Coleridge and himself. Coleridge, who had perhaps a tenuous commitment to the political status quo, was primarily interested in religion and morality; he wished to convert the nation through the medium of a review journal. Through Coleridge, Southey wished to use book reviews to defend the established political order, to counter the influence of the unstamped weekly press, and to achieve one of his original objectives in joining the ranks of the *Quarterly* reviewers, create a pocket moral revolution by modelling dis-interestedness and civility in reviewing. He believed that under the influence of William Gifford and John Wilson Croker, Sir William Drummond's prediction had come true: the *Quarterly* was 'a gentle Inquisition', a 'bully of orthodoxy', intolerant and full of malice. His confidence in Coleridge, the scourge of Hunt and Shelley, was therefore oddly misplaced. After all, typical of many appeals to Murray was his criticism of the *Quarterly*'s (that is to say, Coleridge's) attack on Leigh Hunt. Southey admonished Murray that

> any undue severity, any gratuitous attack, any wound wantonly inflicted makes a man your enemy when he might as well have been your friend. ... [L]ess than justice was done to Leigh Hunt, a conceited writer, and a man of the most villainous principles, – but of no inconsiderable powers. Let us differ from the Edinburgh as much in our principles of criticism as in every thing else.[20]

However imperfectly Southey had read his friend's temperament and motives, his brief was accepted. On 13 November Murray , who around this time made 'conditional' promises to Coleridge regarding his becoming editor, sent Southey an encouraging response, to which Southey replied, 'I am very glad that you see John Coleridge's qualifications and character in the same light that I do. There is no person in whom you could more entirely rely for discretion, judgment, and that probity which is produced by the union of honourable feeling and virtuous principles'.[21]

Between 1818 and 1822, Murray had come to know and to some extent admire Coleridge, whose moral uprightness and liberal politics appealed to him,[22] so initially he received Southey's suggestion with enthusiasm. As was his wont, having noticed Southey's and Gifford's interest in Coleridge, he had earlier drawn him into his circle to gauge his mettle and attempt to make him one of his literary gentlemen. Murray followed his usual routine of inviting the young man to dine, of plying him with gifts, and of massaging his ego by asking his advice on authors' manuscripts and on books that might be reviewed in the *Quarterly*. In late 1822 conditions looked promising, then, for a successful negotiation.

For a few weeks, talks between Murray and Coleridge proceeded smoothly, but just when it appeared that Southey's delegate was about to be appointed editor, in late November 1822 Murray told Coleridge that Gifford was now well enough to resume his duties and the effort to replace him was therefore suspended. So it was that on 12 December Arnold offered Coleridge words of condolence, not congratulation: 'I am very much interested in all you tell me about the Quarterly and grieve that your accession to the Throne is postponed'. Southey had told Bedford that should Coleridge take Gifford's place, the conspiracy to set up a journal to confront the *Quarterly Review* would fall 'to the ground at once'. With the suspension of Coleridge's candidacy, the High Church effort to replace Gifford with one of their own had failed, so it seemed; yet the conspirators did nothing to advance their plan of setting up a counter review. The reason was because Murray, ever reticent, not to say cowardly, let Coleridge believe his appointment was not set aside but, as Arnold put it, 'postponed'. In giving Coleridge this impression, Murray was disingenuous on two counts: really he had turned against Coleridge and Gifford was still alarmingly ill. The editor was spitting blood in December; at points throughout January 1823 a notice appeared in newspapers: 'The Quarterly Review, which the ill health of the editor has delayed, is nearly ready for publication'; in February Gifford complained his lungs were giving way and he suffered from a debilitating fever; between October 1822 and February 1823 he was unable to write letters of any length.[23]

Murray terminated the negotiation because Coleridge had failed the interview. In the course of his communications with the publisher, apparently in an effort to impress by highlighting the sacrifices he was willing to make Coleridge foolishly admitted his legal duties would place onerous demands on his time. He would therefore have to juggle editorial and professional responsibilities. Worse, he stated that as a lawyer he had been chary of running the '*unnecessary* risque of being thought a dabbler in literature'. To satisfy a higher purpose, he was now willing to accept that risk.[24] Murray, who spent his life dealing in books, must have found Coleridge's philistinism surprising and off-putting. He had plenty of barristers and solicitors among his gentlemen – Turner, Cohen, Grant, Scott, Miller, Stephen – who were not diffident about dabbling in literature. Evidently regarding letters as a shallow pursuit was not endemic to Coleridge's profession. From the evidence of his own reviews of Hemans and Shelley, literature was redeemable for Coleridge if it took the form of a mellifluous sermon. Murray must have seen that, at best, Coleridge wanted the position as a symbolic conquest.

The temporary collapse of Coleridge's candidacy was of great significance in the history of the *Quarterly Review*: it commenced a sea change in the constitutional arrangement between the publisher and the journal's political sponsors. As we have seen, when the *Quarterly* started Murray had less influence in the journal's inner circle than any other founder besides Ballantyne. Through persistence and force of will, by virtue of Gifford's dependence upon his help with the correspondence, the selection of books for review, and the management of contributors, and because he held the purse strings and was perennially present, Murray over time did obtain a degree of editorial control over portions of the journal's content. His influence had therefore grown exponentially, but in 1822–4 it was still not absolute.

Throughout Gifford's tenure, Murray's 'sovereignty over the Review', as Croker put it, was 'a constitutional sovereignty ... exercised thro' his ministers'.[25] As for John Murray's gentlemen, their influence in the inner circle varied, depending upon the man and the issue. In the matter of Gifford's successor, all had the power to nominate but Canning alone could appoint by fiat, though he would not have done so without taking Gifford's advice. Canning excepted, Murray and Gifford had a veto over the other gentlemen who had constitutional authority through the *Quarterly Review*'s informal executive council. Gifford, as Canning's proxy, had the power to override Murray on fundamentals, such as the appointment of an editor. As for Scott, in 1822 his desire to interfere was minimal. The other gentlemen had the equivalent of a single vote each, with the exception of Southey who, because he refused to play the game, had a half-vote. That is, unless he threatened to abandon the *Quarterly*, in which case, to save the journal, Murray would have brought matters to a crisis.

As for Croker and Barrow, whatever power they enjoyed at 50 Albemarle Street was by virtue of their friendship with Murray and their importance as contributors. Barrow, shrewd and scheming, was more efficient and productive than any other man was capable of, imagined possible, or wanted to be, both at the Admiralty and at Albemarle. But, Bentham-like, Barrow regarded literature as push-pin,[26] which severely limited his general utility to Murray and his role in the journal's management. What was left to him was the ability to bully and make trouble. A strutting peacock, he crowded others out by his display.

Croker, too, used hyper-efficiency and mastery of detail to rise above the crowd. Croker's reputation as a back-room manipulator is well deserved; certainly he gained power at Albemarle by making himself useful to Murray behind the scenes. In documents preserved at the Clements Library and in off-hand references in his letters in the John Murray Archive, we catch glimpses of him scuttling about in the dark corners of journalism, pulling the strings of the counterrevolutionary press, feeding Treasury money to shadowy operators such as John Taylor and William Jerdan, trading in secret knowledge. Croker's relationship with Murray during Gifford's reign is worth a chapter in itself.[27] He is often spoken of as the voice of politics in the journal, but that was his role in the 1830s under Lockhart. To the end of Gifford's tenure he confined himself mainly to literary criticism and to chronicling the French Revolution and the Napoleonic years. Murray sidled up to him because he was a reliable reviewer and a powerful political operator. The publisher took advantage of Croker's productivity to fill gaps that would have prevented the journal's timely publication.

January 1823 marked the beginning of a shift in this constitutional structure and the personal relations Murray enjoyed with some of his gentlemen, developments that occurred because the publisher found himself virtually abandoned by the men to whom he was supposed to defer. During the period bounded by the temporary failure of Coleridge's candidacy at the end of 1822 and Murray's unilateral appointment of Lockhart to the editorship at the end of 1825, while his gentlemen often impeded or gainsaid his proposals, frequently they had little or nothing constructive to offer. Their failure adequately to support and guide the publisher during the succession crisis eventually resulted in his gaining control over the *Quarterly Review*.

The process by which Murray ultimately triumphed commenced its long final phase when Gifford was knocked back on his heels by Murray's setting Coleridge aside and by the publisher's refusing, despite Canning's endorsement, even to consider Senior for the editorship.[28] Gifford wished, indeed he needed to retire, retirement was within reach, and then Murray denied Coleridge the editorship and shrugged off Senior. Because Gifford either misunderstood or had no knowledge of the publisher's motives, he thought Murray was acting arbitrarily. Two years elapsed between the time when Murray suspended Coleridge's candidacy and when he finally appointed him, not because Gifford refused to step aside, but because Murray was indecisive and because the incumbent, having once again become wary of his publisher's motives, retarded progress. There was no open hostility between the two men, they continued to regard each other as friends, but they could not agree on whom to appoint.[29] Throughout this period, Gifford had, because of his illnesses, little active power to assist the process of identifying a new editor but much residual power to impede it.

At the end of March 1823, the immediate danger to Gifford's life had passed, but his doctors advised continued rest, so, he told Murray, he would sit out the preparation of Number 56 and then formally resign. The publisher would not hear of it; he needed more time to find a replacement.[30] Gifford continued to be actively involved – he applied his blue pencil to many reviews up to and even beyond the end of 1824 – [31] but to keep the *Quarterly Review* alive, Murray, Croker, and Barrow each took a portion of the editorial duties. The best the four men could manage in 1823, though, was the publication of three issues.

On 22 July 1823, Gifford admonished Murray, 'above all, keep your eye steadfastly on the means of filling my place'. A few days later he confided to Coleridge, with whom he stayed in contact and whose candidacy he continued to support, 'And now what to do, I know not. Murray, who has every thing at stake, either turns a deaf ear to my wishes, or indulges in vague and wild expectations. I tremble at the thought of a new Number in my poor state, and yet I see no present remedy. ... I should grieve to see him opening his eyes too late'. It was Barrow, meanwhile, who had Murray's ear, an Iago who in the final two years of Gifford's editorship sowed doubt and created discord. On 26 July he told Murray, 'I think we have brought Gifford to his bearings. I don't know what he means by your running away from difficulties – I fear that they are *all* of his own making'. What Barrow referred to was Murray's stalled negotiations with a somewhat unlikely candidate for the editorship, William Haygarth, a classicist and poet of minor accomplishment.[32]

Murray's negotiations with Haygarth stalled because Gifford had 'serious doubts' about the man's fitness for the job. Upon Richard Heber's suggestion, Murray approached Haygarth in March 1823. Haygarth readily agreed to Turner's plan, that he at first act as Gifford's assistant and share the editor's salary. In May, Murray assured Haygarth that to complete the appointment he had only to clear the arrangement with the editor. Then for weeks on end, Haygarth heard nothing more from Murray. His candidacy had run into trouble because Gifford suspected his politics and doubted his aptitude. He thought it was 'only the mere drudgery that he could get through'; worse, he was troubled by Haygarth's Whiggish origins.[33] To judge from his articles in the *Quarterly Review*, Haygarth's political orientation had over the years come to resemble more nearly the liberal conservatism of the ideal Canningite reviewer. But Gifford had a long and unforgiving memory. He would have recalled that Haygarth in his poem *Greece* (1814) had expressed views that ran suspiciously close to those of Holland House and the *Quarterly*'s enemies up north, the *Edinburgh* reviewers. Murray had rejected two politically acceptable and otherwise competent candidates, Coleridge and Senior; there was no reason why Gifford would prefer the politically suspect and relatively undistinguished Haygarth over these two men.[34]

The persistent and unexplained delay wore down Haygarth's patience. In late June he complained to Murray, 'I am as completely at a loss to know what your ultimate intentions are, as I was three months ago when you first made the proposition to me'. Unwilling to relinquish Haygarth as an, to him, acceptable successor to Gifford and unable to force the matter, throughout the summer and autumn of 1823 Murray kept the candidate waiting. When in early December the publisher told him there was little likelihood he would become editor, Haygarth, feeling betrayed, irrationally declared he would seek not redress but revenge. Already ill with the disease that within a year would take his life, he declared to Murray that he intended to start a rival periodical for the sole purpose of drawing away the *Quarterly*'s writers and subscribers. His journal would go under, he knew, and he would lose a fortune by it, but his aim was to destroy the *Quarterly*.[35] Haygarth had enough private capital 'to be reckless', as Gifford put it, and start such an enterprise, but his plan was bluff and bluster and nothing came of it.

When April 1824 rolled around, although it was clear Gifford must withdraw, Murray was at an impasse. All probable candidates had been proposed; all declined or had been rejected. The publisher could only think to plead with his editor to stay on 'a little and yet a little further' and to ask Croker temporarily to don Gifford's 'Wig and Spectacles'.[36] Gifford was too ill to accomplish much, but Murray needed him, if only more or less as a figurehead, or his bankers – concerned the journal was about to go under – would not lend him the money to pay his stationer and printer.

Gifford, who saw no sign Murray was willing to pursue Senior's nomination, accept Coleridge, or propose new candidates, felt he had to push him to make a decision. So on 23 April 1824 he took the conclusive step of formally declaring to Canning he would see the journal through one more issue, Number 60, and then lay down his quill forever. By immediately passing Gifford's letter to the prime minister, Canning demonstrated that the Cabinet now regarded the *Quarterly*, if passively, as an important ally. He told Liverpool that to preserve the journal government might have to intervene. The prime minister answered in a 'Most Private' note, 'I return Gifford's letter. The Fall of the Quarterly Review would be a serious calamity, and we must devise some means of keeping it up'.[37] Canning took no action. Apparently he decided to wait for the publication of Number 60 to see how events would unfold.

In the end, there was no need for Ministers to become involved. Helped by Croker and Barrow, Gifford and Murray muddled through. They managed to bring out Number 60, in August 1824, and by the end of the year the *Quarterly Review* had a new editor. In mid-September, with Number 60 out of the way, Murray confronted the impossible prospect of having to pull together the next issue with no editor at the helm, nominal or otherwise. Coleridge appeared to be Murray's only option, but still he could not bring himself to renew the negotiation. With no way forward acceptable to him, Murray wrote to Gifford on 16 September to plead, yet again, 'you can not be aware of the distress and anxiety which I am undergoing, or you would rather commiserate my suffering than be angry at an indecision which, even you, have not boldness enough to fix'. He asked Gifford to assist him in bringing out one final number. In stating his case, he anticipated Gifford's objection that he should hire Coleridge. Coleridge was out of town, Murray claimed, as were Canning, Croker and 'those other friends' whom he needed to consult. That the publisher was making excuses is confirmed by the ease with which Gifford himself contacted Coleridge. In a letter composed on 23–24 September, he wrote:

> Thursday. Private
> I waited for a call by Murray, who is grown quite timid and afraid to look his situation in the face. I have formally resigned the dictatorship, from absolute debility – but he haunts me in forma pauperis and begs of charity that I will go on for a few weeks longer to give him time to make arrangements! He has had two years, and has done nothing. I have not yet decided, nor shall I, till I see him here – meanwhile there is a sort of interregnum, and nothing done.
> – Friday
> I have seen Murray, and have promised to assist him for a few weeks, not as *Editor*, but as a *friend*. Keep this to yourself at present.[38]

At the end of September, Barrow tried to convince Murray that the time for action was at hand. Still the publisher hesitated; October and November passed without a decision. One problem Murray faced was that, Barrow aside, the publisher could get no advice from the *Quarterly*'s putative steering committee. Having seen his and his brother's several nominees refused, Heber was no longer disposed to help. Scott was now so uninvolved it appears he was not even contacted. And, for reasons that are not entirely clear, Croker had become uncooperative. Though Murray tried to consult 'Mr. Croker at the beginning, middle, and end' of the process of appointing an editor, he 'could get no advice from him'.[39]

Finally, in mid-autumn, Murray made up his mind; he would have to appoint Coleridge. He wished not to appear to have made the decision on his own, and he felt he at least had to make a show of gaining the assent of the journal's sponsors. He later told Lockhart that sometime in the fall of 1824 he mentioned to Croker that Gifford had promised to buttress Coleridge during the initial months of his editorship. Gifford's promise (supposing it was made) partly removed the excuse Murray apparently had used at an earlier date, that Coleridge was too young and inexperienced. According to Murray, when Croker heard of Gifford's willingness to assist during a transition period, he impatiently told the publisher, '*Then take him*'. Relieved now that he could plausibly claim he acted under direction, Murray 'did so accordingly'.[40]

On 9 December 1824, the publisher made a verbal offer to Coleridge with a request that he work out the formal details with F. H. Locker, a lawyer.[41] In a letter he sent the next day, Coleridge was ingenuous to the point of stupidity. He told Murray that in accepting his 'kind and flattering offer' he had made up his mind to bear the risk to his professional standing that undertaking the editorship of the *Quarterly Review* would unavoidably entail. These of course were exactly the sentiments that cast a shadow over his candidacy in the first place.[42] By his obtuseness, Coleridge saddled his editorship with a terminal deficit; he had telegraphed to his employer that he was not fully committed to the task of editing the *Quarterly Review*.

Murray must have been crestfallen when he realized he had hired a feckless, unengaged editor. Nevertheless, it was too late; in mid-December he asked Southey as the man who had nominated Coleridge to write to Canning and Croker, 'persons whose confidence it was of great importance to obtain'. Southey agreed to write to Croker, but he wished not to address Canning, 'a person so high in office', even though sometime earlier he had contacted Canning to give him, unsolicited, his opinions on the state of the country.[43] Upon receiving Southey's letter, Croker, who had grown sulky, replied that until now he had not heard of Coleridge's candidacy. Again in an awkward effort to displace responsibility for the appointment, in December Murray brought the editorial coterie and sponsors together after the fact for a figurative laying on of hands. At a dinner at his house in Whitehall Place, Murray introduced Coleridge to Croker, Barrow, Freeling, Heber, and Hay, among others. At the dinner, Barrow, taking Croker aside, said 'he will do, and Croker's answer was, I think so too'.[44] Thus Murray gained the informal board of directors' imprimatur for a decision he had already taken.

From the beginning of Coleridge's editorial labours, Murray was disposed to be critical, and for good reason as his editor was away from London on legal duties for more than half the time between January and October.[45] His absence caused real problems for Murray. In April through July, for example, Captain Procter could get no reply from the editor about his articles. Procter's having to appeal to Murray to act as postman must have confirmed the publisher's worst doubts about Coleridge's commitment. So persistently did Murray complain even early on that in March 1825 Coleridge wrote defensively: 'I am sorry you have found cause for anxiety in my absence on the circuit – but I certainly conceived you were aware that such absences were quite necessary for me before I undertook the task of conducting the review'.[46] Coleridge, who seemed to have no conception of how to manage other men's expectations and perceptions, constantly reminded Murray that legal matters distracted him from his *Quarterly Review* duties. In many of his letters to the publisher he forthrightly admitted he wrote 'in haste' because he had to attend to legal business in Exeter.[47] Indicative of his impatience, the publisher fell silent and he began to usurp some of his editor's privileges. In June, Coleridge found himself having to tell a contributor, Barron Field, 'you must be aware that whatever [the publisher] says respecting the Quarterly, is intended to be understood as subject to such determination as the Editor may find necessary'. In July Coleridge wrote to the now difficult to contact Murray, 'I shall be much obliged to you to communicate to me from time to time whatever you may think important for me to know'.[48]

Despite being preoccupied with his law career, Coleridge was active and fairly efficient and although no single number he edited was sparkling, all but one were published more or less on time. One article stood out for the attention it received from government, Robert Gooch's essay on the plague. Published in Number 65, it was the first article in the journal's history that demonstrably had an impact on legislation.[49] For the most part, though, during Coleridge's year at the helm the *Quarterly* was undistinguished. Scott reflected a consensus when he called Coleridge's editorship 'a most leaden interregnum' and spoke of 'the dull numbers which interfered between Gifford's reign' and Lockhart's. A writer in *Blackwood's Magazine* complained that under Coleridge there was too much politics and science and not enough literature in the *Quarterly*, a deficiency the editor himself admitted to.[50] An imaginary conversation, 'Mornings in Albemarle-Street', published in the April 1825 *London Magazine* was similarly dismissive of the new editor's abilities, *Quarterly Review* Number 62, Coleridge's first, having just appeared:

> MR. D'ISRAELI.
> WELL. – I still must say I regret, Mr. Murray, that I cannot congratulate you on the late change of Editorship, at least as far as the last number of the Quarterly may be regarded as a specimen of the benefit it is to derive from Mr. Coleridge's superintendence.
>
> MR. MURRAY.
> I fear, Sir, the Quarterly has lost much in losing Mr. Gifford. The name of Gifford did a great deal for the Quarterly. It was something for such a work to have a wit, a poet, a scholar, and a satirist, at its head.
>
> MR. LUTTRELL.
> Yes; and now you have got a person who is neither a wit, poet, scholar, nor satirist. I never could conceive what claims Mr. Coleridge had to the eminent office you have assigned to him, and I wonder still more that I have now seen a sample of his management. He is a sort of bad translation of his old uncle.

Although Murray had reason to plot Coleridge's removal, then, there is no evidence he actively did so in the spring and summer of 1825. When the opportunity to set Coleridge aside presented itself, however, he took advantage of it. Coleridge's editorship was doomed when an alternative emerged in September in the midst of Murray's effort to set up a daily newspaper, the *Representative*.[51] Murray's preeminence as the former publisher of Byron and as proprietor of the *Quarterly Review* had made him think too well of himself and to become susceptible to the flattery and enthusiasm of a twenty-year-old, Benjamin Disraeli, the eldest son of his old friend Isaac D'Israeli. In August 1835, Disraeli stoked the idea that Murray could succeed in a 'Great Plan' to rival *The Times*. It was in the course of his attempt to find a director for the projected newspaper that Murray precipitately appointed Sir Walter Scott's son-in-law, John Gibson Lockhart, to the editorship of the *Quarterly Review*.

Details about Lockhart, Scott, and Murray's negotiations over the *Representative* are worth surveying because they expose the convoluted but certain process by which Lockhart gained and Coleridge lost the editorship. If Murray could obtain Lockhart for the directorship of the *Representative* he might secure Scott's active association with his firm and with Scott on board gain credibility for his newspaper with investors and the public. In the course of a few months Murray so deeply committed his finances and his reputation to this venture that he was willing to go to great lengths to ensure its success, even, as it turned out, to placing the editorship of the *Quarterly* in new hands.

In an October 1825 letter to Scott, Murray described how the *Representative* project emerged; the picture he drew was of a man intoxicated by dreams of influence and fame. The enterprise appears to have been conceived in after hours when Murray was in his cups: 'The more we ... thought and talked over our plans, the more certain [we were] of their inevitable success, and of their leading us to certain power, reputation, and fortune'.[52] Thus confused by adulation and excess liquor,[53] in August and September Murray buried himself in the *Representative* with D'Israeli, father and son, with a business partner, J. D. Powles, and with a lawyer, William Wright. He soon found himself in the same predicament he had faced a year earlier over the succession to the editorship of the *Quarterly Review*; he needed someone to edit the *Representative* and he had few suitable prospects. Indeed, Lockhart is the only person he is known to have approached.

Murray's initial contact with Lockhart was in 1817 when the young man wrote to the publisher to offer his services as a translator of German. The two men first met in March 1819 when the Edinburgh publisher William Blackwood supplied Lockhart with a letter of introduction. Having been encouraged by Scott to give him a trial as a contributor to the *Quarterly*, Murray and Gifford contacted him in April 1820. During the balance of Gifford's editorship, Lockhart's name occasionally appears in Murray and Gifford's correspondence. It will be recalled that in 1822 Heber suggested Lockhart for the editorship of the *Quarterly Review*. These were good reasons why Lockhart occurred to Murray in September 1825, but the immediate reason the publisher saw him as a legitimate prospect may have been because he had recently begun to move in Canning's orbit. That development signalled the possibility that Lockhart might now be accepted by members of Murray's wider circle when earlier they had expressed serious doubts about him.[54]

Had Lockhart's character not been impugned by his association with the sometimes scurrilous *Blackwood's Magazine* and by his part in the fatal John Scott-Jonathan Christie duel of 1821, he would have been an uncontroversial candidate to head the *Representative*.[55] But as it was, Murray expected trouble. In

1822 the publisher had enquired of his gentlemen what they thought of Heber's suggestion that Lockhart might make a good editor of the *Quarterly Review*. Their alarmed response, a prequel to Murray's appointment of him to the editorship of the *Quarterly* in 1825, was captured by Heber in a letter of 23 November 1822: 'I was once inclined to suggest Lockhart ... but everybody cried out that he was too great a blackguard'.[56]

Still, in 1825 Murray was ready to place Lockhart at the head of his new enterprise, the *Representative*, because he could identify no other candidate and because Lockhart had some persuasive sponsors. Naturally Lockhart had a loyal advocate in the person of his father-in-law: 'He is a most unexceptionable friend and husband', Scott told Lady Abercorn, 'very clever, very learned, and very handsome, – addicted to satire, though, by which he has made himself many enemies'. It was encouraging to Murray that Canning was willing to entertain Lockhart, and his character and talents were urged by one of the publisher's close friends, the sometime *Quarterly* reviewer Thomas Mitchell, who was Lockhart's correspondent and admirer.[57]

Having gone down this road in 1822 with ill results, in September 1825 Murray devised a scheme to overcome the opposition he knew would arise if he tried to place Lockhart in the directorship of the *Representative*. Surely Scott could silence Lockhart's detractors. He must draw Sir Walter Scott forward as his son-in-law's public defender. To persuade Lockhart to accept the position and Scott to recommend him to influential literary and political associates, Murray sent young Disraeli north as the purveyor of an elaborate and unlikely brief. Disraeli would attempt to convince Scott and Lockhart that through Murray's influence over 'personages of wealth, interests, politics' Lockhart would come to London 'not to be an Editor of a Newspaper, but the Director-General of an immense organ, and at the head of a band of high-bred gentlemen and important interests'. Via Disraeli, Murray intended to make a remarkable suggestion, that the publisher could convince his 'four o'clock visitors' to obtain a parliamentary seat for Lockhart. Disraeli recorded the impression Murray gave him of his influence over high politicos and the support he could expect from other powerful quarters: 'through Powles, all America and the Commercial Interest .... Wilmot H[orton]., &c., not as mere under-secretary, but as [your] private friend .... [T]he West India Interest will pledge themselves and in such situations as Barrow, &c., &c., are distinctly in [your] power'.[58]

Disraeli's visit was prepared for by a letter Wright sent to Lockhart offering him the newspaper directorship. When in mid-September Disraeli arrived in Scotland and knocked at the door of Lockhart's cottage, Chiefswood, on Scott's Abbotsford estate, Lockhart and Scott were momentarily taken aback. It had not occurred to them that Murray would send a boy as his emissary; they understood from Wright's letter that it was Isaac D'Israeli, one of the Murray family's oldest most faithful advisors, who was travelling north to see them. Even then, Disraeli had about him a dash of the *petit-maître* and he was an engaging and persuasive conversationalist. But his primary auditor, Scott, cannot have been impressed. He was too keen an observer of human nature, too personally aware of the pitfalls awaiting those who threw themselves into fantastic schemes to be taken in by Disraeli's sparkling manner. Murray seems to have believed sincerely that he had great influence at Westminster, but his claims were ridiculous. Although Wilmot-Horton, Hay, Canning, Croker, and Huskisson were Murray's acquaintances, they were not about to grant political favours to a publisher. Scott must have seen in an instant how grandly self-deceiving Murray was and he must have wondered at his foolishness in being misled by the sycophantic promptings of a talented near-adolescent.

Additionally, Murray tried through Disraeli to accomplish too much too fast. To obviate the difficulties that arose in 1822 when Murray acted on Heber's proposal that Lockhart take the editorship of the *Quarterly Review*, a most delicate part of Disraeli's commission was that he should gain assurances from Scott about Lockhart's character, assurances Murray could then place before his business partners and political sponsors. To that end, Disraeli took Scott aside; he reported to Murray that their conversation was 'most satisfactory'. Scott was patient with Disraeli, who was protected by his youth and who was, after all, only Murray's agent. For his presumption, though, the publisher was about to get a 'flap with a fox-tail'.[59]

Despite the positive and encouraging tone of Disraeli's letters to Murray from Scotland, Scott and Lockhart were unconvinced. It was obvious Murray had no guaranteed influence at Westminster; certainly he could not secure a parliamentary seat for Lockhart or some long-term, lucrative civil service posting. Effectively, Murray had offered nothing but the editorship of a newspaper. Scott made it clear that he objected to Lockhart's accepting a position that would cause him to 'lose caste', which would certainly happen if he were to become a mere newspaper editor. Even a parliamentary appointment or some similarly dignified position, were it possible to obtain it, which Scott doubted, would fail to secure his assent. A few years as a low-paid parliamentary secretary or as a member of Parliament would not constitute a viable career.[60]

On 7 October 1825, Lockhart therefore wrote to Murray to declare 'the *impossibility* of [his] ever entering into the career of London in the capacity of a newspaper editor'.[61] On October 9, Scott wrote pointedly that he could 'not conceive it advisable that [Lockhart] should leave Scotland on the speculation of becoming editor of a newspaper'.[62] He was not about to countenance his son-in-law abandoning Scotland, forgoing a £1,000 legal practice, and losing caste by becoming a professional journalist. Given Lockhart's vehement letter of refusal, Scott's letter, which should be read in detail for its condescending disparagement of Murray's judgement and his dignity as a book and periodical publisher, would seem redundant except that in it Scott referred to the '*present* state ... of the negotiation'.[63] Evidently he had read the publisher's frame of mind; his object was to encourage Murray to up the ante.

It is perhaps too conspiratorial to suppose that as early as 9 October Scott had the editorship of the *Quarterly Review* in mind for his son-in-law; in any case, he later protested to Southey that he had not 'the most distant idea' of maneuvering for that position.[64] Scott claimed it was sometime between 9 and 16 October when he became aware that Coleridge might have to forgo the editorship of the *Quarterly* because the position was an impediment to his legal career.[65] Still, it is worth pondering why Scott kept negotiations open when he knew as well as any man that Murray genuinely controlled a single desirable office, the editorship of the *Quarterly Review*.

Thus pressed by Scott to proffer a sure, lucrative, and dignified career for Lockhart sufficient to justify his moving to London, Murray turned to the only fungible asset he had that matched the requirement. So it was that on 13 October, in his reply to Scott's letter of 9 October, Murray reported that in conversation with Lockhart (the advocate was visiting London at the publisher's invitation) he had dramatically increased the stakes. To 'obviate any difficulties which have been urged', Murray suggested that Lockhart 'come to London as the editor of the *Quarterly*'. Standing on his dignity, the publisher asserted that the editorship of the *Quarterly Review*, at least, was an appointment 'coveted by many of the highest literary characters in the country, and which, of itself, would entitle its possessor to enter into and mix with the first classes of society'.[66]

Murray's offer was hastily formulated. Possibly the idea of setting Coleridge aside in favour of Lockhart first came up in a conversation between Murray and Wright. In one version it was Wright who originated the plan. Wright and Scott recorded that 'the choice was made on the recommendation of Canning and Gifford'. But the claim that the journal's senior political sponsor and its former editor were involved in Lockhart's appointment sounds like one of Murray's after-the-fact justifications, for if it was true the publisher would have made a great show of it in November when some of the principals objected; he did not. However it first occurred to Murray to appoint a new editor, in late October he signed a three-year contract to pay Lockhart £1,200 per annum to pilot the *Quarterly Review*.[67] At this point, Coleridge knew nothing about the negotiations between Murray, Scott, and Lockhart.

Coleridge's removal from the editorship exposed Murray as 'a slippery chap humorous and variable'. When he made the offer, he assured Scott and Lockhart that Coleridge was set to retire at the end of the year and therefore the position was 'open and disengaged'. By a happy coincidence, Coleridge had indeed 'consulted with his brothers about giving up the Editorship', but Murray only found this out in mid-November when he happened to see a letter John Coleridge sent to John Barrow. In the clearest recorded statement on the matter Murray told Barrow, 'The real fact is, that finding that Mr. Coleridge's business had increased and was increasing to such a degree that he must *in all likelihood* give up the Review the next year, I thought it best at once to apply to Mr. Lockhart as the only man who could fill the appointment'. There is no indication Murray knew from the editor himself that he was considering resigning; certainly in October Coleridge was undecided.[68]

Coleridge, who at the beginning of November found he no longer had easy access to Murray ('I have been very unlucky in several attempts to find you at home ...'), had no inkling of his fate until Murray told him on 16 November, the day before an announcement appeared in *The Times* stating that Lockhart would take over the editorship in the New Year. In a 25 November letter to Scott, Southey recorded information he must have received from Coleridge. When read with Coleridge's letters to Murray and Gifford, Southey's comments leave us in no doubt about 'the manner in which John Coleridge [had] been put out'. Southey concluded, 'If Nature had given [Murray] a tail, it would have been between his legs as often as he thought of me during this dirty and unaccountable transaction'. He was a great bookseller and proprietor of the *Quarterly Review*, Southey allowed, but as a man he lacked honour and rectitude. Southey consoled Coleridge that one 'should not expect to gather grapes from thistles'. He surmised that the publisher was unlikely to have acted without finding someone to prop up his decision. He therefore wished to know who had counselled him; neither Southey nor Coleridge understood the role Disraeli played in firing Murray's imagination or Wright's part in the negotiations. Keble, who was Coleridge's best friend and whose comments reflect private conversations that took place in the aftermath of the dismissal, confirmed that the usurped editor felt ill-treated: 'I am most heartily glad you are free', Keble wrote, 'and certainly if Murray was what it appears he is, the sooner one parted company with him the better'.[69]

The end of this affair was exceptionally messy. When William Stewart Rose found out about Lockhart's appointment, he wrote a heated letter to Barrow to complain that Murray had elevated a man who by his character and actions was unsuited to the dignity and responsibilities of the position. Barrow, who was consistently Coleridge's advocate, tried to escalate his and Rose's displeasure to the level of a crisis. It did not help that in late October and early November when Murray consulted Barrow about appointing Lockhart he did not let on the thing was already done.[70] It required Scott's intervention to dampen the flames of discontent.

A final important development occurred at the end of November. Apparently influenced by Disraeli, Murray had the impression that his old Admiralty friends, Barrow and Croker, had opposed Lockhart's appointment not because they objected to his character or thought he would make a bad editor but because they were trying to torpedo the *Representative*. There was no such conspiracy. Barrow was genuinely upset that a man he liked should be replaced in the editorship by a man he regarded as a blackguard. As for Croker, when Lockhart contacted him on 16 November to try to win his support, he declined to become involved. He had nothing to do with the opposition to Lockhart's appointment.

It was a set of specific actions by Barrow and Croker that caused Murray to draw lines between the First and Second Secretaries and his plans for the *Representative*. By telling Rose about the *Representative*, Barrow had violated Murray's embargo on public discussion of the topic. Croker had strongly objected to the scheme when he first heard about it in August and he thought he had convinced Murray not to go forward with it. On this narrow foundation Murray built a mountain of resentment and suspicion. Tellingly, although Croker played no part whatsoever in the fuss over Lockhart, it was he, not Barrow or Rose, who was the chief object of Murray's wrath. Given how precipitately Murray jumped to conclusions about Croker's actions and motives, it appears he was a chain Murray wished to shake off. Suddenly the publisher saw his long relationship with the Admiralty's First Secretary in an entirely new light. The scales fell from his eyes and now the man who, besides Gifford, had for years been his closest partner in the conduct of the *Quarterly Review* was, in Disraeli's words, 'intriguing, selfish, and narrow-minded'. Murray's 'mind has undergone a revolution', Disraeli told Lockhart, a revolution 'which it has taken ten years to bring about. You would not know him for the same man'. In December, Coleridge confirmed that Murray had soured on Croker.[71]

The Lockhart crisis was a cathartic experience for Murray by which he freed himself of the last vestige of dependence upon his old *Quarterly Review* advisors. Once again without the help of others he had made a crucial appointment. Once again his political masters had given him no good advice but only gainsaid his decisions. Murray had had enough. It was his capital that was at risk; it was he alone who had made hard decisions in the absence of supportive advice. A revolution had indeed taken place, in Murray's sense of ownership over his properties and his schemes.[72] In a matter of months the *Representative* would rise and fall, terminated in July 1826 with Murray having incurred £26,000 in losses. And yet the *Quarterly Review* and John Gibson Lockhart remained, both now firmly under Murray's control. The events of late 1825 and the revolution they precipitated arose over Murray's effort to set up the *Representative*, but their lasting impact was on the publisher's relationship to the *Quarterly Review* and its editor. With Lockhart's only significant outside sponsor, Scott, geographically distant and otherwise preoccupied with his own troubled financial affairs, with Canning and Liverpool satisfied as long as the *Quarterly* remained vaguely supportive of the nation's establishments, and with most of the journal's other key patrons now alienated (Barrow and Croker), exiled (Heber, to continental Europe on rumours of his homosexuality), or too old and ill to be involved (Gifford), Murray was free to conduct the journal as he saw fit.

Coleridge lost the editorship of the *Quarterly Review* when Scott trumped Murray in the negotiation over Lockhart and the *Representative*. Like a gambler desperate to win on the next throw, Murray invested heavily in gaining Lockhart for his newspaper. Scott divined Murray's vulnerability and with great emotional precision cut the publisher's pride to the quick. He forced Murray to cover his wager and in doing so won the *Quarterly Review* for his son-in-law. In October 1808 when Murray visited Scott at Ashiestiel, and in October 1825 when Lockhart visited Murray in London, the publisher fancied he held the best hand, and so perhaps he did, but in both episodes it was Scott, not Murray, who played brilliantly. Scott's mind worked like quicksilver and he could win an opening hand, though his attention soon wandered from the game. But while Murray was not a finesse player and he often lost a deal, he was patient and persistent. He won by waiting others out.

When Lockhart took up the editorship, in January 1826, Murray, truly, was now 'lord paramount'.[72] Between 1822 and 1824, had he tried to dictate who was to become editor of the *Quarterly Review*, he would have had a rebellion on his hands; he had power, but he was not all-powerful. In 1823, Gifford forced him to abandon Haygarth. In 1824, his gentlemen left him with little choice but to appoint Coleridge or Senior or some other man he did not want. But in 1825, Murray achieved a revolution in his relationship to the journal's sponsors. For the twelve months of Coleridge's tenure, the publisher operated the *Quarterly* with minimal interference. By October 1825, he had grown accustomed to treating the journal as his personal property, to do with as he willed. So when he offered the editorship to Lockhart, it did not occur to him to consult the journal's sponsors, who in any case were distracted, dispersed, alienated, or uninvolved. An auditor at Ashiestiel in October 1808 would have been surprised to learn that by virtue of his being the last man at the table, in October 1825 John Murray could have claimed, now without fear of contradiction, that he 'alone created' the *Quarterly Review*, 'the most formidable engine that ever was invented, in support of the laws and Religion of his Country'.[74]

APPENDIX A: LIST OF ARTICLES AND IDENTIFICATION OF CONTRIBUTORS

BCR Barré Charles Roberts
BF Barron Field
CJB Charles James Blomfield
CRM Charles Robert Maturin
DR David Robinson
EC Edward Copleston
EJ Edward Jacob
FC Francis Cohen
GC George Canning
GD'O George D'Oyly
GE George Ellis
GP George Procter
HDW Henry Downing Whittington
HHM Henry Hart Milman
HJS Henry John Stephen
ID'I Isaac D'Israeli
JB John Barrow
JBS John Bird Sumner
JHF John Hookham Frere
JHM John Herman Merivale
JJB John James Blunt
JK John Keble
JM John Murray
JM II John Murray II
JM III John Murray III
JP James Pillans
JPP John Philips Potter
JTC John Taylor Coleridge
JWC John Wilson Croker
OG Olinthus Gregory

OGG	Octavius Graham Gilchrist
PE	Peter Elmsley
RW	Richard Wellesley
RH	Reginald Heber
RL	Robert Lundie
RS	Robert Southey
RWH	Robert William Hay
SD	Sylvester Douglas
TDW	Thomas Dunham Whitaker
TM	Thomas Mitchell
TT	Thomas Thomson
TY	Thomas Young
WG	William Gifford
WJ	William Jacob
WRH	William Richard Hamilton
WS	Walter Scott
WSR	William Stewart Rose
WSW	William Sidney Walker

VOLUME 1, NUMBER 1
(February 1809)
Published 1 March 1809[1]

1   *Affairs d'Espagne*. Article 1, pp. 1–19. George Ellis; assisted by George Canning.
     QR Letters 15, 68. JM MSS: list of paid contributors; GE to JM [February 1809]; WG
     to JM [29 November 1808 p/mark]. JM II's office copy: [in pencil] 'G. Ellis'. JM III's
     Register: Ellis.

2   Cromek's *Reliques of Robert Burns*. Article 2, pp. 19–36. Walter Scott.
     W. B. Todd and A. Bowden, *Sir Walter Scott: A Bibliographical History 1796–1832*
     (New Castle, DE: Oak Knoll Press, 1998). *QR* Letters 15, 20, 34. JM MSS: list of paid
     contributors; GE to JM, 3 March 1810; 1803–23 letterbook, JM to WS, 5 March 1809
     (copy). Compare the entry for #19. JM II's office copy. JM III's Register.

3   Edwards and Walpole's *Anecdotes of Painters*. Article 3, pp. 36–49. John Hoppner.
     JM MS, book loans register, a review copy was sent to 'Hoppner' on 25 November 1808.
     QR Letters 15, 32. JM II's office copy. JM III's Register.

4   Morgan's *Woman; or, Ida of Athens*. Article 4, pp. 50–2. William Gifford.
     JM MSS: list of paid contributors; book loans register, a review copy was sent to 'Mr G'
     on 25 November 1808; 1802–23 letterbook, JM to WG, 7 March 1809 (copy). JM III's
     Register: Gifford, and note, 'See Ellis letter 3d Mar 1809'.

5   *Grammars of the Sanskrita Language* [by Carey, Colebrooke, Wilkins]. Article 5, pp.
     53–69. Sharon Turner; subedited by John Shore, Lord Teignmouth.
     JM MSS: book loans register, one of the works reviewed was sent to 'T' on 5 November
     1808; GE to JM [February 1809]. *QR* Letter 15. JM II's office copy: 'S. Turner'. JM III's
     Register: Turner.

6   Stawell's and Deare's *Translations of the Georgics of Virgil*. Article 6, pp. 69–77. James
    Pillans.
    JM MSS: JP to JM, 29 December 1808; WG to JM [January 1809]. *QR* Letter 15. JM
    III's Register.

7   Zouch's *Life and Writings of Sir Philip Sidney*. Article 7, pp. 78–92. Isaac D'Israeli.
    JM MS, book loans register, a review copy was sent to 'I' on 25 November 1808. *QR* Let-
    ter 15. JM II's office copy. JM III's Register.

8   Cockburn *on the Old Testament*. Article 8, pp. 92–6. John Ireland, probably.
    JM MS, WG to JM [6 February 1809]. JM III's Register: queries D'Israeli.

9   Curran's *Speeches*. Article 9, pp. 96–107. William Erskine; with an interpolation by Wal-
    ter Scott.
    QR Letters 15, 20. *SL*, vol. 2, p. 179. Smiles, *Memoir*, vol. 1, pp. 118–19, 148. JM II's
    office copy: [in pencil] 'Erskine'. JM III's Register: Erskine.

10 Laplace's *Supplement to the Mécanique Céleste*. Article 10, pp. 107–12. Thomas Young.
    Young's list. JM III's notes. JM MSS: WG to JM [6 February 1809]; GE to JM, 3 March
    1810. JM II's office copy. JM III's Register.

11 Pinkerton *on Medals*. Article 11, pp. 112–31. Barré Charles Roberts.
    JM MSS: WG to JM, 9 February 1809; BCR to JM, 10 March 1809. JM III's Register.

12 *Public Characters of 1809–10*. Article 12, pp. 132–3. William Gifford.
    JM MSS: list of paid contributors; book loans register, a review copy was sent to 'Mr G'
    on 25 November 1808; 1802–23 letterbook, JM to WG, 7 March 1809 (copy). JM II's
    office copy. JM III's Register.

13 Southey's *Chronicle of the Cid*. Article 13, pp. 134–53. Walter Scott.
    Todd and Bowden, *Sir Walter Scott: A Bibliographical History*. JM MS, list of paid con-
    tributors. JM III's Register.

14 Accum *on Mineralogy*. Article 14, pp. 153–61. John Kidd.
    JM III's notes: '1809 ... *WG* ... February 1 Dr Kidd and Dean of Ch[rist], Ch[urch]
    enlisted'. *QR* Letter 31: 'With respect to Dr Kidd, I am perfectly innocent. I entertain
    a sincere regard for him, and have profited by his talents'. JM II's office copy. JM III's
    Register.

15 Barrett's *Life of Swift*. Article 15, pp. 162–77. Walter Scott.
    Todd and Bowden, *Sir Walter Scott: A Bibliographical History*. JM MSS: list of paid con-
    tributors; book loans register, a review copy was sent to 'Mr S' on 25 November 1808.
    JM II's office copy. JM III's Register. See the entry for #13.

16 Carr's *Caledonian Sketches*. Article 16, pp. 178–93. Walter Scott.
    Todd and Bowden, *Sir Walter Scott: A Bibliographical History*. JM MSS: list of paid con-
    tributors; book loans register, a review copy was sent to 'Mr S' on 25 November 1808.
    QR Letters 15, 20. JM II's office copy. JM III's-Register.

17 *Account of the Baptist Missionary Society* [by Scott-Waring, Twining]. Article 17, pp.
    193–226. Robert Southey.
    K. Curry and R. Dedmon, 'Southey's Contributions to the *Quarterly Review*', *Words-
    worth Circle*, 6 (1974), pp. 261–72. JM II's office copy. JM III's Register.

18 Vaughan's *Siege of Zaragoza*. Article 18, pp. 226–31. George Ellis.
    JM MSS: list of paid contributors; GE to JM, 1 February 1809. JM II's office copy. JM
    III's Register.

VOLUME 1, NUMBER 2
(May 1809)
Published 30 May 1809[2]

19 Campbell's *Gertrude of Wyoming*. Article 1, pp. 241–58. Walter Scott.
    Todd and Bowden, *Sir Walter Scott: A Bibliographical History*. JM MS, list of paid contributors. *QR* Letter 20. JM II's office copy. JM III's Register.

20 Poyer's *History of Barbados*. Article 2, pp. 258–68. George Ellis.
    JM MSS: list of paid contributors; WG to JM [6 February 1809]. *QR* Letter 20. JM II's office copy. JM III's Register.

21 *Portuguese Literature*. Article 3, pp. 268–92. Robert Southey.
    Curry and Dedmon, 'Southey's Contributions to the *Quarterly Review*'. JM II's office copy. JM III's Register.

22 Gass's *Voyages and Travels* [of Lewis and Clarke]. Article 4, pp. 293–304. James Pillans.
    JM MSS: JP to JM: 24 April 1809; 25 April 1809. JM II's office copy: [in pencil] 'Barrow'. JM III's Register: 'J Barrow and J Pillans', and note, 'See Pillans letter Apr 24, 1809'. In *An Auto-Biographical Memoir of Sir John Barrow* (London: John Murray, 1847), pp. 500–2, Barrow states that he joined the *QR* in the summer of 1809.

23 Cottin's *Amelie Mansfield*. Article 5, pp. 304–15. William Greenfield.
    JM MS, William Greenfield to JM [17 April 1809 p/mark]. JM II's office copy: [in pencil] 'Rutherford'. JM III's Register: Rutherford, and note, '?Wm Richardson. See his letter Apr 17/09 with WG's'. Walter Scott, who suggested Greenfield to WG as a contributor, refers to him, variously, as Rutherford, Richardson, and Greenshields. See *SL*, vol. 2, pp. 178–9n, 183, 184n, 184–5, 185n, and 189.

24 *Improved Version of the New Testament*. Article 6, pp. 315–36. George D'Oyly; with revisions by William Gifford and John Ireland.
    JM MS, WG to JM [May 1809]. NLS 853 (f. 4) WS to J. B. S. Morritt, 22 July 1809 (copy). *QR* Letter 20. George D'Oyly, *Sermons, with a Memoir by His Son*, 2 vols (London: Rivington, 1847), vol. 1, p. xxiv. JM II's office copy: 'Dr Doyley'. JM III's Register: D'Oyly.

25 Cumberland's *John de Lancaster*. Article 7, pp. 337–48. Walter Scott.
    Todd and Bowden, *Sir Walter Scott: A Bibliographical History*. JM MS, list of paid contributors. JM MS, WG to JM [May 1809]. *QR* Letter 20. JM III's Register.

26 Richardson's *Memoir on Fiorin Grass*. Article 8, pp. 348–55. John Kidd.
    JM MS, list of paid contributors. JM II's office copy. JM III's Register.

27 *Translation of Persius*. Article 9, pp. 355–62. William Gifford, probably.
    QR Letters 6, 8. JM II's office copy. JM III's Register.

28 *Lettres et Pensées du Prince de Ligne*. Article 10, pp. 362–71. George Ellis.
    JM MS, list of paid contributors. JM II's office copy. JM III's Register.

29 *Memoirs of Percival Stockdale*. Article 11, pp. 371–86. Isaac D'Israeli and William Gifford.
    JM MSS: list of paid contributors; WG to JM [May 1809]. JM II's office copy: 'Disraeli'. JM III's Register: D'Israeli.

30 Sydney Smith's *Sermons*. Article 12, pp. 387–98. John Ireland and William Gifford; possibly subedited by George Canning.

JM MS, book loans register, a review copy was sent to 'Mr Gifford' on 8 January 1810. *QR* Letter 20. Smiles, *Memoir*, vol. 1, p. 150. JM II's office copy: 'Dr Ireland and Gifford'. JM III's Register: Ireland and Gifford.

31 Drake's *On Periodical Papers*. Article 13, pp. 398–405. Isaac D'Israeli; with significant edits by William Gifford.
   JM MSS: list of paid contributors; WG to JM [May? 1809; endorsed by JM II, 'Disraeli']; WG to JM [misdated in another hand 'Aug 1809'; states that article proofs are attached]. JM II's office copy: 'D Israeli'. JM III's Register: D'Israeli.

32 Leckie's *State of Sicily*. Article 14, pp. 405–19. Robert Walpole; with significant edits by William Gifford.
   JM MSS: WG to JM: [May 1809, numbered 28]; 30 June 1809. *QR* Letter 20. JM II's office copy: 'Rev. Walpole and Canning'. JM III's Register: 'Revd Walpole and ~~Canning~~ <WG> 'and note, 'See W G's letter No 28'.

33 *Linen Manufactures in Ireland*. Article 15, pp. 419–29. John Kidd; probably with assistance from Thomas Manners-Sutton.
   JM MSS: list of paid contributors; WG to JM [May 1809, numbered 22]. JM II's office copy: 'Oxford'. JM III's Register: Kidd, and note, 'Oxford. See WG's letter (No. 22) May 1809. Dr K was assisted by the Irish Chancellor'.

34 *Parliamentary Reform*. Article 16, pp. 429–37. George Ellis.
   JM MSS: list of paid contributors; book loans register, a review copy was sent to 'Geo. Ellis' on 6 May 1809.

35 *Austrian State Papers*. Article 17, pp. 437–55. Sharon Turner; with significant edits by George Canning and William Gifford.
   JM MSS: WG to JM: 15 May 1809; [22 May 1809; endorsed by JM II, 'Turner's article on Austria']. Smiles, *Memoir*, vol. 1, pp. 157–8. *QR* Letters 20, 23. JM II's office copy: 'Sharon Turner and Canning'. JM III's Register: Turner and Canning.

VOLUME 2, NUMBER 3
(August 1809)
Published 29 August 1809[3]

36 *Pamphlets on West India Affairs* [by Robely, Spencer]. Article 1, pp. 1–24. George Ellis.
   JM MSS: book loans register, a review copy was sent to 'Geo Ellis' on 10 June 1809; GE to JM, 1 June 1809. *QR* Letter 15. JM II's office copy. JM III's Register.

37 *Trans. of the Miss. Soc. in the S. S. Islands*. Article 2, pp. 24–61. Robert Southey.
   Curry and Dedmon, 'Southey's Contributions to the *Quarterly Review*'. JM II's office copy. JM III's Register.

38 Kidd's *Outlines of Mineralogy*. Article 3, pp. 61–74. Thomas Thomson.
   JM MSS: book loans register, a review copy was sent to 'Dr Thos Thomson Edin' on 24 March 1809; WG to JM, 18 June 1809; TT to JM, 30 July 1809; WG to JM, 9 August 1809; WG to JM [n.d], 'On looking over the proof I find a passage (p. 73) which as referring to Dr T. himself, he may not like to lose'. *QR* Letters 27, 29. Smiles, *Memoir*, vol. 1, pp. 161–2. JM III's Register: '1809 ... Thomson (Dr T) Mar 22', and note, 'From Mem book in office, but See WG June 18, 1809'.

39 Paley's *Sermons, and Memoirs*. Article 4, pp. 75–88. George D'Oyly; probably assisted by John Ireland.

JM MS, WG to JM [August 1809]. D'Oyly, *Sermons*, vol. 1, p. xxiv. Smiles, *Memoir*, vol. 1, p. 161. JM II's office copy: [in pencil] 'Dr Doyly'. JM III's Register: D'Oyly.

40   Lord Valentia's *Travels*. Article 5, pp. 88–126. Robert Southey.
Curry and Dedmon, 'Southey's Contributions to the *Quarterly Review*'. JM III's Register: and note, 'From G Ellis's letter Nov 5/09'.

41   Whittington *on Gothic Architecture*. Article 6, pp. 126–45. Thomas Dunham Whitaker, probably.
JM MS, book loans register, a review copy was sent to 'Dr Whitaker' on 9 February 1811. *QR* Letter 35. Smiles, *Memoir*, vol. 1, p. 161. JM II's office copy. JM III's Register.

42   Edgeworth's *Tales of Fashionable Life*. Article 7, pp. 146–54. Henry John Stephen; with an interpolation by William Gifford.
JM MSS: book loans register, a review copy was sent to 'H. J. Stephens [*sic*](Henry John) / 4 Sergts Inn' on 22 June 1809; HJS to JM [n.d.]; WG to JM, 21 July 1809; WG to JM [August 1809]; WG to John Ireland [19 or 22 August 1809]. *QR* Letter 27. *Letters to 'Ivy' from the First Earl of Dudley*, ed. S. Romilly (London: Longmans, Green, 1905), pp. 13–14. Smiles, *Memoir*, vol. 1, p. 163.

43   Haslam, Arnold, *&c. on Insanity*. Article 8, pp. 155–80. Thomas Young.
Young's list. JM III's Register.

44   Pinckney's *Travels through France*. Article 9, pp. 181–7. Author not identified.
JM MSS: book loans register, a review copy was sent to 'J. Pillans' on 16 June 1809; J. Pillans to JM, 5 August 1809; WG to JM [n.d.], 'He [Pillans] will naturally be offended at the omission of his Article'; WG to JM [August 1809], 'I have read Pinckney's Travels ... there is no comparison between the present and that of Mr P'. JM III's Register: Pillans, cites book loans register, and note, 'Mr. Pillan's [*sic*] article appears to have been omitted and one by another hand substituted. See WG Aug 31, 1809'.

45   Middleton's *Doctrine of the Greek Article*. Article 10, pp. 187–203. Frank Sayers.
JM MS, WG to JM [?August 1809, numbered 38x]. JM III's Register: queries 'Dr Sayers', and note, 'Either this article or No. 5 appears to have been written by a Mr Stephens. See W G's July 21, 1809 – See also W G's letter of July 21, 1809, and his letter of Aug 1809 (numbered 35). See also No. 38x'.

46   *Spanish Affairs* [by Clinton, Moore, Neale, Ormsby, Porter]. Article 11, pp. 203–34. George Ellis and George Canning.
JM MSS: GE to JM, 21 August 1809; WG to John Ireland [19 or 22 August 1809]. *QR* Letters 27, 36. *SL*, vol. 2, p. 236n. Smiles, *Memoir*, vol. 1, p. 160. JM III's Register: Ellis and Canning, and note, 'In consequence of my importunity Mr Canning has exerted himself and produced "The best article that ever yet appeared in any review". W.G. August 29, 1809'.

VOLUME 2, NUMBER 4
(November 1809)
Published 23 December 1809[4]

47   Rose's *Observations on Fox's History*. Article 1, pp. 243–55. Allan Maconochie, Lord Meadowbank.
JM MS, William Erskine to JM, 15 July 1809. *QR* Letters 27, 32. JM II's office copy. JM III's Register.

48   De Guignes – *Voyages à Peking, &c*. Article 2, pp. 255–75. John Barrow.

Letter to the editor from John Barrow II, dated 12 February 1844, *GM* (March 1844), p. 246. The author refers to #48 in #82 and #147. JB systematically cross-referenced his articles. Barrow, *Auto-Biographical Memoir*, p. 500. Smiles, *Memoir*, vol. 1, p. 166. JM II's office copy. JM III's Register: Barrow, and note, '?J. Pillans whose letter (1809? April) see'.

49 Jerningham's *Alexandrian School*. Article 3, pp. 275–80. John Ireland.

JM MSS: book loans register, a review copy was sent to 'Dr Ireland' on 19 June 1809. JM MS, WG to JM, 18 June 1809. JM III's Register: and note, 'WG's letter June 18, 1809'.

50 *Poems*, by the Rev. W. L. Bowles. Article 4, pp. 281–7. John Hoppner and William Gifford.

R. B. Clark, *William Gifford: Tory Satirist* (New York: Columbia University Press, 1930), pp. 187–8, 273 n98. JM II's office copy. JM III's Register.

51 Ker Porter's *Travels in Russia, &c.* Article 5, pp. 288–301. Reginald Heber.

NLS 3878 (ff. 239–42), WG to WS [December 1808 or January 1809; Millgate reference 11251]. JM MS, William Erskine to JM, 15 July 1809. NLS 11000 (ff. 138–9), JM to Erskine, 21 July 1809. JM MSS: George Ellis to JM [August 1809]; Erskine to JM, 13 August 1809. [A. S. Heber], *The Life of Reginald Heber, D. D., Lord Bishop of Calcutta*, 2 vols (London: John Murray, 1830), vol. 1, p. 343n. JM II's office copy: [in pencil] 'G. Ellis'. JM III's Register: 'G̶e̶o̶ ̶E̶l̶l̶i̶s̶ Heber'. Regarding the cancelled Ellis attribution, JM III cites JM II's office copy and adds, 'See Ellis's letter Feb 1810'.

52 Wyvill *on Intolerance*. Article 6, pp. 301–9. Robert Walpole, possibly.

The author refers to Walpole's friend, Francis Hodgson. JM III's Register: 'Dr Parr wrote an Art in this No. See WGs letter No 51[;] also Mr Hodgsons[;] see WGs letter No 53'. In these letters, however, 'Parr' refers to a review copy of the book reviewed in #60.

53 Bawdwen's *Translation of the Domesday Record*. Article 7, pp. 310–14. Thomas Dunham Whitaker.

JM MS, WG to JM [October or November 1809], 'Whitaker I think may now stand'. J. G. Nichols, 'Biographical Memoirs of Thomas Dunham Whitaker' in *An History of the Original Parish of Whalley and Honor of Clitheroe*, 2 vols, 4th edn (London: n.p., 1876), p. xxix. JM II's office copy. JM III's Register.

54 Kett's *Emily, a Moral Tale*. Article 8, pp. 314–19. George D'Oyly

JM MSS: book loans register, article transported from Cambridge on 14 November 1809; WG to JM [December 1809], 'D'Oyly ... then Bowles'. *QR* Letter 119. JM II's office copy. JM III's Register.

55 Holmes's *American Annals*. Article 9, pp. 319–37. Robert Southey.

Curry and Dedmon, 'Southey's Contributions to the *Quarterly Review*'.

56 Laplace – *Réfraction extraordinaire*. Article 10, pp. 337–48. Thomas Young.

Young's list. JM II's office copy. JM III's Register.

57 Florian – *William Tell*. Article 11, pp. 348–54. Henry John Stephen.

JM MS, WG to JM, 20 December 1809. Smiles, *Memoir*, vol. 1, p. 165. JM II's office copy: 'Stevens'. JM III's Register: Stevens.

58 *Oxford editions of Herodotus*. Article 12, pp. 354–65. Allen OR Allan.

JM MS, Joseph Parker to JM [6 June 1815], 'Mr Allen, who formerly supplied you with a review of Herodotus and Chalmer's Oxford ...' A number of Allens graduated from Oxford at this time (see *Alumni Oxon.*). JM III's Register: 'Parker of Oxford' and cites JM II's office copy but misinterprets JM II as stating that Parker was the article's author. Instead, in his notation in his office copy, JM II indicates only that Parker forwarded the article. JM II's office copy: 'Parker of Oxford sent it'.

59 Northmore's *Washington*. Article 13, pp. 365–75. William Gifford.
    JM MS, book loans register, a review copy was sent to 'WG' on 6 July 1809. *QR* Letter
    25. JM MS, GE to JM, 2 February 1810. JM II's office copy. JM III's Register.

60 Parr's *Characters of the late Charles James Fox*. Article 14, pp. 375–401. Robert Grant.
    Bodl. Lib. MS Eng. Lett. d. 214 (f. 55), RG to Richard Heber, 'Ireland' 11 October 1809.
    JM MSS: WG to JM [September or October 1809]; WG to JM [?November 1809];
    WG to JM [December 1809]; GE to JM, 2 February 1810. *QR* Letter 34. Smiles, *Mem-
    oir*, vol. 1, p. 169. JM II's office copy, and note, 'This was the first Article that excited
    general admiration'. JM III's Register.

61 Warburton's *Letters*. Article 15, pp. 401–12. James Pillans.
    JM MSS: book loans register, a review copy was sent to 'P' on 9 March 1809 and to
    'G[ifford] for P' on 25 November 1809; WG to JM [19 February 1809]; JP to JM, 8
    March 1809; JP to JM, 25 April 1809. *QR* Letter 20. NLS, 853 (f. 4), WS to J.B.S. Mor-
    ritt, 22 July 1809. JM III's Register: queries Pillans, and note, 'See also W G's letter Feb
    19, 1809. See also J. Pillans Ap 25, 1809'.

62 Mr. Canning's *Letters to Earl Camden*. Article 16, pp. 412–26. George Ellis; assisted by
    George Canning and William Gifford.
    JM MSS: GE to JM [October or November 1809]; WG to JM [8 December 1809]. *QR*
    Letter 32. BL. MS 28099 (f. 69), WG to GE, 12 February [1810]. JM II's office copy: 'G.
    Ellis and Canning'. JM III's Register: Ellis and Canning.

63 [Croker], *The Battles of Talavera*. Article 17, pp. 426–33. Walter Scott.
    Todd and Bowden, *Sir Walter Scott: A Bibliographical History*. *QR* Letter 33. JM II's
    office copy. JM III's Register.

64 Hayley's *Life of Romney*. Article 18, pp. 433–44. John Hoppner and William Gifford.
    JM MSS: WG to JM, 30 June 1809; WG to JM [November 1809]. JM II's office copy.
    JM III's Register.

65 Jackson's *An Account of Morocco, &c.* Article 19, pp. 444–54. Reginald Heber.
    JM MS, WG to JM [8 December 1809]. JM II's office copy: 'Q[UER]Y Jacob'. JM III's
    Register: William Jacob, citing JM II's office copy, and note, 'R. Heber uncertain, see W
    G's letter Dec 8/09'.

66 *Short Remarks on the State of Parties*. Article 20, pp. 454–60. George Ellis and George
    Canning.
    JM MSS: WG to JM [December 1809]; WG to JM [dated by another hand '?February
    1810', but probably December 1809]. JM II's office copy. JM III's Register.

VOLUME 3, NUMBER 5
(February 1810)
Published 31 March 1810[5]

67 *Herculanensia* [by Drummond, Walter]. Article 1, pp. 1–20. Thomas Young.
    Young's list. JM MS, GE to JM, 2 February 1810. *QR* Letters 40, 44, 47. JM II's office
    copy. JM III's Register.

68 Dentrecasteaux – *Voyage à la Recherche de la Pérouse*. Article 2, pp. 21–43. John Bar-
    row.
    JM MS, JB to JM, 6 March 1810. In this article, in #311, and in #347, the author men-
    tions Dentrecasteaux's mistaking the bones of a kangaroo for those of a girl. Barrow,

Auto-Biographical Memoir, pp. 501–2. Smiles, *Memoir*, vol. 1, p. 166. JM II's office copy. JM III's Register.

69 Sir Brooke Boothby's *Fables and Satires*. Article 3, pp. 43–50. Frank Sayers.
JM MS, book loans register, a review copy was sent to 'Dr Sayers, Norwich' on 30 December 1809. JM III's Register: [in pencil] '? Dr Sayer (Norwich)'.

70 Sir Francis D'Ivernois – *Effets du Blocus*. Article 4, pp. 50–63. George Ellis.
QR Letter 47. JM MSS: WG to JM [?February 1810]; GE to JM [October or November 1809]. JM II's office copy. JM III's Register.

71 Holford's *Wallace: or, the Flight of Falkirk*. Article 5, pp. 63–9. Walter Scott, possibly.
Richard Heber looked over the proofs. JM MSS: WG to JM, 2 February 1810; WG to JM [March 1810]; WG to JM [17 March 1810]. *QR* Letters 32, 42, 46. *QR* Letter 47 militates against an attribution to Scott: 'Sotheby has just given us a long poem: – it is, like Wallace, rather too near you for your reviewing. JM III's Register: [in pencil] '? Scott or Heber'.

72 Leroy de Flagis – *Etat de Russie*. Article 6, pp. 69–89. George Ellis.
JM MSS: book loans register, a review copy was sent to 'Geo. Ellis Es*qr*' on 10 June 1809; WG to JM [?1810]; GE to JM, 2 February 1810. *QR* Letter 41. JM III's Register.

73 Peyrard – *Œuvres d'Archimède*. Article 7, pp. 89–110. Olinthus Gregory, probably.
Not in Young's list. In attributing the article to Thomas Young, JM III appears to have been confused by GE to JM, 23 June 1809 (see #43) and by Young's subediting of #103 and #186. Young lived on Welbeck Street, whereas the author, as indicated in JM MS, WG to JM, 13 March 1810, was at Woolwich. OG was mathematical master at Woolwich Academy. JM III's Register: Thomas Young. See also *QR* Letter 41, JM MS, WG to JM, 13 March 1810, and entries for #103 and #186.

74 Churton's *Life of Dean Nowell*. Article 8, pp. 111–14. Thomas Dunham Whitaker, probably.
QR Letter 35. Nichols, 'Biographical Memoirs of Thomas Dunham Whitaker', p. xxix. JM III's Register: 'W Scott??', and note, 'See W G's letter No 76'. See also #53.

75 Ld Grenville and Dr Duigenan *on Catholic Claims*. Article 9, pp. 114–29. George Ellis; assisted by George Canning.
JM MSS: book loans register, one of the pamphlets reviewed was sent to 'George Ellis Es*qr*' on 3 February 1810; GE to JM, 2 February 1810; GE to JM, 4 February 1810; WG to JM, 8 February 1810; WG to JM, 16 March 1810. *QR* Letters 40, 44. JM III's Register: Canning and Ellis, and note, 'See W G's letter Feb 9, 1810 and Nov [March?] 16, 1810 and G Ellis's Feb 2, 1810'. See also #72.

76 Thornton's *Present State of Turkey*. Article 10, pp. 129–43. Reginald Heber.
JM MSS: GE to JM: 4 February 1810; 4 April 1810. [Heber], *Life of Reginald Heber*, vol. 1, pp. 347, 347n. JM III's Register.

77 *Mémoires de la Comtesse de Lichtenau*. Article 11, pp. 144–52. Isaac D'Israeli, probably; and with an unidentified collaborator.
JM MS, WG to JM, 9 February 1810, supplies evidence that ID'I contributed an article to this Number. Article #77 is the only likely candidate.

78 Sir P. Francis and Ricardo *on Bullion*. Article 12, pp. 152–61. Robert Grant; subedited by Edward Copleston.
Bodl. Lib. MS Eng. Lett. d. 214 (f. 55), RG to Richard Heber, 'Ireland' 11 October 1809. JM MS, GE to JM, 4 April 1810. *QR* Letters 40, 42, 67. JM III's Register: queries Ellis, and note, 'See G E's letter Mar 8, 1810 and Ap 4' and, in pencil, 'Coplestone [*sic*] wrote an Art in this No. See G Ellis Feb 1810'.

79   *French Embassy to Persia.* Article 13, pp. 161–7. Author not identified.
80   Burges's *Euripides.* Article 14, pp. 167–85. Author not identified.
     JM MS, book loans register, on 2 February 1810 JM II paid £2 to ship a MS from Cambridge; cash day book 1811–17, p. 4: '6 Dec 1811 *QR* Sophocles sent to Rev. Mr Monk Cambridge'. However, JM MS, C. J. Monk to JM III, 15 January 1858, states that his father's first review was in *QR* Number 9 (#138). JM MS, cash day book 1810–11, p. 7: '1810, Feb 1 Quarterly Review No 5 D[ebi]t Aristophanes Peter Elmsley'. The cash day book reference probably indicates that a copy of Elmsley's Aristophanes was provided to the author of #80. *QR* Letters 25, 44. JM II's office copy: [in pencil] 'Q[UER]Y Monk'. JM III's Register: queries 'Prof Monk', cites JM II's office copy, and note, 'Uncertain'.
81   Sydney Smith's *Visitation Sermon.* Article 15, pp. 185–94. John William Ward, Lord Dudley; with an interpolation by William Gifford and John Ireland.
     JM MSS: WG to JM, 30 March 1810; WG to JM, 31 March 1810 p/mark; GE to JM, 4 April 1810. *QR* Letters 33, 34, 38, 40, 42, 63. JM II's office copy: 'Lord Dudley'. JM III's Register: queries Lord Dudley, and note, '?Dr Ireland. See Ellis letter Apr 4, 1810'.
82   Barrow – *Voyage à la Cochinchine, &c.* Article 16, pp. 194–205. John Barrow.
     The author refers to #48. A passage from #82 is quoted in #600. The article is cross-referenced in #139. JB systematically cross-referenced his articles. JM II's office copy. JM III's Register.
83   Herbert Marsh's *Lectures.* Article 17, pp. 205–18. George D'Oyly, probably.
     QR Letter 35. D'Oyly, *Sermons,* vol. 1, p. xxiv.
84   *Lives of Nelson* [by Charnock, Churchill, Clarke, Harrison]. Article 18, pp. 218–62. Robert Southey.
     Curry and Dedmon, 'Southey's Contributions to the *Quarterly Review*'. JM II's office copy. JM III's Register.

VOLUME 3, NUMBER 6
(May 1810)
Published 21 July 1810[6]

85   Staunton's *Ta Tsing Leu Lee; or, the Laws of China.* Article 1, pp. 273–319. John Barrow.
     JM MSS: JB to WG: 6 March 1810; 20 March 1810; 26 March 1810; 6 April 1810. JM MS, WG to JM, 8 August 1810. The author of #142*WI* claims authorship of #85, #119, #147, #333, and #389. JM II's office copy: 'Sir Geo Staunton'. JM III's Register: cites JM II's office copy, 'S̶i̶r̶ ̶G̶e̶o̶ ̶S̶t̶a̶u̶n̶t̶o̶n̶ J Barrow'.
86   Walsh *on the Genius and Disposition of the French Government.* Article 2, pp. 320–39. George Ellis.
     JM MSS: GE to JM: [n.d.; 1808 w/mark]; 4 February 1810; 4 April 1810. JM MS, WG to JM, 16 July [17 July 1810 p/mark]. *QR* Letter 49. JM III's Register: '?Mr George Ellis', and note, 'See W G's letter of July 6, 1810 and G E's Feb 1810 and Ap 4/10'.
87   [Maturin], *Fatal Revenge; or, the Family of Montorio.* Article 3, pp. 339–47. Walter Scott.
     Todd and Bowden, *Sir Walter Scott: A Bibliographical History. QR* Letters 53, 128. JM III's Register.
88   Dr Milner's *History of Winchester.* Article 4, pp. 347–68. Thomas Dunham Whitaker.

JM MS, book loans register, a review copy was sent to 'Revd. Dr Whitaker' on 28 September 1809 and again 9 February 1811. Nichols, 'Biographical Memoirs of Thomas Dunham Whitaker', p. xxix. JM II's office copy. JM III's Register.

89 Dr Jones's *Account of the Eau Médicinale*. Article 5, pp. 368–74. Thomas Young. Young's list. JM III's Register.

90 *Pursuits of Agriculture*. Article 6, pp. 374–9. Walter Scott, possibly.
JM MSS: WG to JM: [March 1810], WS's article is 'an Ironical imitation of Dr Johnson'; [17 March 1810], 'Mr Heber ... thinks Scott's Article should ... appear'. *QR* Letter 57, WG thanks WS for his 'two little articles in our last'. JM III's Register.

91 Carey and Marshman's *The Ramayuna of Valmeeki*. Article 7, pp. 379–99. Sharon Turner.
JM MSS: WG to JM: [March 1810]; 30 July 1810. JM II's office copy. JM III's Register.

92 Stanley's *Æschylus*. Article 8, pp. 389–98. John Symmons.
JM MSS: book loans register, a review copy was sent to 'John Symmons, Richmond Surrey' on 4 January 1810; JS to JM, 19 January [1810]; WG to JM, 21 May 1810. JM III's Register.

93 Bishop Horsley's *Sermons*. Article 9, pp. 398–407. George D'Oyly, possibly; OR Thomas Dunham Whitaker, possibly.
Attributed to D'Oyly in D'Oyly, *Sermons*. Attributed to Whitaker in Nichols, 'Biographical Memoirs of Thomas Dunham Whitaker', p. xxix. JM MSS: book loans register, 'Horsley's Biblical Criticisms' sent to 'G. D'Oyley' [*sic*] on 1 May [n.y.]. JM III's Register: D'Oyly, citing the book loans register.

94 Shee's *Elements of Art: A Poem*. Article 10, pp. 407–17. John Hoppner and Samuel Rogers, possibly; OR Edmund Lodge, possibly
JM MSS: book loans register, a review copy sent to 'E. Lodge' on 8 November 1809; WG to JM: 18 June 1809; 3 July 1810.

95 Berwick's *Life of Apollonius*. Article 11, pp. 417–31. Thomas Fanshaw Middleton.
JM MSS: book loans register, a review copy was sent to 'Revd Dr Middleton Tansor near Oundle / Northamps' on 2 February 1810; WG to JM, 2 February 1810. NLS 3879 (ff. 215–48), E. Berwick to Walter Scott, 16 October 1810. *SL*, vol. 2, pp. 386–7. JM II's office copy. JM III's Register.

96 Worgan's *Select Poems, &c*. Article 12, pp. 431–9. Charles Abraham Elton.
JM MSS: book loans register, a review copy was sent to 'Chs. A. Elton E*sqr* Portland Place Bath' on 19 February 1810; cash day book 1810–11, p. 13: 'Quarterly Review D[ebi]t 19 Feb 1810 Worgan's Poems sent by coach to C. A. Elton Esq'; WG to JM, 16 July [17 July 1810 p/mark]. JM III's Register.

97 [Vason], *Residence at Tongataboo*. Article 13, pp. 440–55. Robert Southey.
Curry and Dedmon, 'Southey's Contributions to the *Quarterly Review*'. JM II's office copy. JM III's Register.

98 Grahame's *British Georgics*. Article 14, pp. 456–61. Robert Southey.
Curry and Dedmon, 'Southey's Contributions to the *Quarterly Review*'. JM II's office copy. JM III's Register.

99 *Mémoires d'Arcueil*. Article 15, pp. 462–81. Thomas Young; subedited by Olinthus Gregory.
Young's list. JM MS, WG to JM, 8 August 1810. JM III's Register. The following works are introduced for review at the pages indicated: Biot, *Experiments on the Propagation of Sound in Vapours*, p. 467; Laplace, *On the Motion of Light*, p. 471; Malus, *On the Property*

of reflected Light; Lussac and Thénard, *Abstract of Memoirs*, p. 477; Biot, *Experiments on the Propagation of Sound*, p. 479.

100 Aikin *on Song Writing*. Article 16, pp. 481–92. Walter Scott.
Todd and Bowden, *Sir Walter Scott: A Bibliographical History*. *QR* Letters 41, 47. JM II's office copy. JM III's Register.

101 Scott's *The Lady of the Lake*. Article 17, pp. 492–517. George Ellis.
JM MS, GE to JM, Wednesday, June 1810. *QR* Letters 52, 58. *SL*, vol. 2, pp. 322n, 346, 346n. Smiles, *Memoir*, vol. 1, p. 126. JM II's office copy. JM III's Register.

VOLUME 4, NUMBER 7
(August 1810)
Published 27 October 1810[7]

102 *Observador Portuguez*. Article 1, pp. 1–24. Robert Southey.
Curry and Dedmon, 'Southey's Contributions to the *Quarterly Review*'. JM II's office copy. JM III's Register.

103 Leslie's *Elements of Geometry, &c*. Article 2, pp. 25–42. Olinthus Gregory; subedited by Thomas Young.
Not in Young's list. JM MSS: book loans register, a review copy was sent to 'Mr Gifford' on 22 December 1809 and to 'Dr Young' on 11 August 1810; WG to JM: 21 May 1810; [29 July 1810 p/mark]; [18 August 1810 p/mark]. *QR* Letters 40, 46, 54, 58. JM III's Register: Young, and note, 'See W G's letter, July 29, 1810'.

104 Péron – *Voyage de Découvertes aux Terres Australes*. Article 3, pp. 42–60. John Barrow.
JM MSS: JB to WG, 6 April 1810; WG to JM, 8 August 1810; WG to JM [18 August 1810 p/mark]. *QR* Letter 53. The article is cross-referenced in #428. JB systematically cross-referenced his articles. JM II's office copy. JM III's Register.

105 Palmer's *The Daughters of Isenberg*. Article 4, pp. 61–7. William Gifford.
JM MSS: WG to JM: [Ryde, 30 July 1810 p/mark]; [18 August 1810 p/mark]. *QR* Letters 36, 53, 56. Smiles, *Memoir*, vol. 1, p. 180. JM II's office copy. JM III's Register.

106 Dr Wordsworth and Ld Teignmouth *on the Bible Society*. Article 5, pp. 68–80. John Ireland.
JM MSS: WG to JM: 17 July 1810; [18 August 1810 p/mark]; [28 August 1810 p/mark]. *QR* Letter 67.

107 Stewart, *Abu Taleb's Travels in Asia, Africa, and Europe*. Article 6, pp. 80–93. Reginald Heber.
JM MSS: book loans register, a review copy was sent to 'Mr. R. Heber' on 10 July 1810; on 11 September 1810 JM paid for a 'Carriage to Hodnet Hall Shrewsbury', RH's residence; WG to JM [September 1810]. *QR* Letters 52, 59. [Heber], *Life of Reginald Heber*, vol. 1, p. 366. JM II's office copy. JM III's Register.

108 Dr Wordsworth's *Ecclesiastical Biography*. Article 7, pp. 93–103. Thomas Dunham Whitaker.
JM MSS: book loans register, the volume reviewed was sent to 'Dr Whitaker' on 29 March 1810. *QR* Letter 52. Nichols, 'Biographical Memoirs of Thomas Dunham Whitaker', p. xxix. JM II's office copy. JM III's Register.

109 *Memoirs of the Life of Peter Daniel Huet*. Article 8, pp. 103–11. Author not identified.

110 Dr Clarke's *Travels in Russia, &c*. Article 9, pp. 111–53. George Ellis.

JM MSS: book loans register, on 10 September 1810, JM paid £5 for postage to transport a 'Review of Clarkes Travels from Sunning Hill', Ellis's residence and, on 19 September, he paid £2 for 'Postage Clarkes Travels Sunning Hill'; and note, 'd[itt]o first part before [£] 2'; GE to JM, 4 February 1810; GE to JM [*c.* June 1810; 1808 w/mark]; WG to JM, 17 July 1810; GE to JM, 22 July [1810]; WG to JM, 29 July 1810; GE to JM [August 1810]; GE to JM, Sunday [September 1810]; WG to JM [September 1810]; GE to JM, 25 November 1810. *QR* Letters 52, 55, 57, 64. NLS, 853 (ff. 11–12), Walter Scott to J.B.S. Morritt, 3 October 1810 (copy). [Heber], *Life of Reginald Heber*, vol. 1, p. 363. Smiles, *Memoir*, vol. 1, p. 184. *SL*, vol. 2, pp. 381–2, 382n. JM II's office copy. JM III's Register.

111 Green's *Diary of a Lover of Literature*. Article 10, pp. 153–65. John Bird Sumner.
   JM MSS: JBS to JM, 4 June 1810; GE to JM, Sunday [September 1810]. *QR* Letter 25.

112 *Select Poems from Herrick, Carew, &c.* Article 11, pp. 165–76. Barron Field.
   JM MSS: WG to JM: [September] 1810; [?September] 1810; [24] September 1810. 'Scriblerus' referred to at p. 169 is also referred to in #177 (p. 483). *QR* Letter 25. *Notes & Queries*, 10 (8 July 1854), p. 27. JM II's office copy: 'B. Field and Gifford'. JM III's Register: Field and Gifford. Ronald Solomon supplied information for this note.

113 [Copleston], *Replies to Calumnies against Oxford*. Article 12, pp. 177–206. John Davison, Henry Home Drummond, and Edward Copleston.
   JM MSS: WG to JM [18 August 1810 p/mark]; WG to JM [28 August 1810 p/mark]; WG to JM [September 1810, numbered 94]; GE to JM, Sunday [September 1810]; WG to JM, Monday night [24 September 1810]; JM to WG, 25 September 1810. *QR* Letters 34, 40, 47, 51, 55, 56. Smiles, *Memoir*, vol. 1, pp. 181–3. JM III's Register: Davison, and note, '(Home Drummond see WG's letter) See WG's letter No 94 Sept / 10'. JM III's Register: note at Number 7, 'Mr Copleston wrote an art in this No. see WG. Aug 28 [12?]. See also JMs letter to WG. and G Ellis Sept 1810'.

114 Gifford's *Life of the Rt. Hon. W. Pitt*. Article 13, pp. 207–71. Robert Grant; with minor edits by George Canning.
   JM MSS: WG to JM: 1 January 1810; 9 January 1810; 13 January 1810; 3 July 1810; 16 July 1810 [17 July 1810 p/mark]; 3 August 1810; [7 August 1810 p/mark]; 8 August 1810; [18 August 1810 p/mark]; 18 August 1810 [JM II note: 'Recd Oct 6 1810']; [September 1810]; 6 October 1810. *QR* Letters 31, 42, 46, 48, 51, 53, 56, 59, 62, 64, 65, 75. Leeds WYL250 8 66a, WG to GC, 9 October 1810. India Office Library MSS Eur E308 / 26: holograph draft of this article, in RG's hand. JM II's office copy. JM III's Register: and note, 'See also WG's Aug 6–7, 1810'.

VOLUME 4, NUMBER 8
(November 1810)
Published 29 December 1810[8]

115 Crabbe's *Borough*. Article 1, pp. 281–312. Robert Grant.
   JM MSS: WG to JM: [7 August 1810 p/mark]; [September 1810]. *QR* Letters 47, 49, 60, 65. *SL*, vol. 2, pp. 397, 397n. JM II's office copy.

116 Patten's *Natural Defence of an Insular Empire*. Article 2, pp. 313–33. John Barrow; possibly with Robert Southey.
   JM MS, list of paid contributors. *QR* Letter 68. A passage on p. 322 is identical with a passage on p. 192 of JB's *The Life of Richard, Earl Howe* (1838). JM II's office copy: [in

ink] 'Barrow' [in pencil] 'and Southey'. JM III's Register: Barrow, citing JM II's office copy.

117 Landt's *Description of the Feroe Islands*. Article 3, pp. 333–42. Robert Southey.
Curry and Dedmon, 'Southey's Contributions to the *Quarterly Review*'. JM II's office copy. JM III's Register.

118 Chalmers's *Caledonia*. Article 4, pp. 342–60. Thomas Dunham Whitaker.
JM MS, book loans register, a review copy was sent to 'Dr Whitaker' on 7 August 1810. Another entry dated '1810' under 'Dr Whitaker' is glossed 'Q. Rev. No.8'. The article bears similarities to #143. *QR* Letter 78. Nichols, 'Biographical Memoirs of Thomas Dunham Whitaker', pp. xxix, xxxiv n2. JM II's office copy. JM III's Register.

119 Weston's *Conquest of the Miao-tsé*. Article 5, pp. 361–72. John Barrow.
JM MS, list of paid contributors. The author refers to #85 (three times). The article is cross-referenced in #302. JB systematically cross-referenced his articles. The author of #142*WI* claims authorship of #85, #119, #147, #333, and #389. JM II's office copy. JM III's Register.

120 Price *on the Picturesque*. Article 6, pp. 372–82. Author not identified.

121 *Musae Cantabrigienses*. Article 7, pp. 382–92. Thomas Falconer, with an interpolation by Edward Copleston.
JM MSS: WG to JM: [1810 numbered 108+]; [November 1810 numbered 103]. *QR* Letter 78. JM III's Register: 'Arts in this No by Sayers and Falconer / see W Gs letter No 103 / also D'Oyly and Walpole / see W.G. 108.x'.

122 Woodhouse's *Trigonometry*. Article 8, pp. 392–402. Olinthus Gregory, probably.
Not in Young's list. The author refers to #103. On p. 401, Hutton's trigonometry tables are preferred over Sherwin's; cf. #144. Hutton was OG's mentor. See #103.

123 Sir Ralph Sadleir's *State Papers*. Article 9, pp. 403–14. Edmund Lodge; subedited by Walter Scott.
JM MSS: book loans register, a review copy was sent to 'E. Lodge' on 8 November 1809. *QR* Letters 47, 48, 50, 65. JM II's office copy. JM III's Register.

124 Huskisson *on the Depreciation of Currency*. Article 10, pp. 414–53. George Ellis; assisted by George Canning.
JM MSS: list of paid contributors; GE to JM, 1 October 1810; GE to JM, 9 October 1810; GE to JM, 25 November 1810; 1803–23 letterbook, GC to WG, 9 December 1810; WG to JM, 20 December 1810. *QR* Letters 60, 68, 78, 79. BL Add. MS 29281 (ff. 32–3), William Nichol to Henry Boase, 23 January 1811. Leeds WYL250 8 62, WG to GC, 6 October 1810. *SL*, vol. 2, p. 428n. JM III's Register: Ellis, and note, 'see G E's letter Oct 3, 1810'.

125 Southey's *History of Brazil*. Article 11, pp. 454–74. Reginald Heber.
JM MS, WG to JM [20 December 1810 p/mark]. *QR* Letter 62. Graham 41. JM II's office copy. JM III's Register.

126 Britton's *Architectural Antiquities*. Article 12, pp. 474–80. Frank Sayers.
JM MSS: WG to JM: 20 July 1810; [November 1810]. On p. 479, the author recommends Sayers's *Disquisitions*. JM III's Register: Sayers, and with a note at Number 8, 'Arts in this No by Sayers and Falconer. See W G's letter No 103'.

127 [Sedgwick], *On the Evangelical Sects*. Article 13, pp. 480–514. Robert Southey; with excisions by William Gifford and John Ireland.
Curry and Dedmon, 'Southey's Contributions to the *Quarterly Review*'. JM MSS: WG to JM: [December 1810]; [19 December 1810]. *QR* Letter 73. JM II's office copy. JM III's Register.

128 Mary Russell Mitford's *Poems*. Article 14, pp. 514–18. John Mitford and William Gifford; subedited by Richard Heber.

JM MSS: cash day book 1810–11, p. 156, '3 May 1811 *QR* No 8 To Cash Draft No 1814 for VIII – 14 extra £22.17'; WG to JM [November 1810]; WG to JM [December 1810]. Bodl. Lib. MS Eng. Lett. d.309 (f. 5), Charles Edward Grey to Edward Copleston, 22 January 1811. JM II's office copy: 'Mitford'. JM III's Register: 'Rev. J. Mitford', cites JM II, and note, 'aided by W Gifford'.

129 *On the Reports of the Bullion Committee* [by Sinclair]. Article 15, pp. 518–36. George Ellis, George Canning, and William Huskisson; with assistance from John Murray.

JM MSS: GE to JM, Sunday [September 1810]; WG to JM [October or November 1810]; WG to JM [?November 1810]; GE to JM [22 November 1810]; GE to JM [November or December 1810]; WG to JM [9 December 1810], notation in JM II's hand: 'Q Rev No 8 article on Sir John Sinclair – returned with very considerable alterations corrections and additions by Mr C in his own handwriting – J.M'; 1803–23 letterbook, GC to WG, 9 December 1810. *QR* Letter 65, 75, 78. Leeds WYL250 8 66a, GE to GC, Sunday, 2 December [1810]. JM II's office copy: 'Geo Ellis but really Geo Canning' [in lighter ink] 'and Huskisson'. JM III's Register: Ellis and Canning, cites JM II, and with the following note: 'Nominally by G.E. Really by Canning and W. Huskisson'.

VOLUME 5, NUMBER 9
(February 1811)
Published 10 April 1811[9]

130 Clavier – *Histoire des premiers Temps de la Grèce*. Article 1, pp. 1–40. George D'Oyly, possibly.

The evidence for attribution is weak. JM MSS: book loans register, Hale's *Chronology* (discussed on pp. 16–17, 16n) was sent to 'Rev. Geo. Doyley' [*sic*] on 5 December 1809. JM MS, WG to JM [February 1811]. The topic falls within D'Oyly's province. JM II's office copy: 'I never knew. J.M'.

131 Southey's *Curse of Kehama*. Article 2, pp. 40–61. Walter Scott; vetted by Grosvenor Bedford.

Todd and Bowden, *Sir Walter Scott: A Bibliographical History*. JM MSS: WG to JM: [January or February 1811]; [February 1811]. *QR* Letters 69, 73, 75. Morgan MS, Robert Southey to Ebenezer Elliott Jr., 7 February 1811. JM III's Register: Scott, with this note: 'In Drawing Room vols this art is attributed to Grosvenor Bedford'.

132 Sir Robert Wilson – *Campaigns in Poland*. Article 3, pp. 62–84. John William Ward, Lord Dudley, possibly.

JM MSS: book loans register, a review copy was sent to 'R[ichard]. Heber' on 18 December 1810 and to 'Revd. R. Heber, Hodnet' on 19 December 1810; WG to JM, 2 January 1811; [9 May 1811]. *QR* Letters 76, 89. BL Add. MS 28099 (ff. 91–2), WG to George Ellis, 2 February 1811. See also #134 and #146. JM II's office copy: 'Never knew. Croker sent it/ I believe Ld. [?]'. JM III's Register: [in pencil] '? Heber'.

133 Dr Whitaker – *De Motu per Brit. Civico*. Article 4, pp. 84–100. Edward Copleston; subedited by John Ireland.

JM MS, WG to JM [misdated ?May 1811; numbered 119]. *QR* Letters 64, 78, 80, 83, 84, 85. JM II's office copy: 'Coppleston' [*sic*]. JM III's Register: note to Number 9, 'Coplestone [*sic*] wrote an art in this No. See W G's letter no. 119'.

134 Roscoe's *Observations on Lord Grey's Address.* Article 5, pp. 100–10. John William Ward, Lord Dudley; with an excision by George Canning.
JM MSS: book loans register, a review copy was sent to 'Clement Park' (Dudley's residence) on 11 September 1810; WG to JM, 2 January 1811. *QR* Letters 64, 78, 83, 87. JM II's office copy. JM III's Register.

135 Sir R. Colt Hoare's *Ancient Wiltshire.* Article 6, pp. 111–20. Thomas Dunham Whitaker.
JM MSS: book loans register, a review copy was sent to 'Dr Whitaker' on 10 January 1811; WG to JM [18 March 1811]. Nichols, 'Biographical Memoirs of Thomas Dunham Whitaker', p. xxix. JM II's office copy. JM III's Register.

136 Sir John Sinclair's *Remarks, &c.* Article 7, pp. 120–38. George Ellis; with edits and additions by George Canning, Charles Ellis, and John Hookham Frere.
JM MSS: list of paid contributors for No. 9: 'VII Sinclair ... 11 – 17'; WG to JM [18 March 1811]; [25 March 1811]. *QR* Letters 69, 89; 91: 'I have £11.17.0 for your banker'. J. G. Lockhart, *Memoirs of the Life of Sir Walter Scott, Bart*, 7 vols (Edinburgh: Constable, 1837–8), vol. 2, pp. 379–81, 381n. JM II's office copy: 'G. Ellis / Canning'. JM III's Register: Ellis and Canning.

137 *India. – Disturbances at Madras* [by Petrie]. Article 8, pp. 138–203. Robert Grant; subedited by George Canning and possibly by John Wilson Croker; with information from Lord Teignmouth and the elder Charles Grant.
JM MSS: WG to JM [October–November 1810]; [1811], 'I have just received the first 6 pages of India... I should wish to shew the rest to M. C[anning]'; WG to JM, 1 March 1811. JM II's office copy: 'Robert Grant'. *QR* Letter 88. JM III's Register: Robert Grant.

138 Blomfield – *Æsch. Prometheus Vinctus.* Article 9, pp. 203–29. James Henry Monk.
JM MS, WG to JM [May 1810; dated in error May 1811]. *QR* Letters 67, 83, 92. BL Add. MS 34583 (f. 334), Peter Elmsley to Samuel Butler, 17 August 1811. JM MS, C.J. Monk to JM III, 15 January 1858.

139 Grant's *History of Mauritius, &c.* Article 10, pp. 229–41. John Barrow.
JM MS, WG to JM [early 1811], 'I sent the remdr of Barrows slight art'. *QR* Letter 91. The author speaks 'from authority' on naval matters. He expresses interest in the possibility of a connection between the Niger and Nile rivers, JB's hobby horse. The author refers to #82. The article is cross-referenced in #178. JB systematically cross-referenced his articles. JM II's office copy. JM III's Register.

140 *Tracts on the Report of the Bullion Committee* [by Atkinson, Bosanquet, Chalmers, Coutts, Eliot, Fonblanque, Hill, Hoare, Lyne, Maryatt, Ricardo, Rutherford, Smith, Thornton, Trotter, Wilson]. Article 11, pp. 242–62. George Ellis; probably assisted by George Canning and John Barrow.
JM MS, WG to JM [February 1811, numbered 111]. *QR*, 110, p. 744: 'written in conjunction with [Canning's] friend Ellis, and inspired by others'. JM II's office copy: 'Barrow'. JM III's Register: Barrow, cites JM II's office copy and notes, '?revised by G. Canning See W G's letter No 111'.

VOLUME 5, NUMBER 10
(May 1811)
Published 1 July 1811[10]

141 *French Translation of Strabo.* Article 1, pp. 274–303. Thomas Falconer; subedited and with an interpolation by Edward Copleston.

    JM MSS: book loans register, a review copy was sent to 'Rev. T. Falconer' on 10 July 1810; WG to JM, 17 July 1810. *QR* Letters 78, 80, 81, 83, 91, 94. JM III's Register: Falconer.

142 Kirkpatrick's *Account of the Kingdom of Nepaul.* Article 2, pp. 303–32. John Barrow; subedited by John Wilson Croker.

    JM MSS: WG to JM: [May 1811; 'No. 120']; [May 1811, 'No. 123']; [28 May 1811]. The author refers to #85. JB systematically cross-referenced his articles. Nepal is spelled in the article's headnote and running title as above. JM III's Register: '? Mr Barrow', and note, 'See W G's letter No 120 and 123'.

143 Lysons – *Magna Britannia.* Article 3, pp. 332–9. Thomas Dunham Whitaker.

    JM MS, book loans register, a review copy was sent to 'Dr Whitaker' 15 December 1810. There are parallels in treatment and content between #118 and #143: both articles open with a paean to Gough; both works find humour in Chalmers's mermaid. Nichols, 'Biographical Memoirs of Thomas Dunham Whitaker', pp. viii, xiv, xxix, xxxiv. JM III's Register: queries Whitaker.

144 Dealtry's *Principles of Fluxions.* Article 4, pp. 340–52. Olinthus Gregory; subedited by John Ireland and possibly by George D'Oyly.

    The evidence on balance establishes OG as the primary author. JI perhaps monitored references to the 'Saints' (powerful evangelical philanthropists). Mathematics formed no part of JI's expertise, while at this time OG had a monopoly on mathematics in the *QR*. JM MSS: WG to JM: [dated by another hand 'May? 1811']; [17 May 1811]. *QR* Letters 70, 126. The promotion of Hutton's trigonometry table repeats p. 401 of #122. The criticism of Bossut on pp. 340–9 is repeated on pp. 157–8 of #215. Hutton (also mentioned on p. 351) was OG's mentor. JM III's Register: Dr Ireland (crossed out); D'Oyly, and note, 'See W G's letter No. 119 and 121'.

145 *State of the Established Church.* Article 5, pp. 352–65. George D'Oyly.

    JM MSS: WG to JM: [May 1811, 'No. 120']; [17 May 1811]. The author is associated with Cambridge University (p. 358). *QR* Letters 94, 96. JM III's Register: queries Henry Home Drummond [in pencil], and note, 'See W G's Letter No 120'.

146 General Tarleton's *Speech.* Article 6, pp. 366–72. John William Ward, Lord Dudley, probably, and probably assisted by John Wilson Croker; possibly subedited by John Barrow.

    JM MSS: WG to JM: [May 1811]; [9 May 1811]. *QR* Letter 76, 89, 95. The author refers to #134. JWC claimed the article in five Clements Lib. lists; it is bound with the Cambridge Lib. volumes. JM III's Register: Croker, and note, 'Croker revised this, but W.G. writes May 9, 1811 "it is not from Mr C. but comes from Mr B's friend".'

147 Marshman's *A Dissertation on the Chinese Language.* Article 7, pp. 372–403. John Barrow and George Thomas Staunton.

    The author refers to #48, #82, and #85. The article is cross-referenced in #302, #333, #349, and, twice, in #389. The author of #142*WI* claims authorship of #85, #119, #147, #333, and #389. JB systematically cross-referenced his articles. *SL*, vol. 2, pp. 441, 441n.

JM II's office copy: [in pencil] 'Sir G. Staunton'. JM III's Register: Staunton, citing JM II's office copy.

148 Capt. Pasley *on the Military Policy of Gr. Britain.* Article 8, pp. 403–37. Robert Southey; with adjustments by John Wilson Croker; subedited by John Barrow and George Canning.

Curry and Dedmon, 'Southey's Contributions to the *Quarterly Review*'. JM MSS: WG to JM: [8 March 1811]; [May 1811]. *QR* Letters 89, 91, 95. Clements Library MS, JWC to WG, 26 March 1811. JWC claimed the article in four Clements Lib. lists (one entry is queried); the article is not bound in the Cambridge Lib. volumes. JM II's office copy: 'Southey and Croker'. JM III's Register: Southey, citing JM II's office copy and the book loans register, and note, 'Aided by Croker'.

149 *Translations of Pindar* [by Girdlestone, Lee]. Article 9, pp. 437–57. Reginald Heber. JM MSS: book loans register, a review copy was sent to 'Rev. R. Heber, Hodnet' on 8 March 1810; multiple undated letters, WG to JM, all *c.* May 1811; also, WG to JM [12 June 1811]. [Heber], *Life of Reginald Heber*, vol. 1, pp. 350, 350n. JM III's Register.

150 *Reflections on the Licence Trade.* Article 10, pp. 457–71. George Ellis. *QR* Letter 91. BL Add. MS 28099 (f. 93), WG to GE, 19 February 1811.

151 Mrs. Tighe's *Psyche.* Article 11, pp. 471–85. Reginald Heber, probably. JM II's office copy. JM III's Register.

152 Baron von Sack's *Voyage to Surinam.* Article 12, pp. 485–98. John Barrow, probably. The attribution to JB is based on internal evidence. See the entry for #152 in the *QR Archive.*

153 *Letters of Mad. du Deffand, &c.* Article 13, pp. 498–528. Charles Grant, possibly; possibly subedited by John Wilson Croker. JM MSS: book loans register, a review copy was sent to 'Geo. Ellis' on 22 November 1809; GE to JM [October or November 1809]; GE to JM, 3 December 1809; WG to JM [January 1810]; GE to JM, 2 February 1810; WG to JM [12 June 1811]. Not claimed by JWC in his Clements Lib. lists; not bound in the Cambridge Lib. volumes. JM II's office copy: 'Croker'. JM III's Register: Grant (a different attribution having been erased) and note, 'Aided by Croker'.

VOLUME 6, NUMBER 11
(August 1811)
Published 21 October 1811[11]

154 Stewart's *Philosophical Essays.* Article 1, pp. 1–37. Macvey Napier; subedited by Richard Heber and Edward Copleston. *QR* Letters 81, 83, 94, 99, 100, 109. BL Add. MS 34611 (ff. 15–16), WG to MN, 25 August 1811. M. Napier, *Selections from the Correspondence of Macvey Napier*, ed. M. Napier, (London: Macmillan, 1879), pp. 3–5, 5n. Smiles, *Memoir*, vol. 1, p. 194.

155 Sarrazin – *Confession du Général Buonaparté.* Article 2, pp. 38–62. George Ellis; subedited and with a paragraph by George Canning. JM MSS: WG to JM: 28 May 1811; 4 August 1811; [September 1811]. Leeds WYL250 8 66a, WG to GC, 26 July 1811. JM II in his *QR* office copy has glossed on p. 54 from 'We must admit that' to the bottom of the page, 'Entirely by Rt Hon G Canning'. JM III's Register: Ellis, and note, 'See W G's letter May 28, 1811. Also Aug 4 "before it is worked off I will show it to Mr C"'.

156 Milner's *Ecclesiastical Architecture*. Article 3, pp. 62–74. Thomas Dunham Whitaker.
JM MSS: book loans register, a review copy was sent to 'Revd. Dr Whitaker' on 28 September 1809; WG to JM, 4 August 1811. Nichols, 'Biographical Memoirs of Thomas Dunham Whitaker', p. xxix. JM II's office copy. JM III's Register.

157 Cuthbert's *New Theory of the Tides*. Article 4, pp. 74–87. Thomas Young.
Young's list. JM III's Register.

158 Chalmers's *History of the University of Oxford*. Article 5, pp. 87–98. Allen OR Allan; possibly subedited by Edward Copleston.
JM MS, Joseph Parker to JM [6 June 1815]. *QR* Letters 109, 110. See #58.

159 Churton's *Works of the Rev. Dr T. Townson*. Article 6, pp. 98–103. Thomas Dunham Whitaker.
JM MSS: book loans register, a review copy was sent to 'Dr Whitaker' on 19 December 1810; WG to JM, 4 August 1811. Nichols, 'Biographical Memoirs of Thomas Dunham Whitaker', p. xxix. JM III's Register: '?Dr Whitaker', and note, 'See W G's letter August 4, 1811'.

160 Wilks's *Sketches of the South of India*. Article 7, pp. 103–24. John Barrow.
The author promises to review later volumes when published. The article is cross-referenced in #442, JB's review of Wilks's third and fourth volumes. The article is referred to in #688. JB systematically cross-referenced his articles. JM II's office copy. JM III's Register.

161 Hardy's *Life of the Earl of Charlemont*. Article 8, pp. 124–7. John William Ward, Lord Dudley.
QR Letters 84, 101, 103. Claimed by John Wilson Croker in two Clements Lib. lists, but both entries are cancelled; the article is not bound in the Cambridge Lib. volumes. JM II's office copy. JM III's Register.

162 Mathison's *Notices respecting Jamaica*. Article 9, pp. 147–66. Eaton Stannard Barrett, probably; possibly assisted by George Canning.
Leeds WYL250 8 66a, WG to GC, 26 July 1811. JM II's office copy: 'G. Ellis'. JM III's Register: Ellis.

163 Edgeworth's *Essays on Professional Education*. Article 10, pp. 166–91. John Davison.
JM MSS: WG to JM: 4 August 1811; [September 1811]; [October 1811]. *QR* Letters 80, 81, 96, 109. JM II's office copy. JM III's Register.

164 Bishop of Lincoln's *Refutation of Calvinism*. Article 11, pp. 191–210. George D'Oyly and William Gifford.
JM MS, WG to JM [September 1811]. *QR* Letter 110. JM III's Register: queries D'Oyly [in pencil], and note, 'Dr D'Oyly wrote in this No. See No 141–2'.

165 Moor's *Hindu Infanticide*. Article 12, pp. 210–21. John Barrow, probably.
The author is agnostic about the existence of cannibalism (cf. #68, #170, #311, #347, #664). The criticism of Brahmin excesses on p. 216 resembles comments on p. 109 of #160 and p. 418 of #529. JM II's office copy. JM III's Register.

166 Scott's *Vision of Don Roderick*. Article 13, pp. 221–35. Octavius Gilchrist, possibly.
JM MSS: WG to JM: 4 August 1811; [October 1811, 'No. 153']; [9 October 1811]. *QR* Letters 97, 106. BL Add. MS 34567 (f. 248), OGG to Philip Bliss, 23 September 1811.

167 Faber's *Internal State of France*. Article 14, pp. 235–64. John Wilson Croker.
JM MSS: WG to JM, two undated letters; WG to JM [28 May 1811]; JWC to JM, 8 September 1811 and 9 September 1811. *QR* Letter 93. JWC claimed the article in four Clements Lib. lists; Cambridge Lib. volumes. JM II's office copy. JM III's Register.

168 Bell's and Lancaster's *Systems of Education*. Article 15, pp. 264-304. Robert Southey.

Curry and Dedmon, 'Southey's Contributions to the *Quarterly Review*'. JM II's office copy. JM III's Register.

VOLUME 6, NUMBER 12
(December 1811)
Published 1 February 1812[12]

169 *Tracts on the Spanish and Portuguese Inquisitions*. Article 1, pp. 313–57. Robert Southey.
   Curry and Dedmon, 'Southey's Contributions to the *Quarterly Review*'. JM II's office copy. JM III's Register.

170 *Russian Embassy to Japan* [by Krusenstern]. Article 2, pp. 357–91. John Barrow and John Hoppner.
   JM MSS: WG to JM: [26 November 1811; JM II's notation: 'Barrow whose Review was made from the MSS of Hoppner']; [6 December 1811]; [26 January 1812]. The article is referred to in #178, #190, #255, #299, and, twice, in #517. JB systematically cross-referenced his articles.

171 *Courayer sur la Divinité de Jesus Christ* [by Bell]. Article 3, pp. 391–405. John Ireland.
   JM MSS: WG to JM: [24 December 1811]; [3 January 1812]. *QR* Letter 120. JM III's Register: queries Ireland, and note, 'See W G's letters Dec 14 / 11 and Jan 3/12'.

172 Montgomery's *Poems*. Article 4, pp. 405–19. Robert Southey.
   Curry and Dedmon, 'Southey's Contributions to the *Quarterly Review*'. JM III's Register.

173 Ensor *on National Education*. Article 5, pp. 419–33. Edward Copleston.
   QR Letters 94, 113. W. J. Copleston, *Memoir of Edward Copleston, Bishop of Llandaff, with Selections from His Diary and Correspondence* (London: Parker, 1851), p. 347.

174 Baron Smith – *On the Competency of Witnesses*. Article 6, pp. 433–9. John Wilson Croker.
   JWC claimed the article in five Clements Lib. lists; Cambridge Lib. volumes. JM III's Register.

175 Hoare's *Ancient Wiltshire*. Article 7, pp. 440–8. Thomas Dunham Whitaker.
   JM MS, WG to JM [26 November 1811]. The author refers on p. 440 to #135. Nichols, 'Biographical Memoirs of Thomas Dunham Whitaker', p. xxix. JM II's office copy. JM III's Register.

176 Buchanan's *Christian Researches in Asia*. Article 8, pp. 448–62. Thomas Dunham Whitaker, probably.
   JM MSS: WG to JM [26 January 1812; notation on letter in another hand: 'To Mr Sumner an excuse for not using his article on Buchanans Xian Researches']; GE to JM, 22 July [1812]. Nichols, 'Biographical Memoirs of Thomas Dunham Whitaker', p. xxix. JM III's Register: queried attribution to Sumner, and note, '?Mr Sumner's article on this seems to have been forestalled and declined. See W G's Jany 26/12. See Mr Sumners letter Dec 20 1811'.

177 *Ford's Dramatic Works*, by Weber. Article 9, pp. 462–87. Octavius Gilchrist, William Gifford, and Barron Field; subedited by George Ellis.
   JM MSS: WG to OGG, 29 May 1811; WG to OGG, Wednesday, June 1811; WG to OGG, 3 September 1811; WG to JM, [18 January 1812]; WG to OGG, 13 February 1812. *QR* Letter 120. BL Add. MS: 28099 (f. 93), WG to GE, 19 February 1811; 34567

(ff. 222–3), OGG to Philip Bliss, 23 June 1811; (f. 248), OGG to Bliss, 2 September 1811. Smiles, *Memoir*, vol. 1, pp. 200–1. JM II's office copy: 'Baron Field but in fact Gifford'. JM III's Register: repeats JM II's office copy.

178 *On Java and its Dependencies* [by Sonnini]. Article 10, pp. 487–517. John Barrow; vetted by Charles Philip Yorke and Spencer Perceval.

JM MS, WG to JM [24 January 1812; JM II's notation: 'Mr Yorke and Mr Perceval, who were very much afraid that they had allowed Barrow to say too much respecting the future intervention of Government, in regard to their late conquest of Java, in Mr Barrow's article upon the subject. The sheets were however returned on Sunday Jan 26th without any important change']. Shine states: 'Barrow's authorship is indubitable: 11 other MS letters from Gifford to Murray bear upon it, 7 of them annotated' (H. Shine and H. C. Shine, *The Quarterly Review Under Gifford: Identification of Contributors* (Chapel Hill, NC: University of North Carolina Press, 1949), p. 28). *QR* Letter 119. The author refers to #139 and #170. JB systematically cross-referenced his articles. JM III's Register: Barrow and note, 'See W G's letters Jany 3/12 and Jany 5/12'.

179 Trotter's *Memoirs of the Rt. Hon. C. J. Fox*. Article 11, pp. 518–56. George Ellis and George Canning.

JM MSS: book loans register, a review copy was sent to 'G. Ellis, Sunning Hill' on 8 November 1811; WG to JM: [1 January 1812]; [6 January 1812]; [20 January 1812]; [24 January 1812]; [26 January 1812]. . *QR* Letters 110, 120, 122, 123. Smiles, *Memoir*, vol. 1, p. 199. JM II's office copy: 'Entirely by Canning'. JM III's Register: 'Geo Canning? and G Ellis', and note, 'WG's letter Jan 1, 1812'.

VOLUME 7, NUMBER 13
(March 1812)
Published 11 May 1812[13]

180 *America – Orders in Council, &c.* Article 1, pp. 1–34. John Barrow; with materials and subediting by John Wilson Croker, Frederick John Robinson, and George Canning; suggested by John Murray.

JM MSS: book loans register, one of the pamphlets reviewed was sent to 'Geo. Ellis' on 13 May 1809; WG to JM: [7 December 1811]; [1812], 'Our friend B[arrow] proves a tougher piece of work than I expected'; [21 March 1812]. JM II's office copy: 'Barrow'. *QR* Letter 126. JM III's Register: queries Barrow.

181 Hodgson's *Life of Bishop Porteus* Article 2, pp. 34–48. George D'Oyly, probably.

JM MSS: GD'O to JM, 25 October 1811; WG to JM [20 April 1812].

182 Mackenzie's *Travels in Iceland*. Article 3, pp. 48–92. Robert Southey.

Curry and Dedmon, 'Southey's Contributions to the *Quarterly Review*'. JM MSS: book loans register, one of the works reviewed was sent to 'R. Southey' on 4 October 1811. JM II's office copy: 'Barrow'. JM III's Register: 'J Barrow', and note, 'Southey wrote in this No See W G's letter 182'.

183 Lingard's *Antiquities of the Saxon Church*. Article 4, pp. 92–107. Thomas Dunham Whitaker.

JM MSS: book loans register, a review copy was sent to 'Dr Whitaker' on 19 December 1810 and (again?) on 10 January 1811. JM MS, TDW to JM, 11 February 1811. Nichols, 'Biographical Memoirs of Thomas Dunham Whitaker', p. xxix.

184 Cooke's *History of the Reformation in Scotland.* Article 5, pp. 107–20. Thomas Dunham Whitaker.
   JM MSS: book loans register, a review copy was returned by 'Revd. Dr Whitaker' on 15 November 1820; TDW to JM, 11 February 1811; WG to JM [April 1812]. JM III's Register: '? Sir W Scott' [in pencil] and note, in pencil, 'This suggestion is derived from Gifford's letter to Scott, lent to me [JM IV] by D Douglas July 1893'.

185 Haafner's *Travels in India.* Article 6, pp. 120–36. John Barrow.
   JM MS, WG to JM [April 1812]. The article is cross-referenced in #228. JB systematically cross-referenced his articles. JM III's Register: Barrow, and note, 'See W G's letter Mar 14 / 12'.

186 Biot – *Traité Élémentaire d'Astronomie Physique.* Article 7, pp. 136–50. Olinthus Gregory; subedited by Thomas Young and Edward Copleston.
   Not in Young's list. JM MSS: book loans register, a review copy was sent to 'Dr O. Gregory, Woolwich' on 8 November 1811. *QR* Letter 126. JM II's office copy: [in pencil] 'Dr Young'. JM III's Register: Young.

187 Grenville's *Portugal: A Poem.* Article 8, pp. 151–9. John Wilson Croker and William Gifford.
   JM MSS: WG to JM: [April 1812]; [24 April 1812]. *QR* Letter 126. JWC claimed the article in four of the Clements Lib. lists; Cambridge Lib. volumes. JM II's office copy: 'Croker'. JM III's Register: Croker.

188 Sir S. Romilly *on the Criminal Law of England.* Article 9, pp. 159–79. John Davison.
   Reprinted in Davison's *Remains and Occasional Publications* (Oxford: J. H. Parker; London: J. G. F. & J. Rivington, 1841). JM III's Register.

189 *Childe Harold's Pilgrimage, a Romaunt,* by Lord Byron. Article 10, pp. 180–200. George Ellis.
   JM MSS: WG to JM: [November 1811]; [1812], '... Child[e] Harold ... Mr E *expressly* desires may be inserted'. Smiles, *Memoir*, vol. 1, p. 126. JM II's office copy. JM III's Register.

190 Sir J. Nicholl and Dr Daubney, &c. *on Lay Baptism.* Article 11, pp. 201–23. Henry Phillpotts.
   JM MS, book loans register, the works reviewed were sent to 'H. Phillpots' on 6 March 1812. *QR* Letter 126, 130. Smiles, *Memoir*, vol. 1, p. 201. JM II's office copy. JM III's Register.

VOLUME 7, NUMBER 14
(June 1812)
Published 13 August 1812[14]

191 Walton's *Present State of the Spanish Colonies.* Article 1, pp. 235–64. Joseph Blanco White; with significant edits by William Gifford.
   JM MSS: WG to JM: [4 July 1812, numbered 197]; [6 July 1812, numbered 198]. Curry, *NL*, vol. 2, p. 38.

192 Roscoe's *Letters on Reform.* Article 2, pp. 265–81. John William Ward, Lord Dudley.
   JM MS, book loans register, a review copy of one of the works reviewed was sent to 'Clement Park' (Lord Dudley's residence) on 11 September [181?]. *QR* Letter 126. Smiles, *Memoir*, vol. 1, p. 202. JM II's office copy. JM III's Register.

193 Jones's *Biographia Dramatica*. Article 3, pp. 282–92. Octavius Gilchrist; with excisions and an addition by William Gifford.
JM MSS: WG to OGG, Monday [probably 3 February] 1812; WG to OGG, 13–17 February 1812; WG to JM [26 February 1812]; WG to JM [14 March 1812, possibly misdated]; WG to OGG [June or July 1812?]; WG to JM [6 October 1812]. JM II's office copy: [in pencil] 'Field but' [in pen] 'mainly Gifford'. JM III's Register: 'Barron Field but mainly W. Gifford'.

194 Dr Eveleigh's *Sermons*. Article 4, pp. 293–7. George D'Oyly.
JM MS, GD'O to JM, 25 October [1811]. *QR* Letter 89. JM II's office copy. JM III's Register: and note, '?Dr Ireland see W G July 4, 1812'.

195 Galt's *Voyages and Travels*. Article 5, pp. 297–308. John Ferriar, probably.
QR Letter 123. The author refers on p. 301 to 'opposition coaches … between Manchester and London'. Ferriar was a Manchester doctor. JM III's Register: [in pencil] '? Dr Ferriar'.

196 Mrs. Barbauld's *Eighteen Hundred and Eleven*. Article 6, pp. 309–13. John Wilson Croker.
Iowa MS (f. 44), JM to JWC [pencil notation, '1812']. JWC claimed the article in four Clements Lib. lists; Cambridge Lib. volumes. JM II's office copy. JM III's Register.

197 Reid's *Memoirs of the Public Life of John Horne Tooke*. Article 7, pp. 313–28. John William Ward, Lord Dudley; probably assisted by Richard Heber and Edward Copleston.
QR Letters 126, 130, 137. *Byron's Letters and Journals*, ed. L. A. Marchand, 12 vols (London: John Murray, 1973), vol. 2, pp. 235, 235n. The author of the review (or one of the authors) is old enough to remember Tooke's political life (p. 314) and to recall the events of 1794 (p. 328). JWW was born in 1781, EC in 1776, and Heber in 1773. JM II's office copy: 'Heber / Mr Ward / Ld Dudley / and / Coplestone' [*sic*]. JM III's Register: Dudley and Copleston.

198 Miss Edgeworth's *Tales of Fashionable Life*. Article 8, pp. 329–42. John Wilson Croker.
JM MS, WG to JM [July 1812]. *QR* Letter 129. Iowa MS (f. 42), JWC to JM [1812]. JWC claimed the article in five Clements Lib. lists; Cambridge Lib. volumes. Smiles, *Memoir*, vol. 1, p. 202. JM II's office copy. JM III's Register.

199 Mawe's *Travels in the Interior of Brazil*. Article 9, pp. 342–56. John Barrow.
JM MS, WG to JM, 10 July [1812 p/mark].The author refers to #170. JB systematically cross-referenced his articles. JM III's Register.

200 Sismondi – *Histoire des Républiques Italiennes*. Article 10, pp. 357–74. John Herman Merivale, probably.
JM MS, WG to JM, 21 August 1812. *QR* Letter 120. The article is cross-referenced in #256 and #283. JM II's office copy: 'Q[UER]Y Merivale'. JM III's Register.

201 Moore's *Irish Melodies*. Article 11, pp. 374–82. Horace Twiss, possibly.
JM II's office copy.

202 Hurd's *Edition of Bp. Warburton's Works*. Article 12, pp. 383–407. Thomas Dunham Whitaker.
JM MSS: book loans register, a review copy was sent to 'Dr Whitaker' on 26 March 1811; WG to JM [6 July 1812]. *QR* Letter 137. Nichols, 'Biographical Memoirs of Thomas Dunham Whitaker', p. xxix. JM II's office copy: 'Rev. Dr Whittaker'. JM III's Register: Whitaker.

203 Carr's *Descriptive Travels in Spain*. Article 13, pp. 408–11. John Wilson Croker.
JWC claimed the article in four Clements Lib. lists; Cambridge Lib. volumes. JM III's Register.

204 *Lives of the French Revolutionists.* Article 14, pp. 412–38. Robert Southey.
Curry and Dedmon, 'Southey's Contributions to the *Quarterly Review*'. JM III's Register.

205 Spenser's *Poems.* Article 15, pp. 438–40. Author not identified.
JM MS, WG to JM [July 1812], 'Spenser – I am sorry to say – I am almost afraid of. It is but feeble and will do us little good – However, I will look at it again'.

206 Markland's *Euripidis Supplices, &c.* Article 16, pp. 441–64. Peter Elmsley.
JM MSS: WG to JM [July 1812]; PE to JM, 25 June 1813; WG to JM [7 July 1813]; PE to JM, 11 July 1813. JM II's office copy. JM III's Register.

VOLUME 8, NUMBER 15
(September 1812)
Published 15 December 1812[15]

207 *First Report on National Education.* Article 1, pp. 1–27. Hebert Marsh.
Leeds WYL250 8 66a, WG to George Canning, 22 September 1812.

208 Pering and Money *on Ship-building.* Article 2, pp. 28–60. John Barrow.
One in a series by JB on dry rot. JM MSS: WG to JM: 21 August 1812; [21 September 1812]; [6 October 1812]; [26 November 1812]. JM III's Register.

209 *Specimens of a New Translation of Juvenal.* Article 3, pp. 60–5. William Gifford, probably.
JM II's office copy: 'Gifford?'. JM III's Register: Gifford.

210 Davy's *Elements of Chemical Philosophy.* Article 4, pp. 65–86. Thomas Young.
Young's list. JM III's Register.

211 Landor's *Count Julian: a Tragedy.* Article 5, pp. 86–92. Robert Southey.
Curry and Dedmon, 'Southey's Contributions to the *Quarterly Review*'. JM II's office copy. JM III's Register.

212 D'Israeli's *Calamities of Authors.* Article 6, pp. 93–114. Robert Southey.
Curry and Dedmon, 'Southey's Contributions to the *Quarterly Review*'. JM II's office copy. JM III's Register.

213 Macpherson's *European Commerce with India.* Article 7, pp. 114–44. George Ellis; possibly assisted by George Canning.
JM MS, GE to JM, 10 August 1812. *QR* Letters 133, 134. Leeds WYL250 8 66a, WG to GC, 22 Sept 1812 and 21 October 1812. JM III's Register: Ellis, citing unspecified letters.

214 Colman's *Poetical Vagaries.* Article 8, pp. 144–9. John Wilson Croker.
JM MS, WG to JM [3? July 1813 p/mark]. JWC claimed the article in five of his Clements Library MS Lists, though one instance is queried; the article is included in the Cambridge Lib. volumes. JM II's office copy. JM III's Register.

215 Playfair's *Outlines of Natural Philosophy.* Article 9, pp. 149–63. Olinthus Gregory, probably.
Not in Young's list. Internal and circumstantial evidence suggest OG. Note the author's emphasis on mathematical formulae. Mathematics was OG's preserve in the *QR*. Compare #103 and #186. The criticism of Bossut on pp. 157–8 is similar to that in #144. JM III's Register: Thomas Young.

216 Galt's *Life of Cardinal Wolsey.* Article 10, pp. 163–72. Thomas Dunham Whitaker.

JM MSS: WG to JM [October 1812, numbered 205]; WG to Robert William Hay, 22 March 1814. Nichols, 'Biographical Memoirs of Thomas Dunham Whitaker', p. xxix. JM III's Register.

217 *Rejected Addresses* [by Byron]. Article 11, pp. 172–81. John Wilson Croker
JM MSS: book loans register, one of the works reviewed was sent to 'J W Croker' on 8 November 1811. JWC claimed the article in four of his Clements Lib. lists; Cambridge Lib. volumes. JM III's Register.

218 [Woodhouselee], *An Essay on the Life and Character of Petrarch*. Article 12, pp. 181–93. Thomas Penrose; subedited by Walter Scott.
NLS MS 852 (ff. 37–8), WS to JM, 3 December 1810 (copy). JM MS, WG to John Taylor Coleridge, 7 November 1820. *QR* Letters 47, 48, 50, 57, 65, 69. JM II's office copy: [in pencil] 'Rev. Penrose friend of Ld Egremont'.

219 Lowell's *Mr. Madison's War*. Article 13, pp. 193–214. John Barrow.
JM MSS: WG to JM: [21 September 1812]; 26 November 1812. Leeds WYL250 8 66a, WG to George Canning, 22 September 1812. The article continues the defence of the Orders in Council commenced at article #180. The article is cross-referenced in #282. JB systematically cross-referenced his articles. JM II's office copy: [in pencil] 'Q[UER]Y Barrow'.

220 Monk's *Euripidis Hippolytus*. Article 14, pp. 215–27. Charles James Blomfield.
Westminster School MS, CJB to Peter Elmsley, 14 October 1812. [Attribution by C. A. Stray.]

VOLUME 8, NUMBER 16
(December 1812)
Published 5 March 1813[16]

221 *Papers respecting the E. I. Company's Charter*. Article 1, pp. 239–86. John Barrow, probably.
JM MS, WG to JM [March 1813; letter Number '215']. The author refers to #85 and #298. JB systematically cross-referenced his articles. On p. 276, the author quotes Barrow's *Travels in China*. The author is knowledgeable about the Admiralty (p. 286).

222 *Littérateur Française pendant le 18me Siècle* [by Barante]. Article 2, pp. 287–301. John Herman Merivale, probably.
JM MS, JB to JM, 26 April 1813. Note the author's philo-Gallicism, characteristic of JHM, rare in the *QR*. JM II's office copy: [in pencil] 'Merivale'. JM III's Register: 'H Merivale (senior)'.

223 Granberg – *Last Years of the Reign of Gustavus Adolphus IV.* Article 3, pp. 302–18. Reginald Heber.
JM MSS: book loans register, a 'Life of King of Sweden' was sent to 'R Heber' in August 1812. [Heber], *Life of Reginald Heber*, vol. 1, p. 369, 369n. JM III's Register: Heber.

224 *Inquiry into the Poor Laws, &c* [by Weyland]. Article 4, pp. 319–56. Robert Southey.
Curry and Dedmon, 'Southey's Contributions to the *Quarterly Review*'. Curry, *NL*, vol. 2, pp. 50, 318. JM III's Register.

225 Mant's *Bampton Lectures*. Article 5, pp. 356–74. Author not identified.

226 Lichtenstein's *Travels in South Africa*. Article 6, pp. 374–95. John Barrow.

JM MSS: WG to JM, 21 August 1812; JB to JM, 19 December 1812. The author cites John Barrow on p. 375 as the 'textbook' for Lichtenstein's work, and he is mentioned on pp. 387, 390, 391. The article is cross-referenced in #522. JB habitually cross-referenced his own articles and books. JM III's Register.

227 *Electa Tentamina – Scholâ Regiâ Edinensi.* Article 7, pp. 395–406. Walter Scott, possibly; OR William Gifford, possibly.
QR Letter 152.

228 Graham's *Journal of a Residence in India.* Article 8, pp. 406–21. John Barrow, probably. The article follows JB's usual structure (brief *divisio*; lengthy *narratio*) and is in his manner (more descriptive than analytical). The author refers to #185. JB systematically cross-referenced his articles and works. JM II's office copy. JM III's Register.

229 Belsham's *Memoirs of the late Reverend Theophilus Lindsey.* Article 9, pp. 422–37. Thomas Dunham Whitaker.
JM MSS: book loans register, a review copy was sent to 'Revd. Dr Whitaker' on 14 September 1812; TDW to JM, 22 December 1812; WG to JM [1813], 'I like the worthy Dr's Art on Belsham prodigiously'. Nichols, 'Biographical Memoirs of Thomas Dunham Whitaker', p. xxix.

230 Foscolo's *Ultime Lettere di Jacopo Ortis.* Article 10, pp. 438–45. William Stewart Rose, probably.
BL Add. MS 31022 (f. 16), WG to WSR, 27 February 1813. JM II's office copy. JM III's Register.

231 *Campaign of the French in Russia* [by Labaume]. Article 11, pp. 445–84. Robert William Hay; subedited by John Barrow, John Wilson Croker, and Sir George Murray.
JM MSS: WG to JM [16 November 1812]; WG to RWH, 6 February 1813; WG to RWH, 13 February and 16 February 1813. The article is cross-referenced in #329. An article cited as 'Russian [?Campaign]' is claimed by JWC in one Clements Library list; it is not included in the Cambridge Lib. volumes. JM III's Register: 'JW Croker', and note, 'See W G's Nov 16, 1812'.

232 Scott's *Rokeby.* Article 12, pp. 485–517. George Ellis.
QR Letter 144. BL Add. MS 31022 (f. 16), WG to William Rose, 27 February 1813. Smiles, *Memoir*, vol. 1, p. 126. JM II's office copy.

VOLUME 9, NUMBER 17
(March 1813)
Published 16 June 1813[17]

233 *Natural and Political History of Malta* [by Domeier, Eton, Giancinto]. Article 1, pp. 1–29. William Stewart Rose.
JM MS, WG to JM, 12 May 1813. BL Add. MS 31022 (f. 16), WG to WSR, 27 February 1813. The author has visited Malta in wintertime (p. 3). Barrow may have subedited the article. JM III's Register: John Barrow.

234 Horsley's *Sermons.* Article 2, pp. 30–9. Thomas Dunham Whitaker.
JM MSS: book loans register, a review copy was sent to 'Revd. Dr Whitaker' on 14 September 1812; TDW to JM: 22 December 1812; [1813]; and 4 April 1813. Nichols, 'Biographical Memoirs of Thomas Dunham Whitaker', p. xxix. JM III's Register.

235 *Li Romani nella Grecia* [by Barzoni]. Article 3, pp. 39–45. William Stewart Rose.

BL Add. MS 31022 (f. 16), WG to WSR, 27 February 1813. JM II's office copy. JM III's Register.

236 Evelyn's *Sylva*. Article 4, pp. 45–57. Thomas Dunham Whitaker.
JM MS, TDW to JM, 27 November 1812. JM II's office copy. JM III's Register.

237 Kinneir and Morier *on Persia*. Article 5, pp. 57–89. John Barrow.
JM MSS: WG to JM [25 April 1813]; JB to JM, 4 May 1813; WG to JM [1813; JM II's notation: '223 *QR* No 17'] (this letter may apply to #244). JM III's Register.

238 Baron de Grimm's *Correspondence*. Article 6, pp. 89–117. John Herman Merivale.
Cf. #263. *Byron's Letters and Journals*, vol. 3, p. 247. JM II's office copy. JM III's Register.

239 Dr Young's *Introduction to Medical Literature*. Article 7, pp. 117–25. Thomas Young, possibly.
Not in Young's list, but that could be an intentional oversight. *QR* CCX: 741, 741n. JM II's office copy: 'By Dr Young the author'. JM III's Register: Young citing unspecified letters, JM II's office copy, and note, 'by the author of the book'.

240 Feinaigle's and Grey's *Artificial Memory*. Article 8, pp. 125–39. Robert John Wilmot-Horton.
QR Letter 141. [Heber], *Life of Reginald Heber*, vol. 1, p. 391. JM II's office copy. JM III's Register.

241 *Translations of the Comedies of Aristophanes*. Article 9, pp. 139–61. Thomas Mitchell.
JM MS, WG to JM [1813], 'It is odd enough that both Mitchell and Foscolo should have fallen upon the same part of Plato's Banquet'.

242 Clarke's *Travels – Greece, Egypt, and the Holy Land*. Article 10, pp. 162–206. Reginald Heber.
JM MS, RH to JM, 2 July 1816. JM II's office copy. JM III's Register.

243 Rogers's *Poems*. Article 11, pp. 207–18. John William Ward, Lord Dudley.
JM MS, WG to JM, 17 May 1813. Dudley, *Letters to 'Ivy'*, pp. 180, 180n, 224, 224n. JM II's office copy. JM III's Register.

244 Grant *on maintaining the Indian System*. Article 12, pp. 218–53. John Barrow, probably.
JM MS, WG to JM [1813; JM II's notation: '223 *QR* No 17']; JB to JM, 24 May 1813. JM III's Register.

VOLUME 9, NUMBER 18
(July 1813)
Published 25 August 1813[18]

245 *Tracts on the British Fisheries* [by Bernard, Schultes]. Article 1, pp. 265–304. John Barrow.
JM MS, JB to JM, 23 July 1813. *QR* Letter 146. BL Add. MS 34611 (f. 143), JB to Macvey Napier, 22 December 1814. The article is cross-referenced in #260. JB systematically cross-referenced his articles. The author has access to Admiralty records (p. 302). JM II's office copy. JM III's Register.

246 Ferriar *on Apparitions*. Article 2, pp. 304–12. William Stewart Rose.
JM MS, WG to JM [3? 5? July 1813 p/mark]. *QR* Letter 148. Smiles, *Memoir*, vol. 1, pp. 243, 243n. JM II's office copy. JM III's Register.

247 *Correspondence of* Mr. Wakefield and Mr. Fox. Article 3, pp. 313–28. John William Ward, Lord Dudley.
     JM MS, WG to JM, 30 August 1813. JM II's office copy. JM III's Register.

248 D'Oyly's *Letters to Sir W. Drummond.* Article 4, pp. 329–46. George D'Oyly, probably.
     QR Letter 120. JM II's office copy. JM III's Register.

249 Colman's *Vagaries Vindicated.* Article 5, pp. 346–48. John Wilson Croker.
     JM MS, WG to JM [3? or 5? July 1813 p/mark]. JWC claimed the article in five Clements Lib. lists, though one instance is queried; Cambridge Lib. volumes. Smiles, *Memoir*, vol. 1, p. 262. JM II's office copy. JM III's Register.

250 Elmsley's *Euripidis Heraclidae.* Article 6, pp. 348–66. Charles James Blomfield.
     JM MS, Peter Elmsley to JM, 1 April 1813.

251 Montgalliard – *sur la Puissance Russe, &c.* Article 7, pp. 366–87. Robert William Hay.
     JM MSS: WG to RWH, multiple letters from 1813 mention RWH's 'Russia' as in preparation. JM III's Register: queries Hay, and note, 'see Gifford's letters to him'.

252 Meadley's *Memoirs of William Paley.* Article 8, pp. 388–400. Thomas Dunham Whitaker.
     JM MSS: TDW to JM, 24 April 1813; WG to JM [20 May 1813]. JM III's Register: queries Whitaker and cites unspecified letters.

253 Hutton's *Mathematical and Philosophical Tracts.* Article 9, pp. 400–18. Olinthus Gregory, probably.
     OG succeeded Hutton as mathematical master at Woolwich Academy. See p. 418 where OG is mentioned as Hutton's collaborator. The author refers to #73. See also #103 and #186.

254 M'Crie's *Life of John Knox.* Article 10, pp. 418–33. Thomas Dunham Whitaker.
     JM MS, TDW to JM, 24 April 1813. Nichols, 'Biographical Memoirs of Thomas Dunham Whitaker', p. xxix. JM III's Register.

255 Langsdorff's *Voyage round the World.* Article 11, pp. 433–43. John Barrow.
     JM MSS: cash day book, 1810–13, p. 42, Saturday 29 May 1813, 'Quarterly Review / Krusensterns Voyage D[ebi]t / 1 copy to Barrow / Langsdorfs Voyage to J. B. Esq.'; JB to JM, 10 June 1812. The author refers to #170. The author of #299 states that his article continues from #255. JB systematically cross-referenced his articles. JM III's Register.

256 Villani's *Istorie Fiorentine.* Article 12, pp. 444–66. John Herman Merivale, probably.
     The author refers to #200. The author of article #200 mentions Villani. The article is cross-referenced in #283.

257 Blackall *on Dropsies.* Article 13, pp. 466–71. Thomas Young.
     Young's list. JM III's Register.

258 Sir J. Malcolm's *Sketch of the Sikhs.* Article 14, pp. 472–9. John Barrow.
     JM MS, JB to JM, 5 May 1813. JM III's Register: queries Barrow.

259 [Scott], *The Bridal of Triermain.* Article 15, pp. 480–97. George Ellis.
     BL Add. MS 31022 (f. 16), WG to William Stewart Rose, 27 February 1813. JM III's Register.

VOLUME 10, NUMBER 19
(October 1813)
Published 18 December 1813[19]

260 *Papers – On India-built Ships and Naval Timber.* Article 1, pp. 1–30. John Barrow; possibly with information from Sylvester Douglas.
   JM MSS: SD to JM: 30 November 1813; 12 December 1813. The author has access to forests department records (p. 7); SD was commissioner of the forests department. The author refers to #219 and #260. The article is cross-referenced in #297, #328, #514, and #704. JB systematically cross-referenced his articles. Smiles, *Memoir*, vol. 1, p. 284. JM II's office copy. JM III's Register.

261 Mrs. E. Montagu's *Letters.* Article 2, pp. 31–41. Walter Scott, probably.
   Todd and Bowden, *Sir Walter Scott: A Bibliographical History.* JM MS, book loans register, Montagu's first volume of was sent to 'W. Scott' on 13 May 1809. NLS MS 853 (ff. 7–8), WS to J.B.S. Morritt, 17 August 1809 (copy); (ff. 114–15), WS to Morritt, 10 September (1809) (copy). *SL*, pp. 225, 236–7.

262 The Earl of Harrowby's *Speech on the Curacy Bill.* Article 3, pp. 41–57. Edward Copleston.
   JM MS, WG to JM [30 August 1813]. Copleston, *Memoir of Edward Copleston*, pp. 46, 347.

263 Baron de Grimm's *Correspondance. – 3d SERIES.* Article 4, pp. 57–90. John Herman Merivale.
   JM MS, WG to JM [21 September 1813]. A work reviewed at article #222 is quoted on p. 65. The article is cross-referenced in #238. A. W. Merivale, *Family Memorials* (Exeter: For private circulation, 1884), p. 293. JM II's office copy. JM III's Register.

264 *History of Dissenters, &c* [by Bennett, Bogue]. Article 5, pp. 90–139. Robert Southey.
   Curry and Dedmon, 'Southey's Contributions to the *Quarterly Review*'. JM II's office copy. JM III's Register.

265 Bland's *Greek Anthology.* Article 6, pp. 139–57. John Herman Merivale, possibly.
   There is no emphasis here on Christianity, which is uncharacteristic of Sumner (see below). It is possible that the letter cited by JM III points to Sumner as the author of #268. That article treats a subject, the Spanish Inquisition, more along Sumner's line. On p. 155 of #265, two works are discussed that are the subject of reviews by JHM in three articles (#222, #238, #263). The translation of Hodgson on p. 151 is referred to in #289, which is also possibly by JHM (Hodgson and JHM were friends). JM III's Register: Sumner, and note, 'See WG May 14/12' ('12' overwrites '8').

266 Comber *on National Subsistence.* Article 7, pp. 157–75. George Ellis.
   JM MS, WG to JM [3 July 1813]. *QR* Letter 148. BL Add. MS 28099 (ff. 105–6), WG to George Ellis, Thursday night, [?] December 1813. JM III's Register.

267 Hobhouse's *Journey through Albania, &c.* Article 8, pp. 175–203. John Barrow, probably.
   JM MS, WG to JM [5 December 1813]. There are no references in this article to other articles by JB, which is notable as JB systematically cross-referenced his own articles. J. C. Hobhouse, *Recollections of a Long Life*, 6 vols (London: John Murray, 1909), vol. 1, pp. 81, 81n.

268 *Bread and Bulls, and the Inquisition* [by Padrón]. Article 9, pp. 203–11. John Bird Sumner, possibly.

See the discussion at the entry for article #265.

269 *Letter on the Conduct of Denmark*. Article 10, pp. 211–21. Robert William Hay; with excisions by William Gifford.
    JM MSS: WG to JM [5 December 1813]; WG to RWH, 17 December [1813]. JM III's Register: queries Gifford and cites unspecified letters.

270 Eustace's *Tour through Italy*. Article 11, pp. 222–50. Author not identified. Shine suggests Reginald Heber.
    JM MS, WG to JM [10 November 1813]. Robert Bland, John Herman Merivale, and William Stewart Rose are other likely candidates. The author of #270 lived for an extended period in Italy (see. p. 244).

271 Adelung's *General History of Languages*. Article 12, pp. 250–92. Thomas Young.
    Young's list. JM MS, WG to JM [21 September 1813]. BL Add. MS 28099 (ff. 105–6), WG to George Ellis, Thursday night, [?] December 1813. The article is cross-referenced in #356. JM II's office copy. JM III's Register.

VOLUME 10, NUMBER 20
(January 1814)
Published 1 April 1814[20]

272 Miss Edgeworth's *Patronage*. Article 1, pp. 301–22. John William Ward, Lord Dudley; subedited by Edward Copleston.
    JWC claimed the article in five Clements Lib. lists; Cambridge Lib. volumes. However, in the Cambridge volumes a query is entered against this title. Note that JWC was mistaken about his having reviewed Edgeworth's *Tales* (#42). When he compiled his lists (in the 1840s) he seems to have misremembered having written all of the Edgeworth reviews in the *QR*. *Letters of the Earl of Dudley to the Bishop of Llandaff*, ed. E. Copleston (London: John Murray, 1840), pp. 8–9, 10, 13–14, 25. Dudley, *Letters to 'Ivy'*, pp. 170, 170n, 250. JM II's office copy. JM III's Register.

273 Broughton's *Letters from a Mahratta Camp*. Article 2, pp. 323–31. John Barrow; with modifications by William Gifford.
    JM MSS: WG to JM: [8 March 1814]; [25 March 1813]; [22 March 1814]. JM MS, JB to JM, 24 May 1813. JM II's office copy. JM III's Register: Barrow, citing JM II's office copy, and note, 'much edited by Gifford'.

274 Lord Byron's *Giaour, and Bride of Abydos*. Article 3, pp. 331–54. George Ellis.
    JM MS, WG to JM [8 March 1814]. *QR* Letter 148. Smiles, *Memoir*, vol. 1, p. 126. JM III's Register.

275 Madame de Staël Holstein's *De l'Allemagne*. Article 4, pp. 355–409. Reginald Heber.
    JM MS, WG to JM [8 March 1814]. [Heber], *Life of Reginald Heber*, vol. 1, pp. 396, 396n, 418. JM II's office copy. JM III's Register.

276 Butler's *Lives of Bossuet and Fenelon*. Article 5, pp. 409–27. Thomas Dunham Whitaker.
    JM MSS: TDW to JM: 11 September 1813; 27 October 1813; 20 December 1813. *The Letters of Robert Southey to John May 1797 to 1838*, ed. C. Ramos (Austin, TX: Jenkins, 1976), p. 132, Southey states, 'nothing of mine in the last Quarterly'. JM III's Register: R. Southey', and note, '? by Dr Whitaker – see his letter of Oct 27, 1813'.

277 Goethe *on Colours*. Article 6, pp. 427–41. Thomas Young.

Young's list. BL Add. MS 28099 (f. 105), WG to George Ellis, Thursday night, [?] December 1813. JM III's Register.

278 Hermes – *State of the Modern Greeks*. Article 7, pp. 442–63. Stratford Canning.
JM MS, Stanley Lane Poole to JM III, 14 June [1887]. 'I have a letter from George Canning to his cousin, Stratford, in which he says, "I return your proof ... it will do you good in Giff's credit" – dated 20 Feb 1814. The proof appears to have dealt with matters of style and grammar for GC criticizes some of Stratford's remarks about "aorists and paulas" and "the explosion of the dual number". Can this be a Quarterly Review art.?' Notation on the letter in JM III's hand: 'Ansd 15/IV/87, 1st quotn evidently refers to No 20 Art 7'. Compare p. 447: 'The use of the dual number is exploded. All the nice distinctions so laboriously arranged by the ancient grammarians, the delicate shades of first and second future, the paulo post futurum, first and second aorist, the participles, &c. &c. are entirely obliterated'.

279 Paulding's *Lay of the Scottish Fiddle*. Article 8, pp. 463–7. John Wilson Croker.
JM MS, WG to JM [19 January 1814]. JWC claimed the article in four Clements Lib. lists; Cambridge Lib. volumes. JM III's Register.

280 *Resolutions – of the London Ship Owners*. Article 9, pp. 467–81. John Barrow.
The author refers to #260. The article is cross-referenced in #287. JB systematically cross-referenced his articles. The article is one in a series by JB on dry rot.

281 *Intercepted Letters, &c.* [by Napoleon]. Article 10, pp. 481–94. John Wilson Croker.
JM MSS: WG to JM: [19 January 1814]; 7 o'clock, Friday evening, 22 March 1814; [25 March 1814]. *QR* Letter 157. JWC claimed the article in four Clements Lib. lists; Cambridge Lib. volumes. JM II's office copy: [pencil] 'Q[UER]Y Croker'. JM III's Register.

282 [Ingersoll], *Favourable View of the United States*. Article 11, pp. 494–530. John Barrow.
JM MS, JB to JM, November 1813 (several letters). The author refers to #219. The article is cross-referenced in #297, #282, #468. JB systematically cross-referenced his articles. JM III's Register: Barrow, and note.

VOLUME 11, NUMBER 21
(April 1814)
Published 16 July 1814[21]

283 Ginguené and Sismondi's *Literary History of Italy, &c.* Article 1, pp. 1–32. Robert Bland, possibly.
R. Marshall, *Italy in English Literature, 1755–1815* (1934), p. 382, cited in Shine, *The Quarterly Review Under Gifford*.

284 Galt's *Tragedies*. Article 2, pp. 33–41. John Wilson Croker.
JWC claimed the article in four Clements Lib. lists; Cambridge Lib. volumes. JM III's Register.

285 Malus, Biot, and Brewster *on Light*. Article 3, pp. 42–56. Thomas Young.
Young's list. JM III's Register.

286 *Missionaries' Letters on the Nicobar Islands*. Article 4, pp. 57–72. Robert Southey.
Curry and Dedmon, 'Southey's Contributions to the *Quarterly Review*'.

287 *Letters of Lord Nelson to Lady Hamilton, &c.* Article 5, pp. 73–7. John Wilson Croker.
JWC claimed the article in four Clements Lib. lists; Cambridge Lib. volumes. JM II's office copy. JM III's Register.

288 Montgomery's *World before the Flood*. Article 6, pp. 78–87. Robert Southey.

Curry and Dedmon, 'Southey's Contributions to the *Quarterly Review*'. JM III's Register: Southey and Gifford.

289 Busby's *Lucretius*. Article 7, pp. 88–103. Henry Drury, possibly, and possibly with John Herman Merivale.

JM II's office copy: [pencil] 'Rev [H] Drury'. JM III's Register: 'Rev [H] Drury'. On Merivale, see the note for #289 at the *QR Archive*.

290 Jameson's *Travels through Norway, Lapland, &c*. Article 8, pp. 103–23. Robert William Hay.

JM MSS: WG to RWH: 14 March 1814; 15 July 1814; 17 December [1814]. JM III's Register: queries Hay, and note, 'one of Gifford's letters to him'.

291 D'Arblay's *Wanderer*. Article 9, pp. 123–30. John Wilson Croker.

JWC claimed the article in four Clements Lib. lists; Cambridge Lib. volumes. JM III's Register.

292 Kirwan's *Sermons*. Article 10, pp. 130–8. Author not identified.

JM MS, WG to JM [3 June 1814]. JM III's Register: 'A friend of Mr Hebers' W.G'.

293 Lacretelle's *Histoire de France*. Article 11, pp. 138–77. Richard Chenevix, possibly.

The article is cross-referenced in #662.

294 Coleridge's *Remorse*. Article 12, pp. 177–90. John Taylor Coleridge.

JM MS, WG to JTC, 13 February 1814. Bodl. Lib. MSS Eng. Lett. d.134, John Keble to JTC (f. 14) [1 February 1814]; (f. 16) [22 February 1814]. JM II's office copy. JM III's Register.

295 *History of the Azores* [by Ashe]. Article 13, pp. 191–203. John Barrow, probably.

JM MS, WG to JM, 3 June 1814. On p. 199, the author refers to Barrow. The author has visited Sete Cidades (p. 200), a volcano in San Miguel Island, the Azores. The debunking strategy adopted by the author is similar to JB's approach in other articles.

296 Dr Bancroft *on permanent Colours*. Article 14, pp. 203–15. Thomas Young.

Young's list. JM MSS: WG to JM [2 July 1814]; TY to [WG], 29 August 1814. JM III's Register.

297 *Papers – on the Thames Ship-builders, &c*. Article 15, pp. 217–52. John Barrow.

JM MS, WG to JM [3 June 1814]. The article is a defence of #280 and develops its arguments. The article is one in a series by JB on dry rot. JM III's Register: queries Barrow.

VOLUME 11, NUMBER 22
(July 1814)
Published 8 November 1814[22]

298 Brand's *Popular Antiquities*. Article 1, pp. 259–85. Francis Cohen

Smiles, *Memoir*, vol. 1, pp. 284–5, 285n. F. Palgrave, *Collected Historical Works*, ed. Sir R. H. Inglis Palgrave (Cambridge: Cambridge University Press, 1919–22). JM II's office copy. JM III's Register.

299 Langsdorff – *Russian Voyages round the World*. Article 2, pp. 285–304. John Barrow.

The author asserts that this article is a continuation of #170 and #255. JB systematically cross-referenced his articles.

300 Mathias – *Mason's Life and Writings of Gray*. Article 3, pp. 304–18. Thomas Dunham Whitaker.

JM MS, book loans register, the review copy was returned by 'Revd. Dr Whitaker' on 15 November 1820. Nichols, 'Biographical Memoirs of Thomas Dunham Whitaker', pp. xxix, xxxiv.

301 Davy's *Agricultural Chemistry*. Article 4, pp. 318–31. Thomas Young.
Young's list. The article is reprinted in Young's *Works*. JM III's Register.

302 *Progress of Chinese Literature in Europe* [by Marshman, Morrison]. Article 5, pp. 332–46. John Barrow.
The author refers to #84, #119, and #147 and states that the present article is a continuation of these. The article is cross-referenced in #389. JB systematically cross-referenced his articles.

303 Adams *on Diseases of the Eye*. Article 6, pp. 347–54. Thomas Young.
Young's list.

304 [Scott], *Waverley; or, 'tis Sixty Years since*. Article 7, pp. 354–77. John Wilson Croker.
QR Letter 161. JWC claimed the article in three Clements Lib. lists; Cambridge Lib. volumes. JM III's Register.

305 Badham's *Translation of Juvenal*. Article 8, pp. 377–98. William Gifford.
QR Letter 161. JM MS, WG to JM [p/mark 27 July 1814]. JM II's office copy. JM III's Register.

306 Baron De Grimm's *Correspondance Littéraire*. Article 9, pp. 399–423. John Herman Merivale, probably.
JM MS, WG to JM, 15 July 1814 (may instead refer to #289). The author states that the present article is a continuation of #238 and 263. The author refers to #263. JM III's Register: queries Southey, and note, 'Apparently Mr Merivale had an Art in this No'.

307 Wewitzer's *School*, Kett's *Flowers, of Wit*. Article 10, pp. 423–8. John Herman Merivale, possibly; with revisions by William Gifford.
JM MSS: WG to JM: 15 July 1814 (may instead refer #289); [20 October 1814 p/mark]. *QR* Letter 161. JM III's Register: Merivale and Gifford.

308 Lord Byron's *Corsair, and Lara*. Article 11, pp. 428–57. George Ellis.
JM MS, WG to JM [20 October 1814 p/mark]. *QR* Letter 158. JM II's office copy. JM III's Register.

309 Leake's *Researches in Greece* Article 12, pp. 458–80. Charles James Blomfield.
Westminster MS, 7 October 1814 CJB to Peter Elmsley. [Attribution by C. A. Stray.] G. Peacock, *Life of Thomas Young* (London: John Murray, 1855), pp. 246–7. JM III's Register.

310 Chalmers's *English Poets*. Article 13, pp. 480–504. Robert Southey; with excisions by William Gifford.
Curry and Dedmon, 'Southey's Contributions to the *Quarterly Review*'. JM MSS: cash day book 1810–14, books sent to Southey regarding 'Quarterly Review No. 22'; WG to JM [20 October 1814 p/mark]. JM II's office copy. JM III's Register.

VOLUME 12, NUMBER 23
(October 1814)
Published 6 January 1815[23]

311 Flinders's *A Voyage to Terra Australis*. Article 1, pp. 1–46. John Barrow.
JM MSS: WG to JM: [26 July 1814]; [20 October 1814 p/mark; JM II's notation: 'Flinders, Q.R. 23'.]. The author quotes a passage from #282 that is also quoted in #297.

The author refers to #104. JB systematically cross-referenced his articles. On p. 23 the author doubts the fact of cannibalism ('anthropophagism'), a position JB consistently took (cf. #68, #165, #170, #347, #664). In this article, in #68, and in #347, the author mentions Dentrecasteaux's mistaking the bones of a kangaroo for those of a girl. JM II's office copy. JM III's Register.

312 Eustace, Shepherd, &c. *on Paris*. Article 2, pp. 46–60. John Wilson Croker.

JM MS, WG to JM [1814], 'Has Mr Croker seen the other little publication Mon voyage de huit Jours? It is more comical than Wanseys'. JWC claimed the article in four Clements Lib. lists; Cambridge Lib. volumes. JM III's Register.

313 Chalmers's *English Poets*. Article 3, pp. 60–90. Robert Southey; with excisions by William Gifford.

Curry and Dedmon, 'Southey's Contributions to the *Quarterly Review*'. JM II's office copy.

314 Wells *on Dew*. Article 4, pp. 90–9. Thomas Young.

JM MS, WG to JM [18 or 21 November 1814]. Not in Young's list in [H. Gurney], *Memoir of the Life of Thomas Young* (London: John & Arthur Arch, 1831), pp. 56–60, but it is in Young's list reproduced in *Quarterly Journal of Science*, 28 (1829), p. 157 and in another version of Young's list reproduced in T. J. Pettigrew, *Biographical Memoirs of the Most Celebrated Physicians, Surgeons, etc., etc.* (London: Fisher, Son and Co., 1840), vol. 4, p. 21. JM III's Register: Young.

315 Wordsworth's *Excursion*. Article 5, pp. 100–11. Charles Lamb; with excisions by William Gifford.

Bodl. Lib. MS Eng. Lett. d.52 (ff. 100–1), Grosvenor Bedford to Robert Southey, 30 October 1814 (ff. 117–18); same, 1 February 1815; (ff. 121–2), same, 15 February 1815. NLS MS 866 (f. 149), WG to Walter Scott, 11 September 1817. J. I. Ades, 'Lamb on Wordsworth's Excursion', *Review of Arts and Letters* 3 (1969), pp. 1–9. *Letters of Charles and Mary Anne Lamb*, ed. E. W. Marrs, 3 vols (Ithaca, NY: Cornell University Press, 1976–9), vol. 3, pp. 131–3, 133n.

316 Schlegel's *Cours de Littérature Dramatique*. Article 6, pp. 112–46. Francis Hare-Naylor.

JM MS, WG to JM [26 July 1814]. JM III's Register: 'F. Hare Naylor or Coleridge', and note, 'from a letter of F. H N's. July 21st 1814 [and] from a letter of STC's Sept 10. 1814. See also WG July 26/14'. No other evidence connects Coleridge with this article.

317 *On improving the Condition of the Poor* [by Myers, Salis]. Article 7, pp. 146–59. John Bird Sumner.

Claimed by JBS in J. B. Sumner, *A Treatise on the Records of the Creation, and on the Moral Attributes of the Creator*, 2 vols (London: J. Hatchard, 1816), vol. 2, p. 306n, 'In an article in the Quarterly Review for October 1814, the author attempted to show with how much ease county banks might be universally established through the medium of Government'. D. Sorenson, D. Southern, and A. M. C. Waterman assisted in the attribution of this article to Sumner.

318 [Brown], *Paradise of Coquettes*. Article 8, pp. 159–79. Francis Cohen, probably.

JM MS, Peter Elmsley to JM, 16 January 1815. Smiles, *Memoir*, vol. 1, pp. 284–5, 285n. JM III's Register.

319 Forbes's *Oriental Memoirs*. Article 9, pp. 180–227. Robert Southey; with excisions by William Gifford.

Curry and Dedmon, 'Southey's Contributions to the *Quarterly Review*'. JM II's office copy. JM III's Register.

320 Layman *on Trees, Timber, the Dry-rot, &c*. Article 10, pp. 227–38. John Barrow.

JM MS, JB to JM, 27 November 1814. The article is cross-referenced in #514 and #704. JB systematically cross-referenced his articles. The article is one in a series by JB on dry rot. Smiles, *Memoir*, vol. 1, p. 284. JM III's Register.

321 *Memoirs of Buonaparte's Deposition, &c.* Article 11, pp. 238–66. John Wilson Croker. JM MSS: WG to JM: [3 June 1814]; [26 July 1814]. JWC claimed the article in four Clements Lib. lists; Cambridge Lib. volumes. JM III's Register.

VOLUME 12, NUMBER 24
(January 1815)
Published 23 March 1815[24]

322 Stewart's *Elements of the Philosophy of the Human Mind.* Article 1, pp. 281–317. William Rowe Lyall.
JM MS, WG to JM [27 January 1815]. Smiles, *Memoir*, vol. 1, pp. 284, 284n. JM II's office copy. JM III's Register.

323 Lewis and Clarke's *American Travels.* Article 2, pp. 317–68. Robert Southey.
Curry and Dedmon, 'Southey's Contributions to the *Quarterly Review*'. BL Add. MS 47886 is the holograph MS of this article.

324 Gibbon's *Miscellaneous Works.* Article 3, pp. 368–91. Thomas Dunham Whitaker, probably.
Nichols, 'Biographical Memoirs of Thomas Dunham Whitaker', pp. xxii and xxix. JM III's Register.

325 Louis Buonaparte's *Marie.* Article 4, pp. 391–8. John Wilson Croker.
JWC claimed the article in four Clements Lib. lists; Cambridge Lib. volumes. The author refers to #321. JM III's Register.

326 Colquhoun *on the Wealth, Power, &c.* Article 5, pp. 398–433. John Barrow; subedited by William Huskisson.
JM MS, WG to JM [14 November 1814]. BL Add. MS 38740 (ff. 71–2), WG to WH, 9 February 1815. JM III's Register.

327 Cunningham's *The Velvet Cushion.* Article 6, pp. 433–44. Author not identified.

328 Seppings's *Improvements in Ship-building.* Article 7, pp. 444–66. John Barrow.
JM MSS: JB to JM, 21 December 1814; WG to JM [27 January 1815]. Two later articles, #704 and 710, discuss the same topic. The author refers to #260, in which Seppings is praised (p. 25). The article is cross-referenced in #514 (twice). JB systematically cross-referenced his articles. The article is one in a series by JB on dry rot. JM II's office copy. JM III's Register.

329 *Buonaparte's Russian Campaign* [by Bourgeois, Labaume and Porter]. Article 8, pp. 466–501. Robert William Hay.
JM MSS: WG to RWH, 5 January [1815]; WG to RWH, 20 March 1815; WG to JM [26 July 1814]; WG to JM [27 January 1815]. The author refers to #231. JM III's Register.

330 [Scott], *Guy Mannering, or the Astrologer.* Article 9, pp. 501–9. John Wilson Croker.
JWC claimed the article in four Clements Lib. lists; Cambridge Lib. volumes. JM II's office copy. JM III's Register.

331 Roberts's *Letters and Miscellaneous Papers.* Article 10, pp. 509–19. Robert Southey.
Curry and Demon. JM III's Register.

VOLUME 13, NUMBER 25
(April 1815)
Published 20 June 1815[25]

332 Miot's *Mémoires de l'Expédition en Egypte, &c.* Article 1, pp. 1–55. Robert Southey.
Curry and Dedmon, 'Southey's Contributions to the *Quarterly Review*'. JM II's office
copy. JM III's Register.

333 De Guignes's *Dictionnaire Chinois.* Article 2, pp. 56–76. John Barrow.
JM MS, JB to JM, 13 January 1815. The author refers to #85 and #147. The article is
cross-referenced in #349 and #389. JB systematically cross-referenced his articles. The
author of #142*WI* claims authorship of #85, #119, #147, #333, and #389. JM II's office
copy. JM III's Register.

334 Mason's *Statistical Account of Ireland.* Article 3, pp. 76–82. John Wilson Croker.
JWC claimed the article in four Clements Lib. lists; included in the Cambridge Univ.
vols. JM III's Register.

335 Southey's *Roderick.* Article 4, pp. 83–113. Grosvenor Charles Bedford; assisted by Robert Southey and William Nichol.
JM MS, WG to JM, [28 January 1815]. Bodl. Lib. MS Eng. Lett. d. 52, GB to RS: (f.
123), 18 February 1815; (f. 125), 25 February 1815; (f. 127), 27 February 1817. JM II's
office copy: 'Bedford'. JM III's Register: Bedford, citing JM II's office copy.

336 [Styles], *A New Covering to the Velvet Cushion.* Article 5, pp. 113–19. Author not identified.

337 Park's *Journal of a Mission to the Interior of Africa.* Article 6, pp. 120–51. John Barrow.
BL Add. MS 35611 (f. 299), JB to Macvey Napier, 23 October 1815. The article is cross-
referenced in #457 (twice) and #531. JB systematically cross-referenced his articles.

338 Elton's *Specimens of the Classic Poets.* Article 7, pp. 151–8. Henry Hallam, probably.
JM II's office copy: 'H. Hallam'.

339 Gall and Spurzheim's *Physiognomical System.* Article 8, pp. 159–78. Author not identified.

340 Rice – *on the Irish Grand Jury Laws.* Article 9, pp. 178–82. John Wilson Croker.
JWC claimed the article in four Clements Lib. lists; included in the Cambridge Univ.
vols. JM III's Register.

341 Routh's *Reliquiae Sacrae.* Article 10, pp. 183–92. Charles James Blomfield, possibly.
Compare the author's recommending Marsh on p. 187 with #346.

342 Wraxall's *Historical Memoirs of My Own Time.* Article 11, pp. 193–215. John Wilson
Croker.
JWC claimed the article in four Clements Lib. lists; included in the Cambridge Univ.
vols. JM II's office copy. JM III's Register.

343 Elliott's *Life of Wellington.* Article 12, pp. 215–75. Robert Southey.
Curry and Dedmon, 'Southey's Contributions to the *Quarterly Review*'. JM II's office
copy. JM III's Register.

VOLUME 13, NUMBER 26
(July 1815)
Published 1 December 1815[26]

344 Scott's *The Lord of the Isles.* Article 1, pp. 287–309. George Ellis, probably.

JM II's office copy.

345 Campbell – *Missionary Travels in South Africa*. Article 2, pp. 309–40. John Barrow.
JM MS, WG to JM, 6 September 1815. The author of #368, #522, and of #641 claims this article. JB systematically cross-referenced his articles. JM MS, Robert Southey to JM, 26 June 1815. JM II's office copy: [in pencil] 'Barrow'.

346 Marsh's *Horæ Pelasgicæ*. Article 3, pp. 340–51. Charles James Blomfield.
JM MS, JM to CJB, 1 April 1815 (copy). JM II's office copy. JM III's Register: 'Ugo Foscolo?' [the query is in red ink] and note, 'Bp Blomfield of London' and another 'See also Blomfield's letter July 2/15'. The suggestion that Ugo Foscolo wrote the article probably derived from the unreliable note in *GM* 21 (1844), p. 140.

347 Porter's *Cruize in the Pacific Ocean*. Article 4, pp. 352–83. John Barrow.
The author refers to #68. JB systematically cross-referenced his articles. Compare the author's doubts about the existence of cannibalism on p. 367 with #68, #165, #170, #311, #664. Dentrecasteaux's mistaking 'the bones of a kangaroo for those of a young girl' (pp. 367–8) is also mentioned in #68 and #311. The author quotes Admiralty correspondence (pp. 376–7) and supplies new information about one of JB's preoccupations, the *Bounty* mutiny. JM III's Register: queries Barrow.

348 Dunlop's *History of Fiction*. Article 5, pp. 384–408. Francis Cohen; substantially rewritten by George Taylor.
JM MS, WG to JM, 21 Sept 1815. Claimed by GT in his *Memoir of Robert Surtees* (Durham: Surtees Society [1852]), p. xiv. JM III's Register: Cohen.

349 *Translations from the original Chinese*. Article 6, pp. 408–18. John Barrow, probably; possibly with another writer.
JM MS, WG to JM, 21 September 1815. The author implies that the other *QR* articles on the same subject are his (#85, #119, #147, #333). JB systematically cross-referenced his articles. The author of #142*WI* claims authorship of #85, #119, #147, #333, and #389, but not this article. JM III's Register: [in pencil] '? Barrow'.

350 Gentz – *On the Fall of Prussia*. Article 7, pp. 418–42. Robert William Hay.
JM MSS: WG to RWH: [17 February 1815]; [24 June 1815]; 20 July 1815; 30 November [1815]. *QR* Letters 164, 165. JM III's Register.

351 Pillet – *L'Angleterre, vue à Londres, &c.* Article 8, pp. 442–8. John Wilson Croker and John Barrow.
JM MS, WG to JM, 21 September 1815. *QR* Letter 164. JWC claimed the article in four of his Clements Lib. lists; included in the Cambridge Univ. vols. JM II's office copy: [in pencil] 'Croker'. JM III's Register: JWC, citing unspecified letters.

352 *Life of Wellington* [by Elliott]. Article 9, pp. 448–526. Robert Southey; with adjustments by John Wilson Croker acting for the Duke of Wellington.
Curry and Dedmon, 'Southey's Contributions to the *Quarterly Review*'. *QR* Letters 164, 165. Iowa MS (f. 105), JM to JWC, 30 October 1815. JM MS, WG to JM [25 November 1815]. *NL*, vol. 2, p. 124 ff. *Selections from the Letters of Robert Southey*, ed. J. W. Warter, 4 vols (London: Longman, et al., 1856), vol. 2, pp. 411, 413, 416–17, 418, 421–2, 425, 429–30, vol. 3, pp. 5–6, 13. JM II's office copy. JM III's Register.

VOLUME 14, NUMBER 27
(October 1815)
Published 12 March 1816[27]

353 *Ceylon*. Article 1, pp. 1–38. John Barrow.
JM MS, book loans register, the works reviewed were sent to 'John Barrow' on 16 August 1815 and were returned 2 December 1815. The author promises to review Beckmann's *History of Inventions* (cf. #370). JM III's Register.

354 *The Bishop of London – Mr. Belsham*. Article 2, pp. 39–53. George D'Oyly.
JM MS, WG to JM [6 September 1815]. JM III's Register.

355 *Buonaparte* [by Bowerbank, Haye, Martillière, Pradt, Trucheses-Waldbourg, Williams]. Article 3, pp. 53–96. John Wilson Croker.
The author refers to #321. JWC claimed the article in four Clements Lib. lists; included in the Cambridge Univ. vols. JM II's office copy. JM III's Register.

356 *Jamieson and Townsend on Ancient Languages*. Article 4, pp. 96–112. Thomas Young.
Young's list. The author refers to #271. JM III's Register.

357 Lord Blayney's *Forced Journey through Spain, &c*. Article 5, pp. 112–20. John Wilson Croker.
JWC claimed the article in four Clements Lib. lists; included in the Cambridge Univ. vols. See #384. JM II's office copy. JM III's Register.

358 *Mendicity*. Article 6, pp. 120–45. John Barrow, possibly.
Southey's topic (cf.# 224, 385, 454, 469). The article, however, is not in Southey's definitive MS list of his *QR* articles published in Curry and Dedmon, 'Southey's Contributions to the *Quarterly Review*'. JM III in his 'Register' does not substantiate his assertion that the article is by JB. The article's style and strategies suggest JB, but as it was JB's practice in his *QR* articles to refer to his own works, it is perhaps significant that there are no references in #359 to other articles by JB, nor is this article referred to in any of his later articles. JM III's Register: Barrow.

359 Beatson's *St. Helena*. Article 7, pp. 146–52. John Wilson Croker.
JWC claimed the article in four Clements Lib. lists; included in the Cambridge Univ. vols. JM III's Register.

360 Elphinstone's *Account of the Kingdom of Caubul*. Article 8, pp. 152–88. John Barrow and William Gifford.
NLS MS 3886 (ff. 261–2), JM to WS, 25 December 1815. JM MS, WG to JM [24 February 1816]. The article is cross-referenced in #435. JB systematically cross-referenced his articles. Note the discussion of the Himalayas (pp. 184–5), a topic that is JB's preserve. JM III's Register.

361 [Austen], *Emma*. Article 9, pp. 188–201. Walter Scott.
Todd and Bowden, *Sir Walter Scott: A Bibliographical History*. NLS MSS 3886 (ff. 261–2), JM to WS, 25 December 1815; 3887 (f. 17), WG to WS, 6 March 1816. JM MS, WS to JM, 19 January 1816. JM II's office copy. JM III's Register.

362 Wordsworth's *White Doe*. Article 10, pp. 201–25. William Rowe Lyall, probably.
JM MS, WG to JM [16 February 1816], may instead refer to #364. JM II's office copy: [pencil] 'Archdn Lyell'. JM III's Register: Lyall. Attributed to Whitaker in Nichols, 'Biographical Memoirs of Thomas Dunham Whitaker', p. xxix. At p. 211 the author refers to a legend given in Whitaker's history of Craven. The review is incorrectly attributed to John Keble by J. R. Griffin in 'John Keble and the *Quarterly Review*', *Review of Eng-*

lish Studies, 29 (November 1978), pp. 454–5 and in *John Keble, Saint of Anglicanism* (Macon, GA: Mercer University Press, 1987).

363 Tweddell's *Remains*. Article 11, pp. 225–36. Charles James Blomfield; subedited by Robert William Hay and probably with information from Lord Elgin.
JM MSS: WG to RWH [n.d.], 'I return Lord E[lgin]'s letter'; WG to RWH, 29 December 1815; WG to JM: [6 September 1815]; [13 February 1816]; [24 February 1816]. JM III's Register: Blomfield.

364 *Lives of Melancthon and Taylor* [by Bonney and Coxe]. Article 12, pp. 236–57. Thomas Dunham Whitaker.
JM MSS: book loans register, one of the books reviewed, Bonney's *Taylor*, was sent to 'Revd. Dr Whitaker' on 12 April 1815; it was returned by TDW on 15 November 1820; WG to JM [16 February 1816]; TDW to JM, 30 December 1815. Nichols, 'Biographical Memoirs of Thomas Dunham Whitaker', p. xxix. JM III's Register.

365 *Elgin*. Article 13, pp. 257–73. John Wilson Croker; subedited by Robert William Hay and probably with information from Lord Elgin.
JM MS, WG to RWH, 29 December 1815. *QR* Letters 169, 170. JWC claimed the article in three Clements Lib. lists; included in the Cambridge Univ. vols. JM III's Register: Croker.

VOLUME 14, NUMBER 28
(January 1816)
Published 18 May 1816[28]

366 Forbes's *Culloden Papers*. Article 1, pp. 283–333. Walter Scott.
Todd and Bowden, *Sir Walter Scott: A Bibliographical History*. JM II's office copy: 'Scott'. JM III's Register.

367 Alfieri's *Life and Writings*. Article 2, pp. 333–68. Robert Southey.
Curry and Dedmon, 'Southey's Contributions to the *Quarterly Review*'. JM III's Register.

368 Humboldt's *Travels*. Article 3, pp. 368–402. John Barrow.
BL Add. MS 34611 (f. 363), JB to Macvey Napier, 14 March 1816. The article is cross-referenced in #345, #394, #446, #505, and #590. JB systematically cross-referenced his articles. JM II's office copy. JM III's Register.

369 [Polwhele], *The Fair Isabel of Cotchele*. Article 4, pp. 402–5. Walter Scott.
Todd and Bowden, *Sir Walter Scott: A Bibliographical History*. *QR* Letter 69. Smiles, *Memoir*, vol. 1, p. 290. JM III's Register: '? Sir W Scott', and note, 'See a letter from Sir WS to JM (undated)'. The article begins: 'The valuable manuscript of the poem before us was inclosed, it seems, in a bureau of Mr. Walter Scott, which was "for some time inaccessible". ... The key, however, was at length luckily found, or a blacksmith procured; and the Cornish Romance emerged from the obscurity of its seclusion. ... In the drawer of this mystic cabinet were some papers belonging to Mr. Scott himself ...'

370 Beckmann's *A History of Inventions*. Article 5, pp. 405–29. John Barrow.
The author of #353 promised to continue this topic. JM III's Register.

371 Alison's *Sermons*. Article 6, pp. 429–43. William Rowe Lyall.
JM MS, book loans register, a review copy was sent to 'Wm Lyall' on 12 December 1815. JM III's Register. See #362.

372 Hobhouse's *Letters from Paris*. Article 7, pp. 443–52. John Wilson Croker.

JWC claimed the article in four Clements Lib. lists; included in the Cambridge Univ. vols. JM III's Register.

373 *Tombuctoo* [by Adams]. Article 8, pp. 453–75. John Barrow.
Timbuktu is spelled 'Tombuctoo' in the article's headnote and running title. The author's discussion of the Niger River and Lake Wangara and his argument that the Niger connects with the Nile (pp. 469–71) repeats #337 (pp. 140–51), #410 (pp. 317–19), #457 (pp. 347–9), and #544 (passim). The article is one in a series by JB in which he judges the veracity of a travel narrative, in this case favourably. Compare #383, on a similar topic. JM III's Register.

374 Leigh Hunt's *Rimini*. Article 9, pp. 473–81. John Wilson Croker.
JWC claimed the article in five Clements Lib. lists; included in the Cambridge Univ. vols. JM II's office copy. JM III's Register.

375 De Pradt's *Congrès de Vienne*. Article 10, pp. 481–505. Robert William Hay.
JM MSS: WG to RWH: 2 February 1816; [late March or early April 1816]. The author refers to #355. JM III's Register.

376 Lord Barrington's *Political Life*. Article 11, pp. 505–13. Henry Phillpotts, probably. JM III's Register.

377 Lord Elgin's *Collection of Sculptured Marbles*. Article 12, pp. 513–47. John Wilson Croker.
JWC claimed the article in four Clements Lib. lists; included in the Cambridge Univ. vols. JM II's office copy. JM III's Register.

VOLUME 15, NUMBER 29
(April 1816)
Published 10 August 1816[29]

378 La Roche Jaquelein – *La Vendée*[by Barante, Beauchamp, Bourniseaux, Bouvier-Desmortiers, Prudhomme, Rousselin, Turreau]. Article 1, pp. 1–69. Robert Southey.
Curry and Dedmon, 'Southey's Contributions to the *Quarterly Review*'. JM II's office copy. JM III's Register.

379 Milman's *Fazio*. Article 2, pp. 69–85. John Taylor Coleridge.
JM MS, WG to JM [13 February 1816]. JM II's office copy. JM III's Register.

380 Pottinger's *Travels in Beloochistan and Sinde*. Article 3, pp. 85–111. John Barrow.
JM MS, book loans register, a review copy was sent to 'John Barrow' on 4 May 1816 and returned 2 August 1816. The author states on p. 36 that the review is one in a series. Compare #237 and #360. JM III's Register.

381 Monk's *Alcestis*. Article 4, pp. 112–25. Charles James Blomfield, probably. JM III's Register.

382 [Scott], *The Antiquary*. Article 5, pp. 125–39. John Wilson Croker.
JM MS, JWC to JM, 3 June 1816. JWC claimed the article in three Clements Lib. lists; included in the Cambridge Univ. vols. JM II's office copy. JM III's Register.

383 *The Barbary States* [by Croker, Keatinge, Macgill, Smith]. Article 6, pp. 139–83. John Barrow.
JM MSS: book loans register, four of the works reviewed were sent to 'John Barrow' on 4 May 1816; JB to JM, 27 November 1814. Compare #373, on a similar topic. JM II's office copy. JM III's Register.

384 Lord Blayney's *Sequel to his Travels*. Article 7, pp. 183–7. John Wilson Croker.

JWC claimed the article in four Clements Lib. lists; included in the Cambridge Univ. vols. Compare #357, on the same topic. JM II's office copy. JM III's Register.

385 *The Poor* [by Prunelle, Weyland]. Article 8, pp. 187–235. Robert Southey.
Curry and Dedmon, 'Southey's Contributions to the *Quarterly Review*'. JM III's Register.

386 Malcolm's *History of Persia*. Article 9, pp. 236–92. Reginald Heber.
JM MSS RH to JM: 17 January 1816; 2 July 1816; 14 August 1816. [Heber], *Life of Reginald Heber*, vol. 1, pp. 418, 418n. JM II's office copy. JM III's Register.

VOLUME 15, NUMBER 30
(July 1816)
Published 12 November 1816[30]

387 *Travels of Ali Bey*. Article 1, pp. 299–345. Robert Southey.
Curry and Dedmon, 'Southey's Contributions to the *Quarterly Review*'. JM MS, book loans register, a review copy was sent to 'John Barrow' on 3 July 1815. JM II's office copy: 'Barrow'. It appears that JM II mixed up #387 and #389. The article's author says of Barrow what Barrow would never have said of himself, that, as a traveller (to South Africa and China), had he some of Ali Bey's spirit, he 'would have borne with him a sounder judgement and a more observant eye' (p. 345). JM III's Register.

388 Webster's *Waterloo*. Article 2, pp. 345–50. John Wilson Croker.
JWC claimed the article in four Clements Lib. lists; included in the Cambridge Univ. vols. Smiles, *Memoir*, vol. 1, p. 371n. JM II's office copy. JM III's Register.

389 *Missionary Chinese Works* [by Marshman, Morrison]. Article 3, pp. 350–75. John Barrow.
JM MS, JB to JM, 20 August 1816. *QR* Letter 173. The author of #142*WI* claims authorship of #85, #119, #147, #333, and #389. JB systematically cross-referenced his articles. JM II's office copy: [in pencil] 'Southey'. It appears that JM mixed up #387 and #389. JM III's Register: Barrow.

390 *Works of Mason*. Article 4, pp. 376–87. Thomas Dunham Whitaker.
JM MSS: WG to JM [13 February, 1816]; WG to JM [24 February, 1816]; TDW to JM, 9 October 1816. Nichols, 'Biographical Memoirs of Thomas Dunham Whitaker', p. xxix. JM III's Register.

391 *Insanity and Madhouses* [by Bakewell, Hill, Sharpe, Tuke]. Article 5, pp. 387–417. David Uwins, probably.
Compare the methodical *divisio* in this article with that of #483. Internal evidence suggests Uwin: the author, a medical man (p. 395), seems familiar with Edinburgh Infirmary (p. 391); he defends serious religion (p. 401); he faults democratizing expectations (p. 400); and he cites Morgagni (p. 402). The article is cross-referenced in #564 (twice). JM II's office copy. JM III's Register.

392 Rundall's *Symbolic Illustrations*. Article 6, pp. 418–19. Octavius Gilchrist, possibly.
Although the article is attributed to Croker by JM II and JM III (the latter derives his attribution from the former), Croker does not claim the article in any of his Clements Lib. lists and the article is not included in the Cambridge Univ. volumes of Croker's articles. This tentative attribution to OGG is based on JM MS, WG to OGG, 16 October 1816: 'you must finish your Art as soon as you conveniently can'. The article's brevity is suggestive of WG himself, or to a regular contributor to the *QR* whom WG would

have indulged. For that reason Croker is a good candidate, but an attribution to Croker amounts to a guess. JM II's office copy: [in pencil] 'Q[UER]Y Croker'. JM III's Register: Croker and note, 'Not mentioned in Mr Croker's own list'.

393 Chateaubriand's *Monarchy*. Article 7, pp. 419–40. John Wilson Croker.
JM MS, WG to JM [1816]. JWC claimed the article in four Clements Lib. lists; included in the Cambridge Univ. vols. JM III's Register. See #362.

394 Humboldt's *American Researches*. Article 8, pp. 440–68. John Barrow.
QR Letter 173. JM MSS: JB to JM, 20 August 1816; WG to JM [October 1816]. The author refers to #368. The article is cross-referenced in #505 and #590. JB systematically cross-referenced his articles. JM II's office copy. JM III's Register.

395 Hogg's *The Poetic Mirror*. Article 9, pp. 468–75. John Wilson Croker.
JWC claimed the article in five Clements Lib. lists (two entries are queried); included in the Cambridge Univ. vols. The author refers to #214 and #217. JM III's Register.

396 *Tracts on Baptismal Regeneration* [by Biddulph, Laurence, Mant, Scott]. Article 10, pp. 475–511. John Davison; subedited by John Keble.
Oriel College MS 10 (f. 992), JK to James E. Tyler, 4 September 1816. JM III's Register.

397 James's *Travels in Sweden, Prussia, &c.* Article 11, pp. 511–36. Robert William Hay.
JM MSS: WG to JM [October 1816]; WG to RWH [n.d.], states that RWH has done well to take up 'James'; WG to Hay [n.d.] 'Wednesday' [1812 w/mark], 'surprised and grieved at the idea that I destroyed your paper ... Nor did I intend to hurt Mr. James'. The author refers to #350. JM II's office copy. JM III's Register.

398 *Works on England* [by Anderson, Levis, M.***, Napea, Say, Silliman, Simond]. Article 12, pp. 537–74. Robert Southey.
Curry and Dedmon, 'Southey's Contributions to the *Quarterly Review*'. JM II's office copy: [in pencil] 'Southey'. JM III's Register.

VOLUME 16, NUMBER 31
(October 1816)
Published 11 February 1817[31]

399 Legh's *Narrative of a Journey in Egypt and Nubia*. Article 1, pp. 1–27. John Barrow.
JM MSS: book loans register, a review copy was sent to 'John Barrow' on 9 November 1816. The author refers to #472. JB systematically cross-referenced his articles. JM II's office copy. JM III's Register.

400 Counsellor Phillips's *Poems and Speeches*. Article 2, pp. 27–37. John Wilson Croker.
JWC claimed the article in five Clements Lib. lists; included in the Cambridge Univ. vols. JM III's Register.

401 Sumner's *Prize Essay*. Article 3, pp. 37–69. John Weyland, probably.
The Works and Correspondence of David Ricardo, ed. P. Sraffa, 10 vols (Cambridge: Cambridge University Press for the Royal Economic Society, 1951–5), vol. 7, p. 247, Ricardo to Hutches Trower, 26 January 1818, in regard to this article: 'Report says that Mr Weyland was the reviewer'. JM III's Register: D'Oyly.

402 Campbell's *Shipwreck and Voyage*. Article 4, pp. 69–85. John Barrow, probably.
On p. 82, using the example of Robert Adams of Pitcairn Island of *Bounty* mutiny fame, the author illustrates his idea that Christianity elevates women's morals. The identical

sentiment and illustration appear in #347 (p. 380). The author doubts the existence of cannibals (p. 80; cf. #68, #165, #170, #311, #347, #664). JM III's Register: Barrow.

403 Beckett's *Shakespeare's Himself Again!* Article 5, pp. 85–9. William Gifford, probably.
JM MS, book loans register, a review copy was sent to 'W. Gifford' on 20 January 1816. The article's brevity and caustic tone suggest WG. WG was an editor of Elizabethan texts. The article is cross-referenced in #462. JM II's office copy. JM III's Register.

404 *Tracts on Savings Banks* [by Duncan, Rose, Taylor]. Article 6, pp. 89–116. Robert Lundie.
JM MS, RL to JM, 15 July 1816. G. Duncan, *Memoir of the Rev. Henry Duncan* (Edinburgh: Oliphant, 1848), p. 95.

405 Cowper's *Poems and Life*. Article 7, pp. 116–29. William Sidney Walker.
Cambridge Lib., Add. MS 5492, I. 34, WSW to his parents, 18 June [1817], refers to his article on Cowper in the *QR*. Claimed for WSW in *The Poetical Remains of W.S.W. ... by J. Moultrie* (London: n.p.,1852). JM III's Register.

406 *Lord Selkirk, and the North-west Company* [by Amoretti, Selkirk]. Article 8, pp. 129–72. John Barrow.
The article is cross-referenced in #474, #585, and #625 as part of a series by the same author. JB systematically cross-referenced his articles. JM II's office copy. JM III's Register.

407 [Lord Byron], *Childe Harold, Canto III. – and other Poems*. Article 9, pp. 172–208. Walter Scott.
Todd and Bowden, *Sir Walter Scott: A Bibliographical History*. JM II's office copy. JM III's Register.

408 Warden's *Conversations with Buonaparte*. Article 10, pp. 208–24. John Wilson Croker.
JM MS, JWC to JM, 18 September 1816. JWC claimed the article in four Clements Lib. lists; included in the Cambridge Univ. vols. The author refers to #281, #321, and #355. The author of #661 indicates his article is one in a series: #408, #418, and #439. JM II's office copy. JM III's Register.

409 *Parliamentary Reform*. Article 11, pp. 225–78. Robert Southey; with excisions by William Gifford.
Curry and Dedmon, 'Southey's Contributions to the *Quarterly Review*'. JM III's Register.

VOLUME 16, NUMBER 32
(January 1817)
Published 17 May 1817[32]

410 Riley's *Shipwreck, and Captivity, &c.* Article 1, pp. 287–321. John Barrow.
The author refers to #337. The article is cross-referenced in #431, twice in #457, and in #531. JB systematically cross-referenced his articles. The author's discussion of the Niger River and Lake Wangara and his argument that the Niger connects with the Nile (pp. 317–19) is identical with the discussion in #337 (pp. 140–51), #373 (pp. 469–71), #431 (pp. 325–7), #457 (pp. 347–9), and #544 (*passim*).

411 *Ambrosian Manuscripts*. Article 2, pp. 321–37. Charles James Blomfield, probably.
Note the ostentatious display of classical learning characteristic of CJB. JM III's Register.

412 Miss Plumptre's *Narrative of a Residence in Ireland*. Article 3, pp. 337–44. John Wilson Croker.

JM MS, JWC to JM, 14 May 1817. Leeds WYL250 8 66a, WG to George Canning, 25 October 1816. JWC claimed the article in five Clements Lib. lists; included in the Cambridge Univ. vols. Smiles, *Memoir*, vol. 2, p. 44. JM III's Register.

413 Koster's *Travels in Brazil*. Article 4, pp. 344–87. Robert Southey; with excisions by William Gifford.

Curry and Dedmon, 'Southey's Contributions to the *Quarterly Review*'. *Selections from the Letters of Robert Southey*, vol. 3, p. 484, vol. 4, p. 520. JM III's Register.

414 Miss Porden's *Veils, a Poem*. Article 5, pp. 387–96. Author not identified.

Perhaps Francis Cohen, who in the *QR* took an interest in occult knowledge, the general topic of this article. The author, however, is not sympathetic to the material. The article is as much about Darwin as it is about Porden. The article is in Croker's style, but it is not claimed by him in any of his lists preserved at the Clements Library.

415 *Chinese Drama – Lord Amherst's Embassy*. Article 6, pp. 396–416. John Barrow.

The article is cross-referenced in #438. JB systematically cross-referenced his articles. Twice the author quotes Barrow (pp. 401, 421). There are frequent references in the article to JB's friend, George Staunton. The description of Amherst's Chinese embassy in #438 at p. 489 resembles the description in this article at p. 410.

416 Repton's *Fragments on Landscape Gardening*. Article 7, pp. 416–30. Author not identified.

417 [Scott], *Tales of My Landlord*. Article 8, pp. 430–80. Walter Scott; subedited by William Erskine.

Todd and Bowden, *Sir Walter Scott: A Bibliographical History*. JM II's office copy. JM III's Register.

418 *Buonaparte's Appeal to the British Nation* [by Barnes, Napoleon, Santini]. Article 9, pp. 480–511. John Wilson Croker.

JWC claimed the article in three Clements Lib. lists; included in the Cambridge Univ. vols. The author of #661 indicates his article is one in a series: #408, #418, and #439. JM II's office copy. JM III's Register.

419 *Rise and Progress of Popular Disaffection* [by Hermit of Marlow (Shelley)]. Article 10, pp. 511–52. Robert Southey.

Curry and Dedmon, 'Southey's Contributions to the *Quarterly Review*'. JM III's Register.

VOLUME 17, NUMBER 33
(April 1817)
Published 6 September 1817[33]

420 *Accounts of the Tonga Islands* [by Burney, Martin]. Article 1, pp. 1–39. Robert Southey.

Curry and Dedmon, 'Southey's Contributions to the *Quarterly Review*'. JM III's Register.

421 Stewart's *Dissertation*. Article 2, pp. 39–72. William Rowe Lyall, probably.

JM III's Register: Lyall, and note, 'on the authority of his nephew Canon Pearson'.

422 Raffles's *History of Java*. Article 3, pp. 72–96. John Barrow, probably.

The author refers to #178, a review on the same topic as #422. The reviewer quotes with approval a passage from #178. The article's author also refers to #353. JB systematically cross-referenced his articles.

423 Edgeworth's *Comic Dramas*. Article 4, pp. 96–107. Charles Robert Maturin.
JM MSS: CRM to JM: 27 September 1817; 3 October 1817; 28 January 1818. The evidence for Maturin is unassailable. Claimed by John Wilson Croker in three Clements Lib. lists; included in the Cambridge Univ. vols. Note, however, that in these lists Croker mistakenly claims #42 (on Edgeworth's *Tales*). Apparently he misremembered having written all of the *QR*'s Edgeworth reviews. Also, while the review appears in two of his comprehensive lists, it does not appear on a third list that is demonstrably later and more complete.

424 *East India College* [by Malthus, Wellesley]. Article 5, pp. 107–54. Robert William Hay, possibly.
JM MS, WG to RWH, 1 September 1817.

425 Hazlitt's *Round Table*. Article 6, pp. 154–9. John Taylor Coleridge, probably.
JM MS, book loans register, a review copy was sent to 'J. T. Coleridge' on 14 July 1817 and returned 21 August 1817. Internet auction sale item, 2 March 2004, holograph MS letter: JTC to an unidentified correspondent, 23 October 1817, returns review copies, states, 'The Round Table has already met its due castigation; and I found that nothing was to be made, at least I could make nothing worth sending you on Harold the Dauntless ...'. Smiles, *Memoir*, vol. 2, p. 44. JM III's Register: [in pencil] '? A Mr Russell in [Smiles's] memoir'.

426 Clarke's *Travels – Vols. III. and IV.* Article 7, pp. 160–217. Reginald Heber.
JM MSS: book loans register, volume III of Clarke's *Travels* was sent to 'Rev. R. Heber' on 19 September 1816 and returned 29 July 1817; volumes IV and V were sent to 'Rev. R. Heber' on 9 June 1817; cash day book 1817–19, p. 36, dated 10 June 1817, 'Carriage of Parcel to Rev. R. Heber'; RH to JM: 2 July 1816; 14 August 1816.

427 [Croly], *Paris in 1815. A Poem.* Article 8, pp. 218–29. John Wilson Croker.
JWC claimed the article in four Clements Lib. lists; included in the Cambridge Univ. vols. JM III's Register.

428 Péron – *Voyage de Découvertes. Tome II.* Article 9, pp. 229–48. John Barrow.
The author refers to #104, a review of the first volume of this work; it is a continuation of its arguments, especially its promotion of Captain Flinders. JB systematically cross-referenced his articles. JM III's Register: Barrow.

429 [Sheil], *The Tragic Drama. – The Apostate.* Article 10, pp. 248–60. Charles Robert Maturin; with significant edits by William Gifford.
JM MS, WG to JM [1817; notation in another hand, 'Maturin's Review of Shiell's Apostate']. NLS MS 866 (ff. 145–6), JM to WS, 27 May 1817. JM MS, CRM to JM, 3 October 1817. JM III's Register.

430 *France*, by Lady Morgan. Article 11, pp. 260–86. John Wilson Croker and William Gifford; subedited by John Hookham Frere.
JM MSS: JHF to JM [n.d.; pencil notation in JM II's hand: '*QR* 33 Art 11']; WG to JM [1817; erroneous notation in another hand, '1819–20']. *QR* Letter 180. Iowa MS (f. 142), WG to JM [n.d.]. JWC claimed the article in four Clements Lib. lists; included in the Cambridge Univ. vols. The author refers to #412 (specific ref. on p. 261n). Proofs of part of the article and part of the manuscript in JWC's hand are preserved in the JM Archive. *The Correspondence and Diaries of the Right Honourable John Wilson Croker, LL.D., F.R.S., Secretary to the Admiralty from 1809 to 1830*, ed. L. J. Jennings, 3 vols (London: John Murray, 1884), vol. 1, p. 102. JM III's Register: Croker, citing unspecified letters, and note, [in pencil] '? Frere. See his letter here enclosed'.

VOLUME 17, NUMBER 34
(July 1817)
Published 1 December 1817[34]

431　*History of Discoveries in Africa* [by Murray]. Article 1, pp. 299–338. John Barrow.
JM MS, JB to JM: 25 August 1817; 1 September 1817. The reviewer surveys the disastrous 1816 Niger expedition under Major Peddie that was organized by JB and others. The author's discussion of Lake Wangara and the Niger River and his argument that the Niger connects with the Nile (pp. 325–7) is identical with discussion of the topic in #337 (pp. 140–51), #373 (pp. 469–71), #410 (pp. 317–19), #457 (pp. 347–9), and #544 (passim). JM III's Register.

432　Heber's *Bampton Lectures*. Article 2, pp. 338–47. George D'Oyly.
D'Oyly, *Sermons*, vol. 1, p. 24.

433　*History of Hofer. – Transactions in the Tyrol* [by Forster]. Article 3, pp. 347–69. John Hookham Frere, probably; probably with materials from Samuel Taylor Coleridge.

434　Malthus *on Population*. Article 4, pp. 369–403. John Bird Sumner.
JM MSS: WG to JM, 21 September 1817; TRM to JM, 1 December 1817. D. Ricardo, *Letters of David Ricardo and Hutches Trower and others: 1811–23*, ed. J. Bonar and J. H. Hollander (Oxford: Clarendon Press, 1899), pp. 46–7, 47n.

435　*Himalaya Mountains, and Lake Manasawara* [by Colebrooke, Moorcroft]. Article 5, pp. 403–41. John Barrow.
JM MS, JB to JM, 1 September 1817. The author refers to #360. The article is cross-referenced in #529 (three times). JB systematically cross-referenced his articles. JM III's Register.

436　*French Theatres*. Article 6, pp. 441–51. John Wilson Croker.
JWC claimed the article in five Clements Lib. lists; included in the Cambridge Univ. vols. JM III's Register.

437　Chalmers – *On the Christian Revelation*. Article 7, pp. 451–63. Thomas Dunham Whitaker.
JM MSS: book loans register, a review copy was sent to 'Revd. Dr Whitaker' on 9 June [1817?]; cash day book 1817–19, p. 36, dated 10 June 1817, 'Carriage of Parcel to / Rev. Dr Whitaker'; earlier, a review copy was sent to 'Rev. D'Oyley', on 1 February 1817; John Barrow to JM, 25 August 1817. Nichols, 'Biographical Memoirs of Thomas Dunham Whitaker', p. xxix.

438　*Embassy to China* [by Ellis]. Article 8, pp. 463–506. John Barrow.
JM MSS: JB to JM, 25 August 1817; JB to JM 2 September 1817; WG to JM, 21 September 1817. The author refers to #415. JB systematically cross-referenced his articles. JM III's Register.

439　O'Meara's *Answer to Mr. Warden*. Article 9, pp. 506–30. John Wilson Croker.
JWC claimed the article in four Clements Lib. lists; included in the Cambridge Univ. vols. The author refers to #418, which is also by JWC. The author of #661 indicates his article is one in a series: #408, #418, and #439. JM III's Register.

440　*Spain and her Colonies* [by Pradt]. Article 10, pp. 530–62. Richard Wellesley and William Jacob; OR Richard Wellesley alone; OR William Jacob alone.
JM MSS: RW [to JM], 28 August 1817; RW [to JM], 3 October 1817; WJ to JM, 5 October 1817. JM III's Register: [in pencil] '? R Wellesley'.

VOLUME 18, NUMBER 35
(October 1817)
Published 21 February 1818[35]

441 Lord Holland's *Life and Writings of Lope de Vega*. Article 1, pp. 1–46. Robert Southey. Curry and Dedmon, 'Southey's Contributions to the *Quarterly Review*'. JM III's Register.

442 Wilks's *Sketches of the South of India*. Article 2, pp. 47–73. John Barrow. The author refers to #160 and #442. The author of #160 promised to review Wilks's additional volumes when published. JB systematically cross-referenced his articles. The author states that he is a friend of the late Sir George Staunton. Staunton was JB's patron and JB was the close friend of Staunton's son.

443 *Lives of Haydn and Mozart* [by Stendhal]. Article 3, pp. 73–99. Isaac D'Israeli, possibly; possibly with John Ireland. JM MS, WG to JM [1818 w/mark], 'I cannot complete the revise until I receive Mr. D'Israeli. I wished Dr Ireland to see it'. Note the comment on p. 80: 'We knew Haydn, and well remember the circumstance of his sitting for the picture' (i.e., Joshua Reynolds's portrait). The author has access to Haydn's correspondence (see p. 97). Note reflections on the nature of biography (pp. 82, 91), an interest of ID'I's. The article is not by Burney. Burney would not have written the statement on p. 98, 'the history of man appears to us more interesting than that of music', and probably not '... music and musical instruments of the ancients; a subject that is still involved in considerable obscurity, notwithstanding Dr Burney's acute and elaborate investigation' (p. 87).

444 Southey's *History of Brazil. – Vol. II*. Article 4, pp. 99–128. Reginald Heber. JM MS, book loans register, a review copy was sent to 'Revd. R. Heber' on 9 June 1817. Smiles, *Memoir*, vol. 2, p. 38. [Heber], *Life of Reginald Heber*, vol. 1, pp. 456, 456n, 482. JM III's Register.

445 Bentham's *Plan of Parliamentary Reform*. Article 5, pp. 128–35. Robert William Hay, possibly. RWH appears to have had an article in this Number. JM MSS: WG to Hay: 1 September 1817; 5 January 1818.

446 Humboldt's *Travels. – Part II*. Article 6, pp. 135–58. John Barrow. The author refers to #368 and #394. The article is cross-referenced in #474, #503, #585, and #705. JB systematically cross-referenced his articles.

447 Sir William Adams *on Cataract*. Article 7, pp. 158–68. Author not identified.

448 Savigny's *Naufrage de la Méduse*. Article 8, pp. 168–76. John Barrow, possibly. There author refers to #438. JB systematically cross-referenced his articles.

449 Godwin's *Mandeville*. Article 9, pp. 176–7. John Wilson Croker. JWC claimed the article in six Clements Lib. lists; included in the Cambridge Univ. vols. JM III's Register.

450 Kendall's *Appeal of Murder and Trial by Battle*. Article 10, pp. 177–98. Author not identified. The article reflects on the case of Abraham Thornton (*c.* 1793–1860) who, in 1817–19, was tried twice on the same murder charge. See the *ODNB* entry on Thornton; see also J. Hall, *Trial of Abraham Thornton* (1926). Leeds WYL250 8 66a, WG to George Canning, 27 March [1818 w/mark] 'I will take care to let our coy friend know your opinion. He is now in Scotland ... He was, of course, handsomely paid'.

451 *On the Polar Ice and Northern Passage into the Pacific* [by Chapell]. Article 11, pp. 199–223. John Barrow.

JM MS, WG to JM [1818]. The article is cross-referenced in #474, #503, #585, and #705. JB systematically cross-referenced his articles. Smiles, *Memoir*, vol. 2, pp. 45, 45n. Barrow, *Auto-Biographical Memoir*, pp. 505–6, 506n. JM III's Register.

452 M. C. Malo – *Panorama d' Angleterre*. Article 12, pp. 223–9. John Wilson Croker.

JWC claimed the article in five Clements Lib. lists; included in the Cambridge Univ. vols. JM III's Register: Croker.

453 *Life of Richard Watson, Bishop of Llandaff.* Article 13, pp. 229–53. Thomas Dunham Whitaker.

JM MSS: book loans register, 'Bishop Burnet's Memorial' was sent to 'Revd. Dr Whitaker' on 12 April 1815. On pp. 230, 259–60, the author compares Burnet and Watson. JM MS, WG to JM [August 1818]. Nichols, 'Biographical Memoirs of Thomas Dunham Whitaker', p. xxix. JM III's Register.

VOLUME 18, NUMBER 36
(January 1818)
Published 9 June 1818[36]

454 *On the Poor Laws* [by Sheffield]. Article 1, pp. 259–308. John Rickman; assisted by Robert Southey.

Not in RS's definitive list published in Curry and Dedmon, 'Southey's Contributions to the *Quarterly Review*'. JM MS, cash day book, 1817–18, p. 186: 'Quarterly Review No. 36 ... Recomposing RS 2 sheets 5£'. JM MS, WG to John Taylor Coleridge [4 April; 1818 p/mark]. 'Some Unpublished Letters of Robert Southey', *Blackwood's Edinburgh Magazine*, 164 (August 1898), pp. 167–85, Curry. *NL*, vol. 2, pp. 178, 317, and N. L. Kaderly, 'Southey and the Quarterly Review', *Modern Language Notes* 70: 4 (April, 1955), pp. 261–3 show that JR wished not to be known by the *QR* editorial coterie as the author of this review, that he had RS present his review to WG, and that WG and JM mistakenly believed the article was from RS himself. JM III's Register: Southey.

455 Hall's *Account of the Loo-choo Islands*. Article 2, pp. 308–24. John Barrow, probably.

Shine (*The Quarterly Review Under Gifford*, p. 59) demonstrates that in ascribing the article to [Walter] Hamilton, JM III in his so-called 'Register' mistook a reference in JM MS, WG to JM [June 1818] as applying to #455 that points instead to the authorship of #457. JM MS, WG to JM [June 1818], 'I wish you would look at the Revise – you can form a better guess than I can whether what I have struck out, will leave room for the insertion of those parts of Mr Hamilton's MS which are no[t] crossed. If not – the note on the Memnon on p. 308 [actually p. 368] must be struck out ...The note is certainly creditable to Mr Hamilton's judgment and taste'. The author of the article quotes from JB's *Travels* and refers to articles on the same topic, #428, #438, and #446. JB systematically cross-referenced his articles. JM MSS: book loans register, a review copy was sent to 'W Jacob' on 14 July 1817. No additional evidence has been identified to support an attribution to Jacob. JM III's Register: 'Mr Hamilton'.

456 *'Foliage'*, by Leigh Hunt. Article 3, pp. 324–55. John Taylor Coleridge.

JM MSS: WG to JTC [4 April 1818 p/mark]; 24 April 1818. The evidence for Coleridge is unassailable. J. W. Croker claimed the article in two Clements Lib. lists; however, in what is demonstrably the later of these two lists, the entry is first queried and then crossed out. The article is not included in the Cambridge Univ. Lib. volumes of Croker's articles. JM III's Register: 'J. W. Croker', citing unspecified letters.

457 *The Congo Expedition – African Discoveries* [by Tuckey]. Article 4, pp. 335–79. John Barrow; with materials from Henry Salt and William Hamilton.
   JM MSS: WG to JM [June 1818]; JB to JM, 17 November 1818. The author refers to #337 (twice) and makes two references to JB. The article is cross-referenced in #472 (twice), #531 (three times), and in #578. JB systematically cross-referenced his articles. *The Life and Correspondence of Henry Salt*, 2vols (London: H. Bentley, 1834), vol. 1, p. 491 states, 'compiled from documents sent over by Mr Salt'. JM III's Register: ' – Salt (Consul in Egypt)'.

458 [Shelley], *Frankenstein, or the Modern Prometheus*. Article 5, pp. 379–85. John Wilson Croker.
   JWC claimed the article in six Clements Lib. lists; included in the Cambridge Univ. vols. *QR* Letter 190. JM III's Register.

459 *Origin and State of the Indian Army* [by Williams]. Article 6, pp. 385–423. John Malcolm.
   JM MSS: Walter Hamilton (of Liverpool) to JM, 15 May 1818; WG to JM [June 1818]. JM III's Register.

460 Douglas *on the Passage of Rivers*. Article 7, pp. 423–31. Walter Scott; with assistance from an unidentified person.
   Todd and Bowden, *Sir Walter Scott: A Bibliographical History*. *QR* Letter 188. JM III's Register.

461 Burney – *Behring's Strait and the Polar Basin*. Article 8, pp. 431–58. John Barrow.
   The article is one in a series by JB on Arctic exploration. The article is cross-referenced in #503 (twice) and in #667. JB systematically cross-referenced his articles. JM III's Register. In the running title, Bering Strait is rendered as above.

462 Hazlitt's *Characters of Shakespear's Plays*. Article 9, pp. 458–66. William Gifford, possibly.
   The reviewer taunts Hazlitt for his association with the working class and attacks his politics and morals. The author refers to #403, which was probably written by WG. Shakespeare is spelled in the article's running title as above.

463 *Account of the Pindarries* [by Saabye]. Article 10, pp. 466–80. William Jerdan; possibly subedited by John Barrow.
   Leeds WYL250 8 66a: WG to George Canning, 21 February 1818; same to same, 28 February 1818, sends the whole of Jerdan's proofs. *The Autobiography of William Jerdan*, 3 vols (London: Hall, Virtue, 1852–3), vol. 3, p. 55. The author states in the article's opening sentence, 'The rise and progress of the Mahratta States have been fully detailed by us in the course of our critical labour from more elaborate works than the little volume before us'. Articles that appeared before this on India include #160, #273, and #442. But the article is not in John Barrow's manner, and the opening sentence can be seen as apologetic. Because it was WG's usual practice to have articles subedited by specialists, it is possible that JB looked at the article before its publication and that he added the first sentence.

464 *Ancient and Modern Greenland*. Article 11, pp. 480–96. Francis Cohen.
   JM MS, WG to JM [18 May 1818]. F. Palgrave, *Collected Historical Works*. Smiles, *Memoir*, vol. 2, pp. 46–7. JM III's Register.

465 *Ecclesiastical Computation of Easter*. Article 12, pp. 496–502. Alexander Boswell, probably.

JM MS, WG to JM [May–June 1818], 'What if between Greenland and Pindarries, we place Boswell (if he can be got ready)'.

466 Kirkton's *History of the Church of Scotland*. Article 13, pp. 502–41. Walter Scott.
Todd and Bowden, *Sir Walter Scott: A Bibliographical History*. NLS MS 852 (ff. 56–7), WS to JM, 15 May [1818] (copy). JM III's Register.

VOLUME 19, NUMBER 37
(April 1818)
Published 26 September 1818[37]

467 Evelyn's *Memoirs*. Article 1, pp. 1–54. Robert Southey.
Curry and Dedmon, 'Southey's Contributions to the *Quarterly Review*'. JM III's Register.

468 Birkbeck's *Notes on America*. Article 2, pp. 54–78. John Barrow and William Gifford.
JM MSS: WG to JM: 19 July [1818]; Ramsgate [August 1818]; Ramsgate, 4 August 1818; [1818 p/mark], 'I have not had … the last revise of Birkbeck which I sent to Mr. B to look at'. The author refers to p. 532 of #282. JB systematically cross-referenced his articles. Smiles, *Memoir*, vol. 2, p. 51. JM III's Register: [in pencil] '?Barrow and Gifford'.

469 *On the Means of Improving the People* [by Bennet, Courtenay, Myers, Nicoll]. Article 3, pp. 79–118. John Rickman; assisted by Robert Southey.
Not in RS's definitive list published in Curry and Dedmon, 'Southey's Contributions to the *Quarterly Review*'. *Life and Correspondence of Robert Southey*, ed. C. C. Southey, 6 vols (London: Longman, et al., 1849–50), vol. 3, pp. 361–2. *Selections from the Letters of Robert Southey*, vol. 3, p. 100. O. Williams, *Lamb's Friend the Census-Taker: Life and Letters of John Rickman* (London: Constable, 1911), pp. 10, 124, 134, 195–204. JM III's Register: Southey.

470 Walpole's *Letters to Mr. Montagu*. Article 4, pp. 118–34. Walter Scott.
Todd and Bowden, *Sir Walter Scott: A Bibliographical History*. JM MS, WG to JM [4 August 1818 p/mark]. NLS MS 3889 (ff. 38–9), JM to WS, 17 March 1818. NLS MS 852 (f. 55), WS to JM, 26 April [1818] (copy). NLS MS 3889 (ff. 79–80), WG to WS, 30 April 181[8]. JM III's Register: 'J W Croker', citing unspecified letters; 'Sir W Scott' citing unspecified letters, and note, 'Not mentioned in Mr Croker's own list'.

471 Wilson's *Military and Political Power of Russia*. Article 5, pp. 131–77. Reginald Heber.
JM MS, WG to JM [4 August 1818 p/mark]. Smiles, *Memoir*, vol. 2, pp. 77–8. JM III's Register: [in pencil] '? Reg Heber'.

472 Light's *Travels in Egypt, Nubia, &c*. Article 6, pp. 178–204. John Barrow; with materials from Henry Salt.
JM MSS: book loans register, a review copy was sent to 'John Barrow' on 9 November 1816; WG to JM [1818 p/mark], 'I have not had Mr. B's review of Light'; JB to JM, 24 July 1818. The author refers to #399 and, twice, to #457. The author of #514 cites the note on p. 195. The article is cross-referenced in #486 (twice) and in #563. JB systematically cross-referenced his articles. The reviewer mentions a manuscript of Henry Salt's (p. 195). *Life and Correspondence of Henry Salt*, vol. 1, p. 491. JM III's Register: Barrow.

473 Keats's *Endymion*. Article 7, pp. 204–48. John Wilson Croker.
JWC's holograph manuscript of this article is in the JM Archive. JWC claimed the article in six Clements Lib. lists; included in the Cambridge Univ. vols. JM III's Register.

474 O'Reilly's *Voyage to Davis's Strait*. Article 8, pp. 208–14. John Barrow.

The article is one in a series by JB on Arctic exploration. The author refers to #406 and #451. The article is cross-referenced in #503. JB systematically cross-referenced his articles. The author has access to official Admiralty documents (pp. 208–10). JM III's Register.

475 Byron, *Childe Harold. – Canto IV.* Article 9, pp. 215–32. Walter Scott.

Todd and Bowden, *Sir Walter Scott: A Bibliographical History*. JM MS, WG to JM [Ramsgate, August 1818 p/mark]. NLS MSS: 3889 (ff. 79–80), WG to WS, 30 April 1818; 852 (ff. 56–7), WS to JM, 15 May [1818]; 3889 (ff. 185–6), JM to WS, 3 September 1818.

476 Walpole's *Memoirs on Turkey*. Article 10, pp. 233–46. Charles James Blomfield.

JM MSS: WG to JM: Ryde, 19 July [1818]; Ramsgate, 6 August [1818]. JM III's Register: '? 10 Bp Blomfield (London)'.

477 [Barrett], *Woman: a Poem*. Article 11, pp. 246–50. John Taylor Coleridge.

JM MSS: WG to JM: Ramsgate, August 1818; Ramsgate [August 1818 p/mark]. JM III's Register.

478 Bellamy's *Translation of the Bible*. Article 12, pp. 250–80. George D'Oyly.

JM MSS: book loans register, a review copy was sent to the 'Rev. D'Oyly' on 17 May 1817; WG to JM: [1818], 'I send you Bellamy for D'Oyly'; Ramsgate [August 1818 p/mark]. JM III's Register: D'Oyly, citing unspecified letters, and note, 'See G D'O's letter Oct 30/18'.

VOLUME 19, NUMBER 38
(July 1818)
Published 2 February 1819[38]

479 [Henderson], *Iceland*. Article 1, pp. 291–321. John Barrow, possibly; possibly with Robert Southey.

JM MSS: WG to JM: 24 July 1818; 6 August [1818; annotation on letter in another hand suggests '*QR* No. 38, Art. 1'.]; [Ramsgate, 6 August 1818, p/mark]. In content, structure, and language the article resembles Robert Southey, not JB: the article is more analytical than descriptive (the former RS's, the latter JB's usual manner); the author's interest is political and social, not anthropological and geographical (the former RS's, the latter JB's usual interests). Note also sentiments characteristic of RS, not of JB: the emphasis on religious language and a 'moral' view (p. 292); concern for pastoral care (p. 298); an interest in the Sabbath (p. 299); a concern over the prevalence of 'popish' religion (p. 301). As it was JB's signature practice in his *QR* articles to refer to his own works, it is relevant that the article contains no references to works by him and yet, twice, the author refers to #182, an article by RS on Iceland. However, the article is not in Southey's definitive MS list of his *QR* articles published in Curry and Dedmon, 'Southey's Contributions to the *Quarterly Review*', and, moreover, Shine quotes the following letter that appears to rule out a contribution by RS to this Number: BL Add. MS 28603, RS to William Peachey, 9 February 1819: 'there is nothing of mine in the last Quarterly' (*The Quarterly Review Under Gifford*). *QR* Number 38, the most recent issue, was published 2 February 1819. A series of letters preserved at the Bodl. also appears to preclude RS. Bodl. Lib. MS Eng. Lett. d.47 (ff. 128–9), RS to Grosvenor Bedford, 28 November 1818, speaks of Copyright (#502) and the Catacombs (#507) as the two articles he is presently working on, that when he completes them he will write nothing more for the

QR for the next six months; d.47 (ff. 134), RS to Bedford [30 January 1819], says that WG has postponed both of his articles for a future Number; d.47 (ff. 136–7), RS to Bedford, 8 February 1819, is disappointed in the current Number of the *QR*. He does not mention having contributed an article to the issue. JM III's Register: '? Barrow', and note, 'See letter of J B July 24'.

480 [Maturin], *Women: By The author of 'Bertram'.* Article 2, pp. 321–8. John Wilson Croker.
JWC claimed the article in six Clements Lib. lists; included in the Cambridge Univ. vols. JM III's Register.

481 Milman's *Samor.* Article 3, pp. 328–47. John Taylor Coleridge.
JM MSS: WG to JTC, 7 January 1819; JTC to WG, 22 January 1822. Bodl. Lib. MS Eng. Lett. d.130 (ff. 13–14), Thomas Arnold to JTC, 5 February 1819. JM MS, WG to JTC, 12 March 1819, Friday.

482 Fulton – *Torpedos, Steam-Boats, &c.* Article 4, pp. 347–57. John Barrow.
JM MS, WG to JM, 6 August [1818]. The author has personal knowledge of official Admiralty proceedings (pp. 350–1). The article is cross-referenced in #54*WI*. JB systematically cross-referenced his articles. 'Torpedoes' is spelled in the running title as above.

483 *History of Small-Pox and Vaccination* [by Moore]. Article 5, pp. 357–75. David Uwins.
JM MS, WG to JM, [4 August 1818 p/mark].

484 Sir R. Phillips *on the Phenomena of the Universe.* Article 6, pp. 375–9. Author not identified.

485 Brown's *Northern Courts.* Article 7, pp. 379–90. Author not identified.
The author speaks authoritatively in defence of government ministers and diplomats (including Pitt and Canning). A number of the works alluded to in the article were reviewed by Reginald Heber (#51, #76, #471). The subject of #342, by Croker, Wraxall's spurious Memoirs, is alluded to in the article. But there is no indication in any of Croker's Clements Lib. lists that he wrote #485.

486 [Davison], *Antiquities of Egypt.* Article 8, pp. 391–424. John Barrow and Thomas Young; with materials from Henry Salt.
Young's list. TY's translation of the inscription on the Sphinx appears on pp. 411–12. JM MS, JB to JM, 17 November 1818, states that he and TY want proofs of Greek inscriptions (see pp. 411–15), to ensure that they are correct. The author refers to #472 (twice). The article is cross-referenced in #536, #563 (twice), and #651. JB systematically cross-referenced his articles. JM III's Register: [in dark ink] 'Dr Young' [in lighter ink, and superscript] '? and Barrow'.

487 Hazlitt's *Lectures on the English Poets.* Article 9, pp. 424–34. Eaton Stannard Barrett.
JM MSS: WG to JM: [Ramsgate, August 1818 p/mark], 'Mr Barrett's parcel'; [Ramsgate, 4 August 1818 p/mark]

488 *Cambridge Botanical Professorship* [by Smith]. Article 10, pp. 434–46. George D'Oyly, probably.
JM MS, WG to JM [1818]. Linnaean Society MS, Sir James Smith correspondence (12.84), Samuel Goodenough, Bishop of Carlisle, to Sir James Smith, discusses a rumour that D'Oyly wrote the review, but he 'cannot think it possible, that so very Gentlemanly and quiet a man as D'Oyly, should overhand apply to you for information of which he has made material use, and underhand attack you in the dark, anonymously in a Review'. A footnote in the article that discusses Cambridge Univ. policy would more likely come from a Cambridge than an Oxford man.

489 Bellamy's *Reply to the Quarterly Review.* Article 11, pp. 446–60. William Goodhugh.

JM MS, William Goodhugh to JM, 24 December 1835. Laing MSS, vol. 2, pp. 784–5, WG to Lord John Russell, 1 June 1839. Claimed for Goodhugh in the *ODNB* article on him (that also, incorrectly, attributes #546 to him). JM III's Register: 'Goodhugh'.

490 Dangeau's *Mémoires de Louis XIV.* Article 12, pp. 460–78. John Wilson Croker.
JWC claimed the article in six Clements Lib. lists; included in the Cambridge Univ. vols. JM III's Register.

491 Sir R. Wilson's *Letter to the Borough Electors.* Article 13, pp. 478–92. William Carr Beresford; with material supplied by Arthur Wellesley, Duke of Wellington.
Southampton MS WP/1/613/4, James Stanhope to the Duke of Wellington, 2 January 1819.

492 Mr. Brougham. – *Education Committee.* Article 14, pp. 492–569. James Henry Monk and George Canning; with excisions and an insertion by John Wilson Croker; vetted by Charles Manners-Sutton, and others.
JM MSS: Thomas Mitchell to JM, 29 May 1820 [JM II's notation: '*QR* 38 last article'.]; C.J. Monk to JM III, 25 March 1875. *QR* Letters 195, 197–215, 268. JWC claimed the article in four Clements Lib. lists; in what appears to be the latest of these lists, his contribution is noted as partial. [Anon.], 'Edinburgh Critics and Quarterly Reviewers', *Athenaeum*, 2473 (20 March 1875), pp. 393–5. JM III's Register: 'Rev Prof Monk (in part)', and note [in pencil], 'Canning – Croker and Gifford assisting'.

VOLUME 20, NUMBERS 39 and 40
GENERAL INDEX to Numbers 1 to 38
(1820)
Published: Part I: 20 May 1820
Part II: June 1820[39]

VOLUME 21, NUMBER 41
(January 1819)
Published 4 June 1819[40]

493 Bristed – *Statistical View of America.* Article 1, pp. 1–25. John Barrow, probably.
It appears that a review of this work by William Jacob was received and set up, but it was cancelled at the last moment in favour of JB's. JM MSS: book loans register, 'W. Jacob' was sent a number of works on America, including 'North America by a North American', on 10 February 1818 and 5 December 1818; cash day book, 1818–20, p. 107: 'Quarterly Review No. 41 … Cancelled [pages], Bristed 16 1/4'; book loans register, a review copy was sent to 'John Barrow' on 16 January 1818. The author quotes a passage from #282. JB systematically cross-referenced his articles. The virulent characterization of 'Jacobinism' is typical of JB. Compare 'polluted trash of our Jacobinical press … irreligious and levelling principles of the Jacobins' (p. 19) with 'the scum and feculence of the worst Jacobinical journals' (#482, p. 356n). JM III's Register: 'W. Jacob Senr'.

494 Wilkins's *Translation of Vitruvius.* Article 2, pp. 25–40. Edward Copleston, possibly.
JM MS, EC to JM, 26 March 1819, encloses an article for the next number of the *QR*. The only unattributed article in Number 41 is #494. Note, however, that the evidence suggests only that EC forwarded an article to WG; it does not demonstrate

that he was the author. JM III's Register: ' – Wilkins'. Shine (*The Quarterly Review Under Gifford*, p. 65) doubts JM III's attribution to Wilkins, citing 'passages in the article', especially p. 40.

495 Gisborne's *Natural Theology*. Article 3, pp. 41–66. Thomas Dunham Whitaker.
JM MSS: book loans register, a review copy was sent to 'Revd. Dr Whitaker' on 8 October [1818?]; TDW to JM, 15 November 1818. Nichols, 'Biographical Memoirs of Thomas Dunham Whitaker', p. xxix. JM III's Register.

496 Abel's *Journey in China*. Article 4, pp. 67–91. John Barrow.
The author refers to #415 and #438 (including a specific ref.). The discussion of infanticide (p. 76) repeats a similar discussion in #422. JB systematically cross-referenced his articles. JM III's Register.

497 [Tabart], *Antiquities of Nursery Literature*. Article 5, pp. 91–112. Francis Cohen.
Palgrave, *Collected Historical Works*. JM III's Register.

498 Bowdler – *Select Pieces in Prose and Verse*. Article 6, pp. 112–24. John Impey, possibly.
John Impey (d. 1829), a legal writer who flourished in the 1780s, seems an unlikely person to write on this topic. JM III's Register: ' – Impey'.

499 Fearon's *Sketches of America*. Article 7, pp. 124–67. John Barrow.
JM MS, book loans register, a review copy was sent to 'John Barrow' on 7 October 1818. The author refers to #493 (twice) and alludes to it as a companion piece. The author of #629 quotes #499 (twice). JB systematically cross-referenced his articles. JM III's Register.

500 Bentham's *Church-of-Englandism*. Article 8, pp. 167–77. William Gifford, probably with an unidentified collaborator.
JM III's Register: 'Wm Gifford mainly'.

501 Marsden's *Marco Polo*. Article 9, pp. 177–95. John Barrow, probably.
JM MS, book loans register, a review copy was sent to 'Revd R Heber' on 23 February 1819, which therefore puts the attribution to JB in doubt. As a subject, China is JB's preserve in the *QR*. The author of #568 cross-references this review. JB systematically cross-referenced his articles. JM III's Register.

502 *Inquiry into the Copyright Act* [by Brydges, Christian, Montagu]. Article 10, pp. 196–213. Robert Southey; with adjustments suggested by Sharon Turner and John Murray.
Curry and Dedmon, 'Southey's Contributions to the *Quarterly Review*'. Bodl. Lib. MS Eng. Lett. d.47. (f. 155), RS to Grosvenor Bedford, 28 May 1819. JM III's Register.

503 Ross's *Voyage of Discovery*. Article 11, pp. 213–62. John Barrow.
JM MS, book loans register, a review copy was sent to 'John Barrow' on 28 January 1818. The article is one in a series by JB on the search for a Northwest Passage. The author alludes to #406, #451, #461 (including a specific ref.) and #474. On p. 261 of the article, JB refers to himself. The author of #705 (pp. 233, 265) refers to his earlier articles on Captain Ross (#451 and #503). JB systematically cross-referenced his articles. JM III's Register: Barrow.

VOLUME 21, NUMBER 42
(April 1819)
Published 10 September 1819[41]

504 [Schlegel], *View of Grecian Philosophy. - The Clouds, &c*. Article 1, pp. 271–320. Thomas Mitchell; possibly with William Richard Hamilton and John Hookham Frere.

JM MSS: TM to JM: 1 December 1818; 21 January 1819, he does not mind if WRH and JHF look at his manuscript article on Schlegel. JM III's Register: Mitchell.

505 Humboldt's *Travels*. Article 2, pp. 320–52. John Barrow.
The author refers to other reviews of Humboldt, #368, #394, #446. The article is cross-referenced in #590. JB systematically cross-referenced his articles. JM III's Register.

506 Hawkins's *Dissertation on Tradition*. Article 3, pp. 352–59. Richard Whately.
QR Letter 207. JM III's Register.

507 [Thury], *Cemeteries and Catacombs of Paris*. Article 4, pp. 359–98. Robert Southey.
Curry and Dedmon, 'Southey's Contributions to the *Quarterly Review*'. JM III's Register.

508 *State of the Laws of Great Britain*. Article 5, pp. 398–430. John Miller; vetted by George Canning and John Backhouse.
QR Letters 200, 211. JM MSS: WG to JM, 6 July 1819; John Miller to JM, 21 August 1819. JM III's Register.

509 *Past and Present state of Hayti* [by Lacroix, Vastey]. Article 6, pp. 430–60. John Barrow; probably with William Gifford.
JM MSS: WG to JM, 6 July 1819; [1819], 'Hayti I will set about immediately'. JM III's Register: Barrow, and note, 'Wm. Gifford (mainly)'.

510 Shelley's *Revolt of Islam*. Article 7, pp. 460–71. John Taylor Coleridge.
JM MSS: WG to JM, Ramsgate, pm 4 August 1818; same, Ryde, 6 July 1819; WG to JTC, 7 June 1819. *QR* Letter 168. JM III's Register.

511 Parnell's *Maurice and Berghetta*. Article 8, pp. 471–86. John Wilson Croker.
JM MS, WG to JM, 19 July 1819. JWC claimed the article in five Clements Lib. lists; included in the Cambridge Univ. vols. JM III's Register.

512 [Frere and Rose], *Narrative and Romantic Poems of the Italian*. Article 9, pp. 486–556. Ugo Foscolo.
JM MSS: WG to JM: 6 July 1819; [1819], 'I send a little of Foscolo to break up into pages ... He must, I suppose, have a copy, which may then be given to Cohen ...'; cash day book 1818–20, p. 113: '13 May 1819 To Cash Paid to U. Foscolo Esq as per cheque in Q.R. Book. £115'; Copies Ledger B, May 13 [1818], 'Cash to Mr. Foscolo Esq. 115.8 -'. Smiles, *Memoir*, vol. 2, p. 52. JM III's Register.

VOLUME 22, NUMBER 43
(July 1819)
Published 11 December 1819[42]

513 Abernethy, Lawrence, Morgan, Rennell, *on the Theories of Life*. Article 1, pp. 1–34. George D'Oyly.
JM MSS: WG to JM, Ryde 6 July 1819; G. D'O [1819], '... a parcel ... will contain the article I have been preparing on Laurence, Rennell, etc'. D'Oyly, *Sermons*, vol. 1, p. 25. JM III's Register.

514 Dupin – *on the Marine Establishments of France and England*. Article 2, pp. 34–59. John Barrow.
The author refers to #260, #320, #328 (twice), #451, and #472 (specific ref. to 'No. XXXVII. p. 195'). JB systematically cross-referenced his articles. The article is one in a series by JB in which the problem of dry rot is addressed. Compare #600, on a related

subject, and #738, a review attributed to JB of Dupin's *Commercial Power of Great Britain*. JM III's Register.

515 Fosbrooke – *British Monachism*. Article 3, pp. 59–102. Robert Southey.
Curry and Dedmon, 'Southey's Contributions to the *Quarterly Review*'. JM III's Register.

516 Ensor's *Restoration of Usurped Rights*. Article 4, pp. 102–7. William Jacob.
JM MS, WG to JM, 6 July 1819.

517 Golownin's *Captivity in Japan*. Article 5, pp. 107–29. John Barrow.
JM MS, book loans register, one of the works reviewed was sent to 'John Barrow' on 7 October 1818. The author refers to #170. JB systematically cross-referenced his articles. JM III's Register.

518 Woodhouse – *Physical Astronomy*. Article 6, pp. 129–49. Olinthus Gregory, possibly; OR, John Brinkley, possibly.
An earlier book by Woodhouse was reviewed in #122, probably by OG; that article is referred to in a note on p. 130. JM III's Register: 'Dr Brinkley'.

519 Gally Knight's *Eastern Sketches*. Article 7, pp. 149–58. Stratford Canning; subedited by Robert William Hay.
JM MSS: WG to RWH, 4 October 1819; 12 October 1819. JM III's Register: Stratford Canning.

520 Hazlitt's *Sketches of Public Characters*. Article 8, pp. 158–63. William Gifford, possibly; OR, Edward Jacob, possibly.
Despite its running title, the article answers Hazlitt's *Letter to W. Gifford*. There is no evidence independent of JM III to suggest that the article is by EJ. Shine gives priority to a queried attribution to WG, but while the article does resemble WG's writing, no objective evidence has been identified to suggest that it is his (*The Quarterly Review Under Gifford*). JM III's Register: 'Jacob junr'.

521 *State of Female Society in Greece* [by Hill]. Article 9, pp. 163–203. Thomas Mitchell.
JM MSS: TM to JM: 1 December 1818, proposes an article on this subject; TM to JM, 8 March 1819; 4 October 1819, sends the conclusion of the 'Greek women'. JM III's Register.

522 *The Cape of Good Hope* [by Burchell, Fisher, Latrobe, Wilson, Ross]. Article 10, pp. 203–46. John Barrow.
JM MS, book loans register, 'Latrobe's Visit to S. Africa' was sent to 'John Barrow' on 22 April 1819. The author refers to #226, #345, and #479. The author puffs JB's *Travels in South Africa*, four times. On p. 246 JB identifies himself as the article's author. JM III's Register.

523 M. Cottu. – *Criminal Law of England*. Article 11, pp. 247–64. John Wilson Croker, probably.
JWC claimed the article in five Clements Lib. lists. In what is demonstrably the latest of the comprehensive lists, the article is queried. The article is included in the Cambridge Univ. JM III's Register: Croker, and note, 'Not mentioned in Croker's own list'.

VOLUME 22, NUMBER 44
(January 1820)
Published 17 March 1820[43]

524 Bowdich's *Mission to Ashantee*. Article 1, pp. 273–302. John Barrow.

The article is cross-referenced in #657. JB systematically cross-referenced his articles. The discussion of the river Niger's possible connection with the Nile (pp. 291–3) is a favourite topic of JB's (see #544). JM III's Register.

525 Stephens's *Thesaurus*. Article 2, pp. 302–48. Charles James Blomfield.
JM MSS: WG to JM: [n.d.], refers to an article on Bowdich (#524) and states, 'I have nothing from Blomfield this morning – this is trifling with us'; [n.d.], 'Mr Blomfield has sent three or four pages more', A. Blomfield (ed.), *A Memoir of Charles James Blomfield, with Selections from His Correspondence*, 2 vols (London: John Murray, 1863), vol. 1, p. 27. JM III's Register.

526 *Popular Mythology of the Middle Ages* [by Dobeneck, Garinet, Plancy]. Article 3, pp. 348–80. Francis Cohen.
Palgrave, *Collected Historical Works*. JM III's Register: Cohen (Palgrave).

527 *Strategics – The Archduke Charles*. Article 4, pp. 380–401. Robert William Hay.
JM MS, WG to RWH, 28 December 1819. JM III's Register.

528 [Payne], *Brutus* and [Shiel], *Evadne*. Article 5, pp. 402–15. John Taylor Coleridge.
JM MSS: JTC to WG, 22 January 1819, asks if 'Brutus Tarquin' is engaged; WG to JTC, 12 March 1819, accepts JTC's proposal to review these works. JM III's Register.

529 Humboldt – *Passage of the Himalaya Mountains*. Article 6, pp. 415–30. John Barrow.
The author refers to #435 (three times). JB systematically cross-referenced his articles. JM III's Register.

530 Lysias – *Letter to the Prince Regent*. Article 7, pp. 430–6. Robert Grant, probably.
JM III's Register.

531 Burckhardt's *Travels in Nubia*. Article 8, pp. 437–81. John Barrow.
JM MSS: book loans register, a review copy was sent to 'John Barrow' on 28 January 1818; WG to JM [n.d.], 'Mr Barrow says he is hard at work on Burckhardt's Travels'; JB to JM, 1 July 1820. The author refers to #337 and, three times, to #457. The article is cross-referenced in #544 and #651. JB systematically cross-referenced his articles. The publisher of the volume under review is the Association for promoting the Discovery of the interior Parts of Africa. The Association was a forerunner of the Royal Geographical Society, whose primary founder was JB. A leading purpose of the Association (founded in 1788 and headed by JB's geographical mentor, Sir Joseph Banks) was to encourage the effort to discover the source of the Niger, a major preoccupation of JB's. JM III's Register.

532 Jerome Buonaparte – *Court of Westphalia*. Article 9, pp. 481–92. John Wilson Croker.
JM MS, WG to JM [16 February 1820]. JWC claimed the article in five Clements Lib. lists; included in the Cambridge Univ. vols. JM III's Register.

533 *State of Public Affairs* [by Canning, Greville, Plunket]. Article 10, pp. 492–560. Robert Grant.
JM MSS: WG to JM: [16 February 1820]; [25 February 1820]. JM III's Register.

VOLUME 23, NUMBER 45
(May 1820)
Published 27 May 1820[44]

534 Coxe – *Life of Marlborough*. Article 1, pp. 1–73. Robert Southey.
Curry and Dedmon, 'Southey's Contributions to the *Quarterly Review*'. JM III's Register.

535 *Van Diemen's Land – The Bush Ranger* [by Howe]. Article 2, pp. 73–83. Barron Field.
JM MSS: BF to JM: 24 August 1819; BF to JM, 1 February 1821. In the first sentence, the author refers to Van Diemen's Land as a 'state only fifteen years old', therefore dating the manuscript of this article to 1818, coincident with Field's letter to JM cited above. At page 78, the author states, 'the Judge of the Supreme Court of New South Wales has lately made a circuit to the island'. BF is the Judge referred to. JM III's Register. Mr Ronald Solomon materially assisted in the preparation of this note.

536 Forbin – *Voyage dans le Levant*. Article 3, pp. 83–96. John Barrow.
JM MS, JB to JM, 1 July 1820. The author refers to #476 and #486. JB systematically cross-referenced his articles. JM III's Register.

537 *Roads and Highways* [by Edgeworth, McAdam, Peterson]. Article 4, pp. 96–111. Edward Berens.
JM MS, Edward Berens to JM, 26 September 1820. JM III's Register.

538 *Parga* [by Bosset, Duval]. Article 5, pp. 111–36. John Barrow, probably; OR Ugo Foscolo, possibly; possibly subedited by John Barrow.
JM MSS: WG to Robert William Hay, 28 December 1819, states that he cannot get John Wilson Croker to work on Parga (perhaps as subeditor; Croker sometimes subedited JB's articles); JB to JM, 29 May 1820, requests the return of 'Dr Holland's two volumes' once the article is printed (he does not state which article). JB probably meant from the printer, who may have been using the volumes to copy a quotation; conversely, Holland's volumes may have been lent to JM either by JB or another party for use by the reviewer. (See pp. 114n and 128 for references to Dr Holland.) The reviewer has access to official correspondence (p. 117). The author refers to #82. The subjects of #267 and #547 are alluded to on p. 128 and p. 125, respectively. JB systematically cross-referenced his articles. The author refers to *Edinburgh Review* writers as 'Northern Seers' (cf. 'Northern Philosophers' in #493, p. 13). 'JM II's office copy: [in pencil, and partly erased] 'Foscolo'. JM III's Register: Barrow. Parga' is the subject of *ER* #886, October 1819, a review by Ugo Foscolo. The British Library holds a proof copy of an 'unfinished and never to be published volume on Parga' by Foscolo. John Murray is on the proof's imprint (BL shelf mark: C.142.aa.24).

539 [Coray], *Decline and Corruption of the Greek Tongue*. Article 6, pp. 136–54. Robert Walpole; possibly subedited by Charles James Blomfield.
JM MS, RW to JM, 29 May 1820. JM III's Register: 'By Blomfield', and note, '?Robt Walpole. See his letter, May 1820'.

540 *Private Life of Voltaire and Madame du Châtelet*. Article 7, pp. 154–66. John Wilson Croker.
JWC claimed the article in six Clements Lib. lists; included in the Cambridge Univ. vols. JM III's Register.

541 Clare's *Poems*. Article 8, pp. 166–74. Octavius Graham Gilchrist.
JM MS, WG to OGG, 22 May 1820 [24 May 1820 p/mark]. BL Add. MS 2245 (ff. 84–5), OGG to John Clare, 10 April 1820. See also BL Add. MS 2245 (ff. 92, 93, 134, 135), letters from OGG to Clare in which he keeps him abreast of his progress on the article and comments on it post publication. JM III's Register.

542 Rubichon – *De l'Angleterre*. Article 9, pp. 174–98. Richard Chenevix, probably.
The article is alluded to in #87*WI* (p. 47), which is attributed to RC. Note the author's use of the form 'Lewis XIV.', characteristic of RC. JM III's Register.

543 Milman's *Fall of Jerusalem*. Article 10, pp. 198–225. Reginald Heber.

NLS MSS 142: (f. 14), WS to John Gibson Lockhart, 11 April [1820]; (f. 15), WG to Walter Scott, 18 April [1820]. *SL*, vol. 6, pp. 170–1, 171n, 177. JM III's Register.

544 Mollien – *The Course of the Niger.* Article 11, pp. 225–44. John Barrow.
The author refers to #531. The article is cross-referenced in #636. JB systematically cross-referenced his articles. JM III's Register.

545 D'Israeli' – *Manners of the Athenians.* Article 12, pp. 245–79. Thomas Mitchell.
JM MSS: TM to JM: [n.d.], 'I shall pursue D'Israeli as soon as I can who is however too much of a "Hellus", to please me altogether'; 29 May 1820, states that the *QR* has just arrived and he has detected a misprint on p. 277: for 'more virgins, more speed' read 'more vigour, more speed'! JM III's Register.

VOLUME 23, NUMBER 46
(July 1820)
Published 5 October 1820[45]

546 Whittaker, Bellamy, Sir J. B. Burges, Todd – *Translation of the Bible.* Article 1, pp. 287–325. George D'Oyly.
JM MS, GD'O to JM, 24 April 1820. JM III's Register.

547 Douglas – Haygarth – *Modern Greece.* Article 2, pp. 325–59. John Barrow.
JM MS, book loans register, one of the works reviewed was sent to 'John Barrow' on 8 February 1818. The author refers to books reviewed in #278 and #476. JB systematically cross-referenced his articles. JM III's Register.

548 Parnell's *A Letter to the Editor of the Quarterly Review.* Article 3, pp. 360–73. John Wilson Croker.
JM MS, JWC to JM, 13 July 1820. JWC claimed the article in six Clements Lib. lists; included in the Cambridge Univ. vols. JM III's Register.

549 Grece – Stuart – Strachan – *Emigration to Canada.* Article 4, pp. 373–400. Richard Whately.
JM MS, WG to JM [1820]. R. Whately, *Miscellaneous Lectures and Reviews* (London: Parker, Son and Bourn, 1861), pp. 211–45. JM III's Register.

550 Spence's *Anecdotes*; Bowles's *Invariable Principles of Poetry.* Article 5, pp. 400–34. Isaac D'Israeli.
JM MS, WG to JM, Ramsgate, Sunday noon [c. July] 1820 [p/mark], 'I hope you will bring Mr D'Israeli's revise'. *The Letters of John Murray to Lord Byron*, ed. A. Nicholson (Liverpool: Liverpool University Press, 2007), p. 386. Smiles, *Memoir*, vol. 2, p. 53. JM II's office copy. JM III's Register.

551 Hodgskin – *State of Society, &c. in Germany.* Article 6, pp. 434–54. Robert William Hay.
JM MSS: WG to JM: 23 August [1820]; Sunday noon [1820], 'Mr Hay, I suppose will let you have his revise. JM III's Register.

552 [John Matthews], *Fables from La Fontaine.* Article 7, pp. 455–65. Henry Matthews, probably.
JM III's Register.

553 Clarke. – *Glass Blow-pipe.* Article 8, pp. 466–73. Edward Daniel Clarke, possibly.
JM III's Register.

554 Mitchell's *Translations of Aristophanes.* Article 9, pp. 474–505. John Hookham Frere; with a significant excision by William Gifford.

JM MS, WG to JM [September or October 1820], 'I am a great deal embarrassed about Aristophanes.... the light matter ... though very good, seems out of place in our Review.... yet what will Frere say to cutting out four pages of what he probably considers very highly! And yet, if it must be done, it must'. WG cut from the article a passage he thought was too much in the flippant acerbic tone of *Blackwood's Magazine*. Duke MS, WG to George Canning, 3 Oct [1820]. The article is signed 'W', for Whistlecraft, JHF's pseudonym. JM II's office copy. JM III's Register.

555 [Luttrell], *Advice to Julia*. Article 10, pp. 505–10. John Wilson Croker.
QR Letter 225. JWC claimed the article in six Clements Lib. lists; included in the Cambridge Univ. vols. JM III's Register.

556 M. Edgeworth's *Memoirs of R. L. Edgeworth, Esq*. Article 11, pp. 510–49. John Wilson Croker; possibly with information from Thomas Casey.
Florida MS, JWC to T. Casey, 20 July 1820. JM MSS: WG to JM [September or October 1820], 'I saw our friend yesterday – he has his reasons for wishing Edgeworth to appear'; JM to JWC, 1 September 1820. *QR* Letter 224. JWC claimed the article in six Clements Lib. lists; included in the Cambridge Univ. vols. JM III's Register.

557 *New Churches* [by Elmes, Haydon, Yates]. Article 12, pp. 549–91. Robert Southey.
Curry and Dedmon, 'Southey's Contributions to the *Quarterly Review*'. JM III's Register.

VOLUME 24, NUMBER 47
(October 1820)
Published 19 December 1820[46]

558 Southey's *Life of Wesley*. Article 1, pp. 1–55. Reginald Heber.
JM MSS: book loans register, a review copy was sent to 'Revd. R. Heber' on 22 April 1820; WG to JM [1820], 'Wesley was finished last night and I sent the whole with the exception of the 1st sheet which had gone before to Hodnet [Heber's residence, Hodnet Hall]'. [Heber], *Life of Reginald Heber*, vol. 2, p. 39. JM III's Register.

559 Wentworth. – Oxley. – *New South Wales*. Article 2, pp. 55–72. Barron Field.
JM MSS: BF to JM: 13 December 1817; 24 August 1819. JM III's Register: Barrow. In this review, there are no references to previous articles by John Barrow, which is significant, as he habitually cross-referenced his reviews.

560 Manzoni. – Foscolo. – *Italian Tragedy*. Article 3, pp. 72–102. Henry Hart Milman.
JM MSS: HHM's autograph list of his *QR* articles; book loans register, the books reviewed were sent to 'H. H. Milman' in September 1816. JM III's Register.

561 Fraser – *Tour through the Snow Range of the Himālā*. Article 4, pp. 102–30. John Barrow, probably.
JB wrote on the Himalayas for *Encyclopaedia Britannica*. However, the author refers to no other articles by JB and this review is not referred to in his later articles, which is significant, as JB systematically cross-referenced his articles. JM III's Register: Barrow.

562 Mrs. Hemans's *Poems*. Article 5, pp. 130–9. John Taylor Coleridge.
JM MSS: WG to JM [1820], 'I shall set up that part of Mr Coleridge which relates to Mrs Hemans'; WG to JTC, 25 October 1820; WG to JTC, 21 December 1820. JM III's Register.

563 Belzoni's *Operations and Discoveries in Egypt, &c*. Article 6, pp. 139–69. John Barrow; with information from Henry Salt.

The author refers to #472 and, twice, to #486. The author takes credit for having introduced Belzoni, in #472 and #486, to an English audience. JB systematically cross-referenced his articles. JM III's Register.

564 Burrows – *Inquiries relative to Insanity*. Article 7, pp. 169–94. David Uwins, probably. JM III's Register.

565 *Report from the Select Committee on Criminal Laws*. Article 8, pp. 195–270. John Miller.
Duke MS (Backhouse collection), WG to George Canning, 3 October [1820]. JM MS, John Miller to JM, 19 December 1820. JM III's Register.

VOLUME 24, NUMBER 48
(January 1821)
Published April 1821[47]

566 *Freedom of Commerce*. Article 1, pp. 281–302. M. Fletcher, probably.
M. Fletcher, the author of *Reflexions on the Causes Which Influence the Price of Corn* (1827). Compare #620 and #626. JM MS: M. Fletcher to JM, 77 Guilford St, 9 June 1821. Note that while this letter suggests 'M. Fletcher' corresponded with JM at this time, the letter supplies no evidence of Fletcher's authorship of this article. JM III's Register: ' – Fletcher'.

567 Maturin – *Melmoth, the Wanderer*. Article 2, pp. 303–11. John Wilson Croker.
JM MSS: JWC to JM, 29 July [1820]; WG to JM [25 January 1821]. JWC claimed the article in six Clements Lib. lists; included in the Cambridge Univ. vols. JM III's Register.

568 Murray's *Asiatic Discoveries*. Article 3, pp. 311–41. John Barrow.
JM MS, WG to JM [25 January 1821]. The author refers to #501. The article is cross-referenced in #633. JB systematically cross-referenced his articles. JM III's Register.

569 Accum – *On Culinary Poisons*. Article 4, pp. 341–52. John MacCulloch, possibly.
JM III's Register.

570 [Austen], *Modern Novels*. Article 5, pp. 352–76. Richard Whately.
JM MS, WG to JM [25 January 1821]. R. Whately, *Miscellaneous Lectures and Reviews*, pp. iii, iv, 282. JM III's Register: 'Sir W Scott' citing unspecified letters, and note, 'By Dr Whately – from Lockhart's Life of Scott in wh book, however, it is inserted by mistake'.

571 Barker – *Aristarchus Anti-Blomfieldianus*. Article 6, pp. 376–400. James Henry Monk; probably subedited by Charles James Blomfield.
JM MS, G. J. Monk to JM III, 15 January 1858. Blomfield, *Memoir*, vol. 1, pp. 27–8, states the article is by JHM. JM III's Register: James Henry Monk.

572 *Rise and Progress of Horticulture*. Article 7, pp. 400–19. John Claudius Loudon, possibly
JM MS, WG to JM [19 July 1822 p/mark]. JM III's Register.

573 Motte-Fenélon – *Manners of the Athenians*. Article 8, pp. 419–61. Thomas Mitchell.
JM MS, TM to JM, 13 April 1821. JM III's Register.

574 Huntington, S. S. *Works and Life*. Article 9, pp. 462–510. Robert Southey.
Curry and Dedmon, 'Southey's Contributions to the *Quarterly Review*'. JM III's Register.

575 Hope's *Anastasius*. Article 10, pp. 511–29. Henry Matthews.

JM MS, HM to JM, 9 August 1820. JM III's Register.

576 Mad. de Genlis – *Pétrarque et Laure*. Article 11, pp. 529–66. Ugo Foscolo.
A footnote on p. 549 reads, 'Two letters written with his [Petrarch's] own hand, now existing in the library of Lord Holland, are the only two specimens we have seen'. UF was patronized by Holland House. In a footnote on p. 555 the author states: 'This passage is taken from the 14th of those Letters which are not to be found amongst Petrarch's works. The manuscript is preserved in the Library of Saint Mark, at Venice'. JM III's Register.

VOLUME 25, NUMBER 49
(April 1821)
Published 28 June 1821[48]

577 *The Spanish Drama*. Article 1, pp. 1–24. Henry Hart Milman.
JM MSS: HHM's autograph list of his *QR* articles; HHM to JM, 15 January 1821. JM III's Register.

578 Lyon. – *Northern Africa, and the Niger*. Article 2, pp. 25–50. John Barrow.
JM MS, cash day book 1821–4, the same person was paid for articles 2 and 9 in this Number. The author refers to #457. The article is referred to in #692. JB systematically cross-referenced his articles. JM III's Register: Barrow.

579 Irving's *The Sketch Book of Geoffrey Crayon, Gent*. Article 3, pp. 50–67. Henry Matthews.
JM MSS: WG to JM, [n.d.], 'I enclose to you the letter for our friend Matthews as I know not whether he lives with his father, or where to find him'; WG to JM, [1820], 'If our friend Matthews does not give us a much better review of the Sketchbook than theirs [*ER* 34 (August 1820) 160–76], I will, without ceremony, fling it into the fire'; HM to JM, 9 August 1820. JM III's Register.

580 Dupin – *Military Force of Great Britain*. Article 4, pp. 67–95. George Procter; subedited by Sir George Murray.
JM MSS: WG to Robert William Hay: 2 October [1820]; 11 October 1820; GP to JM, 11 April 1821. JM III's Register.

581 *The Etonian*. Article 5, pp. 95–112. William Sidney Walker, possibly.
JM III's Register: 'Rev – Walker'.

582 Pugin – *Normandy – Architecture of the Middle Ages*. Article 6, pp. 112–47. Francis Cohen.
JM MS, cash day book, 1821–4, p. 62: 'Quarterly Review 49 ... Cancelled [pages], Architecture 28 1/2'. Palgrave, *Collected Historical Works*. The article is referred to in #639. JM III's Register: Cohen.

583 Galt's *Annals of the Parish*. Article 7, pp. 147–53. John Wilson Croker.
QR Letter 228. JWC claimed the article in six Clements Lib. lists; included in the Cambridge Univ. vols. JM III's Register.

584 Mitford's *The History of Greece*. Article 8, pp. 154–74. William Haygarth.
Present writer's private correspondence with Stella G. Miller. JM III's Register.

585 Parry's *Voyage of Discovery*. Article 9, pp. 175–216. John Barrow.
JM MSS: cash day book 1821–4, the same person was paid for articles 2 and 9 in this Number; JB to JM, 28 May 1821. The article is one in a series by JB on Arctic exploration. The author refers to #406 and #451. JB systematically cross-referenced his articles.

In #163*WI*, JB claims this article and other *QR* articles on Parry (#705 and #97*WI*). JM III's Register.

586 Scudamore *on Mineral Waters*. Article 10, pp. 216–28. David Uwins, possibly.

At this time, DU was an occasional contributor to the *QR* on medical topics. On p. 217 the author indicates that he is a professor (or student) of medicine.

587 Fergusson – *Reports of Decisions in Actions of Divorce*. Article 11, pp. 229–72. James Glassford.

QR Letter 222. JM III's Register.

VOLUME 25, NUMBER 50
(July 1821)
Published 17 October 1821[49]

588 *Life of Cromwell* [by Cromwell, Villemain]. Article 1, pp. 279–347. Robert Southey; with an excision by William Gifford.

Curry and Dedmon, 'Southey's Contributions to the *Quarterly Review*'. JM MSS: cash day book, 1821–4, p. 76: 'Quarterly Review No. L ... to cheque for article 1 [£]100'. One hundred pounds was RS's usual payment; WG to JM, James Street, Wednesday night [1821], 'Southey's conclusion may perhaps have lost a little spirit but I saw nothing so valuable in the two paragraphs as to make one wish to retain them and they might, as you think, have at this time given displeasure'. JM III's Register.

589 Hone – *Apocryphal New Testament*. Article 2, pp. 347–65. Hugh James Rose.

JM MS, 25 October 1821, William Hone to WG, complains of ad hominem remarks in this article. The reviewer is identified on the letter, in pencil, as 'Rev. H. Rose'. JM MS, WG to Hone, 26 October 1821 [draft]. JM III's Register.

590 Humboldt's *Personal Narrative*. Article 3, pp. 365–92. John Barrow.

JM MSS: cash day book 1821–4, the same person was paid for articles 3, 5, and 8 in this Number; WG to JM: Ramsgate [July] 1821: 'I send ... the first part of Humboldt for Mr Barrow'; 26 August 1821. The author states that he reviewed Humboldt's previous volumes (#368, #394, #446, #505). JB systematically cross-referenced his articles. JM III's Register.

591 Lord Waldegrave's *Memoirs*. Article 4, pp. 392–414. John Wilson Croker.

JM MSS: cash day book 1821–4, the same person was paid for articles 4 and 11 in this Number; WG to JM, Ramsgate [July] 1821: 'I suppose we may follow Humboldt with Mr Croker's clever paper on Waldegrave'. JWC claimed the article in six Clements Lib. lists; included in the Cambridge Univ. vols. JM III's Register.

592 Staunton – *Embassy to Tourgouth Tartars*. Article 5, pp. 414–26. John Barrow.

JM MSS: cash day book 1821–4, the same person was paid for articles 3, 5, and 8 in this Number; WG to JM, 26 August 1821. The author refers to #415. JB systematically cross-referenced his articles. JM III's Register.

593 Hunt – *Tasso's Jerusalem Delivered*. Article 6, pp. 426–37. Reginald Heber and —; with significant edits by William Gifford.

JM MSS: WG to JM: [n.d; notation on the letter in JM II's hand, 'QR 50'], 'Our friend Heber has sent me by this morning's post a short review of Hunt's translation of Tasso – not our friend Leigh H but a country clergyman of that unfortunate name. It is not all written by himself but tis smart enough'; Ramsgate [n.d.], 'I think, too, we must have

Heber's Tasso. I have gone over it very carefully'. [Heber], *Life of Reginald Heber*, vol. 1, p. 486. JM III's Register.

594 Martyn's *Memoir – Religious Missions*. Article 7, pp. 437–53. William Gilly, probably. JM MS, WG to JM, 31 December 1824. JM III's Register.

595 [Blount], *Notes on the Cape of Good Hope*. Article 8, pp. 453–66. John Barrow.
JM MS, cash day book 1821–4, the same person was paid for articles 3, 5, and 8 in this Number. The author refers to #522. JB is cited on p. 454. JB systematically cross-referenced his articles. JM III's Register.

596 *Report – On the State of Agriculture*. Article 9, pp. 466–504. Nassau William Senior.
JM MS, WG to JM [15 August 1812 frank]. S. L. Levy [and F. W. Fetter], *Nassau W. Senior: The Prophet of Modern Capitalism* (Boston, MA: Bruce Humphries, 1943), pp. 102–4: 'S. Leon Levy saw the original manuscript of this article, which was in the Senior papers in the possession of ... the granddaughter of Senior. He reprints a passage that was not published in the *Quarterly* in which Senior argues, as against the view of Ricardo, that taxes on agricultural products and tithes fall on the landlord and not on the consumer'. JM III's Register.

597 Blomfield – *Æschyli Agamemnon*. Article 10, pp. 505–29. John Symmons.
JM MS, WG to JM, 26 August 1821. Westminster School uncatalogued MS ALS (Elmsley papers), CJB to Peter Elmsley, 12 Nov 1821. JM III's Register.

598 Lady Morgan's *Italy*. Article 11, pp. 529–34. John Wilson Croker.
JM MS, cash day book 1821–4, the same person was paid for articles 4 and 11 in this Number. JWC claimed the article in six Clements Lib. lists; included in the Cambridge Univ. vols. JM III's Register.

599 *England and France*. Article 12, pp. 534–75. Richard Chenevix.
JM MSS: WG to JM: Ramsgate, 18 July 1821; 26 August 1821. JM III's Register.

VOLUME 26, NUMBER 51
(October 1821)
Published 22 December 1821[50]

600 Dupin – *The Navy of England and of France*. Article 1, pp. 1–37. John Barrow.
JM MS, cash day book 1821–4, the same person was paid for articles 1, 3, and 10 in this Number. The author refers to #81. JB systematically cross-referenced his articles. JM III's Register.

601 *Russian Church Architecture* [by Geissler, Hempel, Richter]. Article 2, pp. 37–51. Henry Downing Whittington.
JM MSS: WG to JM, 26 August 1821; HDW to JM, Brighton [1 October 1821 p/mark]. JM III's Register.

602 *Fernando Po – State of the Slave-Trade* [by McQueen]. Article 3, pp. 51–82. John Barrow.
JM MSS: cash day book 1821–4, the same person was paid for articles 1, 3, and 10 in this Number; WG to JM [28 December 1821; JM II's notation: '*QR* 51 *ER* 71']. The article is referred to in #609. JB systematically cross-referenced his articles. JM III's Register.

603 Copleston – Whately – *Inquiry into the Doctrines of Predestination*. Article 4, pp. 82–102. Charles James Blomfield.

JM MSS: CJB to JM: 27 September 1821; 6 November 1821. NLW MS 21743C (17/4), WG to Edward Copleston, Friday, 4 January 1822. Blomfield, *Memoir*, vol. 1, p. 82. JM III's Register.

604 Hazlitt's *Table Talk*. Article 5, pp. 103–8. John Matthews.
Smiles, *Memoir*, vol. 2, pp. 54, 54n. JM III's Register: 'Col. Matthews'.

605 [Scott], *Novels, by the author of Waverley*. Article 6, pp. 109–48. Nassau William Senior.
QR Letter 193. JM III's Register.

606 Godwin and Malthus *on Population*. Article 7, pp. 148–68. George Taylor.
Taylor, *Memoir of Robert Surtees*, p. xiv.

607 Shelley – *Prometheus Unbound, &c.* Article 8, pp. 168–80. William Sidney Walker, probably.
JM III's Register.

608 Moore – Brand – *Astrology and Alchemy*. Article 9, pp. 180–209. Francis Cohen.
JM MSS: WG to JM, 26 August 1821; FC to JM, 21 December 1821. Palgrave, *Collected Historical Works*. JM III's Register.

609 Della-Cella – *Route from Tripoli to Egypt*. Article 10, pp. 209–29. John Barrow.
JM MS, cash day book 1821–4, the same person was paid for articles 1, 3, and 10 in this Number. The author refers to #602. The article is cross-referenced in #614. JB systematically cross-referenced his articles. JM III's Register.

610 Morellet – *Memoirs of the French Revolution*. Article 11, pp. 229–42. John Wilson Croker.
JWC claimed the article in six Clements Lib. lists; included in the Cambridge Univ. vols. JM III's Register.

611 Dalzel – *Lectures on the Ancient Greeks*. Article 12, pp. 243–71. Thomas Mitchell.
JM MS, WG to JM [1821], 'It was my design to give Mitchell whose paper has much beautiful writing in it'. *QR* Letter 230. JM III's Register.

VOLUME 26, NUMBER 52
(January 1822)
Published 30 March 1822[51]

612 Dorbrizhoffer – *Account of the Abipones*. Article 1, pp. 277–323. Robert Southey.
Curry and Dedmon, 'Southey's Contributions to the *Quarterly Review*'. JM III's Register.

613 Burgess – Griesbach – *Vindication of 1 John v. 7*. Article 2, pp. 324–41. Thomas Turton, possibly.
JM MS, WG to JTC, 21 February 1822. The article was submitted by JTC for an acquaintance of his. In #769, a continuation of #613, the author states that his manuscript lay unpublished for some time. That article, attributed to Thomas Turton, was published when JTC was editor of the *QR*.

614 Kotzebue – *Voyage of Discovery*. Article 3, pp. 341–64. John Barrow.
JM MS, cash day book 1821–4, the same person was paid for articles 3, 8, and 14 in this Number. The article is specifically referred to in #619 and #667. JB systematically cross-referenced his articles. JM III's Register.

615 [Galt], *Memoirs of a Life passed in Pennsylvania*. Article 4, pp. 364–74. John Wilson Croker.

JM MSS: cash day book 1821–4, the same person was paid for articles 4, 7, and 10 in this Number; JWC to JM, 13 December 1821. JWC claimed the article in six Clements Lib. lists; included in the Cambridge Univ. vols. JM III's Register.

616 Buckingham's *Travels in Palestine*. Article 5, pp. 374–91. William John Bankes.
JM MSS: WJB to JM: 24 November 1821; 16 January 1822; 29 June 1826. BL Add. MS 34585 (f. 170), T. Hughes to Samuel Butler, Cambridge, 16 April 1822. JM III's Register: '?JW' replaced by 'W J Bankes', and note, 'Apparently Mr. Bankes was sued by Buckingham in consequence of this article. See Bankes's letter to J M June 29, 1826 (Safe)'. JM means the letter is in the company safe.

617 Arrowsmith – *Instruction of the Deaf and Dumb*. Article 6, pp. 391–405. Author not identified.

618 *Mémoires du Duc de Lauzun*. Article 7, pp. 405–9. John Wilson Croker.
JM MS, cash day book 1821–4, the same person was paid for articles 4, 7, and 10 in this Number. JWC claimed the article in six Clements Lib. lists; included in the Cambridge Univ. vols. JM III's Register.

619 Harmon – *Western Caledonia*. Article 8, pp. 409–16. John Barrow.
JM MSS: cash day book 1821–4, the same person was paid for articles 3, 8, and 14 in this Number; JB to JM, 28 December 1821.

620 *State of Weights and Measures*. Article 9, pp. 416–25. M. Fletcher, probably.
JM MS, cash day book 1821–4, the same person was paid for articles 9 and 15 in this Number. See #626.

621 *Memoirs of the Kit-Cat Club* [by Kelly, Tarbé]. Article 10, pp. 425–37. John Wilson Croker.
JM MSS: cash day book 1821–4, the same person was paid for articles 4, 7, and 10 in this Number; JWC to JM, 13 December 1821. JWC claimed the article in six Clements Lib. lists; included in the Cambridge Univ. vols. JM III's Register.

622 Ker Porter – Morier – *Travels in Georgia, Persia, &c.* Article 11, pp. 437–54. John Barrow, possibly; OR Barron Field, possibly.
The author refers to #237. JB systematically cross-referenced his articles. However, as JM MS, cash day book 1821–4 states that the same person was paid for articles 3, 8, and 14 in this Number, but not article 11, it appears that he did not write this review. In private correspondence. with the present writer, Ronald Solomon has argued that Barron Field wrote the review, Dr J. M. R. Cameron, that Barrow was its author.

623 [Scott], *The Pirate*. Article 12, pp. 455–74. Nassau William Senior.
Lockhart, *Life*, vol. 6, pp. 179–80. N. W. Senior, *Essays on Fiction* (London: Longman, Green, Longman, Roberts & Green, 1864), p. 76.

624 Stewart's *Second Dissertation*. Article 13, pp. 474–514. William Rowe Lyall, probably.
The article's author defends #322, which is by WRL.

625 Malt-Brun's *Spurious Voyages*. Article 14, pp. 514–22. John Barrow.
JM MS, cash day book 1821–4, the same person was paid for articles 3, 8, and 14 in this Number. JM III's Register: Barrow, and note, 'See letter from JB Nov 26/21'.

626 *Colonial Policy*. Article 15, pp. 522–40. M. Fletcher, probably.
JM MS, cash day book 1821–4, the same person was paid for articles 9 and 15 in this Number. See #566 and #620. See also #669. On the article's first page, the author refers to #566, which is probably by Fletcher.

VOLUME 27, NUMBER 53
(April 1822)
Published 4 July 1822[52]

627 *Life and Writings of Camoens* [by Adamson]. Article 1, pp. 1–39. Robert Southey.
Curry and Dedmon, 'Southey's Contributions to the *Quarterly Review*'. JM III's Register: Southey.

628 Penn – *History of the Æolic Digamma*. Article 2, pp. 39–70. Ugo Foscolo.
Smiles, *Memoir*, vol. 2, p. 137. JM III's Register.

629 Harris – Flower – *Views, Visits, and Tours in North America*. Article 3, pp. 71–99. John Barrow.
JM MS, cash day book 1821–4, the same person was paid for articles 3, 4, 7 and 10 in this Number. JM MS, WG to JM [10 August 1824 p/mark]. The article is referred to in #630 and #686. JB systematically cross-referenced his articles.

630 Evans – *Van Diemen's Land*. Article 4, pp. 99–110. John Barrow.
JM MS, cash day book 1821–4, the same person was paid for articles 3, 4, 7 and 10 in this Number.

631 Reid – *On Nervous Affections*. Article 5, pp. 110–23. Robert Gooch probably.
Letters of Charles and Mary Anne Lamb, vol. 3, p. 132n.

632 *Cases of Walcot v. Walker, &c.* [on copyright] Article 6, pp. 123–38. Nassau William Senior.
NLW MS 21743C (17/1), WG to Edward Copleston, 27 June [1822].

633 Nazaroff – *Expedition to Kokania*. Article 7, pp. 138–45. John Barrow.
JM MS, cash day book 1821–4, the same person was paid for articles 3, 4, 7 and 10 in this Number. The author refers to #568. The article is cross-referenced in #131*WI* (twice). JB systematically cross-referenced his articles.

634 Montlosier – *De la Monarchie Française, &c.* Article 8, pp. 146–78. Richard Chenevix, probably.
The article is twice referred to in #599. Note the author's use of the form 'Lewis XIV.', 'Lewis XV.', characteristic of RC. French history and society are preoccupations of RC in his *QR* articles.

635 Walpole's *Memoires*. Article 9, pp. 178–215. John Wilson Croker.
JWC claimed the article in six Clements Lib. lists; included in the Cambridge Univ. vols. The author refers to #591, which is also by JWC. JM III's Register.

636 Waddington's *Visit to Ethiopia*. Article 10, pp. 215–39. John Barrow.
JM MS, cash day book 1821–4, the same person was paid for articles 3, 4, 7 and 10 in this Number. The author refers to #544. The article is cross-referenced in #651. JB systematically cross-referenced his articles. The article's author discusses the course of the Nile, a favourite theme of JB's.

637 *State of the Currency*. Article 11, pp. 243–67. Edward Copleston.
Copleston, *Memoir of Edward Copleston*, p. 347. *Letters of the Earl of Dudley to the Bishop of Llandaff*, pp. 312, 322, 322n, 333. Reprinted in an anonymous pamphlet, *An Examination of the Currency Questions, and the Project for Altering the Standard of Value* (1830), attributed to EC in *National Union Catalogue Pre-1956*.

VOLUME 27, NUMBER 54
(July 1822)
Published 23 October 1822[53]

638 Bankes – *Early History of Rome*. Article 1, pp. 273–308. William Haygarth.
  JM MSS: WH to JM, 4 Jan 1822; WG to John Taylor Coleridge, 19 December 1822.
  JM III's Register.

639 Cottingham – *Application and Intent of the various Styles of Architecture*. Article 2, pp.
  308–36. Francis Cohen.
  JM MSS: WG to JM, 18 July 1822; WG to JM, Ramsgate, 27 July 1822; FC to JM, 13
  August 1822. The author refers to p. 116 of #582 and implies that the present article is a
  continuation from it. JM III's Register.

640 [Scott], *The Fortunes of Nigel*. Article 3, pp. 337–64. Nassau William Senior.
  Senior, *Essays on Fiction*, pp. 97–137. JM III's Register: [in pencil] '?Nassau Senior'.

641 Campbell – *Missionary Travels in South Africa*. Article 4, pp. 364–77. John Barrow.
  JM MSS: cash day book 1821–4, the same person was paid for articles 4 and 9 in this
  Number; JB to JM, 13 July 1822; WG to JM [19 July 1822 p/mark]. JM III's Register.

642 Bentham – *On the Art of Packing Juries*. Article 5, pp. 377–82. Author not identified.

643 *Panegyrical Oratory of Greece* [by Auger, Planche]. Article 6, pp. 382–404. Thomas
  Mitchell.
  JM MSS, WG to JM: 18 July 1822; Ramsgate, 19 July 1822. JM III's Register.

644 James – Thomson – Prevost – *Campaigns in the Canadas*. Article 7, pp. 405–49. George
  Procter.
  JM MSS: WG to JM: Ramsgate, 18 July 1821; 27 July 1822. JM MSS: GP to JM: 20
  August, 31 October 1821; 5 December 1821; 18 February 1822; 15 July 1822; 12
  November 1822. The article is cross-referenced in #724. JM III's Register: Procter.

645 Mayow – *Sermons and Miscellanies*. Article 8, pp. 450–9. Author not identified.

646 Buckland – *On Antediluvian Fossil Bones*. Article 9, pp. 459–76. John Barrow.
  JM MSS: cash day book 1821–4, the same person was paid for articles 4 and 9 in this
  Number; WG to JM [July 1823].

647 Lord Byron's *Dramas*. Article 10, pp. 476–524. Reginald Heber.
  [Heber], *Life of Reginald Heber*, vol. 2, pp. 59, 59n. JM III's Register: attribution to
  'W Gifford', and note, 'author's name given in letter of Sir G. Dallas. November 1822';
  attribution revised to 'W Gifford or Bb Heber', and note, 'Bp Heber. See Byron's Life,
  8vo Ed. p. 570 note'.

648 *Contagion and Quarantine* [Faulkner, Hancock, Maclean, Thomason]. Article 11, pp.
  524–53. Robert Gooch, probably.
  Sketches of Eminent Medical Men (London: Religious Tract Society, n.d.), p. 140.

VOLUME 28, NUMBER 55
(October 1822)
Published 15 February 1823[54]

649 Gregoire – *History of Religious Sects*. Article 1, pp. 1–46. Robert Southey.
  Curry and Dedmon, 'Southey's Contributions to the *Quarterly Review*'. JM III's Register.

650 Sir C. H. Williams's *Works*. Article 2, pp. 46–59. John Wilson Croker.

JM MS, cash day book 1821–4, the same person was paid for articles 2 and 13 in this Number. Clements Library MS, Croker Papers, Letters Index entry: '1822 ... 8 June review of Walpole'. JWC claimed the article in four Clements Lib. lists; included in the Cambridge Univ. vols. JM III's Register.

651 *Egypt, Nubia, Berber, and Sennaar* [by Drovetti, Edmonstone, Henniker, Jomard, Richardson, Saint-Martin, Saulnier]. Article 3, pp. 59–97. John Barrow.
   JM MSS: cash day book 1821–4, the same person was paid for articles 3, 5, 8, 9, and 11 in this Number; JB to JM, 25 December 1822. The author refers to #486, #531 (twice), and #636. JB systematically cross-referenced his articles. JM III's Register.

652 Jouy – *Sylla*. Article 4, pp. 97–111. John Taylor Coleridge.
   JM MS, WG to JTC, 18 February 1823. Bodl. Lib. MS Eng. Lett. d. 130 (ff. 64–5), Thomas Arnold to JTC, 1 March 1823. JM III's Register.

653 Crawfurd – *The Indian Archipelago*. Article 5, pp. 111–38. John Barrow; probably with information from Sir Thomas Stamford Raffles.
   JM MSS: cash day book 1821–4, the same person was paid for articles 3, 5, 8, 9, and 11 in this Number; WG to JM [Ramsgate, 19 July 1822 p/mark]. JM III's Register: 'Sir Stamford Raffles and J. Barrow'.

654 Moore's *Irish Melodies*. Article 6, pp. 138–44. Henry Taylor.
   H. Taylor, *Autobiography, 1800–1875*, 2 vols (London: John Murray, 1885), vol. 1, pp. 41–2. JM III's Register: [in pencil] 'Sir H. Taylor'.

655 Whately – *Party-Feeling in Matters of Religion*. Article 7, pp. 144–57.
   Author not identified.

656 Strangeways – *The Poyais Bubble*. Article 8, pp. 157–61. John Barrow.
   JM MS, cash day book 1821–4, the same person was paid for articles 3, 5, 8, 9, and 11 in this Number. On the first page, the author mentions 'Barrow's Strait'. The review is one in a series by JB in which he debunks schemes and claims related to geography. JM III's Register.

657 *The Slave Trade*. Article 9, pp. 161–79. John Barrow; vetted by George Canning and Charles Rose Ellis.
   JM MS, cash day book 1821–4, the same person was paid for articles 3, 5, 8, 9, and 11 in this Number. *QR* Letter 236. The author refers to #602. JB systematically cross-referenced his articles. JM III's Register.

658 [Ireland] – Tebbs – *Adultery* – *Prize Essay*. Article 10, pp. 179–88. Author not identified.

659 Champollion's *Hieroglyphical Alphabet*. Article 11, pp. 188–96. John Barrow.
   JM MS, cash day book 1821–4, the same person was paid for articles 3, 5, 8, 9, and 11 in this Number. On p. 192, the author alludes to #651. JB systematically cross-referenced his articles. JM III's Register.

660 *The Opposition*. Article 12, pp. 197–219. David Robinson and William Gifford.
   JM MSS: DR to WG: 19 February 1823; 2 September 1823. JM III's Register: 'all that is excellent by Wm Gifford. David Robinson', and note, 'David Robinson nominally the author. See his own letter Sep 2 1823'.

661 O'Meara – Gourgaud – Montholon – *Voice from St. Helena, &c*. Article 13, pp. 219–64. John Wilson Croker, as compiler; with information from Sir Hudson Lowe, Sir Thomas Reid, Gideon Gorrequer, Robert Wilmot Horton, and Arthur Wellesley, Duke of Wellington.
   JM MSS: WG to JM, 18 July 1822; [October 1822], 'We can hardly have O'Meara for this No. I suppose. ... I own I shall not, unless Mr C expects it, wish to wait'; John Taylor

Coleridge to WG, 15 February 1823; JWC to JM, 19 February 1823, asks JM, if anyone should ask, to deny that he, JWC, is the author of this article. States, 'tho' I agree in most if not all, the sentiments of the said article, I do not wish to wear borrowed feathers ...'. Yet JWC claimed the article in five Clements Lib. lists; it is included in the Cambridge University bound volumes of Croker's articles, and, JM MS, cash day book 1821–4, the same person was paid for articles 2 and 13 in this Number. *QR Letters* 238–240, 246. JM III's Register.

VOLUME 28, NUMBER 56
(January 1823)
Published 8 July 1823[55]

662 Lacretelle – *The Constituent Assembly*. Article 1, pp. 271–314. Richard Chenevix.
JM MS, WG to JM, Ramsgate [July 1823], asks if the 'Dramatic papers' (#676) have been sent to Chenevix and states that he hears great praise for Chenevix's last article (therefore, #662). The author refers to #599 (twice) and to the volume under review as a continuation of Lacretelle's *Histoire de France*, reviewed, possibly by Chenevix, in #293. Note the author's use of the form 'Lewis XIV.', 'Lewis XV.', also used in #293 and #634, probably by Chenevix. JM III's Register.

663 Burton's *Antiquities and other Curiosities of Rome*. Article 2, pp. 315–32. John James Blunt.
JM MS, JJB to JM, 23 July 1823. JM III's Register: 'Rev. T. J. Blunt' [*sic*].

664 Arago – *Voyage round the World*. Article 3, pp. 332–49. John Barrow.
JM MS, cash day book 1821–4, the same person was paid for articles 3 and 6 in this Number. The author is agnostic about the existence of cannibalism (pp. 342–3); cf. #68, #165, #170, #311, and #347. JM III's Register.

665 Chalmers – *Poor-Laws*. Article 4, pp. 349–65. George Gleig; subedited by John Wilson Croker.
JM MSS: WG to JM [1823], 'I found here a Rev of Chalmers by Dr Gleig'; JWC to JM, 29 March 1823 [JM II's notation: 'Gleig's in no.56'], 'I return the Poor article with its additions. Let the author's amendments be attended to, and let his termination be inserted between his former conclusion and that which I have written'. JWC's additions cannot have been very extensive, for he does not claim a part-contribution in any Clements Lib. lists, nor is the article included in the Cambridge Univ. JM III's Register: '?Mr Gleig'.

666 Ducas – *Travels*. Article 5, pp. 365–72. George Procter, possibly.
This is an odd topic for Procter, and it does not seem to be in his style. The author is knowledgeable about Italian literature. JM III's Register: Procter.

667 Franklin's *Journey to the Polar Sea*. Article 6, pp. 372–409. John Barrow.
JM MSS: cash day book 1821–4, the same person was paid for articles 3 and 6 in this Number; JB to JM, 7 April 1823, refers to the Franklin article as his. The article is one in a series by JB on Arctic exploration. There is a specific ref. on p. 391 to #406 (the compositor made an error, mistaking No. XXXI for No. XXXII); and on p. 406 the author refers to #614. JB systematically cross-referenced his articles. On p. 292 reference is made to Cape Barrow.

668 Moore's *Pindar*. Article 7, pp. 410–30. John Taylor Coleridge.

JM MSS: WG to JTC: 19 December 1822; 12 February 1823; 11 July 1823; WG to JM [March 1823], refers to JTC's 'Pindar' article. *QR* Letter 244. JM III's Register.

669 *Navigation Laws* [by Andrewes]. Article 8, pp. 430–49. M. Fletcher, probably; subedited by John Barrow

JM MS, JB to JM, 7 April 1823. Compare #566, #620, and #626. JM III's Register: ' – Fletcher'.

670 Madame Campan – *Memoirs of Marie Antoinette*. Article 9, pp. 449–63. John Wilson Croker.

JM MS, cash day book 1821–4, the same person was paid for articles 9 and 10 in this Number. JWC claimed the article in six Clements Lib. lists; included in the Cambridge Univ. vols. The author refers to #661. JM III's Register.

671 *Memoirs by the Royal Family of France* [by Angoulême, Campan]. Article 10, pp. 464–74. John Wilson Croker.

JM MS, cash day book 1821–4, the same person was paid for articles 9 and 10 in this Number. JWC claimed the article in six Clements Lib. lists; included in the Cambridge Univ. vols. In the first sentence of the article the author states that the article is a continuation of #670. JM III's Register.

672 *The Cause of the Greeks* [by Raffenel]. Article 11, pp. 474–93. William Haygarth.

JM MSS: WG to JM: 20 June 1823; [July 1823], 'As for Greece, let it go as it is ... Mr Haygarth is very anxious about its appearance: so pray indulge him'. The author has visited Greece (see p. 485). JM III's Register.

673 Grégoire – *Progress of Infidelity*. Article 12, pp. 493–536. Robert Southey.

Curry and Dedmon, 'Southey's Contributions to the *Quarterly Review*'. JM III's Register.

674 *Affairs of Spain* [by Guerra, Pechio]. Article 13, pp. 536–60. Robert William Hay; subedited by William Jacob.

JM MSS: WG to RWH, 26 May 1823, promises to show him revisions to the 'Spanish Art'; WG to JM: [1823], 'somebody should have an eye to Hay's Article'; [July 1823], 'I send the remr of Spain. It is not necessary that I should see it again; but Mr H or some one for him, should look at the revise. The pencil m.s. at the end is by Mr Jacob, who read it as I believe I told you, in my absence. I have not seen him since'. JM III's Register: Hay.

VOLUME 29, NUMBER 57
(April 1823)
Published 27 September 1823[56]

675 Schoolcraft – Nuttall – *The Valley of the Mississippi*. Article 1, pp. 1–25. John Barrow and William Gifford.

JM MSS: cash day book 1821–4, p. 265, the same person was paid for articles 1 and 4 in this Number; WG to JM: Ramsgate [July 1823], 'I thought Barrow was in forwardness. His Ionia Art [#678] would be good to begin with, or if that is not ready perhaps his America, which I suppose is finished'; [September 1823], 'Let Mr Barrow have a revise of his Art. He has quite forgotten all that we have said of America, and is quite full of admiration of the country. I have mentioned it to him, and altered his language – but I must see the Article again'; 'I return Mr Barrows revise[.] [H]ad I not been very ill the last four days, it should have been sent before'. The author alludes on p. 13 to p. 377 of #667. JB systematically cross-referenced his articles. JM III's Register.

676 Bis – Arnault – Giroux – Soumet – *French Tragedy*. Article 2, pp. 25–53. Richard Chenevix.

JM MSS: WG to JM: [July 1823], 'Have you sent proofs of Crim Tatary to Mr. W. [#679] Or the Dramatic papers to Chenevix?'; [September 1823], 'Chenevix I thought of putting into one Article but the first part, at all events, may be set up'. See #689 for the second part of the material. On p. 53 the author promises additional articles on the French drama. Note the author's use of the form 'Lewis XIV.', characteristic of Chenevix. JM III's Register.

677 Southey's *History of the Peninsular War*. Article 3, pp. 53–85. George Procter; subedited by John Wilson Croker.

JM MS, GP to JM, 25 November 1822. Smiles, *Memoir*, vol. 2, pp. 57–8. JM III's Register.

678 Goodisson – *The Ionian Islands*. Article 4, pp. 86–116. John Barrow; subedited by George Canning.

JM MSS: cash day book 1821–4, the same person was paid for articles 1 and 4 in this Number; WG to JM [July 1823], 'I thought Barrow was in forwardness. His Iona Article would be good to begin with'; JB to JM, 18 August 1823. The author of #704 states in a note on p. 229 that he is the author of #678 and that he has received, via the publisher of the *QR*, correspondence from a person mentioned in #678. The author refers to #538. JB systematically cross-referenced his articles. JM III's Register: Barrow, citing unspecified letters, and note, 'from the Notes (signed) of Sir F Hervey'; [in pencil] '?'; [in ink] 'corrected by Mr Canning'; 'See J Barrows letter Aug 18/23'.

679 Holderness – *Manners of the Crim Tatars*. Article 5, pp. 116–38. Henry Downing Whittington, probably.

JM MS: HDW to JM, Brighton [1 October 1821 p/mark]; WG to JM [July 1823], 'Have you sent proofs of Crim Tatary to Mr. W. or the Dramatic papers to Chenevix?' The author of #601 briefly discusses the Tatars (pp. 42–3). JM III's Register: [in pencil] '?' [in ink] 'Whittington'.

680 Buckland – *Reliquiæ Diluvianæ*. Article 6, pp. 138–65. Edward Copleston; vetted by William Buckland.

JM MSS: WG to JM: [July 1823], 'Mr Buckland, I know complains that he has been treated solely as a geological writer – but he aspires to something higher, and it was this which made me wish for a more philosophical view of the subject: and this the Provost could well have given'; [July 1823], 'The Provost of Oriel has written to me this morning to say that he has an Article on Buckland, taking a philosophical view of the subject'; [September 1823], 'The Provost, from whom I heard today, promises to be ready in three or four weeks, but wishes for a later place. He will take pains'. NLW MS 21743C (17/2), WG to EC, Thursday [?July 1823; notation in EC's hand: 'Wrote to Buckland – from Exeter – July 14.1823']. JM MS, cash day book 1821–4, p. 264: 'Quarterly Review 57 23 Sept 1823 ... 1 Dr Copleston / 1 Revd T R Malthus [#682] / 1 Prof Buckland / 1 Revd Blanco White [#683] .... Rejected ... Reliq Diluv'. The rejected article might be Barrow's (see below). BL Add. MS 59416 (f. 93), EC to Lord Grenville, Sidmouth, 10 December 1823. JM III's Register: attribution and note, 'Provost of Oriel. An article was written by Mr Barrow and withdrawn in favour of this one – See Dr Buckland's letter Feb 3/1823'.

681 Burnet – *History of his Own Times*. Article 7, pp. 165–214. Robert Southey.

Curry and Dedmon, 'Southey's Contributions to the *Quarterly Review*'. JM III's Register.

682 Tooke – *on High and Low Prices*. Article 8, pp. 214–39. Thomas Robert Malthus.
JM MS, cash day book 1821–4, p. 264: 'Quarterly Review 57 23 Sept 1823 ... 1 Revd T R Malthus'. T. R. Malthus, *Five Papers on Political Economy*, ed. C. Renwick (Sydney: University of Sydney, Reprints of Economics and Economic History, No. 3, 1953), pp. 41–67. JM III's Register.

683 Quin – *Spain*. Article 9, pp. 240–76. Joseph Blanco White.
BL Add. MS 28603, Robert Southey to William Peachey, 4 October 1823. JM MS, cash day book 1821–4, p. 264: 'Quarterly Review 57 23 Sept 1823 ... 1 Revd Blanco White'. JM III's Register.

VOLUME 29, NUMBER 58
(July 1823)
Published 30 December 1823[57]

684 Maury – Irving – *Pulpit Eloquence*. Article 1, pp. 283–313. Henry Hart Milman.
JM MS, Milman's autograph list of his *QR* articles. JM MS, WG to JM [September 1823], 'Milman's promised paper, if well written, may be serviceable. JM III's Register.

685 Planche – *Legal Oratory of Greece*. Article 2, pp. 313–38. Thomas Mitchell.
[Anon.], 'Note on the Quarterly Reviewers', *Blackwood's Edinburgh Magazine*, 15 (January 1824), p. 84. *GM*, 24 (1845), p. 203. The author refers to #643. JM III's Register.

686 Faux – *Memorable Days in America*. Article 3, pp. 338–70. John Barrow.
JM MS, cash day book 1821–4, the same person was paid for articles 3, 5, and 9 in this Number. *QR* Letter 252. JM III's Register.

687 Lord John Russell – *Don Carlos, a Tragedy*. Article 4, pp. 370–82. Henry Taylor and William Gifford.
Taylor, *Autobiography*, vol. 1, pp. 51, 51n. JM III's Register: Taylor and Gifford, citing unspecified letters.

688 Malcolm – *Memoir of Central India*. Article 5, pp. 382–414. John Barrow.
JM MS, cash day book 1821–4, the same person was paid for articles 3, 5, and 9 in this Number. *QR* Letter 253. The author refers to #442. JB systematically cross-referenced his articles. JM III's Register.

689 Duval – Mirmont – Etienne – Scribe – *French Comedy*. Article 6, pp. 414–40. Richard Chenevix.
Blackwood's Edinburgh Magazine, 15 (January 1824), p. 84. JM MS, WG to JM [September 1823], 'Chenevix I thought of putting into one Article but the first part, at all events, may be set up'. The author refers to #676. The subject was promised in #676. Note the author's use of the form 'Lewis XIV', typical of Chenevix. JM III's Register.

690 *Superstition and Knowledge*. Article 7, pp. 440–75. Francis Cohen; with significant excisions by William Gifford.
JM MSS: FC to JM [September 1822], 'I send my article on superstitions'; WG to JM [July 1823], 'Cohen must have mistaken me or I him ... I never thought of opening with his Article nor is it proper for it. I have read it this evening, and have many doubts about its tendency: – it must, at all events, be carefully pruned. It is clever but rash'; FC to JM, 31 August 1823 [1 September 1823 p/mark]'. JM III's Register.

691 Wilberforce – Clarkson – *Condition of the Negroes in our Colonies.* Article 8, pp. 475–508. Joseph Lowe, probably; possibly subedited by John Barrow.
Joseph Lowe published an *Inquiry into the State of the British West Indies* (1807). The author refers to #602, which is by JB. JB systematically cross-referenced his articles. The author refers to #701, which is by William Jacob. JM III's Register: ' – Low'.

692 Adams – *Bornou.* Article 9, pp. 508–24. John Barrow.
JM MS, cash day book 1821–4 articles 3, 5, and 9 in this Number. The author refers to #578. JB systematically cross-referenced his articles. JM III's Register.

693 Thackeray – *Ecclesiastical Revenues.* Article 10, pp. 524–60. Edward Edwards.
JM MSS: EE to WG: 20 March 1823; 23 March 1823. The article was reprinted in an anonymous pamphlet, *The Revenues of the Church of England Not a Burden upon the Public* (1830). JM III's Register.

694 *Savary, and the Duke d'Enghien* [by Dupin, Enghien, Hulin, Marquart, Rovigo, Touche]. Article 11, pp. 561–85. John Wilson Croker.
JWC claimed the article in five Clements Lib. lists; included in the Cambridge Univ. vols. JM III's Register.

VOLUME 30, NUMBER 59
(October 1823)
Published 17 April 1824[58]

695 Dwight – *Travels in New England and New York.* Article 1, pp. 1–40. Robert Southey; with a significant alteration by William Gifford.
Curry and Dedmon, 'Southey's Contributions to the *Quarterly Review*'. *Selections from the Letters of Robert Southey*, vol. 3, p. 417. JM II's office copy. JM III's Register.

696 Rose's *Orlando Furioso.* Article 2, pp. 40–61. John James Blunt, possibly.
JM MS, WG to JM [May 1824], '... have the proof forwarded to Mr. Blunt'. JM III's Register: 'Rev T J Blunt' [*sic*].

697 *Recollections of the Peninsula, &c.* [by Batty, Sherer]. Article 3, pp. 61–79. George Procter, probably.
JM MS, cash day book 1821–4, the same person was paid for articles 3 and 9 in this Number. During this period, military analysis was GP's preserve in the *QR*. JM III's Register.

698 Belsham – *Translation of St. Paul's Epistles.* Article 4, pp. 79–115. Hugh James Rose.
JM MS, John Taylor Coleridge to JM, 10 November 1825, asks if JM knows Rose, who wrote 'the Belsham article ... he lives at Horsham'. HJR was Vicar of Horsahm 1821–7. *QR* Letter 254. JM III's Register: Rose.

699 Brooke's *Travels to the North Cape.* Article 5, pp. 115–33. John Barrow.
JM MS, cash day book 1821–4, the same person was paid for articles 5, 10, and 11 in this Number. The author comments on the possible conjunction of the Nile and the Niger, a preoccupation of JB's. JM III's Register.

700 *Mal'aria* [by Foderé, Julia, Koreff]. Article 6, pp. 133–51. Robley Dunglisson, possibly. JM III's Register.

701 *Mexico* [by Baily, Guerra, Robinson]. Article 7, pp. 151–85. William Jacob.
JM MS, WJ to JM, 17 February 1824. JM III's Register.

702 Johnson – *Private Correspondence of Cowper.* Article 8, pp. 185–99. John Philips Potter.

JPP reprinted this article in *Essays on the Lives of Newton, Cowper, and Heber* (1830). The article is cross-referenced at article #721. JM III's Register.

703 [Morier], *Adventures of Hajji Baba*. Article 9, pp. 199–216. George Procter, probably. JM MS, cash day book 1821–4, the same person was paid for articles 3 and 9 in this Number. JM III's Register.

704 *Dry Rot* [by Burridge]. Article 10, pp. 216–30. John Barrow. JM MS, cash day book 1821–4, the same person was paid for articles 5, 10, and 11 in this Number. Public Record Office (Kew), ADM 1/4371: the pamphlet in the article's headnote is among the papers of the Secretaries of the Admiralty (Croker and JB). The article's author refers to #208, #260, #320, and #678. JB systematically cross-referenced his articles. The article is one in a series by JB on dry rot in the navy's ships. JM III's Register.

705 Parry – *North-West Passage – Parry's Second Voyage*. Article 11, pp. 231–72. John Barrow. JM MS, cash day book 1821–4, the same person was paid for articles 5, 10, and 11 in this Number. The article is one in a series by JB on Arctic exploration. The author of the article alludes to his former articles in the *QR* on Captain Ross (#451 and #503). The author refers to #667. JB systematically cross-referenced his articles. JM II's office copy. JM III's Register.

706 *Court of Chancery*. Article 12, pp. 272–91. John Wilson Croker; probably with materials from William Wright. JM MS, JWC to JM, 4 April 1824. JWC claimed the article in six Clements Lib. lists; included in the Cambridge Univ. vols. JM III's Register: Croker, and note, 'with valuable information from Mr Wright a barrister'.

VOLUME 30, NUMBER 60
(January 1824)
Published 28 August 1824[59]

707 McCulloch – *Political Economy*. Article 1, pp. 297–334. Thomas Robert Malthus. D. Ricardo, *Letters of David Ricardo and Hutches Trower and others: 1811–1823*, ed. by J. Bonar and J.H. Hollander (1899), p. 179n. JM III's Register.

708 Meyrick – *On Ancient Armour*. Article 2, pp. 334–51. George Procter. The author refers to #580. JM III's Register.

709 White – *Cambodia*. Article 3, pp. 351–68. John Barrow. JM MS, cash day book 1821–4, the same person was paid for articles 3, 4, and 9 in this Number. JM III's Register.

710 Dupin – *Commercial Power of England*. Article 4, pp. 368–82. John Barrow. JM MS, cash day book 1821–4, the same person was paid for articles 3, 4, and 9 in this Number. The author refers to #328 and #514. JM III's Register.

711 Smyth – *Sicily and its Islands*. Article 5, pp. 382–403. John James Blunt. JM MSS: JJB to JM: 23 July 1823; 30 April 1824. JM III's Register.

712 Holford – Roscoe – Buxton – *Prisons and Penitentiaries*. Article 6, pp. 404–40. John Taylor Coleridge. JM MSS: cash day book 1821–4: JM paid £50 for article 6 in Number 60; WG to JTC, 31 August 1824, states that he has £50 for him. Bodl. Lib. MS Eng. Lett. d. 130 (ff.

68–9), Thomas Arnold to JTC, 12 October 1823. BL Add. MS 47553 (ff. 32–3), Robert Southey to JTC, 21 October 1823 [27 October 1823 p/mark]. JM III's Register.

713 Schmidtmeyer – Graham – Hall – *Chili, Peru, &c.* Article 7, pp. 441–72. William Jacob, possibly; possibly subedited by John Wilson Croker.

JM MS, WG to JM [July 1824], 'By way of saving time I send a few pages of America – let them be revised as soon as possible, and then put into Mr C hands as I should wish him to have the final view. This critique is very amusing. I am sorry it is so long' [pencil notation on letter in another hand: 'Coleridge?']. 'Mr C' here more likely refers to JWC than to John Taylor Coleridge. JM III's Register.

714 Hone – *Aspersions Answered.* Article 8, pp. 472–81. Hugh James Rose, probably.
The article is a defence of #589. JM III's Register.

715 Mengin – *Modern Egypt.* Article 9, pp. 481–508. John Barrow; with information from an unnamed correspondent, possibly Henry Salt.

JM MSS: cash day book 1821–4, the same person was paid for articles 3, 4, and 9 in this Number; JB to JM, 30 April 1824; WG to JM, 10 July 1824. The author states on p. 482: 'To these notices we are enabled to add, from documents in our possession, some circumstances of considerable interest, from a source equally authentic'. At about this time, Henry Salt was in communication with JM and JB about Egypt. The author mentions Salt on p. 491 and on the same page alludes to an unnamed 'correspondent'. JM III's Register.

716 Landor – *Imaginary Conversations.* Article 10, pp. 508–19. Henry Taylor; with significant excisions by William Gifford.

Taylor, *Autobiography,* vol. 1, p. 79. JM MS, WG to JM [22 July 1824 p/mark]. JM III's Register.

717 Paulding – *Sketch of Old England.* Article 11, pp. 519–42. John Wilson Croker; with some additions by William Gifford.

JM MSS: WG to JM: [22 July 1824 p/mark]; Ramsgate, 31 July 1824; [August 1824], 'I sent by yesterday's post Mr Croker's revise, with my own remarks'; [August 1824], 'I put Mr C [*sic*] revise, a most ridiculous passage that struck me in Paulding'; [August 1824], 'All that I do this morning is to return Mr C's revise for press. I have added a bit of note'. JWC claimed the article in six Clements Lib. lists; included in the Cambridge Univ. vols. JM III's Register.

718 *Correspondence of Lady Suffolk.* Article 12, pp. 542–59. Walter Scott; subedited by John Wilson Croker.

Todd and Bowden, *Sir Walter Scott: A Bibliographical History.* JM MSS: WG to JM: Ramsgate, 9 August 1824 p/mark; Ramsgate, 10 August 1824 p/mark. JM III's Register.

719 Canning – Stephen – McQueen – *West India Colonies.* Article 13, pp. 559–87. Robert John Wilmot Horton and Charles Rose Ellis; with materials from Robert William Hay and others.

JM MSS: WG to John Taylor Coleridge, 9 December 1823; WG to JM: July 1824: 'You have not sent me the whole of America ... nor mentioned whether Mr C[roker] has revised what is forwarded. I do not understand Wilmot's note. Has neither he nor Hay seen the proofs?'; Ramsgate, 22 July 1824; Ramsgate, 10 August 1824; [August 1824], 'It can do no harm to forward a copy of the revise to Mr Ellis – I can go on with mine again – and if anything comes in time so much the better – Where Mr Wilmot is I do not know'; [August 1824], 'I enclose Wilmot, which is a sound and useful paper – Thanks in the first place to our good friend C.E. I think Wilmot cannot have much to do to it'; Ramsgate, Sunday [August 1824], 'I only wait for Mr Wilmot, who I hope will not meddle with what is done; but content himself with additions – if he has anything important to say'; RWH to JM: 16 June 1824; 28 August 1824; 20 October 1824. *QR* Letter 247. JM III's Register.

VOLUME 31, NUMBER 61
(April 1824)
Published 30 December 1824[60]

720 Graham – Von Spix – Von Martius – *Travels in Brazil.* Article 1, pp. 1–26. William Jacob, possibly.
JM III's Register.

721 Scott – Newton – Cecil – *Memoirs of Scott and Newton.* Article 2, pp. 26–52. John Philips Potter.
JPP reprinted this article in *Essays on the Lives of Newton, Cowper, and Heber* (London: B. Fellowes, 1830). The author refers to #702. JM III's Register.

722 Cruise – *New Zealand.* Article 3, pp. 52–65. John Barrow.
JM MS, cash day book 1821–4, the same person was paid for articles 3, 8, and 13 in this Number. JM III's Register.

723 *Life of Joanna, Queen of Naples.* Article 4, pp. 65–76. George Procter.
JM MS, cash day book 1821–4, the same person was paid for articles 4, 5, and 9 in this Number. JM III's Register.

724 Hunter – Buchanan – *The North American Indians.* Article 5, pp. 76–111. George Procter.
JM MS, cash day book 1821–4, the same person was paid for articles 4, 5, and 9 in this Number. JM MS, WG to JM [October 1824], 'Be so good as to send the inclosed to Mr Procter'. The author refers to #644. JM III's Register.

725 Biddulph – *Operation of the Holy Spirit.* Article 6, pp. 111–25. Thomas Turton, possibly.
JM III's Register.

726 Joplin – *Savings Banks and Country Banks.* Article 7, pp. 126–45. George Taylor.
Claimed by GT in his *Memoir of Robert Surtees*, p. xiv. NLW MS, Robert Southey to Charles William Watkins Wynn, 11 February 1826.

727 Lyall – *Character of the Russians.* Article 8, pp. 146–66. John Barrow.
JM MS, cash day book 1821–4, the same person was paid for articles 3, 8, and 13 in this Number. The article is referred to in #732. JM III's Register: Barrow, and note, 'see Mr Lyall's letters Feb 1825'.

728 Mitford – *Village Sketches.* Article 9, pp. 166–74. George Procter.
JM MS, cash day book 1821–4, the same person was paid for articles 4, 5, and 9 in this Number. JM III's Register.

729 Russell – *Tour in Germany.* Article 10, pp. 174–97. John James Blunt, probably.
JM MS, John Taylor Coleridge to JM, 16 June 1825. JM III's Register.

730 Dale – *The Tragedies of Sophocles.* Article 11, pp. 198–210. Thomas Smart Hughes.
JM MS., John Taylor Coleridge to JM, 4 Sept. 1825. JM III's Register: 'Canon Hughes'.

731 Young – *Angerstein's Collection of Pictures.* Article 12, pp. 210–15. George James Welbor Agar Ellis, possibly.
JM MS, John Taylor Coleridge to JM, 30 Jan. 1825. JM III's Register.

732 Cochrane's *Pedestrian Journey*. Article 13, pp. 215–29. John Barrow.
   JM MS, cash day book 1821–4, the same person was paid for articles 3, 8, and 13 in this Number. The author refers to #727. JB habitually cross-referenced his own articles. JM III's Register: Barrow.

733 Newman – *New Churches – Progress of Dissent*. Article 14, pp. 229–54. Henry Hart Milman.
   JM MS, Henry Hart Milman's holograph list of his *QR* articles. JM MSS: HHM to JM, August 1824, he sends his article on religious dissent; WG to JM [24 December 1824]. The author refers to #684 and #721. JM III's Register.

VOLUME 31, NUMBER 62
(March 1825)
Published 11 March 1825[61]

734 Hayley's *Life and Writings* Article 1, pp. 263–311. Robert Southey.
   Curry and Dedmon, 'Southey's Contributions to the *Quarterly Review*'. JM MS, John Taylor Coleridge to JM, 28 January 1825. *Life and Correspondence of Robert Southey*, vol. 5, p. 177.

735 Ravenstone – *Funding System*. Article 2, pp. 311–27. William Jacob; subedited by William Huskisson.
   JM MS, WJ to JM, 24 January 1825; 30 January 1825; 3 February 1825; 16 February 1825; 13 March 1825.

736 Hubertsberg – *Prussian ReforMS* Article 3, pp. 327–41. Henry Crabb Robinson.
   Henry Crabb Robinson on Books and Their Writers, ed. E. J. Morley (London: J. M. Dent, 1938), vol. 1, pp. 299, 318–19. JM III's Register: 'Robinson (barrister)'.

737 Campbell's *Theodric*. Article 4, pp. 342–49. Edward Smedley, probably.
   JM III's Register.

738 Cumming – Sylvester – Sandars – *Canals and Rail-roads*. Article 5, pp. 349–78. John Barrow.
   JM MS, cash day book, the same person was paid, £100, for articles 5 and 9 in this number; JB to JM, 28 January 1825, 25 July 1825.

739 Baillie – *Lisbon*. Article 6, pp. 378–90. Robert Southey.
   Curry and Dedmon, 'Southey's Contributions to the *Quarterly Review*'.

740 *Artizans and Machinery*. Article 7, pp. 391–419. Charles Ross.
   JM MSS: John Taylor Coleridge to JM, 24 January 1825; CR to JM, 30 January 1825; CR to JM 3 February 1825.

741 Daru's *Venice*. Article 8, pp. 420–45. Thomas Whitaker.
   Not by George Procter as stated in *WI* I, citing JM III's Register. JM MS, John Taylor Coleridge to JM, 30 December 1824, states that TW is preparing an article on this topic. The author is Thomas Whitaker (1762/63–1839).

742 Laing – *Interior of Africa*. Article 9, pp. 445–73. John Barrow.
   JM MS, cash day book, the same person was paid, £100, for articles 5 and 9 in this number; JB to JM, 21 July 1825. JM III's Register.

743 Washington Irving's *Tales*. Article 10, pp. 473–87. John Hughes.
   JM MS, John Taylor Coleridge to JM, March 1825. Beinecke MSS: draft of article #743 and covering letter WG to JH.

744 Rose's *Anecdotes of Monkeys*. Article 11, pp. 487–91. Nassau William Senior.

N. W. Senior, *Biographical Sketches* (London: Longman, Green, Longman, Roberts & Green, 1863). JM III's Register.

745 *The Church in Ireland.* Article 12, pp. 492–528. George Arthur Arden Dealtry and John Taylor Coleridge.

JM III's Register: Rev. Dealtry, and note, 'see Venn', and in another hand, '& Coleridge, whose letter (September 21/25) see'.

VOLUME 32, NUMBER 63
(June 1825)
Published 10 June 1825[62]

746 *Church of England Missions.* Article 1, pp. 1–42. Robert Southey.
Curry and Dedmon, 'Southey's Contributions to the *Quarterly Review*'.

747 *Palladian architecture of Italy.* Article 2, pp. 42–66. Spencer Compton.
JM MS, Henry Hart Milman to JM, 27 September 1824. JM III's Register.

748 Niebuhr – Wachsmuth – Creuzers – *Early Roman History.* Article 3, pp. 67–92. Thomas Arnold.
A. P. Stanley, *The Life and Correspondence of Thomas Arnold, D.D.* , 2 vols (New York: D. Appleton & Co., 1846), vol. 1, p. 49.

749 Hammond – Jeremy – Flather – *Origin of Equitable Jurisdiction.* Article 4, pp. 92–125. Francis Palgrave.
Palgrave, *Collected Historical Works*. JM III's Register.

750 Cladcleugh – *South America.* Article 5, pp. 125–52. John Barrow.
JM III's Register: and note, 'from a letter of JB's April 1825'.

751 Dibdin's *Library Companion.* Article 6, pp. 152–60. George James Welbor Agar Ellis.
JM MS, John Taylor Coleridge to JM, 30 January 1825. JM III's Register: and note, 'from Coleridge's letter, January 30, 1825'.

752 Lowe – *Past and Present State of the Country.* Article 7, pp. 160–97. William Jacob.
BL Add. MS 34613, WJ to Macvey Napier, 24 June 1826.

753 [Croker], *Irish Fairy Tales.* Article 8, pp. 197–211. William Stewart Rose, probably.
T. Keightley, *The Fairy Mythology* (London: n.p., 1850), p. 396n (noted in *WI*).

754 Conder – *The Star in the East – Sacred Poetry.* Article 9, pp. 211–32. John Keble.
JM MS, John Taylor Coleridge to JM, March 1825. J. Keble, *Occasional Papers and Reviews* (Oxford: J. Parker, 1887). JM III's Register.

755 Henderson – *Wines, Ancient and Modern.* Article 10, pp. 232–62. George Procter.
JM MS, John Taylor Coleridge to JM, 11 February 1825. JM III's Register: and note, 'from Capt. P's letter, February 1825'.

VOLUME 32, NUMBER 64
(October 1825)
Published 27 October 1825[63]

756 Roscoe – Warton – Bowles – *Pope's Works and Character.* Article 1, pp. 271–311. George Taylor.
The Correspondence of Robert Southey with Caroline Bowles, ed. E. Dowden (Dublin: Hodges, Figgis, & Co., 1881), p. 93. JM III's Register.

757 Wentworth – Curr – Field – *The Australian Colonies*. Article 2, pp. 311–42. John Barrow.
JM MS, cash day book, the same person was paid, £63, for articles 2 and 5 in this number.
JM III's Register.

758 Pichot's *Literary Tour*. Article 3, pp. 342–55. John Wilson Croker.
JWC claimed the article in five Clements Lib. lists; it is bound with the Cambridge Lib.
volumes. JM III's Register.

759 *Memoirs of Bayard*. Article 4, pp. 355–97. Robert Southey.
Curry and Dedmon, 'Southey's Contributions to the *Quarterly Review*'.

760 Partington – *The Century of Inventions* [Marquis of Worcester]. Article 5, pp. 397–410.
John Barrow.
JM MS, cash day book, the same person was paid, £63, for articles 2 and 5 in this number.

761 Brougham – Grinfield – *Mechanics' Institutes and Infant Schools*. Article 6 pp. 410–28. John
Bird Sumner and John Taylor Coleridge.
JM MS, JTC to JM, 4 September 1825. *Selections from the Letters of Robert Southey*, vol. 3,
p. 511. JM III's Register: 'Rev. J. B. Sumner (Durham)'.

762 Teonge's *Diary*. Article 7, pp. 429–42. John Wilson Croker.
JWC claimed the article in five Clements Lib. lists; it is bound with the Cambridge Lib.
volumes. JM III's Register.

763 Sumner – *Milton, On Christian Doctrine*. Article 8, pp. 442–57. Henry Hart Milman.
JM MS, HHM's autograph list of his *QR* articles. JM III's Register.

764 Southey's *Tale of Paraguay*. Article 9, pp. 457–67. John Taylor Coleridge.
See *WI*. JM III's Register.

765 Wordsworth – *Icôn Basilikè*. Article 9, pp. 467–505. John Leycester Adolphus.
JM MS. JTC to JM, 8 July 1825. JM III's Register.

766 McDonnell – Barham – *West Indian Slavery*. Article 10, pp. 506–43. John Miller and John
Taylor Coleridge.
JM MS, JTC to Murray, five letters, 21 May to 19 October 1825. JM III's Register: William
Ellis and Nassau William Senior supplied materials; Wilmot Horton recommended adjust-
ments; Coleridge re-wrote much of it.

VOLUME 33, NUMBER 65
(December 1825)
Published 29 December 1825[64]

767 Merlin – Butler – Andrews – Cobbett – *The Reformation in England*. Article 1, pp. 1–37.
Henry Hart Milman.
JM MS, HHM's autograph list of his *QR* articles. JM III's Register.

768 Judson – *American Mission to the Burmans*. Article 2, pp. 37–63. John Barrow.
JM MS, John Taylor Coleridge to JM, 10 November 1825.

769 Burgess – David – *Controversy on 1 John v. 7*. Article 2, pp. 64–104. Thomas Turton, probably.
JM III's Register: and note, 'of Catherine Hall, Cambridge'.

770 Crawford's *Mission to Siam and Hué*. Article 3, pp. 104–33. John Barrow.
The author refers to #709. JB systematically cross-referenced his articles. JM III's Register.

771 Gilly – *History of the Vaudois*. Article 4, pp. 134–76. Robert Southey.
Curry and Dedmon, 'Southey's Contributions to the *Quarterly Review*'. JM MS, John
Taylor Coleridge to JM, 24. January 1825.

772 Antommarchi – *Last Moments of Napoleon*. Article 5, pp. 176–86. Robert Gooch.
JM MS, John Taylor Coleridge to JM, 31 November 1825; 14 December 1825. JM III's
Register.

773 *The Usury Laws.* Article 6, pp. 186–205. Francis Palgrave.
JM MSS, John Taylor Coleridge to JM: 2 February 1825; 16 February 1825, 13 March 1825.

774 Gutierrez's *Don Esteban.* Article 7, pp. 205–17. Joseph Blanco White.
See *WI.* JM III's Register.

775 Macmichael – *Plague, a Contagious Disease* Article 8, pp. 218–57. Robert Gooch.
QR Letter 267. JM MSS: John Taylor Coleridge to JM: 4 November 1825; 19 November 1825. JM III's Register.

776 Campbell – *The London University.* Article 9, pp. 257–75. Edward Copleston.
JM MSS: John Taylor Coleridge to JM: 10 November 1825; 19 December 1825. JM III's Register.

APPENDIX B: PUBLICATION STATISTICS

Initial Print Run

Tracing the journal's print run opens a window on Murray's personality and business practice; it is also an objective way to measure the journal's setbacks and successes. Murray's determination of how many copies to print for a given number (issue) was generally dictated by the market, although the publisher's cautious and indecisive nature also influenced his judgements. The rapid sale and quick exhaustion of one number would encourage him to print additional copies the next time around; or, conversely, a slow sale and a clogged inventory might lead him to reduce the print run. When despite increased demand Murray printed the same number of copies from one issue to the next, which happened often, we discover why Byron called him the most timid of God's booksellers.

[Table B.1: Initial Print Run, Numbers 1–60]

Issue Number	Copies Printed	Issue Number	Copies Printed	Issue Number	Copies Printed
1	3,000	21	‡	41	13,000
2	3,000	22	‡	42	‡
3	4,000	23	7,000	43	‡
4	4,000	24	‡	44	13,000
5	5,000	25	‡	45	13,000
6	5,000	26	8,000	46	13,000
7	5,000	27	7,000	47	13,000
8	5,000	28	8,000	48	12,500
9	6,000	29	8,500	49	12,500
10	6,000	30	8,500	50	12,500
11	5,000	31	10,000	51	12,000
12	5,000	32	12,000	52	12,500
13	5,000	33	12,000	53	12,500
14	5,000	34	12,000	54	12,000
15	5,500	35	12,000	55	‡
16	6,000	36	13,000	56	12,500
17	‡	37	13,000	57	12,000

Issue Number	Copies Printed	Issue Number	Copies Printed	Issue Number	Copies Printed
18	‡	38	13,000	58	12,500
19	5,500	39	‡	59	12,250
20	‡	40	13,000	60	12,250

Source: see the notes to Appendix A.
‡ signifies that there is no known record.

Profit and Loss, Numbers 1–11

During the journal's first three years, Murray pored over his ledger books, amazed at the huge outlay required to see the journal through the press. In 1807 and 1808 he assured Canning and Scott that he was a man of capital. In 1810 and 1811 he repeatedly complained of being 'so confoundedly poor'.[1] In August 1810, under the stress of two years' labour to bring the *Quarterly Review* into existence and make it a success, and with financial problems weighing heavily on his mind, Murray's health broke down.[2] Ill and in a dark mood, he harried his editor to the point where Gifford thought of giving up the post. In October of that year, Murray told Gifford he had 'expended nearly £5,000 upon the Review', an assertion he repeated to Ellis. He had 'barely paid the [cost] of producing [the *Quarterly*] and paying the contributors', he claimed. To Southey he said he had 'not gained a farthing' by the *Quarterly*, 'only 10,000 Numbers of dead stock'.[3] In November he baldly stated that 'no one number ha[d], hitherto, paid its own expenses'.

Those statements are contradicted by the firm's records and even by John Murray's own testimony. In April 1809 he informed his editor that the journal's 'regular sale [was] ... on the increase' and in July he assured his wife that the *Quarterly* was doing as well as one might expect.[4] For three years he manipulatively used the journal's lateness and his apparent failure to make a profit as a stick to beat his editor with. Over the years, exaggerating his financial concerns was a strategy he habitually used with authors, even with Byron, by whom he made a fortune.

Because rudimentary inventory and ledger books survive, we can test the truth of Murray's claims. The clearest record from the early period is an accounting of circulation, sales, and expenses that Murray prepared in November 1811 of Numbers 1–11, epitomized in the present volume as Table B.2. Murray's outlay over the course of eleven numbers was £10,200.[5] The sale of initial runs when complete (clearing his stock for a given number sometimes took several months) generated £10,457. By October 1811, because Number 11 had yet to sell out, Murray had not quite covered his expenses. When in a few more months he finally emptied his warehouse of first edition copies of Numbers 1–11, he generated a small profit, £257.

[Table B.2: Epitome of Profit and Loss, Numbers 1–11]

Issue Number	On hand, Nov. 1811*	Initial Print Run	Break even point†	Initial Sale	Total Expenses‡	Payment to Editor and Contributors**			Potential Profit (Loss)‡	Stated Profit (Loss)‡
		number of copies			£	£	s.	d.	£	£
1	800	3,000	–	3,000	544	213	10	11	(19)	(19)
2	160	3,000	–	3,000	546	200	18	6	(21)	(21)
3	1,200	4,000	3,646	3,454	638	206	2	6	62	(17)
4	800	4,000	3,835	3,715	671	202	15	10	29	(21)
5	700	5,000	3,924	3,487	875	224	8	9	205	(119)
6	900	5,000	3,660	4,100	793	198	6	9	290	
7	800	5,000	4,020	4,200	871	230	14	5	212	not stated
8	600	5,000	3,798	4,400	823	220	15	6	260	
9	1,740	6,000		missing		248	1	–	missing	
10	1,950	6,000				210	–	3		
11	850	5,000	4,431	4,150	960	no record			123	not stated
	10,500									

Source: JM MS, epitome of Numbers 1–11.

* Includes Edinburgh and Dublin unsold copies and unsold copies of second and third editions.
† The minimum number of sales required to cover expenses.
‡ Murray calculated his cost per copy at 3s. 6d. for Nos. 1–4 and 4s. 4d. for Nos. 5–11. His greatest single expense was paper, £324 for No. 5, for example.
** Except for Southey, to whom he paid £100 per article, Murray paid contributors £10 10s per sheet. He paid the editor £50 per issue for Nos. 1–9, £100 for Nos. 10 and 11.

In the meantime, Murray began to speculate on the future value of the *Quarterly Review*. He did so by printing second and third editions of specific numbers that he then offered to the book-buying public as individual copies or as part of complete runs. Without exactly revealing to his coadjutors the true state of affairs, he did admit that 'every penny of [his] gain [was] in the Warehouse' in the form of inventory of first, second, and third 'editions'.[6] In late 1811, he had in his warehouse 'more than *Ten Thousand Numbers*'. Most of those 10,500 copies were not unsold stock from first editions – which is what he let his editor and contributors believe – but speculative inventory.[7]

The journal as such was not a source of financial problems for Murray. His troubles were due to his tying up capital in inventory and in contracting partnerships that drained his coffers. Scott's *Edinburgh Annual Register*, which in 1808–11 damaged the *Quarterly* by distracting Scott and drawing off potential contributors, was an unwanted expense. By the end of March 1811, Murray had sold fewer than fifty copies of the *Register* and he had lost £300 by it.[8] Much more seriously, throughout this period he carried debt for his two major partners, Ballantyne and Constable, who, in treating Murray as a loans officer, abused what was meant to be a mutually advantageous relationship.[9]

A reason why Murray was not making more money on the *Quarterly* was because of his tug of war with Gifford over editorial control, a contest that is documented in Murray's accounts. Their combat involved much costly second guessing. For any given number Murray's bookkeeper regularly recorded 'Extra' costs for off-hours work – 'Sunday work' and 'Night work'. 'Cancelled 11 pages' (or a similar number) is an oft-repeated entry in the accounts, the result of the publisher and editor disagreeing with each other about the suitability of this or that article. Articles that were worked up and never used include 'Milton' in Number 2 and 'Clarkes marbles' in Number 4. The amount of cancelled and corrected copy increased from number to number. There were £16 3*s.* worth of corrections in Number 6. That was followed by £17 18*s.* 6*d.* of cancelled matter in 'Leslie' in Number 7. Corrections for Number 8 cost £21 5*s.* Also for that number £2 was paid to the printer for 'Sunday and Night work' and an additional £1 to the printer for 'Extra Trouble'. Number 11 cost Murray £28 17*s.* for corrections. For Numbers 1 through 11 Murray paid out about £200 in 'Extra' costs,[10] approximately the equivalent of Gifford's current annual salary.

Especially for initial runs, producing the *Quarterly* was a costly venture, which is why Murray worked with Gifford to make it as much as possible an encyclopaedia-like repository of permanent knowledge. The goal was to make the *Quarterly* a resource that readers would wish to purchase in complete runs. Epitomizing the accounts gives us a clear understanding of where Murray incurred his expenses, the relative cost of each element of the physical book, the cost of procuring articles, and the cost of administration, advertising, and distribution.

Taking Number 7 as an example – the number in which Robert Grant's review of a life of William Pitt appeared – we find that Murray paid thirteen authors a total of £189 for their labours at a rate of 10 pounds 10 shillings per sheet (a sheet consisted of 16 pages). It was characteristic of Murray to pay a handsome bonus for extraordinary work, not as an act of largesse so much as to encourage more of the same. Consequently, he paid Grant double for article number 13 – £85 for sixty-five pages. The editor was remitted £50 plus £2 10*s.* for copyright. 'Books, Postage, Incidents' for Number 7 cost Murray £10, an amount that appears regularly in the accounts and was therefore a budgeted estimate. Editorial costs and the cost of obtaining articles for this number, then, amounted to about £310. With the addition of £19 19*s.* 2*d.* for advertising, non-production costs equaled about £330 or about thirty-eight percent of the total cost of publishing Number 7.

Printing and Paper costs, Numbers 48–65

About two thirds of the cost of producing the *Quarterly Review* was absorbed by the printer's shop. Continuing with Number 7 as our example, printing and assembling the physical book cost Murray about £540. Each of the 5,000 copies of Number 7 consisted of 271 pages of articles, 136 leaves. For printing the 680,000 leaves required for *Quarterly Review* Number 7, Charles Rowarth of

Bell-yard, Temple Bar, charged Murray £135 at a rate of £7 10s. per sheet. The 5,000 wrappers on which appeared the title, publisher's imprint, the printer's name and the price, cost £2 19s. 'Cancelled matter in Leslie & in Quarterly List, corrections, Remaking up &c' cost Murray £17 18s. 6d. Paper, his single greatest expense, cost an extraordinary £319 10s. 10d. for 180 reams at £35 6s. a ream.[11] For the wrappers Murray used heavier, more costly, paper, so to produce these he paid more, £8 15s. for two reams at seventy shillings a ream. Other large incidental expenses included £10 for 'Books, Postage, Carriage &c', a budgeted estimate as the same figure appears in the ledger book for number after number. Advertising was a heavy expense at about £30 per issue. Stitching cost Murray £3 2s. For 5,000 copies of Number 7, that amounted to £72 18s. 4d.

Much investment in human labour went into the making of a single copy of the *Quarterly Review*, and much of that investment was expended in the printer's shop. The printer's shop was in many ways equal to Murray's offices in importance, though we know less about what went on there than about activities in the editorial department. When the printer's office does enter the record, it was because it had become a site of conflict between the publisher, the editor, and their contributors. That happened rather too often for the health of the *Quarterly*'s editorial machine. Sometimes, the printer's shop was a scene of deception and subterfuge. Early on, Murray occasionally took a manuscript away from Gifford before he was done with it to have it printed in slips. To retaliate for Murray's humiliating practice, Gifford sometimes then held onto the slips and made 'retarding corrections' that prevented the number from going forward.[12] Contributors, too, sometimes used the printer against the editor. To bypass Gifford, Barrow and Croker often worked directly with the printer. When Coleridge was editor he was 'surprised and vexed' to find that one of his contributors, Miller, had gone over his head by directly ordering the printer to make changes to his article.[13] Entering the printer's shop without the editor's or publisher's connivance was fraught with social and professional significance.

[Table B.3: Printing and Paper Costs, Numbers 48–65]

Date Paid	To	For *QR* Number	Amount £.s.d
7.2.1821	*Rowarth	48	329.13.–
28.6.1821	Rowarth	49	286.9.–
17.10.1821	Rowarth	50	319.19.–
22.12.1821	Rowarth	51	279.4.–
28.3.1822	Rowarth	52	308.9.–
1.8.1822	Rowarth	53	294.4.6
23.9.1822	Rowarth	54	295.11.6
15.2.1823	Rowarth	55	306.13.6
8.7.1823	†Magnay	56	562.17.6
29.9.1823	Rowarth	57	299.6.–
27.9.1823	Magnay	57	506.12.6
27.1.1824	Rowarth	58	326.19.–
30.12.1824	Magnay	58	583.13.6
19.4.1824	Rowarth	59	432.14.6

Date Paid	To	For *QR* Number	Amount £.s.d
1.9.1824	Magnay	60	552.12.6
1.9.1824	Rowarth	60	316.17.–
1.1.1825	Rowarth	61	506.12.6
1.3.1825	Rowarth	61	291.8.–
14.3.1825	Rowarth	62	294.6.6
11.3.1825	Magnay	62	518.2.6
11.6.1825	Magnay	63	518.2.6
24.10.1825	Rowarth	64	292.13.6
25.10.1825	Magnay	64	762.2.6
28.10.1825	Rowarth	65	312.17.–
1.2.1826	Magnay	65	663.2.6

Source: JM MS, bills payable ledger.
*C. Rowarth, printer.
†C. Magnay, stationer

Publication Dates and Publication Record, Numbers 1–65

[Table B.4: Publication Dates, Numbers 1–65]

Volume	Number	Title Page Date	Appearance Date
1	1	February 1809	1 March 1809
1	2	May 1809	30 May 1809
2	3	August 1809	29 August 1809
2	4	November 1809	23 December 1809
3	5	February 1810	31 March 1810
3	6	May 1810	21 July 1810
4	7	August 1810	27 October 1810
4	8	November 1810	29 December 1810
5	9	February 1811	10 April 1811
5	10	May 1811	1 July 1811
6	11	August 1811	21 October 1811
6	12	December 1811	1 February 1812
7	13	March 1812	11 May 1812
7	14	June 1812	13 August 1812
8	15	September 1812	15 December 1812
8	16	December 1812	5 March 1813
9	17	March 1813	16 June 1813
9	18	July 1813	25 August 1813
10	19	October 1813	18 December 1813
10	20	January 1814	1 April 1814
11	21	April 1814	16 July 1814
11	22	July 1814	8 November 1814
12	23	October 1814	6 January 1815
12	24	January 1815	23 March 1815
13	25	April 1815	20 June 1815
13	26	July 1815	1 December 1815
14	27	October 1815	12 March 1816
14	28	January 1816	18 May 1816
15	29	April 1816	10 August 1816
15	30	July 1816	12 November 1816
16	31	October 1816	11 February 1817
16	32	January 1817	17 May 1817
17	33	April 1817	6 September 1817
17	34	July 1817	1 December 1817
18	35	October 1817	21 February 1818
18	36	January 1818	9 June 1818
19	37	April 1818	26 September 1818
19	38	July 1818	2 February 1819
20	39	Index Pt I	20 May 1820
20	40	Index Pt II	June 1820

Volume	Number	Title Page Date	Appearance Date
21	41	January 1819	4 June 1819
21	42	April 1819	10 September 1819
22	43	July 1819	11 December 1819
22	44	January 1820	17 March 1820
23	45	May 1820	27 May 1820
23	46	July 1820	5 October 1820
24	47	October 1820	19 December 1820
24	48	January 1821	12 or 19 April 1821
25	49	April 1821	28 June 1821
25	50	July 1821	17 October 1821
26	51	October 1821	22 December 1821
26	52	January 1822	30 March 1822
27	53	April 1822	4 July 1822
27	54	July 1822	23 October 1822
28	55	October 1822	15 February 1823
28	56	January 1823	8 July 1823
29	57	April 1823	27 September 1823
29	58	July 1823	30 December 1823
30	59	October 1823	17 April 1824
30	60	January 1824	28 August 1824
31	61	April 1824	30 December 1824
31	62	March 1825	11 March 1825
32	63	June 1825	10 June 1825
32	64	October 1825	27 October 1825
33	65	December 1825	29 December 1825

Sources: See the notes to Appendix A.

For students of the *Quarterly Review*, sorting out the journal's real and putative publication dates is important for the proper understanding of references to articles in letters and other documents.[14] The question is also of interest more generally, for it casts light on William Gifford's conduct of the *Quarterly* and on his relationship with John Murray. The journal's irregular appearance was a matter of grave concern to publisher and editor and the cause of serious friction between the two men.[15] When because of the journal's non-appearance topical comments in the review were overtaken by events, the *Quarterly* became at best a historical journal. Chronic lateness was professionally embarrassing and it probably affected sales. Subscribers were left frustrated and booksellers inconvenienced. In the end, it was nonsensical in a journal whose title advertised regularity to be reliable only in being reliably late.

Only a handful of times during Gifford's editorship are the title page date and the real publication date identical for any given issue of the *Quarterly Review*. Indeed this understates the problem, for there is also often a lack of congruence between the date that appears on an issue's original wrapper and the date on the same number's inside title page. For a single issue it is not unusual for a researcher to be faced with four or more 'publication' dates, no two of which agree: the title page date, the date on the wrapper, the date (or very often dates) the journal was advertised to appear, and the date when the journal was made available for sale. To give a typical example: the title page date of Volume 21 Number 41 is January 1819; on May 28th the issue was advertised to appear 'on June 1st'; and then on June 4th Murray announced in newspapers that Number 41 was published 'this day'; indeed, the Number did appear at booksellers on 4 June 1819, but the date on the original wrappers reads 'May 1819'.

Because of Gifford's frequent illnesses, the publisher and his editor never found a way to bring the *Quarterly* out on a regular schedule. As illustrated in Table B.5, for thirty-five out of the sixty-one numbers published during his tenure, Gifford took more than three months to prepare the journal.[16] There was an interval of five months between Numbers 25 and 26 because Gifford fell ill. Worst of all, in five years – 1811, 1814, 1818, 1822, and 1824 – only three numbers appeared. The editor deflected some of the responsibility for the journal's lateness onto the shoulders of his contributors. 'My friends', he told Murray, 'will never, I fear, learn the virtue of punctuality'. Regardless, the *Quarterly*'s lateness was not excused by booksellers and subscribers. It caused them to doubt Murray's reliability, the projectors' commitment, and the editor's ability to attract and keep contributors. 'Hence', Ellis told Murray in 1810, 'I infer that *punctuality* is, in our present situation our great and only desideratum'.

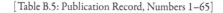

[Table B.5: Publication Record, Numbers 1–65]

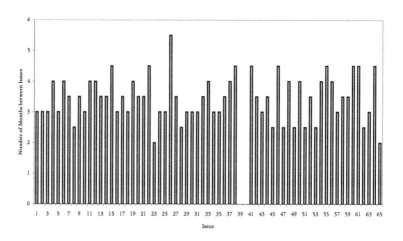

The *Quarterly Review* should have appeared once every three months. The table demonstrates how often Gifford and Coleridge hit that mark. Issues 39 and 40, blank in the chart, were Parts I and II of the index.

APPENDIX C: JOHN MURRAY'S 1808 LISTS OF PROSPECTIVE CONTRIBUTORS

In late October or early November 1808, a few weeks after John Murray's seminal meeting with Walter Scott at Ashiestiel, the publisher began to fill a notebook with ideas about the proposed journal. In his memoranda, in categorizing the *Quarterly*'s prospective audience he embraced the whole reading nation, 'The Parson – Soldier – Lawyer – Statesman', and so on. He then ambitiously concluded, 'there should be one article in every number appropriate to each of these classes – the rest to be filled up with subjects of general interest and importance'. His reasoning, though plausible, was impractical as it presupposed the thing most difficult to supply, a stream of ideologically correct writers who could produce copy four times a year specifically targeted to each of these audiences.

More immediately useful were his lists of 'Books on Subjects desirable for the Review', subdivided into 'Already published' and 'Books or Subjects already in [the press]'. Having done this preliminary work, on 15 November 1808 he wrote a long letter to Scott in which, apparently for the first time, he took ownership of 'the plan' of establishing the new journal, he advocated a temperate tone, and he worried about how effective Gifford would be in the editor's chair. At the end of the letter he promised to share 'a list of Literary men we may both now and hereafter more or less engage as contributors' (*QR* Letter 8). The progenitor of his promised list is preserved in Murray's *Quarterly Review* planning notes. In his notebook he arranged the prospective contributors' names under the heads of the three men principally responsible for bringing out the first number – Scott, Gifford, and himself. There are reasons to believe that Murray drew up these lists in consultation with Scott and Gifford and that they record one aspect of his discussions with Scott at Ashiestiel.[1]

Even though only 35 of the 123 men and women in Murray's lists eventually contributed to the *Quarterly Review*, the lists bear close study, for, taken together, they are a window on the founders' understanding of the types of articles the journal should cover, the audiences it should address, and the *Quarterly*'s ideology. Whatever the amorphous nature of political parties in this period – no 'Tory' party existed, for instance – men such as John Murray were aware of the fine shadings of conservatism in Parliament, Church, and Nation and they knew who belonged to which camp.[2] So it is that all of the political men in Murray's lists are – risking an oxymoron – at the liberal end of the conservative spectrum: Hawkesbury, Palmerston, Long, Canning, Hammond, Ellis, Rose, Huskisson, and the Grant brothers. There is at least one surprising political name in Gifford's column, that of Lord Dudley who in 1808 was still in the Whig camp. He had however expressed himself dissatisfied with the Whigs on at least one of the litmus test issues that defined the Canningites – he was for prosecuting the war against Napoleon. Instructive, too, is the presence in John Murray's lists of John Wilson Croker, a man who would become one of the *Quarterly*'s 'sheet anchors' but who was not then and never became formally allied with Canning. He is present in Murray's lists because he held the right opinions, he was known as a political journalist, and he was trusted by many of the men in power.

The lists also include key Saints, William Wilberforce and James Stephen, their City coadjutor Henry Thornton, and William Gifford's friend, Lord Teignmouth. These men, despite their conservative reputation among scholars, were, in certain respects, radicals willing to reshape the foundational institutions of Great Britain for the sake of moral if not political reform. The Saints had been frequent contributors to the *Edinburgh Review* and they collaborated with Henry Brougham in the effort to abolish the slave trade. Thornton, a banker and leading political economist, had his classic treatise on *Paper Credit* favourably reviewed in the *Edinburgh*'s first number. But recently, Sir William Drummond published anti-Christian sentiments in the *Edinburgh*, Francis Jeffrey savaged the evangelical poet James Montgomery, and Sydney Smith roughly treated the Saints over their plans for the evangelization of India. The Saints were therefore ready to abandon the *Edinburgh*, and it was because Teignmouth had offered the Saints' support for the prospective *Quarterly* journal that Murray added their names to his lists.

Among the literary figures in Murray's lists are friends of Scott and fashionable authors, including Baillie, Edgeworth, and Barbauld. One literary name stands out as anomalous. Murray thought well of the radical author Leigh Hunt's talents and he had his eye on him to write a grand review of the English drama. Though he wrote repeatedly to Hunt with that object in mind, the author contemptuously spurned him. Other prominent literary names include the Romantic poets, Wordsworth, Coleridge, and Southey. Except for Southey, though, their presence is mere musing on Murray's part. He did not meet Wordsworth until 1818 and, as for Coleridge, he thought him unreliable as a man and as a prose writer too obscure for a popular journal. That Southey should have made the lists is somewhat surprising. At the end of 1808 he was in the minds of most of the reading public a dangerous radical. But Southey was legitimately in Murray's lists because he supported the war against Napoleon.

There are some notable gaps. One kind of mental ruminator popular in the period, the antiquary, is only lightly represented and there is also no one connected with music. Murray perhaps saw no point in competing with the specialist journals that served these constituencies. Indeed, he may have intuited that including subject matter of this sort would alienate more subscribers than it would attract.

The reader should note that in his lists Murray sometimes recorded only initials or last names. Given the context and from strong clues from correspondence and other documentation in the John Murray Archive it has not, however, proved difficult to arrive at a positive identification of the men and women he had in mind.

Names Listed under Murray

Anstey, John (d. 1819), barrister and comic poet
Barbauld, Anna Letitia (1743–1825), poet and essayist
Barclay, John (1758–1826), anatomist
Barrett, Eaton Stannard (1786–1820), *QR* contributor, poet and satirist
Black, John (1783–1855), journalist and newspaper editor
Bowdler, Henrietta Maria (1750–1830), writer and literary editor
Burney, Charles (1757–1817), schoolmaster
Burney, James (1750–1821), *QR* subscriber, naval officer, writer
Chalmers, Alexander (1759–1834), biographer and literary editor
Cockburn, William (d. 1858), Christian Advocate, Cambridge
Coleman, Edward (1765–1839), Surgeon General, Veterinary College, St Pancras, London
Colman, George, the younger (1762–1836), playwright
Crombie, Alexander (1760–1840), philologist and schoolmaster
Cumberland, Richard (1732–1811), playwright and novelist
Davy, Sir Humphry, baronet (1778–1829), chemist and inventor
Dibdin, Thomas Frognall (1776–1847), bibliographer
D'Israeli, Isaac (1766–1848), *QR* contributor, writer
Douce, Francis (1757–1834), antiquary and collector
Drake, Nathan (1766–1836), essayist and physician
Dubois, Edward (1774–1850), writer
Duppa, Richard (bap. 1768, d. 1831), writer and draughtsman
Edgeworth, Maria (1768–1849), novelist and educationist
Elmsley, Peter (1773–1825), *QR* contributor, classicist
Ferriar, John (1761–1815), *QR* contributor, medical professional
Frere, John Hookham (1769–1846) *QR* contributor, diplomat. His name also appears under Gifford.

Gilchrist, Octavius Graham (1779–1823), *QR* contributor, scholar, grocer

Greenfield, William (1755–1827), *QR* contributor, disgraced university professor

Hamilton, William Richard (1777–1859), antiquary and diplomat

Heber, Reginald (1783–1826), *QR* contributor, clergyman

Hoare, Prince (1755–1834), playwright and artist. His name also appears under Gifford.

Huddesford, George (bap. 1749, d. 1809), satiric poet

Hunt, (James Henry) Leigh (1784–1859), poet and journalist

Inchbald, Elizabeth (1753–1821), writer and actress

Kirwan, Richard (1733–1812), chemist and mineralogist

Knight, Richard Payne (1751–1824), art collector and writer

Lawrence, James Henry (1773–1840), writer

Malthus, Thomas Robert (1766–1834), *QR* contributor, clergyman, political economist

Marsh, Herbert (1757–1839), *QR* contributor, clergyman

Middleton, Thomas Fanshaw (1769–1822), clergyman

Mill, James (1773–1836), political philosopher, historian, civil servant

Monk, James Henry (1784–1856), *QR* contributor, clergyman, classicist

Murray, Hugh (1779–1846), geographer

Ouseley, Sir William (1767–1842), orientalist, diplomat

Park, Thomas (1758/59–1834), antiquary and bibliographer

Penrose, John (1778–1859) *QR* contributor, teacher. His name also appears under Gifford.

Pillans, James (1778–1864), *QR* contributor, teacher

Planta, Joseph (1787–1847), diplomat

Playfair, John (1748–1819), mathematician and geologist

Porden, William (bap. 1755, d. 1822), architect

Reeve, Henry (1780–1814), physician

Rennell, James (1742–1830), cartographer

Roberts, Barré Charles (1789–1810), *QR* contributor, antiquary

Shaw, George (1751–1813), natural historian

Shee, Sir Martin Archer (1769–1850), portrait painter and writer

Shipley, William Davies (1745–1826), clergyman

Smith, James (1775–1839), writer and humorist

Stephen, Henry John (1787–1864), *QR* contributor, lawyer

Stoddart, John (1773–1856), journalist

Thomson, John (1765–1846), physician and surgeon

Thomson, Thomas (1773–1852), *QR* contributor, scientist

Turner, Sharon (1768–1847), *QR* contributor, lawyer

Walker, Joseph Cooper (1761–1810), antiquary

Walpole, Robert (1781–1856), *QR* contributor, classicist

Westall, Richard (1765–1836), painter

Whitaker, Thomas Dunham (1759–1821), *QR* contributor, clergyman, antiquary

Young, Thomas (1773–1829), *QR* contributor, scientist

Names Listed under Gifford

Bagot, Sir Charles (1781–1843), parliamentary undersecretary

Batten, Joseph Hallett (d. 1837), principal of Hertford College, East India Company

Canning, George (1770–1827), *QR* co-founder, statesman

Canning, Stratford (1786–1880), *QR* co-founder, diplomat

Conybeare, John Josias (1779–1824), geologist and antiquary

Croker, John Wilson (1780–1857), *QR* contributor, politician

Drummond, Henry Home (1783–1867), member of Parliament

Ellis, Charles Rose, 1st Baron Seaford (1771–1845), politician

Ellis, George (1753–1815), *QR* contributor, diplomat, writer

Elton, Charles Abraham (1778–1853), *QR* contributor, poet, theologian

Frere, John Hookham (1769–1846), *QR* contributor. His name also appears under Murray.

Gaisford, Thomas (1779–1855), classical scholar and college dean

Grant, Charles, Baron Glenelg (1778–1866), statesman

Grant, Sir Robert (1779–1838), *QR* contributor, politician

Gutch, John Mathew (1776–1861), journalist, author, and bookseller

Herries, John Charles (1778–1855), politician

Hoare, Prince (1755–1834), playwright and artist. His name also appears under Murray.

Hoppner, John (1758–1810), *QR* contributor, portraitist

Ireland, John (1761–1842), *QR* contributor, clergyman

Ivory, James (1765–1842), mathematician

Jenkinson, Robert Banks, 2nd Earl of Liverpool (1770–1828), *QR* patron, prime minister

Jordan, John (1746–1809), local historian and poet

Kidd, John (1775–1851), *QR* contributor, physician

Long, Charles (1760–1838), *QR* patron, politician

Mackintosh, Sir James (1765–1832), writer and politician

Peltier, Jean-Gabriel (bap. 1760, d. 1825), journalist and political exile

Penrose, John (1778–1859), *QR* contributor, teacher. His name also appears under Murray.

Rickman, John (1771–1840), *QR* contributor, civil servant

Robinson, (John) Thomas Romney (1793–1882), astronomer and physicist

Rose, George (1744–1818), *QR* patron, politician

Seyer, Samuel (1757/58–1831), clergyman and antiquary

Shore, John, 1st Baron Teignmouth (1751–1834), *QR* patron, governor-general of Bengal

Smythe, Percy, 6th Viscount Strangford (1780–1855), diplomat

Sotheby, William (1757–1833), poet and translator

Southey, Robert (1774–1843), *QR* contributor, writer

Stephen, James (1758–1832), *QR* subscriber, lawyer

Stevenson, William (c. 1750–1821), antiquary

Temple, Henry John, third Viscount Palmerston (1784–1865), *QR* patron, prime minister

Thornton, Henry (1760–1815), *QR* patron, banker and political economist

Ward, John William, Earl of Dudley (1781–1833), *QR* contributor, member of parliament

Wellesley, Richard (1787–1831), *QR* contributor, diplomat

Wilberforce, William (1759–1833), politician, philanthropist

Names Listed under Scott

Alison, Archibald (1757–1839), associationist philosopher, writer on aesthetics

Baillie, Joanna (1762–1851), dramatist and poet

Campbell, Thomas (1777–1844), *QR* subscriber, poet

Coleridge, Samuel Taylor (1772–1834), *QR* contributor, poet

Copleston, Edward (1776–1849), *QR* contributor, clergyman, teacher, political economist

Dundas, Robert Saunders, 2nd Viscount Melville (1771–1851), *QR* patron, politician

Erskine, William, Lord Kinneder (1769–1822), *QR* contributor, lawyer

Gordon, George Hamilton -, 4th Earl of Aberdeen (1784–1860), *QR* patron, prime minister

Heber, Richard (1774–1833), *QR* co-founder, bibliophile, member of Parliament

Leyden, John (1775–1811), linguist and poet

Marriott, John (1780–1825), poet and clergyman

Mathias, Thomas James (1753/4–1835), satirist and Italian scholar

Morritt, John Bacon Sawrey (1771–1843), traveller and classical scholar

Murray, John (1778–1820), chemist and public lecturer

Nott, John (1751–1825), physician and classical scholar

Tytler, Alexander Fraser, Lord Woodhouselee (1747–1813), historian

Wordsworth, William (1770–1850), poet

NOTES

Introduction

1. For a discussion of deviations from this generalization, see my 'A Plurality of Voices in the *Quarterly Review*' in J. Cutmore (ed.), *Conservatism and the Quarterly Review: A Critical Analysis* (London: Pickering and Chatto, 2007), pp. 61–85.
2. D. H. Reiman, *The Romantics Reviewed: Contemporary Reviews of British Romantic Writers*, 5 vols (New York: Garland, 1972), Part C, vol. 2, p. 751.
3. The *Victorian Periodicals Review* articles are, 'The *Quarterly Review* under Gifford: Some New Attributions,' 24:3 (1991), pp. 137–42; 'The Early *Quarterly Review* 1809–24: New Attributions and Sources,' 27:4 (1994), pp. 308–18; 'The Early *Quarterly Review*: New Attributions of Authorship,' 28:4 (1995), pp. 305–25. Portions of this section of the introduction and parts of the acknowledgements repeat material first published in the *Quarterly Review Archive*. The material appears with acknowledgement to the editors of *Romantic Circles*.
4. P. N. Furbank and W. R. Owens, *Defoe De-Attributions: A Critique of J. R. Moore's Checklist* (London: Hambledon Continuum, 2003), p. xiii.
5. In most cases, the date of the journal's initial sale differed significantly from the title page date. See the notes to individual numbers in Appendix A, the introduction to Appendix B, and the note on Publication Dates in Appendix B.
6. Originally assigned in H. Shine and H. C. Shine, *The Quarterly Review under Gifford: Identification of Contributors* (Chapel Hill, NC: University. of North Carolina Press, 1949).

1 Origins

1. The journal's publication dates are documented in Appendix A of the present volume. For an explanation of the notation '*QR* Letters' and for a list of the letters referred to, see Cutmore (ed.), *Conservatism and the Quarterly Review*, pp. 179–88.
2. *QR* Letters 1, 3.
3. At least the *Quarterly*'s projectors saw it this way. Some years later, James Mill argued in the *Westminster Review* that both the *Quarterly* and the *Edinburgh* supported the establishment. See James Mill, 'Periodical Literature: The Edinburgh Review, Vol. 1, 2, &c', *Westminster Review*, 1 (January 1824), pp. 206–49 and 'Periodical Literature: The Quarterly Review', *Westminster Review*, 2 (October 1824), pp. 463–503. The French traveller Louis Simond remarked, 'The philosophic and political adversaries of

the Edinburgh Review, have set up a similar work in London, (the Quarterly Review), an imitation as to plan and manner, but, at the same time, in direct opposition on almost every subject' (*Journal of a Tour and Residence in Great Britain* (Edinburgh: Constable, 1817), p. 60).

4. In *English Bards and Scotch Reviewers* (London: Cawthorne, 1809), Byron's nickname for the *Edinburgh Review*.

5. On philosophic Whiggism see for instance B. Hilton, *A Mad, Bad, And Dangerous People?: England 1783–1846* (Oxford: Oxford University Press, 2006), pp. 346–52.

6. D. Roper, *Reviewing Before the Edinburgh, 1788–1802* (Cranbury, NJ: University of Delaware Press, 1978). Simond commented, 'The Edinburgh reviewers ... must be allowed the merit of having founded a new school, destined to be the model for the critics of the nineteenth century' (*Journal of a Tour*, p. 60).

7. 'Criticism', in N. Bosworth et al. (eds), *Pantologia. A New Cabinet Cyclopædia*, 12 vols (London: G. Kearsley, et al., 1808–13), vol. 3, unpaginated.

8. *QR* Letter 1. *Life and Correspondence of John Foster*, ed. J. E. Ryland, 2 vols (New York: Wiley and Putnam, 1848), vol. 1, p. 310.

9. Josiah Conder, the editor of the *Eclectic Review*, spoke for many of the *Edinburgh*'s otherwise admiring readers when he detected arbitrariness and grandstanding. The reviewers, he lamented, 'are demagogues, who are striving to raise their own importance, by levelling the distinctions of literary merit. The authors whose works a former age would have received with gratitude, and inspected with reverence, are brow-beaten, cross-examined, and held up to ridicule by the anonymous Critic, with cold professional arrogance.' Of the authors Conder mentions as having been unfairly reviewed in the *Edinburgh*, Thomson, Young, and Gregory became writers for the *Quarterly* (J. Conder, *Reviewers Reviewed* (Oxford: J. Bartlett, 1811), pp. 26, 39, 59, 60). Samuel Romilly thought that 'the editors seem[ed] to value themselves principally on their severity', and, like Conder, he concluded that they were egoists who 'reviewed some works seemingly with no other object than to show what their powers in this particular line of criticism are' (S. Romilly, *Memoirs of the Life of Samuel Romilly*, 2 vols (London: John Murray, 1841), vol. 1, p. 426).

10. Variant of 'fugleman', a military drill instructor. Throughout his adulthood, Bedford was Southey's abiding friend, as Southey himself testified in 1820: 'You are my only *frequent* and constant correspondent, the only person, with whom correspondence has become a habit; with whom I can be grave or nonsensical ...' (quoted in *NL*, vol. 2, p. 481). Bedford's letters to Southey, preserved at the Bodleian, provide valuable insight into the development of many of Southey's articles for the *QR* and into Murray's back-office machinations. He was Gifford's friend as well and as a frequent visitor to Murray's Fleet Street and later Albemarle Street shop he was privy to Murray and Gifford's chatter and their private behaviour, which he gleefully retailed to the ever-receptive Southey. His assessments are often uncharitable – he portrays Murray as a boozer, Gifford as the untalented butcher of other men's prose – but he gives the impression that in these cruel portraits he is reflecting Southey's frustration over having to labour for pay and, pleased to be the confidential friend of a man greater than himself, he is happy to play the role of enabler.

11. Bodl. Lib. MS Eng. Lett. d. 52 (ff. 112–14), 29 December 1814.

12. *Life and Correspondence of Robert Southey*, ed. C. C. Southey, 6 vols (London: Longman, et al., 1849–50), vol. 3, pp. 125–6. Southey wrote to Scott in June 1807, 'I have scarcely one opinion in common with it [the *Edinburgh Review*] upon any subject.

...Whatever of any merit I might insert there would aid and abet opinions hostile to my own, and thus identify me with a system which I thoroughly disapprove. This is not said hastily. ... But my moral feelings must not be compromised'. Southey's refusal was an event of some importance in the history of the *QR*. It was one of the factors that inspired Scott to reconsider his relationship to the *Edinburgh* as a contributor and subeditor. NLS MS 3876 (ff. 137–8), quoted in Smiles, *Memoir*, vol. 1, pp. 94–5. JM MS, Southey to Murray, 18 March 1810. On Southey's role in the *QR* see L. Pratt's 'Hung, Drawn and Quarterlyed: Robert Southey, Poetry, Poets, and the *Quarterly Review*' and B. Speck's 'Robert Southey's Contribution to the *Quarterly Review*' in Cutmore (ed.), *Conservatism and the Quarterly Review*, pp. 151–64 and 165–77, respectively.

13. The Montgomery review is *WI* #332; Cowper (part 1), *WI* #57, (part 2), *WI* #160; Moncreiff, *WI* #218; Hoyle, *WI* #249; More, *WI* #294; Curates' Salaries Bill, *WI* #427. Up to the end of 1808, the *Edinburgh*'s literary reviews that caused the greatest offence were Jeffrey's reviews of Southey's *Thalaba, WI* #8; and his *Madoc, WI* #245; Thelwall's *Poems, WI* #73; Wordsworth's *Poems, WI* #383; and Scott's *Marmion WI* #398.

14. BL Add. MS 34567 (f. 42), Henry White to Philip Bliss, Lichfield Cathedral, Thursday, 16 March 1809. Celestial metaphors were common in sometimes-complimentary, sometimes-facetious contemporary nicknames for the *Edinburgh*, its editor and its writers. The *Satirist*, for instance, referred to the *Edinburgh* as 'the aurora-*borealis* (great *Northern* Light) in its chilling splendour' (*Satirist*, 1 (December 1807), p. 318). Cf. Simond, *Journal of a Tour*, p. 60.

15. *QR* Letters 1, 41.

16. *ER* #364. J. Clive, *Scotch Reviewers: The Edinburgh Review, 1802–1815* (London: Faber and Faber, 1957), p. 104, quoted by B. Hilton in '"Sardonic Grins" and "Paranoid Politics": Religion, Economics, and Public Policy in the *Quarterly Review*' in Cutmore (ed.), *Conservatism and the Quarterly Review*, pp. 41–60.

17. *ER* #422. See D. Saglia, *Poetic Castles in Spain: British Romanticism and Figurations of Iberia* (Atlanta, GA: Rodopi, 1999), pp. 21–2.

18. *QR* Letter 1. The Don Pedro Cevallos article is well summarized by H. Ben-Israel in *English Historians on the French Revolution* (Cambridge: Cambridge University Press, 2002), pp. 40–1.

19. While Scott, Gifford, Canning and the others supported the Established Church, they also backed Pitt's policy of Roman Catholic Emancipation. They believed the measure would preserve national unity by accommodating the Irish.

20. *QR* Letters 3, 24, 31. In March 1875, Stratford Canning told the third John Murray that the walk along Pall Mall took place 'when the 8th year of the century [1807, counting from 1800] was passing out of spring into summer'. An end-of-May date for the walk is probable because of Canning's description and for two other reasons: Cambridge Easter Term would soon end, which perhaps explains why Canning and his university friends could be in London; and on 28 May 1807 John Murray distributed *Edinburgh Review* Number 19 (*Courier*, 28 May, the *Edinburgh* 'has just arrived'), which might have initiated the young men's discussion (JM MS, S. Canning to John Murray III, 20 March 1875, transcribed in Cutmore (ed.), *Conservatism and the Quarterly Review*, p. 254 n2); cf. S. Lane-Poole, *The Life of the Right Honourable Stratford Canning*, 2 vols (London: Longmans, Green, 1888), vol. 1, p. 192.

21. JM MS, S. Canning to John Murray III, 20 March 1875.
22. So Byron called him, Byron to Murray, 23 August 1811 (*Byron's Letters and Journals*, ed. L. A. Marchand, 12 vols (London: John Murray, 1973–82), vol. 1, p. 78). The fairly uniform assessment by Gifford's contemporaries that he was the greatest satirist 'since the days of Pope' bewilders modern critics. Thus, for example, 'Nothing in the present study requires a greater leap for our historical imagination than the esteem many readers felt for the satires of Gifford' (G. Dire, *British Satire and the Politics of Style, 1789–1832* (Cambridge: Cambridge University Press, 1997), pp. 23–4).
23. See note 21, above.
24. *QR* Letter 1.
25. No reply from Canning is preserved in the John Murray Archive. As Murray kept every scrap of correspondence, had he received a reply from Canning he certainly would have preserved it as a special prize.
26. C. Knight, *Passages of a Working Life during Half a Century*, 3 vols (London: Bradbury and Evans, 1864), vol. 1, p. 66. JM MS, bound collection of letters of the younger Thomas Rennell, Gally Knight, and Stratford Canning relating to 'The Miniature'. 'The Miniature' in its connection with Murray's fortune is noted in Smiles, *Memoir*, vol. 1, pp. 67–9. Murray was formally introduced to George Canning by William Gifford in December 1808. In March 1809, the publisher wrote to Stratford Canning, the 'Quarterly Review ... owes its birth to your obliging countenance' (quoted in Smiles, *Memoir*, vol. 1, p. 152).
27. JM MS, S. Canning to Murray, Thursday, 7 January 1807: 'I have seen Mr Gifford this morning and mentioned your name to him. / If you will have the goodness to call on him tomorrow morning before one or two, he will be glad to see you. He lives in James's Street, Buckingham House [*sic*], No. 6; his name is on the door'. Cf. *QR* Letter 4; Smiles, *Memoir*, vol. 1, pp. 94, 152.
28. See the postscript to *QR* Letter 6, transcribed in Cutmore (ed.), *Conservatism and the Quarterly Review*, p. 199. Apparently deciding that the better part of valour is discretion, and because the Foreign Secretary's silence might have been read as disapproval, evidently Murray at no point mentioned to Gifford that he had written to George Canning.
29. Spring Gardens was also the neighbourhood of one of the *Quarterly*'s future 'sheet anchors', John Barrow. In statements in his planning notes, through *gratis* subscriptions to the *Quarterly*, and in other ways John Murray showed that he regarded these men – all of whom were close to George Canning – as the journal's original political sponsors. Other later key sponsors in government, business, and the civil service were: Lord Lonsdale, George Ellis, Charles Rose Ellis, Francis Freeling, John Wilson Croker, John Barrow, Robert William Hay, Robert John Wilmot (later Wilmot-Horton), and four evangelical Saints, Lord Teignmouth, Henry Thornton, James Stephen, and Zachary Macaulay. Had George Canning attended the Spring Gardens meeting, his presence would have been remarked upon. On the meeting, see J. Bagot (ed.), *Canning and His Friends*, 2 vols (London: John Murray, 1909), vol. 1, p. 51n, and H. E. C. Stapylton, *Two Under-Secretaries* (London: William Clowes and Sons, *c*. 1891), p. 3.
30. Lane-Poole, *Life*, vol. 1, p. 43.
31. In an effort to define a distinctive British identity in the wake of the Anglo-Scottish Union of 1701, the French Revolution, and the 1800 Act of Union, state propaganda portrayed canonical 'British' literature as a national 'establishment' level with the Monarchy, Parliament, and the Church. Like these other establishments, literature was therefore

to be protected from erosion by foreign interlopers. Consequently, to preserve and defend the nation, during the French Revolution and the Napoleonic era conservatives such as William Gifford defined British literature, character, manners, and politics as distinct from and superior to French models with Gifford attacking the Della Cruscans, for instance, in part for their Gallic sensuousness. Martin Wechselblatt points out that in the early nineteenth century 'ancient Scottish poetry was being "recovered" south of the border for a history of British literature culminating in and establishing a genealogy for the "native genius" of something very like great England'. George Ellis, William Stewart Rose, and Walter Scott, among others who were engaged in this project, continued their nationalist programme in the *QR*. See M. Wechselblatt, 'The Canonical Ossian', in Greg Clingham (ed.), *Making History: Textuality and the Forms of Eighteenth Century Culture* (Lewisburg, PA: Bucknell University Press, 1998), pp. 19–34; p. 25. On the development of British nationalism see especially L. Colley, *Britons: Forging the Nation 1707–1837* (New Haven, CT: Yale University Press, 1992). On the role of literature in the promotion of English nationalism see L. Lipking, *Ordering of the Arts in Eighteenth-Century England* (Princeton, NJ: Princeton University Press, 1970), G. Newman, *The Rise of English Nationalism: A Cultural History 1740–1830* (London: Weidenfeld and Nicolson, 1987) and J. Sorenson, *The Grammar of Empire* (Cambridge: Cambridge University Press, 2000). On canon formation and nationalism see, for a start, J. B. Kramnick, *Making the English Canon: Print-Capitalism and the Cultural Past, 1700–1770* (Cambridge: Cambridge University Press, 1998) and M. Gamer, *Romanticism and the Gothic: Genre, Reception, and Canon Formation* (Cambridge: Cambridge University Press, 2000). In addition to Clingham, on the nationalists' use of ancient British literature, see K. Trumpener, *Bardic Nationalism: Romantic Novel and the British Empire* (Princeton, NJ: Princeton University Press, 1997).

32. Smiles, *Memoir*, vol. 1, p. 110.
33. JM MS, James Ballantyne to Murray, 5 June 1807.
34. JM MS, 20 December 1808.
35. JM MS, 14 July 1807.
36. Smiles, *Memoir*, vol. 1, pp. 322–5. Murray hoped to establish a periodical for the predictable income it would supply, to keep his firm's name before the public, to help establish a relationship with a stable of authors, and, so he hoped, to enhance his reputation.
37. *SL*, vol. 2, pp. 45–6; Campbell to Murray, 3 March 1806, quoted in Smiles, *Memoir*, vol. 1, p. 324.
38. JM MS, Ballantyne to Murray, 14 November 1806.
39. In 1806 and in 1808 Ballantyne arranged for Murray to contact Scott; he connived with the publisher; and he acted as go-between. The impression that in planning the *Quarterly* in 1808 Murray looked back to his 1806 experience with Campbell, Scott, and Ballantyne is reinforced by the curious detail that Murray mimicked an idea he received from Campbell. In 1806 Campbell kept in a 'memorandum book all [his] desultory ideas respecting the publication' and 'many respectable names' of potential contributors. From October 1808, in setting up the *QR* Murray kept exactly such a memorandum book. The lists of prospective contributors from that book appear in the present volume as Appendix C. Campbell to Murray, 3 March 1806, quoted in Smiles, *Memoir*, vol. 1, p. 324. JM MS, JM II's 1808 *QR* planning notes.
40. Prior to October 1808, Murray saw Ballantyne in London in 1805, in Edinburgh in 1806, and again in London in 1808. As for Murray and Stratford Canning, though they undoubtedly got together at other times, in this period the only recorded meeting took

place at 31 Hertford St on 15 January 1808 at S. Canning's command. JM MSS: Murray to Ballantyne, 14 November 1806; Ballantyne to Murray, 24 August 1807; Ballantyne and Co. to Murray, 30 March 1808; S. Canning to Murray, 14 January 1808.

41. The London trip finally took place with Murray's connivance and, indeed, his financial support. To pay for the trip, Ballantyne and Company requested a note from Murray in the amount of £241. When in the summer of 1807 Ballantyne pondered whether to make his way to London to solicit additional contracts, he sought the publisher's advice: 'You are so much in the very heart of the circle from which I might expect advantage, and know so completely what is doing or likely to be done, in it, that your opinion would have the highest authority with me; and, as my friend, I trust you will not with hold it'. JM MSS: 24 August 1807; 30 March 1808.

42. Ballantyne set out on 29 March and returned to Edinburgh in June. No known record exists to prove that Ballantyne and Murray met in London and that when they met Ballantyne retailed confidences about Scott, but about both matters there can be no doubt. Ballantyne came to London on Murray's advice; he was terribly upset when in the autumn of 1806 Murray accused him of failing to return the hospitality he, Murray, had offered Ballantyne when he was in London in 1805; and, perennially in his correspondence with Murray, Ballantyne made his knowledge of Scott's activities, opinions, and prejudices a point of central interest. JM MS, Ballantyne and Co. to Murray, 28 March 1808. The Ballantyne-Murray correspondence is JM MSS, NLS Acc. 12604/ 1042, 1043, 1044. See also E. Johnson, *Sir Walter Scott: The Great Unknown*, 2 vols (London: Hamish Hamilton, 1970), vol. 1, pp. 234, 280.

43. J. G. Lockhart, *Memoirs of the Life of Sir Walter Scott*, 7 vols (Edinburgh: Constable, 1837–8), vol. 2, pp. 200–1, quoted in Smiles, *Memoir*, vol. 1, p. 96.

44. As Stratford Canning had introduced Gifford to Murray, so Murray by this means hoped to introduce Gifford and Scott, possibly with the same motive, to position Gifford as an advisor in setting up a new review journal. In late May–early June, Murray proposed, through Gilchrist, that Scott edit the plays of Beaumont and Fletcher. Had Scott accepted, he undoubtedly would have worked closely with Gifford, who was an expert on Jacobean dramatists. On 5 June, Gilchrist wrote to Scott about Murray's intention. NLS MS 3877 (f. 79).

45. Smiles, *Memoir*, vol. 1, 96. Murray arrived at Edinburgh on 11 September. JM MS, Murray to Anne Murray, 12 September 1808.

46. JM MS, 21 September 1808.

47. Murray's idea of forming a closer partnership with Ballantyne can therefore be dated to mid-June 1808, when Ballantyne was in London.

48. In 1806–7 there was much discussion between Murray and Ballantyne about the publisher's 'beautiful plan of the Novels', a uniform set to be printed by Ballantyne and published by Murray. Now the idea occurred to them to involve Scott in that project as a way to draw him away from Constable. JM MS, Ballantyne to Murray, 24 August 1807.

49. Scott's country residence is variously spelled 'Ashestiel' and 'Ashiestiel'. Following Corson, I have regularized the spelling as 'Ashiestiel' (J. C. Corson, *Notes and Index to Sir Herbert Grierson's Edition of the Letters of Sir Walter Scott* (Oxford: Clarendon Press, 1979), p. 357).

50. *Familiar Letters of Sir Walter Scott*, ed. D. Douglas, 2 vols (Edinburgh: Douglas, 1894), vol. 1, p. 115, Scott to Lady Abercorn, 9 June 1808.

51. Smiles, *Memoir*, vol. 1, p. 101.

52. In his youth, Ellis had been a Whig and a contributor to the anti-Pittite *Rolliad* (1784–5), but the Revolution, and especially the Terror, caused him to shift his support to Pitt and his war policy. Despite his intimacy with four of the *QR*'s principals – Scott, Canning, Heber, and Gifford – Ellis was the last of the co-founders to hear about the plan to establish a journal to rival the *Edinburgh Review*. Canning told Ellis about the nascent *Quarterly* when in mid or late October he showed him a letter from Campbell-Colquhoun in which Scott's plan 'was mentioned' (*QR* Letter 7). From that moment to the time of his death, Ellis was an indefatigable and effective theorist, recruiter, and reviewer. He was one of Gifford's best writers and his most cogent, active, and concerned adviser.

53. *QR* Letter 4. *SL*, vol. 2, p. 121, Scott to Ellis, 2 November 1808.

54. *SL*, vol. 2, p. 164, 15 February [1809].

55. *SL*, vol. 2, p. 79, Scott to Constable and Company, 25 July 1808.

56. Smiles, *Memoir*, vol. 1, p. 95; *SL*, vol. 2, p. 154; Lockhart, *Life*, vol. 3, p. 32.

57. K. Curry, *Sir Walter Scott's Edinburgh Annual Register* (Knoxville: University of Tennessee Press, 1977), pp. 5–6.

58. NLS MS 3877 (ff. 134–55), Ellis to Scott, 23 September 1808. NLS MS 3878 (ff. 6–7), C. K. Sharpe to Scott, 20 January 1809.

59. Besides Rose, men such as Glenbervie, Frere, Gilchrist, Canning, Douce, Ellis, Heber, Hoppner, Rogers, Sotheby and Turner corresponded with Scott about old Romances and later became in one way or another associated with the *QR*. NLS MS 3877 (ff. 45–6), Rose to Scott, 6 May 1808. T. Constable, *Archibald Constable and His Literary Correspondents* (Edinburgh: Edmonston and Douglas, 1873) vol. 1, p. 117, cited in Curry, *Scott's Edinburgh Annual Register*, p. 6.

60. *SL*, vol. 2, 153–4, 14 January [1809]. Emphasis added.

61. Ibid.

62. Quoted in Curry, *Scott's Edinburgh Annual Register*, ch. 1.

63. That his failure to mention Murray in this passage is significant becomes clear later in the journal's history.

64. In a letter to George Ellis dated 18 November 1808, Scott referred to the *Edinburgh Annual Register* as 'Another bomb [that was] about to break on [Constable] besides the [*Quarterly*] *Review*'. It would be, he noted, '*valde* anti-Foxite'. *SL*, vol. 2, pp. 127–30; vol. 12, pp. 305–7.

65. Quoted in Curry, *Scott's Edinburgh Annual Register*, p. 8. *SL*, vol. 2, pp. 124–7, 134, 165, Scott to Murray, 15 November 1808; Scott to Ellis, 13 December 1808; Scott to Patrick Murray, 15 February [1809].

66. *SL*, vol. 2, p. 160, Scott to Southey, 31 January 1809.

67. *QR* Letter 4.

68. Heber's metropolitan residence, 'Pimlico Lodge', was a short walk from Gifford's accommodations in James Street. Heber was a friend to all of the *QR*'s principals and some of its leading writers, including Scott, Canning, Murray, Gifford, Dudley, Ellis, and Frere. Alone among Gifford's coadjutors, Heber took it upon himself not only to recommend prospective reviewers but, without bothering to tell the editor or the publisher, to assign review books. More than once he thus put Gifford in the unenviable position of having to tell a co-founder such as Scott or Erskine to stop working on a particular article because a writer nominated by him had supplied one on the same topic. In May 1810 Gifford wrote to Heber requesting 'that in future no distribution may be made without my being instantly informed of it' (*QR* Letter 48).

69. Smiles, *Memoir*, vol. 1, p. 94.
70. *QR* Letter 2.
71. Murray recorded that statement in his 15 November 1808 letter to Scott (*QR* Letter 8). It is the only known instance when he referred to a two-year gestation period for the journal; he usually dated the commencement of his plan to his September 1807 letter to George Canning. He seems to have had in mind his approaching Scott in 1806 about Campbell's projected literary magazine. In this context, whether it is significant that Murray was in Edinburgh in October-November 1806, at which time he had meetings with Constable and Ballantyne, is unclear.
72. *SL*, vol. 2, p. 143, 30 December 1808, quoting *1 Henry IV*.
73. Constable's practice turned high-end periodical writing into a commodity of exchange whereby talented writers of whatever class or means were amply rewarded for researching and writing quality work. Insisting that without exception even wealthy aristocrats must accept payment, Jeffrey, and later Gifford, answered the scruples of middle class writers who wished not to be stigmatized by writing for pay. The practice helped journalism become a socially acceptable profession.
74. *QR* Letters 4, 7. Scott recorded the quoted stipulation in a letter of 30 December 1808 to Sharpe, but as he picked up the same theme in his letter to Gifford of 25 October 1808, the notion was evidently integral to his plan.
75. *SL*, vol. 2, pp. 101–2n, W. Erskine to A. Campbell-Colquhoun, 23 October 1808. *SL*, vol. 2, 130–1, W. Scott to T. Scott, 19 November 1808.
76. Smiles, *Memoir*, vol. 1, p. 124.
77. *QR* Letter 5, Scott to Ellis, 2 November 1808.
78. *QR* Letter 4.
79. Jeffrey was aware of the plan by 6 December (*SL*, vol. 2, p. 138n; p. 141). On 9 January 1809, Douce wrote to his friend Ellis, 'About 6 weeks ago I received so broad a hint from an acquaintance of ours on the subject of the new review, that I could not well mistake it, yet, as in delicacy bound, I forbore to press the matter, but the day only before your last letter arrived, I received from another quarter, a full and confidential disclosure, now useless to regard as such, of the whole plan and design' (BL Add. MS 28099, f. 53). On 23 February 1809, Murray's office assistant, Thomas Underwood, informed Messers Rees and Curtis, 'Mr Murray is so much occupied with his new Review, prevents him writing you himself' (JM MS, March 1803 to September 1823 letterbook, p. 243).
80. Letters in November 1808 through March 1810 to Ellis, Morritt, Sharpe, and Patrick Murray. See J. Millgate (ed.), *The Millgate Union Catalogue of Walter Scott Correspondence* – National Library of Scotland <www.nls.uk> (accessed 8 November 2007).
81. In an important letter to Morritt dated 14 January 1809, Scott associates Murray not so much with the start of the *QR* as with his effort to set up John Ballantyne in business. Indeed, in that letter he brings Murray in as an afterthought ('not to mention an alliance ... with young John Murray'). In his 2 November letter to Ellis, in a passage in which he states that Murray came to Ashiestiel to 'canvass *a* most important plan', his syntax obscures the plan's origins and owner. Scott saw the plan as 'important' not because Murray introduced it but because Canning was behind it. In the next sentence in the same letter, Scott makes clear his own sense of ownership of the plan. He excludes Murray entirely and places himself and the Lord Advocate at the centre: 'I had most strongly recommended to our Lord Advocate to think of some counter-measures against the Edinburgh Review ...' Here he tells Ellis that the *QR* commenced with news Murray brought from London: Canning was convinced that the time was ripe to start a conserv-

ative literary tribunal in opposition to the *Edinburgh*; like Scott, the Canningites were poised to act. Scott diminished Murray's importance at this time because, in an age when everyone from king to climbing boy was daily conscious of their slot in the hierarchies of place and power, he regarded the publisher, a mere tradesman, as lower in the pecking order than any other man involved in planning the *QR* (James Ballantyne not excepted). For additional discussion see S. Ragaz, 'Walter Scott and the *Quarterly Review*' in Cutmore (ed.), *Conservatism and the Quarterly Review*, pp. 107–32.

82. *Selections from the Letters of Robert Southey*, ed. J. W. Warter, 4 vols (London: Longman, et al., 1856), vol. 2, p. 42.
83. *QR* Letters 4, 5, 26, 29, 41. NLS MS 3879 (ff. 222–3), Ellis to Scott, 22 October 1810.
84. *QR* Letter 216. JM MSS: note in the third person in JM II's hand, beginning, 'In 1811 – JM – had just started – by his own sagacity ...'; Murray to William Johnstone, 3 November 1837.
85. So Murray designated the *QR* in an advertisement in the *Courier*, 10 January 1809.
86. Unhappy, because Scott's connection with the Ballantynes led to financial disaster. On Scott's bankruptcy, see J. Sutherland, *The Life of Walter Scott* (London: Blackwell, 1995), pp. 272–98.
87. *QR* Letter 40.

2 Launching the *Quarterly Review*

1. *QR* Letter 8.
2. JM MS. Ballantyne was mistaken; the Dryden review had already appeared, in the October number. The 'Great Plan' consisted of: the *QR*; the set of romance novels Murray hoped to interest Scott in; and the combination Murray and Ballantyne intended to form with each other.
3. *QR* Letter 5.
4. Lockhart, Smiles and others relate that Scott made his hint to the Lord Advocate after Murray set out on his return journey to London, but Scott nowhere clearly states when the communication took place. He did, however, imply in his 25 October letter to Gifford and in his letter to Ellis that his overture to Campbell-Colquhoun was unconnected with Murray's visit.
5. JM MS, Ballantyne to Murray, 28 October 1808.
6. *QR* Letter 30. In his letter to Copleston, Gifford stated that Murray was appointed publisher before he, Gifford, came on board. A letter G. Bedford sent to P. Elmsley on 26 January 1809 confirms that Scott told others (as he later put it) that he had 'the principal share in erecting this Review' (*The Journal of Sir Walter Scott: from the Original Manuscript at Abbotsford* (Edinburgh: D. Douglas, 1891), p. 15). In summarizing the origins of the soon-to-be published *Quarterly*, Bedford wrote that the 'idea originated with Walter Scott about three months ago' (Bedford to P. Elmsley, 26 January 1809, Westminster School Library MS). Bedford's information came from Scott via Southey. That Scott claimed to be the originator is confirmed as well in *QR* Letters 7, 41.
7. *QR* Letter 6.
8. *SL*, vol. 2, pp. 101–2n.
9. That information could only have come from Canning via the Lord Advocate, not from Murray who was in transit from 6 to 16 October. He did not communicate again with Scott until 26 October.

10. J. O. Hayden employs this nice description, 'letter of policy', in his *The Romantic Reviewers 1802–1824* (Chicago, IL: University of Chicago Press, 1968), p. 26.
11. *QR* Letter 6.
12. *QR* Letter 30.
13. *SL*, vol. 2, pp. 109–11, Scott to Lady Abercorn, 27 October 1808. Dundas's father, Viscount Melville, as Pitt's Scottish manager was the most powerful politician in Scotland.
14. *QR* Letter 5, Scott to Ellis, 2 November 1808. Ellis's 11 November 1808 reply is *QR* Letter 7.
15. *QR* Letters 3–7. In advance of Scott's letter, Ballantyne wrote to Murray on 28 October, in reply to a letter from Murray to say that Scott had contacted Canning. Ballantyne did not mention Gifford, however.
16. *SL*, vol. 2, pp. 114–15; *QR* Letter 8; Smiles, *Memoir*, vol. 1, pp. 98–9.
17. *QR* Letter 8.
18. *SL*, vol. 2, pp. 130–1; Smiles, *Memoir*, vol. 1, p. 5.
19. JM MSS. 'Hunter has excited a degree of boiling rage in the breast of Mr. Scott ...', Ballantyne told Murray in the 20 December letter.
20. The exact publication date of the October *Edinburgh Review* (No. 25) has proved elusive. In the *Edinburgh Evening Courant* for Saturday 1 October, *ER* No. 25 is not listed among the month's new publications for 'the use of subscribers at Mackay's Circulating Library'. At no point in October (or in September for that matter) is there an advertisement in the *Edinburgh Evening Courant* announcing the publication of No. 25, or in the London *Courier*, *The Times*, or the *Morning Chronicle*. The *Monthly Literary Advertiser*, which appeared regularly on the tenth of every month, in its forty-second issue, 10 October 1808, announced *ER* No. 25 as published. In the second week of October, book advertisements in newspapers cite or quote from No. 25. A 'Review of the Exposition of Don Pedro Cevallos [in the *Edinburgh Review*]' appeared in the *Examiner* on 16 October 1808. Staff at the Edinburgh Room of the Edinburgh Central Library supplied information used in this note.
21. *SL*, vol. 2, pp. 124–7, Scott to Murray, 15 November 1808.
22. Double underscored in the manuscript.
23. JM MS, Ballantyne to Murray, 21 November 1808, quoted, with excisions and adjustments, in Smiles, *Memoir*, vol. 1, p. 115. Ballantyne's comments in this letter also tend to confirm that 'Don Pedro Cevallos' did not motivate discussions during the Ashiestiel conference.
24. *Selected Letters of Sydney Smith*, ed. N. C. Smith (Oxford: Oxford University Press, 1981), pp. 46–8: Smith to Jeffrey, [November or December 1808]; Smith to Jeffrey, [November or December 1808]; Smith to Lady Holland, 10 January 1809; Smith to Lady Holland, [after Christmas, 1808].
25. *Memoirs and Correspondence of Francis Horner*, ed. L. Horner, 2 vols (London: John Murray, 1843), vol. 1, p. 464. P. Flynn, *Francis Jeffrey* (Newark: University of Delaware Press, 1978), p. 124.
26. *Selected Letters of Sydney Smith*, p. 45, Smith to Jeffrey, [November or December 1808]. *SL*, vol. 2, pp. 138–9. Two years later Jeffrey, still trying to recover Scott's favour, apologized for any pain he caused in his review of *Marmion*. NLS MS 3879 (ff. 161–2), Jeffrey to Scott, 11 August 1810.
27. Constable remonstrated with Scott not to let Hunter spoil their friendship or their business arrangements. *SL*, vol. 2, pp. 154–5, Scott to Constable, 22 January 1809.

28. *QR* Letter 258. Gifford's 9 November letter is *QR* Letter 6; Ellis's 11 November letter is *QR* Letter 7.
29. JM MS, March 1803 to September 1823 letterbook, p. 228.
30. *Memoirs and Correspondence of Francis Horner,* vol. 2, p. 215. *SL,* vol. 2, p. 169, Scott to Murray, 25 February 1809.
31. *SL,* vol. 2, p. 144, 30 December 1808.
32. Copleston to Richard Heber, 2 March 1811, quoted in *The Heber Letters, 1783–1832,* ed. R. H. Cholmondley (London: Batchworth Press, 1950), p. 238.
33. *QR* Letters 4, 8.
34. Scott alludes to the Bible, Numbers 4:15.
35. As K. Wheatley points out in 'Plotting the Success of the *Quarterly Review*' in Cutmore (ed.), *Conservatism and the Quarterly Review,* pp. 19–39.
36. *SL,* vol. 2, pp. 128–9, Scott to Ellis, 18 November 1808; quoted in Smiles, *Memoir,* vol. 1, p. 103.
37. In early 1809 Horner gave Jeffrey the same advice, that the *QR* should never be named in the *Edinburgh Review.*
38. *QR* Letter 7.
39. *QR* Letter 41, Ellis to Scott, 8 March 1810.
40. In mid-November, Scott wrote to Murray, alarmed that Gifford wished to wait for his 'arrival to town to set the great machine a-going'. Smiles, *Memoir,* vol. 1, p. 113.
41. For Murray's lists, see Appendix C.
42. When Sharpe heard that Moore was involved, Scott reassured him, 'Your opinion quite coincides with mine about Mr Moore. He is not at all deeply concerned in the Review; the bookseller only mentioned his name to me *en passant*' (*SL,* vol. 2, p. 149). Murray repeatedly wrote to Leigh Hunt to solicit a review on the drama. Citing the *Quarterly*'s political complexion, Hunt turned him away (BL Add. MS 38523 (f. 8), Murray to Hunt, 13 March 1809).
43. Young was motivated to become a *Quarterly* reviewer in part because of Brougham's 1803 review of his *Bakerian Lecture on Light and Colours* (*ER* #46). This ridiculous article, now laughed at by scientists for its vehemence in upholding Newton's corpuscular theory of light in opposition to Young's correct championing of Huygens's wave theory, cast a pall over Young's reputation that he never entirely shook off. George Ellis, who was Young's patient and one of his 'most intimate and most valued friends', used these circumstances to convince him to become a contributor (Young to Ellis, late 1808, quoted in Smiles, *Memoir,* vol. 1, p. 123). Young played an important role in the history of the early *Quarterly* as a contributor, recruiter, and subeditor. His articles in turn were vetted by subeditors, mainly by Olinthus Gregory, the mathematical master at Woolwich military school, and by John Barrow, the Admiralty's Second Secretary. Knowledge of the full extent of Young's *Quarterly*-related activities is just out of reach; his papers, in private hands, are inaccessible.
44. Turner was Murray's and Southey's solicitor and the publisher's sometime literary advisor. An important pioneer in the study of Anglo Saxon history and literature, he was a man of high standing in London intellectual circles. That he was a serious Christian is proved in Murray's correspondence with Annie Murray and is suggested by his leading Isaac D'Israeli out of Judaism into the Church of England and his standing godfather to Benjamin Disraeli upon the boy's baptism, in 1817. He was himself of Jewish origin: he was D'Israeli's cousin (Smiles, *Memoir,* vol. 1, p. 77); there is a record of Murray asking Turner to come around to his office on the weekend, 'despite your Saturday regu-

lations' (JM MS, *c.* January 1810); in 1807 Alexander Hunter included Turner in a list of Jews who were in attendance at a party at D'Israeli's house: 'The whole company except ourselves I believe, were Jews and Jewesses! ... Our male part of the company consisted mainly of literary men – Cumberland, Turner, Disraeli, Basevi, Prince Hoare, and Mr. Cervetto' (quoted in M. Ragussis, *Figures of Conversion: "The Jewish Question" and English National Identity* (Durham, NC: Duke University Press, 1995), p. 181). Turner's Puritan sensibilities appealed to Murray's skittish desire not to offend middle-class readers of his books and journals.

45. Now remembered as the father of the prime minister, D'Israeli was in his own right a respected man of letters. He gained early notice with a satire on John Wolcot (*pseud.,* Peter Pindar), Gifford's literary nemesis. From 1791, when the first John Murray published D'Israeli's *Curiosities of Literature,* he enjoyed a lifelong intimacy with the Murray family. Whenever the second John Murray was on the road, he would habitually remind his wife not to forget to pay her compliments to Mr and Mrs D'Israeli. About one of D'Israeli's works Gifford wrote: 'It is like all of his; abundant in good thoughts and happy expressions, but without the lucidas ardour, of which he has *naturally* no idea' (*QR* Letter 132).

46. *SL*, vol. 2, p. 156, Scott to Sharpe, 26 January 1809.

47. *SL*, vol. 2, pp. 141–2, 148, 152–3, Scott to Sharpe, 30 December 1808 and 13 January 1809; Scott to Morritt, 13 January 1809.

48. Ireland and Gifford were friends from childhood. Helped at crucial points along the way by generous patrons, these two clever capable boys together rose from the humblest of origins to the ante-rooms of some of the most powerful men in the British establishment. The importance of Ireland's influence on the early *QR* cannot be overstated. He was the editor's 'steady and affectionate assistant' (Smiles, *Memoir,* vol. 2, p. 161, Ireland to Murray, 8 July 1824; *QR* Letter 257). Murray and some members of the *QR*'s staff, however, distrusted Ireland's influence over Gifford. Southey thought him 'a dead-weight' (BL Add. MS, 47553, f. 30, Southey to J. T. Coleridge, 17 February 1823); Ellis advised Murray that 'Gifford must guard against the bad taste of Dr Ireland' (JM MS, 4 April 1810); and Murray spoke of him as Gifford's 'evil genius' (*QR* Letter 62). Murray and the others mainly disliked Ireland because he encouraged Gifford to dedicate the *Quarterly* to a defence of the Established Church and orthodox Christianity. Ireland's association with the journal ceased with the retirement of the *Quarterly*'s first editor.

49. Although he and his relatives were Whigs and republicans, and although, as portrait painter to the Prince of Wales from 1789, Whigs patronized him, Hoppner was a welcome figure in the circle of Canning, Frere, Gifford, Ireland, and D'Israeli. Hoppner first made Gifford's acquaintance in the 1780s at the home of Gifford's patron, Lord Grosvenor. As confirmed by Farington in his diary, the two men sometimes quarrelled violently over politics, but they were fast friends – Gifford in his *The Maeviad* states that Hoppner was, next to Ireland, highest in his affections.

50. Smiles, *Memoir,* vol. 1, pp. 116–17. For an account of the Saints' early association with the *Quarterly,* see my 'A Plurality of Voices in the *Quarterly Review*' in *Conservatism and the Quarterly Review,* pp. 61–85. As early as September 1808, the Saints were plotting to set up a journal to counter the *Edinburgh.* See Henry Thornton to Zachary Macaulay, 14 September [1808], quoted in S. Meacham, *Henry Thornton of Clapham, 1760–1815* (Cambridge, MA: Harvard University Press, 1964), pp. 92, 189n. *QR* Letter 12.

51. These linkages can be established by tracing family, school, and professional background and by noting patterns of membership in clubs and organizations. Following these leads,

it is possible to reveal what would otherwise not be readily apparent, that Reginald and Richard Heber, for example, were personally or professionally connected with a remarkable number of *Quarterly* reviewers, including Blunt, the Cannings, Cohen, Coleridge, Copleston, Ellis, Erskine, Ferriar, Grant, Hallam, Hare-Naylor, Hay, Hoppner, Milman, Mitford, Penrose, Scott, Stephen, Ward, Whitaker, Whittington, and Wilmot-Horton. The preferred clubs of many *Quarterly* reviewers included the Literary, Alfred, and Travellers'. Indicative of their high standing in the establishment, many reviewers were members of premier intellectual organizations, such as the Society of Antiquaries and the Royal Society. Several were members of 'The Club', an exclusive literary association founded by Dr Johnson in 1764, including Canning, Frere, Ellis, Heber, Glenbervie, Scott, Blomfield, Hallam, Young, and Copleston. See the list of 'Club' members in J. Boswell, *The Life of Samuel Johnson, LL. D.: Including a Journal of a Tour to the Hebrides*, ed. J. W. Croker, 2 vols (New York: George Dearborn, 1833–4) vol. 1, pp. 533–4.

52. *SL*, vol. 2, p. 143, Scott to Sharpe, 30 December 1808.

53. Under Gifford and Coleridge, the following men who qualify as liberals or radicals contributed to the *Quarterly*: Thomas Arnold, William John Bankes, Robert Bland, Charles James Blomfield, Richard Chenevix, Peter Elmsley, Octavius Gilchrist, Henry Hallam, Francis Hare-Naylor, John Hoppner, Henry Matthews, John Herman Merivale, Macvey Napier, James Pillans and John Symmons.

54. *QR* Letters 6, 8. G. Carnall, *Robert Southey and His Age: The Development of a Conservative Mind* (Oxford: Oxford University Press, 1960), p. 97. JM MS, Gifford to Murray, 29 November 1808, 'I leave town this morning for Claremont, with Canning. We shall there meet G. Ellis, and come to something decisive. This appears to me to be the only promising mode. I shall be very explicit.' JM MS, Gifford to Murray, 'Saturday noon', [17 December 1808]. Gifford was small of stature, around five feet tall.

55. *QR* Letters 4, 12. Smiles, *Memoir*, vol. 1, p. 118. *SL*, vol. 2, p. 146, Scott to Murray, 4 January 1809. JM MSS, Ballantyne to Murray: 11 January 1809; 18 January 1809; 22 January 1809.

56. JM MSS: Ballantyne to Murray, 3 January 1809; Murray to Anne Murray, 6 January 1809.

57. JM MSS: Ballantyne to Murray, 3 January 1809; Murray to Anne Murray, 5 January 1809, 6 January 1809. *SL*, vol. 2, p. 146, Scott to Murray, 4 January 1809. Smiles, *Memoir*, vol. 1, p. 141.

58. *QR* Letter 15. In the *Courier* (30 January 1808), an increase in printing and paper costs was announced for 1 February. *Courier*, 31 January 1809.

59. *SL*, vol. 2, pp. 157, 163–4, Scott to Murray, 28 January 1809; 10 February [1809].

60. JM MS, Ballantyne to Murray, 18 January 1809. Evidently, Scott had by this point given up the first number as a lost opportunity and now pinned his hopes on the future. On 1 February, Ballantyne told Murray that Scott was 'bold as a lion in respect to your *second* Number'. JM MS, Ballantyne to Murray, 22 January 1809.

61. *QR* Letters 8, 3, 6.

62. *QR* Letters 10, 3, 4.

63. *QR* Letter 64. The *Quarterly*'s habitual lateness inspired John Coleridge to quip, 'Hazlitt would say that among other courtly-favours the Review was about to change its name from Quarterly to Half-Yearly'. JM MS, Coleridge to Gifford, 25 May 1819.

64. *QR* Letters 8, 12.

3 Competition for Editorial Control

1. JM MSS, John Ballantyne to Murray: 4 March 1809; 5 March 1809; 1 March 1809; 6 March 1809; 9 March 1809. Copies arrived in Scotland by land and by sea. The first two shipments, by coach, a more expensive and faster mode, consisted of 200 and of 50 copies. The third and fourth shipments were by sea, 200 copies in each shipment. By month end Ballantyne had sold about 500 copies. On 5 June he still had 135 copies on hand. JM MSS, John Ballantyne to JM, 17 March 1809; 29 March 1809; 5 June 1809.

2. Ballantyne was however critical of some of the reviews, even of Scott's article on Burns. 'What a myriad of pities', he told Murray, 'that he had not taken a more enlarged view of the poetical character! He could have done it so well'. JM MS, 28 February 1809.

3. That is, 'chain mail'. Bodl. Lib. MS Eng. Lett. d. 51 (ff. 24–5), Southey to Bedford, 14 March 1809.

4. *SL*, vol. 2, p. 173, Scott to Sharpe, 3 March 1809.

5. *QR* Letter 8.

6. *SL*, vol. 2, p. 167, 25 February 1809; cf. *SL*, vol. 2, p. 173, Scott to Sharpe, 3 March 1809, 'I am a little disconcerted with the appearance of one or two of my own articles, which I have had no opportunity to revise in proof'.

7. JM MS, Ballantyne to Murray, 13 March 1809.

8. *SL*, vol. 2, pp. 161–2, Scott to Murray, 2 February 1809.

9. *SL*, vol. 2, pp. 164–5, 15 February [1809]; p. 167, 17 February 1809.

10. The letter has not been preserved, but its contents can be gleaned from Ballantyne's letter to Murray of 13 March and Scott's to Murray of 19 March. *SL*, vol. 2, pp. 182–4; *QR* Letter 18.

11. As publisher, Murray managed the relationship with the printing house; delays in publication due to problems with the printer were therefore his responsibility. To generate sufficient revenue to cover his costs, Murray should have printed at least 3,050 copies; he printed 3,000, so he ensured a loss of at least £19. Of the 650 copies assigned to John Ballantyne, 200 hundred reached Scotland too late to be immediately saleable. See also Table B.2 in Appendix B, 'Epitome of Profit and Loss, Numbers 1–11'.

12. *QR* Letter 18; Ballantyne's emphasis. Scott's letter to Gifford is missing. His letter to Canning, dated 24 March 1809, is preserved at the West Yorkshire Archives, Leeds (Har/GC 66a). Canning's reply, dated 1 May 1809, is NLS MS 3878 (f. 51). Scott to Murray, 19 March 1809, quoted in Smiles, *Memoir*, vol. 1, pp. 149–50.

13. Scott to Murray, 11 May 1809, quoted in Smiles, *Memoir*, vol. 1, pp. 156–7. *SL*, vol. 2, p. 196, 4 May 1809; NLS MS 853, copy.

14. *SL*, vol. 2, p. 150, 19 March 1809. JM MS, Gifford to Murray, April 1809.

15. Smiles, *Memoir*, vol. 1, pp. 149.

16. *QR* Letter 61. JM MSS, Murray to Anne Murray: 24 August 1809; 8 July 1809.

17. *QR* Letter 4.

18. *SL*, vol. 2, p. 157, Scott to Murray, 28 January 1809. When Scott finally made it to London, in April 1809, Murray covered his expenses. JM MS, letterbook, copy in a secretary's hand, Murray to Scott, 24 March 1809: 'In other words if there be no plea for charging it to government, I will undertake that the Review shall pay it as far as One Hundred Guineas – If this will do I entreat the favor of you to hasten your departure'. NLS MS 853 (f. 93), Scott to Southey, 16 July 1809, copy. *SL*, vol. 2, pp. 206, 224–6. He arrived in London on April 3rd. JM MS, James Ballantyne to JM, 1 April 1809.

19. NLS MS 3878 (ff. 90–1), Morritt to Scott, 17 July [1809]. *QR* Letters 24, 4. NLS MS 3878 (ff. 90–1), Morritt to Scott, 17 July 1809. Scott's spelling here is 'hurld' and 'listend'.

20. *SL*, vol. 2, p. 211, Scott to Morritt, 22 July [1809]. *SL*, vol. 2, pp. 211, 225, Scott to Morritt, 17 August 1809; same, 22 July [1809]. *SL*, vol. 2, p. 211, Scott to Morritt, 22 July [1809]; *SL*, vol. 2, p. 249, Scott to Ellis, 26 September 1809.

21. See Appendix A, note to article #38.

22. *QR* Letter 31. JM MS, Gifford to Hay, 5 March 1813. Within the inner circle, he was prepared to criticize Murray if he thought it would benefit the *QR*. In a letter to Copleston, for instance, he blamed the publisher for the 'unmannerly rejection' of an article by John Penrose. See the discussion later in this history.

23. *QR* Letter 41. JM MSS: Murray to Gifford, 19 July 1809; Murray to Anne Murray, 4 August 1809 and 8 August 1809.

24. JM MSS: Murray to Anne Murray, 4 August 1809; Murray to Gifford, 24 August 1809. *QR* Letter 29.

25. Smiles, *Memoir*, vol. 1, p. 154. *QR* Letters 29, 44, 45, 57. JM MS, Gifford to Murray, 12 May 1809, quoted in Smiles, *Memoir*, vol. 1, p. 157. BL Add. MS 18204 (f. 273), Gifford to an unidentified correspondent, 20 August 1809.

26. *QR* Letter 31. JM MS, Gifford to Murray 18 June 1809. In a 26 January 1809 letter to Elmsley, Bedford stated that the *Quarterly* was 'set up on the same plan as the Edinburgh but with different principles in politics *and* theology'. Westminster School Library MS. Emphasis added. JM MS Gifford to Murray, 18 June 1809, quoted in Smiles, *Memoir*, vol. 1, p. 158. 'The base servility of the British Critic disgusts me completely', Gifford told Murray. 'How does it find readers?' JM MS, 3 August 1810.

27. *QR* Letter 48.

28. *QR* Letters 3, 4.

29. Bodl. Lib. MS Eng. Lett. d. 134 (f. 6), Keble to Coleridge, 20 September 1812. JM MS, Gifford to Coleridge, 12 March 1819.

30. JM MSS: Gifford to Hay, 6 February 1813; same, 20 March 1815; Gifford to Coleridge, 7 January 1819. *QR* Letters 4, 204, 123.

31. JM MSS: Gifford to Murray, Friday, n.d., after 1812; Gifford to Hay, February 1813; same, 6 February 1813; same, 2 July, n.y. (1822 w/mark). Bodl. Lib. MS Eng. Lett. d. 134 (f. 15), Keble to Coleridge, 15 February 1819.

32. *QR* Letter 246. JM MS, 10 March 1815. Beinecke MS, draft of article #743.

33. JM MS, letterbook, Murray to Lockhart, 16 December 1837. *QR* Letter 109.

34. JM MS, Ellis to Murray, 4 April 1810.

35. JM MSS, Gifford to Barrow, 6 February 1813; Gifford to Hay, 20 March 1815.

36. *Life and Correspondence of Robert Southey*, vol. 5, p. 336.

37. Gifford's early history is a famous tale of self-help. He was born at Ashburton, Devonshire, on 24 April 1756, in humble circumstances to a family whose once considerable wealth was squandered by its patriarchs. His father, Edward Gifford, was a glazier and sailor; his mother, Elizabeth Cairn of Ashburton, was a carpenter's daughter. Orphaned at age thirteen, he fell into the clutches of a man named Carlile, his godfather, who set him to work for a farmer and later for a fisherman. Pressed by the people of his home town to treat him more civilly, in 1770 Carlile sent him to Ashburton School. There he exhibited strength in mathematics, assisted the Master, and entertained thoughts of becoming a schoolteacher. But when Gifford was age fifteen, his godfather forced him into a seven-year apprenticeship to a shoemaker, Carlile's cousin; apparently the shoe-

maker was the father of Richard Carlile, the radical bookseller (S. Tunnicliffe, 'A Newly Discovered Source for the Early Life of William Gifford', *Review of English Studies*, n.s. 16 and 61 (1965), pp. 25–34; p. 31). His master refused to let him study; denied paper, Gifford secretly scratched out sums on discarded leather.

Some satirical verses Gifford wrote about a Methodist meeting caught the attention of William Cookesley, a local surgeon. In 1775 Cookesley took pity on him, raised a subscription to release him from his apprenticeship, and, when Gifford was twenty years of age, supplied a tutor in the person of the Reverend Thomas Smerdon. In 1779 Cookesley and Thomas Taylor of Denbury helped him complete his education by procuring a Bible Clerkship for him at Exeter College, Oxford (BA 1782). Through a Devonshire clergyman, he then made contact with Earl Grosvenor, who consented to be his patron. Gifford resided with Grosvenor, tutored the earl's son, Lord Belgrave, and in the 1780s toured the continent with Grosvenor's family (BL Add. MS 22976, f. 138).

Gifford's first foray into editing was a 1789 collection of minor verse contributed by himself and some of his friends, *The Eaton Chronicle, or, The Salt-box.* He attracted major literary attention with his *The Baviad* (1791) and *The Maeviad* (1795), two satires on the so-called Della Cruscans, a group of Florentine English expatriates who were writers of light sentimental verse. These works, highly thought of except by his literary and political enemies, made Gifford a public figure; even Byron, who called Gifford his 'literary father' (*Byron's Letters and Journals*, vol. 11, p. 117), regarded him as a model satirist, though really his poems were not for the ages. He later made a more notable contribution as a translator of Juvenal and as an editor of the plays of Massinger, Ford, and Jonson. Each of his editions is still respected by scholars; two hundred years later his Jonson and Juvenal remain in print. The greatest boost to his career came in 1797 when George Canning, John Hookham Frere, and George Ellis enlisted him to edit their political journal, the *Anti-Jacobin; or, Weekly Examiner* (November 1797 to July 1798). Clark states that they hired Gifford in part because he was a friend of Pitt, though how he met Pitt is unclear. It seems as likely that Canning and the others made his acquaintance through John Wright, the publisher of the *Anti-Jacobin* and of Gifford's poems, whose Piccadilly shop Gifford frequented (see Farington's *Diary* and the *Annual Register* for 1827). By his editorship of the *Anti-Jacobin* Gifford established a lifelong professional and personal relationship with these men; it led to his appointment as editor of the *Quarterly Review.*

38. Gifford lived alone except for his housekeeper, Anne (sometimes Ann or Annie) Davis, twenty years his servant, whom he loved unabashedly. His enemies snickered and Barrow pruriently referred to Davis as Gifford's 'strumpet', but the evidence suggests a deeply affectionate, platonic friendship. The strongest indication of the innocence of Gifford's love for Davis is its transparency. He directed in his will that he be buried near Davis in South Audley Chapel in Hanover Square (his executor, Dean Ireland, overruled him), and he left significant legacies to her relatives. Gifford, who never married, felt his isolation deeply, even more so after Hoppner's and Davis's deaths. It does not reflect well on his character, though, that too often he invited sympathy for his condition. In one such bout of self-pity he told Hay that a person 'does well to marry' so as not to find home 'cheerless and life unprofitable; and go down to the ground, like me, without a single comfort, among strangers and hirelings' (JM MS, 2 July, n.y. 1822 w/mark).

39. Among the *Quarterly* reviewers, James Pillans was one such victim.

40. H. Taylor, *Autobiography, 1800–1875*, 2 vols (London: John Murray, 1885), vol. 1, p. 48.

41. *QR* Letter 20. Bodl. Lib. MS Eng. Lett. c. 4 (f. 20), 28 July [1824] Ramsgate.

42. *QR*, 2 (article #38). JM MSS: Gifford to Hay, 2 July, n.y., (1822 w/mark); same, 6 February 1813. Smiles, *Memoir*, vol. 1, p. 162.

43. W. Hazlitt, *A Letter to William Gifford, Esq*, ed. A. R. Waller and A. Glover, 12 vols (London: J. M. Dent, 1902–6), vol. 1, p. 365.

44. Quoted in Smiles, *Memoir*, vol. 2, p. 22. K. Gilmartin, *Writing Against Revolution: Literary Conservatism in Britain, 1790–1832* (Cambridge: Cambridge University Press, 2007), p. 108. In 1822, an unsympathetic American writer predicted that the *Quarterly* would attack Lord Byron's politics in the guise of a defence of morals and religion. 'The Quarterly always attacks under cover of this mask' (J. K. Paulding, *A Sketch of Old England*, 2 vols (New York: Wiley, 1822), vol. 2, p. 118).

45. *QR* Letter 180. Morgan called Gifford 'the direst, darkest enemy I ever had ... he hated me for my success and my principles' (S. Morgan, *Lady Morgan's Memoirs: Autobiography, Diaries and Correspondence*, 2 vols (London: William H. Allen, 1868), vol. 2, p. 281; vol. 1, p. 345, quoted in *British Fiction 1800–1829* <www.british-fiction.cf.ac.uk> (accessed 8 November 2007)).

46. *QR*, 1 (article #4), p. 52.

47. William Carey (1761–1834), head of a famous Baptist mission to Calcutta, is a subject also of Southey's defence of Christian missions in the same Number. Henry Thomas Colebrooke (1765–1836), the son of a chairman of the East India Company, was a seminal member of the Asiatic Society, whose mandate was the scientific study of the Oriental world. Charles Wilkins (1749–1836) was the leading Sanskrit scholar in the West; his grammar was the first in English to be printed in Europe. Students at the East India Company's Haileybury College, where Wilkins was a teacher, were his primary audience. Hastings was one of Wilkins's patrons.

48. John Hoppner introduced Lord Lonsdale to Murray. JM MS, Hoppner to Murray, July 1807. As with the *Edinburgh*, so with the *Quarterly*, a species of literary nepotism was exercised, with 'Reginald Heber puffing Robert Southey, and Robert Southey puffing Reginald Heber ... [with] authors dedicating their books to Mr Gifford, and Mr Gifford, reviewing their books either by himself or by his true legitimate vassals – his nameless knot-headed templars and curates!' ([Anon.], 'Rhapsodies in a Punch Bowel, No. 1', *Blackwood's Edinburgh Magazine*, 11 (1822), pp. 344–8).

49. Croker came into politics in a period of 'non-party loyalism', in William Thomas's phrase, when governments that are sometimes now labelled 'Tory' consisted of fluid coalitions based on professional, personal, and family alliances, on self-interest, on support for the war against France, and in defence of the settlement of 1688. While it is conventional to call Croker a 'High Tory', he was more firmly in the liberal conservative Canningite than the ultra-Tory Eldonite camp. He gained the reputation of an extreme right-winger for his tenacious defence of the old order in the Reform debates; he thought the reform of parliament the Grey ministry proposed, especially the elimination of proprietary boroughs, too radical. Along with many of John Murray's gentlemen, it was fear of revolution that made him what is now called a 'conservative' (a label that had no currency during Gifford's tenure). He was 'a High Churchman, a lifelong champion of prescription as the only way to keep "everything in its place", and a scourge of utilitarianism', as Boyd Hilton puts it (*The Age of Atonement: The Influence of Evangelicalism on Social and Economic Thought, 1785–1865* (Oxford: Oxford University Press, 1988), pp. 92–3). Otherwise, his opinions were generally liberal. He was a supporter of the 1834 Poor Law and though he was a Protestant he saw only inconsequential doctrinal differences between his faith and that of his Roman Catholic fellow Irishmen. He was convinced that Catholic Eman-

cipation would make the Union more secure. He was not averse to gradual, what he called 'rational' reform; besides Catholic Emancipation, he also supported the abolition of the slave trade and the reform of criminal law. These various positions made him the natural ally of the Canningites, but while he worked well with Canning and Canning's friends, he gravitated to the man in power. As Thomas points out, like Burke, to whom he was related by marriage and who was a family friend, and like Wellesley who gave him his first political opportunity, Croker took a European perspective on the question of political order and was deeply and broadly philosophical about the science of politics.

50. Murray cooperated with Hatchard in the form of joint publications, but there was a forced quality about their association because Murray was out of sympathy with Hatchard's evangelicalism. Incidentally, the article illustrates that continental liberal biblical theology and textual studies had yet to have a meaningful impact on the English church.

51. Some years later, Accum's *Treatise on Adulterations of Food and Culinary Poisons* (London: Longman, et al., 1820) created a sensation by revealing that unscrupulous merchants commonly added alum to flour, copper to pickles, and the like. The book was reviewed in the *Quarterly* in No. 48 (article #569).

52. Kearsely's offices were at 46 Fleet Street, a few doors from Murray's at Number 32.

53. C. Dewey in *The Passing of Barchester* (London: Hambledon Press, 1991) numbers D'Oyly among the members of the pre-Tractarian group the 'Hackney Phalanx', partly because of his association with Manners Sutton. It is however difficult to distinguish D'Oyly's brand of churchmanship as he appears in some respects to have crossed party lines. He directed much of his effort in the *Quarterly* to a defence of Trinitarian doctrine and thus challenged Unitarian and other heterodox writers, including Thomas Belsham, Sir James Smith, William Paley, and Sir William Drummond. Gifford looked to D'Oyly to help him achieve one of the chief missions of the *QR*, a defence of Christianity and the constitutional prerogatives of the Church of England. But, as he complained to Canning, he found D'Oyly's writing prolix, so, with John Ireland's help, he liberally pruned and vigorously polished D'Oyly's submissions. 'D'Oyly is a good man', Gifford told Copleston, 'but he is only fit for matter of fact' (*QR* Letter 119). D'Oyly is now remembered, if at all, as the primary founder of King's College, London, which he proposed as a Church of England counterweight to the 'godless institution of Gower Street', the secular London University. In that effort he cooperated with another *Quarterly* reviewer, his curate, the Tractarian Hugh James Rose.

54. The *QR* supplies evidence to support Kevin Gilmartin's thesis that print culture was a key instrument in a counterrevolutionary campaign conservatives engaged in to avoid the social and political upheavals experienced in France. See *Writing against Revolution*, p. 105 and *passim*.

55. [Anon.], 'The Quarterly Review', *London Magazine*, 3 (1821), p. 71.

56. *QR*, 1 (article #46), pp. 173, 176.

57. *QR* Letter 65.

58. *QR* Letter 20. *QR*, 1 (article #25), pp. 337, 348, 347.

59. *QR*, 1 (article #19), p. 243.

60. To meet a condition in a relative's will, in 1809 Henry Vaughan changed his last name to Halford.

61. See the *Quarterly Review Archive* <www. rc.umd.edu.org> (accessed 8 November 2007).

62. JM MSS, March 1803 to September 1823 letterbook, p. 264; quoted in Smiles, *Memoir*, vol. 1, p. 163; 12 September 1809, quoted in Smiles, *Memoir*, vol. 1, pp. 164–5; NLS MS 853 (ff. 253–4), Scott to R. L. Edgeworth, 2 July 1811.
63. *QR* Letters 58, 59; JM MS letterbook, John Wilson Croker to John Gibson Lockhart, 17 August [1834]; *QR* Letter 29.
64. *QR* Letter 28.
65. *QR* Letter 29.
66. When in 1816 Scott returned to the roster of *Quarterly* reviewers, it was not for long. Murray mismanaged the publication of *Tales of My Landlord*, and so Scott felt little incentive to continue to support the publisher's interests. At the end of 1817, he again drifted away from the *Quarterly*.
67. *SL*, vol. 2, p. 148.
68. *QR* Letter 26.
69. *Journal of Sir Walter Scott*, p. 23, quoted in the entry on Scott in the *ODNB*. *SL*, vol. 2, pp. 141–2, 30 December 1808. Ballantyne found he had much work to do to motivate Scott to write. He told Murray, 'I stick to Scott & Erskine, like a leech; creep round them like a ferret – till, lo! I get them to write. Yea, verily, I do cunning things to elicit their exertion'. JM MS, 8 March 1809.
70. Articles #42, #46, #95. NLS MSS: 853 (ff. 253–4), Scott to R. L. Edgeworth, 2 July 1811; 3879 (f. 215), Scott to E. Berwick, 16 October 1810; 3878 (f. 170), Scott to J. Moore, 3 October 1809; (f. 173), same, 17 October 1809. *SL*, vol. 2, p. 157, Scott to C. K. Sharpe, 17 February 1809.
71. *QR* Letter 111.
72. In June 1812 Dudley formally shifted his parliamentary allegiance to Canning. To exchange manuscripts and proofs with Dudley, Copleston had Murray and Gifford use a bookseller, 'Mr. Budd', as a blind post office.
73. It was Richard Heber who first noticed Whitaker and recommended that he contact Murray and Gifford to offer his services as a reviewer. Gifford heard from Whitaker for the first time in February 1810; they met in person in April 1813. Through the frequency and quality of his writings, he became Gifford's 'zealous and able friend'. He wrote for pay because the agricultural depression having devastated his parishioners, he gave up much of his income to charity. That was why he told Murray, '[I need] every Penny which my Pen can procure for the support of my Family'. 'We have not a more valuable correspondent' Gifford assured Murray. *QR* Letters 31, 85; JM MSS: Whitaker to Murray, 24 March 1819; Gifford to Murray, August 1818.
74. The Reverend John Penrose (1778–1859), not to be confused with another man who wrote for the *Quarterly*, the Reverend Thomas Penrose (1769–1851). Without informing Gifford, in January 1809 Murray, who was labouring under the misimpression that Gifford had rejected it, set aside a submission of Penrose's. For the incident, see *QR* Letters 30, 37, 39, 45, and Bodl. Lib. MS Eng. Lett. d. 10 (ff. 107-8).
75. Bodl. Lib. MS Eng. Lett. d. 10 (ff. 109–10).
76. Ibid., emphasis added.
77. Bodl. Lib. MS Eng. Lett. d. 10 (ff. 111–12).
78. *QR* Letter 30.
79. A satire on critical reviewing.
80. *QR* Letter 66. For further discussion of Copleston's role in the journal, see Christopher Stray's 'Politics, Culture, and Scholarship: Classics in the *Quarterly Review*' in *Conservatism and the Quarterly Review*, pp. 87–106.

4 The *Quarterly Review* Ascendant

1. M. F. Brightfield, *John Wilson Croker* (Berkeley: University of California Press, 1940), p. 163. Croker's father who was Surveyor General of Customs and Excise in Ireland had an office in London. The bookseller John Ballantyne, who was in London in early April, may also have attended some of the *Quarterly Review* conferences. JM MS, James Ballantyne to JM, 1 April 1809.
2. De Guignes, *Voyages à Peking* (article #48).
3. Article #60.
4. Smiles, *Memoir*, vol. 1, p. 169. For Number 4, Murray initially printed 3,500 copies, but when he saw how well Grant had handled a topic he knew would be of keen interest to the public, he had his printer, Rowarth, run off another five hundred. As the initial sale alone numbered 3,715 (an improvement by 260 copies over Number 3's initial sale) the publisher's judgement was rewarded. In expectation that the quality of Number 4 would lead to an improved sale for Number 5, Murray increased the print run to 5,000. This time his expectations were disappointed as the initial sale was only 3,487. For sales information, see Table B.1 in Appendix B, 'Initial Print Run, Numbers 1–60'.
5. [A. S. Heber], *The Life of Reginald Heber, D. D., Lord Bishop of Calcutta*, 2 vols (London: John Murray, 1830), vol. 1, pp. 333–4.
6. Article #78.
7. Article #114. *QR* Letters 32, 65. NLS MS 3879 (ff. 222–3), Ellis to Scott, 22 October 1810: 'Pitt' is written with 'too much care', but it is the best essay ever in a periodical work. A holograph draft of Grant's 'Pitt' review is preserved in the India Office deposit at the British Library (MSS Eur 308/26).
8. *The Diaries of Sylvester Douglas*, ed. F. Bickley, 2 vols (London: Constable, 1928), vol. 2, p. 102. Bodl. Lib. Dep. Bland Burges 24 (f. 164), Burges to Croker, 27 November 1810. NLS MS 3880 (ff. 1–2), Ellis to Scott, 9 January 1811.
9. NLS MS 2528 (f. 7), Gifford to Southey, 18 April 1810: 'Sorry I was (and I ask your pardon sincerely for it) to be driven by circumstances to some omissions; but I have the consolation of thinking that not one syllable of yours has been changed'. T. DeQuincey, *The English Mail Coach* (Boston, MA: Ticknor, et al., 1851), p. 128. For the impact of 'Nelson' on the development of English nationalism, see D. Eastwood, 'Patriotism Personified: Robert Southey's *Life of Nelson* Reconsidered', *Mariner's Mirror*, 77.2 (May 1991), pp. 143–9.
10. JM MS, Murray to Turner, [*c.* January 1810]. He asked them to call on him, despite their 'Saturday regulations'. Turner and D'Israeli were Jewish. JM MSS: Ellis to Murray, 4 April 1810; epitome of Numbers 1–11: 'No. 5, art. 18, 28.17.6; extra for 18, 31.10'; cash day book, 1810–11, p. 27: '5 April 1810 Quarterly Review / Article 18 extra £31.10 cheque No 799'. NLS MS 3879 (f. 50), Gifford to Walter Scott, 28 March 1810: '[W]e have also a very well written Article by Southey – indeed excellent. It has cost me an infinity of pains, merely, however, to reduce it, for it originally filled four sheets!' T. F. Dibdin, *The Library Companion; or, The Young Man's Guide, and the Old Man's Comfort, in the Choice of a Library*, 2 vols (London: Harding, et al., 1824), vol. 2, p. 137n.
11. Article #113. JM MS, Ellis to Murray, Sunday [September 1810]. *QR* Letter 30, Gifford to Copleston, 8 December 1809. *QR* Letters 59, 60.
12. Dibdin, *The Library Companion*, vol. 1, p. 103; vol. 1, p. 88. Whitaker's articles are #184 and #202; Elmsley's review is article #206; Southey's articles are #17 and #169.

13. Articles #78, #124, #129. During Gifford's years, controversy followed the publication of monetary articles and reviews of, among others, Byron, Dealtry, Elgin, Hunt, Keats, Mitford, Moore, Morgan, O'Meara, and the Shelleys. The *Quarterly* upset Protestant Constitutionalists because of its imputed support of Roman Catholic Emancipation. Family values readers despised its generally sympathetic reviews of Lord Byron and were suspicious of Murray's association with him as his publisher. Barrow's articles on America were notorious, as was his review of Ross's first Arctic expedition. *QR* Letter 79.

14. G. Bedford to P. Elmsley [1811], quoted in Stray, 'Politics, Culture, and Scholarship', pp. 236–7 n. 68. In 1810 and 1811 Murray had difficulty managing his firm's cash flow. See the introduction to Appendix B. For at time, Murray kept 32 Fleet Street as his warehouse. JM MS, Gifford to Murray, 8 December 1813, quoted in Smiles, *Memoir*, vol. 1, p. 261.

15. Barrow and Croker were more successful than Southey in resisting Gifford's manipulation of their articles. Without exception, however, Gifford had veto power over the political content of submissions to the *QR*.

16. Bodl. Lib. MS Eng. Lett. d. 130 (ff. 60–1), 23 October 1822, Thomas Arnold to John Taylor Coleridge, Arnold spoke of the *QR* as having the 'Tone of Men of the World'. JM MS, letterbook, Murray to William Johnstone, 3 November 1837. [Anon.], 'The Quarterly Review', p. 71.

17. On this general point, see J. J. Sack, *From Jacobite to Conservative: Reaction and Orthodoxy in Britain, c. 1760–1832* (Cambridge: Cambridge University Press, 1993), ch. 1.

18. Hilton, "'Sardonic Grins" and "Paranoid Politics"', p. 41.

19. *QR* Letter 8.

20. Croker to J. Murray III, 6 August 1843, quoted in W. Thomas, *The Quarrel of Macaulay and Croker: Politics and History in the Age of Reform* (Oxford: Oxford University Press, 2000), p. 41. In his autobiography, Barrow reflected an identical understanding of the journal's principles as grounded in 'religion and morality, on loyalty to the throne, and patriotism to the country'. *An Auto-Biographical Memoir of Sir John Barrow* (London: John Murray, 1847), p. 492.

21. *QR* Letter 4. In 'Plotting the Success of the *Quarterly Review*' (p. 25 n.15), Kim Wheatley discusses Scott's paradoxical requirement that Gifford should maintain the journal's political independence while relying upon government for information.

22. *QR* Letters 97, 41. Their 'leaders are unpopular, and even odious', Gifford observed, 'yet the Government is rather suffered than respected; and the want of *ostensible* talent is reproachfully noticed'. The 'present men are ... are obstinate', he complained, 'and will not easily part with office'. *QR* Letters 5, 9, 168, 140.

23. *QR* Letter 256. Cf. *QR* Letters 162, 180. *QR* Letter 183. JM MS, Gifford to Hay, January 1820.

24. *QR* Letter 4.

25. For the Perceval incident, see *QR* Letters 70, 71. In March 1813, Gifford wrote to Murray to tell him that the Secretary of State of the India Board of Control, Thomas Courtenay, conveyed the wish of the prime minister that the *Quarterly* should publish an article supportive of the East India Company's monopoly of the India trade. (The Company's charter was up for renewal). The following day, government sent Croker to Gifford to plead its case. Gifford proudly stood for the journal's independence by insisting that the reviewer would take his own line on the issue (in article #221). JM MS, Gifford to Murray [March 1813]. For the Lonsdale incident regarding article #492, see *QR* Letters 195, 199–210, 212.

26. Article #352.
27. Beinecke Lib. MSS: Gifford to Blomfield, 16 July 1811; Gifford to Twiss, no date, but *c.* 1811.
28. JM MS, 22 March 1814.
29. [Anon.], 'Our Relations with Great Britain', *North American Review*, 27 (1828), pp. 481ff. Emphasis added. Compare these comments from a journal out of Boston, *The Panoplist, and Missionary Magazine, for the Year 1816* (pp. 61–2): 'The *Quarterly Review* is generally supposed to have considerable influence, in controlling the opinions and the feelings of the British nation ... it is principally remarkable for its obstinate attachment to English prejudices, its unceasing labours to inflate English pride, and its contemptuous treatment of foreign nations'.
30. Hazlitt, *A Letter to William Gifford, Esq.*, *Collected Works*, vol. 1, p. 366.
31. See Table B.1 in Appendix B, 'Initial Print Run, Numbers 1–60'. Some of the *Quarterly*'s key men are pictured in the oft-printed '4 o'clock visitors' group portrait, Scott, Canning, Gifford, Barrow, D'Israeli, and Murray. The famous meeting between Scott and Byron thus depicted took place on 7 April 1815 in Murray's first floor drawing room at 50 Albemarle Street. Cf. NLS MS 2245 (ff. 15–16), Murray to James Hogg, 10 April 1815: '... Friday last when I had the honour of presenting Scott to [Byron] for the first time – This I consider as a commemorative event in Literary History ...'. Scott used the phrase '4 o'clock visitors' in *SL*, vol. 4, pp. 318–19, Scott to Murray, 18 December 1816.
32. Thompson's phrase, referring specifically to 1815–19. E. P. Thompson, *The Making of the English Working Class* (New York: Vintage, 1963), p. 603.
33. Boyd Hilton makes this point in his essay '"Sardonic Grins" and "Paranoid Politics"'.
34. *QR* Letters 127, 227. JM MS, letterbook, Croker to John Gibson Lockhart 17 August [1834]. An American commentator remarked that the *Quarterly*, 'though a notorious party journal, pensioned and paid by the government ... continues to be the oracle of ... almost all the higher dignitaries of the church; nearly all the nobility; all those who are both loyal and orthodox by virtue of pension and place – in short, all those worthy people, who are fully convinced by the irrefragable invectives of the Quarterly Review, that religion and loyalty are inseparable' (Paulding, *A Sketch of Old England*, vol. 2, p. 119).
35. On the public debate over the state of the country post-Waterloo, see for example, [Anon.], 'Proceedings in the Present Session of Parliament, *Gentleman's Magazine*, 69:2 (1819), p. 552; *Port Folio*, 13 (1822), p. 488; *Parliamentary Debates* (1823), n.s. 8 (1824), col. 48; n.s. 10, col. 23. JM MS, letterbook, Murray to Lockhart, 25 August 1838, copy in Murray's hand.
36. Murray commissioned Scott's article. NLS MS 3886 (ff. 216–17), Murray to Scott, 'Have you any fancy to dash off an article on Emma? – it wants incident and romance & imagination – does it not – none of the author's other Novels have been noticed & surely Pride & Prejudice merits high consideration'. JM MSS: letterbook, Lockhart to Murray, 30 August 1838; Murray to Lockhart, 25 August 1838, copy in Murray's hand.
37. NLS MS 866 (ff. 89–90), Murray to Scott, 12 April 1816.
38. On the frenzied interest in Scott's novels, see Johnson, *Sir Walter Scott*, vol. 1, p. 691, and Lockhart, *Life*, p. 369, cited in J. Chandler, *England in 1819: The Politics of Literary Culture and the Case of Romantic Historicism* (Chicago, IL: University of Chicago Press, 1998), p. 12n. By 1822, when Scott had reached the apex of his fame, his poems and novels had been reviewed in the *Quarterly* in thirteen articles, #101 , #166, #232 , #259 , #304 , #330 , #344, #382, #396, #417 , #605 , #623, #640. Ragaz, 'Walter Scott and the *Quarterly Review*'.

39. See Table B.1 in Appendix B, 'Initial Print Run, Numbers 1–60'. Number 33 was the first *Quarterly* to appear after the Pentridge Rebellion in June. JM MS, Gifford to Hay, 1 December 1817. Thirteen thousand was the maximum Murray sold for any one issue up to 1829. In a letter dated 19 April of that year, concerned by the decline in sales, Murray told Lockhart that the *Quarterly* sold for each of Nos. 69–71, 12,000; Nos. 72–4, 11,500 each; Nos.75–6, 11,000 each ; and for No. 77, 10,500. Barrow, *Auto-biographical Memoir*, p. 506. John Murray's subscription list, preserved in the John Murray Archive, gives evidence that the *Quarterly* was shared by many readers.

40. In 1818 the *Edinburgh* sold 12,000. R. D. Altick, *The English Common Reader: A Social History of the Mass Reading Public 1800–1900* (Chicago, IL: University of Chicago Press, 1957), p. 392. Its circulation had, however, fallen off from the 13,000 it reached in 1811. See note 36 to Appendix A. For *QR* print runs, see the notes to Appendix A and Appendix B.

41. Article #664, pp. 345–6.

42. As did the Royal Geographical Society, of which Barrow was the chief founder.

43. For a recent discussion of Barrow's contribution to the *Quarterly* see J. M. R. Cameron's 'John Barrow, the *Quarterly*'s Imperial Reviewer' in Cutmore (ed.), *Conservatism and the Quarterly Review*, pp. 133–50.

44. Ross's *Voyage of Discovery made under the Orders of the Admiralty* (London: John Murray, 1819), in quarto, was priced £3 13s. 6d. The price for later accounts, Parry's and Franklin's, exceeded £4, the equivalent in today's values of about £250. Cf. <www.measuringworth.com> (accessed 9 November 2007).

45. Accurate references in the periodical literature of the day to Barrow's authorship of review articles abound. General knowledge and Barrow's own practice of systematically cross-referencing his articles ensured that he was widely recognized as 'the gentleman who travels all over the world in the *Quarterly Review*' (*London Magazine*, 3 (1825), p. 357). In No. 43, article #522, published December 1819, Barrow openly identified himself as the article's author. In his *Library Companion*, Dibdin wrote that Barrow's contribution, 'well known' and 'generally highly appreciated', 'will always secure ... an immediate and extensive sale'. 'The reader, of course, anticipates the mention of notices of various travels, by Mr. Barrow, in the *Quarterly Review*: notices, which, whenever reperused, cannot fail to bring increased pleasure and instruction. They are the productions of an *experienced* head. The Reviewer is at once a traveller and a critic. *Si sic omnia!*' (*Library Companion*, vol. 2, pp. 437–8n). A letter writer in the *Literary Gazette* for 23 May 1818 (pp. 326-7) commented that Barrow, as 'a public man, having free access to Government documents, can scarcely fail of interesting his readers, when he undertakes to describe, *by authority*, the objects contemplated by ministers, in equipping an expensive armament for the purposes of extending science and prosecuting discovery'. For the contest between Scoresby and Barrow, see C. Martin, 'William Scoresby Jr. (1789–1857) and the Open Polar Sea – Myth and Reality', *Arctic*, 41 (1988), pp. 39–47. For biting criticism of Murray's publication and Barrow's reviews of the 'big books', the official Polar accounts, see also the *London Magazine*, n.s. 4 (1826), p. 174. For criticism of the polar explorations, see 'Letter to the Editor from Captain Cochrane', *New Monthly Magazine*, 7 (January–June 1824), pp. 549–59.

46. JM MS, accounts. *The Diary of Joseph Farington*, ed. K. Garlick and A. Macintyre, 17 vols (New Haven, CT: Yale University Press, 1978–98), vol. 15, col. 5328 (entry for 19 February 1819).

47. JM MS, 26 August 1821.

48. JM MSS: 26 March 1813; May, 1813; 26 December 1816. The Lonsdale incident: *QR* Letters 195, 199–210, 212; article #492.
49. *QR* Letters 8, 189.
50. *Citizen: A Monthly Journal of Politics, Literature, and Art*, 1 (November 1839–May 1840), p. 393.
51. Characterizing Gifford as a petty sourpuss crabbed in body and soul, many modern commentators follow Hazlitt's example by stereotyping him as Quilp-like, an evil dwarf ('acrid and deformed pedant' – S. Colvin; 'shriveled deformed' – J. Worham; 'crippled and sour' – J. van Whye). Having often seen Gifford at Hoppner's house when she was five years old, in after years Clarissa Trant vividly recalled 'this little man and his green coat'. It was perhaps antipathetic commentators such as Hazlitt and Hunt who taught her to remember Gifford as a 'small evil genius'. In her remembrance she drew, however, a telling distinction. His was not 'a wicked but a *malign*' evil, she wrote. The child had witnessed nothing vampiric in Gifford's behaviour, but as an adult she was taught to detect in him invisible evil. Following a similar course, others who never met him discovered in Gifford '*innate* meanness' and '*deep-seated* corruption of principle if not of character'. Clarissa Sandford Trant Bramston, *The Journal of Clarissa Trant, 1800–1832*, ed. C. G. Luard (London: J. Lane, Bodley Head, [1925]), p. 4. C. Redding, *Personal Reminiscences of Eminent Men*, 3 vols (London: n.p., 1867), vol. 3, pp. 17, 21. *Athenaeum* 3487 (35 August 1894), p. 267, quoted in *Letters of Charles and Mary Anne Lamb*, ed. E. W. Marrs, 3 vols (Ithaca, NY: Cornell University Press, 1976–9), vol. 3, 132n; emphasis added.
52. 'I never felt more vexed in my life', Lamb wrote to Wordsworth when he saw what Gifford had made of his review of the *Excursion* in the twenty-third number of the *QR*, published on 6 January 1815 (Letter 627, 7 January 1815, in *Letters of Charles and Mary Anne Lamb*, vol. 3, p. 128). Lamb's reaction was only one in a series of farcical incidents in his disastrous relationship with the *QR*. In an earlier episode, in a February 1812 article published in Number 12 (article #177), Gifford had gravely insulted him by calling him a 'poor maniac'. Lamb, who had suffered bouts of insanity, was of course offended that such a crass remark about him should appear in a national publication. When challenged by Southey to explain himself, Gifford abjectly apologized, claiming that in using the epithet he had known Lamb only as a name. Southey accepted the apology on Lamb's behalf and then proceeded to persuade his friend to contribute to the *Quarterly* a review of Wordsworth's *Excursion*. A well-meaning gesture, it was nevertheless a great mistake. Entirely predictably, given his interventionist manner, upon receiving the article Gifford applied his editorial pencil to make it, he said, 'less foolish'; equally predictably, given Lamb's sensitivity and his already finely tuned dislike of Gifford, the author was incensed. He told Wordsworth that by altering a third of the article and excising twelve or so passages, the editor had rendered it completely unintelligible. Lamb, however, almost certainly exaggerated the extent and arbitrariness of Gifford's edits.

    Few writers have come to Gifford's defence (W. Graham, in *Tory Criticism in the Quarterly Review, 1809–1853* (New York: Colombia University Press, 1921) excepted); most – some apparently without looking too deeply into the matter – have sided with Lamb, as does Marrs in *Letters of Charles and Mary Anne Lamb*, vol. 3, p. 132n. Yet a disinterested assessment of the finished article makes it difficult to find grounds for Lamb's complaint. Marrs quotes at length a reviewer in the *Athenaeum* who thought the episode revealed in Gifford a 'deep-seated corruption of principle if not of character'. That assessment is harshly judgmental and definitely unfair if Gifford rescued the article, not to mention inaccurate if Lamb exaggerated Gifford's sins. Grosvenor Bedford, who saw at least a part of Lamb's manuscript, thought the draft 'both feeble and affected' (Bodl. Lib. MS Eng. Lett. d.52, ff. 117–18, 1 February 1815). As Bedford was seldom Gifford's apologist, often his scourge, his verdict carries extra weight. There is another voice in Gifford's favour, that of Frank Sayers who when he saw the article, apparently in draft, wondered if Lamb intended it as a burlesque (ibid.). Too, Gifford consulted Lamb about the excisions and gave him an opportunity to withdraw the review – Bedford told Southey that Gifford returned the review to Lamb for 'some slight alteration', including, crucially in the light of Lamb's later complaints, cutting from the beginning of the article his refutation of the 'Lake Poets' classification (ibid.). But there is no indication either that Lamb confronted Gifford about the edits or that he tried to pull the article back; quite to the contrary, for had he done so, that would be part of the record.

What Gifford preserved of Lamb's original is a lively wide-ranging discussion of the poem and an explication of its Romantic principles. The editor retained wonderfully expressive passages; he permitted Lamb to praise Wordsworth unambiguously and fulsomely; and he kept challenging insightful definitions of Romanticism, including Lamb's suggestive 'Natural Methodism' (p. 105). Too, some of Gifford's excisions make eminent sense. He removed, because he thought it digressive and believed it would unnecessarily bring the *QR* into conflict with the *Edinburgh Review*, an apparently elaborate refutation of Jeffrey's 'Lake Poets' classification in the August 1807 *Edinburgh*. In doing so Gifford obeyed Scott's instruction that, for reasons of honour, he avoid directly confronting the *Edinburgh* (see *QR* Letter 4). We can lament the loss of Lamb's discussion, but Gifford's action is defensible. Gifford's final word on the article is in a letter to Scott: 'He [Southey] forced Lambe [*sic*] upon me for a foolish Article and was then hurt because to save the Review I made it less so' (*QR* Letter 182).

In 1823, the *Quarterly* offended Lamb again, this time in an article on insanity written by Southey's medical friend Robert Gooch (article #631). In quoting Lamb's 'Confessions of a Drunkard', Gooch referred to Lamb's account as a 'fearful picture of the consequences of intemperance, and which we have reason to know is a true tale'. Lamb himself was almost certainly behind the note published in the *London Magazine* in August 1822 that calls the *Quarterly* to account for thus parading a man's misfortunes in public.

The feud continued when in a *QR* article Southey made passing mention of Lamb's *Elia* (article #649). His intention had been kindly, to let readers know about Lamb's work (*NL*, vol. 2, p. 245), but he ran into trouble when he tested *Elia* against the template of his own deeply religious outlook. In the article, Southey called it 'a book which wants only a sounder religious feeling, to be as delightful as it is original'. Incredibly, in a draft of the article Southey wrote 'saner' instead of 'sounder' – though he caught the error in time, it is bizarre that he wrote the word at all. Southey later claimed that had Gifford managed to get proofs to him he would have revised the passage on *Elia* out of existence (*NL*, vol. 2, p. 252). Yet Southey's claim is surely a defensive shifting of responsibility. Just as he had in the case of Gifford's redactions, Lamb now reacted to Southey's unintended provocation out of all proportion to the offence. His *Letter of Elia to Robert Southey* (1823) is savagely abusive. Southey displayed great magnanimity by swiftly offering an apology. Both men then let the matter drop.

53. A. Carmichael, *A Memoir of the Life and Philosophy of Spurzheim* (Boston, MA: Marsh, Capen, and Lyon, 1833), p. 13.

54. Croker repaid Colman's compliment by reviewing *Vagaries Vindicated* itself in No, 18. Delightful too was the response Lady Morgan's sister wrote to an article by Croker:

    Postscriptum – we'd near made a foolish omission,
    And forgotten a slur on her Second Edition.
    Though perhaps, after all, she may have the last word,
    And reply to our "wholesome" remarks – by a Third –
    And thus, like a sly and insidious joker,
    The malice defeat of a *hireling* Croker!!

    (Morgan, *Memoirs*, vol. 2, pp. 58–9).

55. Privately in a letter to Byron and publicly in *Adonais*, Shelley repeatedly and passionately blamed Gifford for Keats's death. In a letter to John Murray, Byron slyly alluded to the episode in his poem, '"Who killed John Keats?" / "I", says the Quarterly, / So savage and Tartarly ...' (JM MS, 30 July 1821). He returned to the theme, again ironically, in Canto XI of *Don Juan*: 'John Keats ... was killed off by one critique ... / 'Tis strange the mind, that very fine particle, / Should let itself be snuffed out by an article'.

56. 25 February 1818 [for 1819], *The Letters of Percy Bysshe Shelley*, ed. F. L. Jones, 2 vols (Oxford: Clarendon Press, 1964), vol. 2, p. 81.

5 The Transition to Lockhart

1. *QR* Letter 225.
2. JM MS, 19 March 1822. [Anon.], 'The Quarterly Review', *London Magazine*, 3 (1821), p. 72. BL Add. MS 34585 (f. 234), Parr to Samuel Butler, [1822?]. *QR* Letter 234; cf. *QR* Letter 239. G. Smith, *Bishop Heber: Poet and Chief Missionary to the East, Second Lord Bishop of Calcutta, 1783–1826* (London: John Murray, 1895), pp. 68, 100.
3. Gifford to Canning, 8 September 1824, quoted in Smiles, *Memoir*, vol. 2, p. 163.
4. JM MS, Gifford to Murray, *c.* 29 March 1825.
5. 'The vanity of being in a secret, is too great for him', Gifford told Copleston. *QR* Letter 120.
6. The speculation about Milman was published in the *Port Folio*, a Philadelphia journal surprisingly well informed about publishing and literary developments in Britain: 'The rumour that Mr. Milman had succeeded Mr. Gifford ... and which had been contradicted, is now revived. It is now understood that Mr. Murray has been corresponding with a celebrated northern writer on the subject of a new editor ... whose voice is decidedly in favour of Mr. Milman' (*Port Folio*, 17 (January–June 1824), p. 86). The rumour's essential truth is confirmed in a postscript to a 6 December 1823 letter from John Taylor Coleridge to Murray (JM MS). Coleridge wrote that Milman 'offered assistance of every kind in the amplest way, saying for himself that his profession and his pursuits would have prevented him from thinking of accepting such a post [as the editorship] if it had been offered to him'.
7. *QR* Letter 235, Cohen to Murray, 13 November 1822.
8. Whately's review is #570. Senior's agricultural article is #596; his Scott reviews are #605, #623, #640.
9. Quoted in J. Shattock, *Politics and Reviewers: The Edinburgh and the Quarterly in the Early Victorian Age* (Leicester: Leicester University Press, 1989), p. 55.
10. BL Add. MS 59416 (f. 90).
11. BL Add. MS 47533 (f. 24), Southey to Coleridge, 2 October 1822. Bodl. Lib. MS Eng. Lett. d. 130 (ff. 62–3), 12 December 1822.

12. JM MS, Barrow to Murray, 18 August 1823. Copleston reluctantly put John Hughes forward at Hughes's own request. Bodl. Lib. MS Eng. Lett. d. 10 (ff. 160–1), Richard Heber to Murray, 17 October 1824. *QR* Letters 251, 253. JM MS, Barrow to Murray, 18 August 1823. Other Noetics who contributed to the *Quarterly* under Gifford – Davison and Potter – were not seriously considered for the editorship.

13. *SL*, vol. 8, p. 375, Scott to Southey, 26 September 1824.

14. Smiles, *Memoir*, vol. 2, p. 162, Barrow to Murray, 24 September 1824. *SL*, vol. 8, p. 375, Scott to Southey, 26 September 1824. Bodl. Lib. MS Eng. Lett. d. 47 (f. 98), Southey to Bedford, 1 June 1818; c.26 (f. 127), same, 28 August 1822; same, 7 December 1822. Quoted in Shattock, *Politics and Reviewers*, p. 44.

15. Details of the 1816–17 scheme are preserved in the Arnold–Coleridge correspondence, Bodl. Lib. MS Eng. Lett. d. 134.

16. Bodl. Lib. MS Eng. Lett. d. 134 (f. 70), Arnold to Coleridge, 11 August 1817; (f. 74), same, 7 October 1817; (f. 124), same, June 1822; d.130 (ff. 58–9), same, 14 August 1822. The primary focus of the 1817 plan was the *British Critic*, but during discussions the *QR* was mentioned as a secondary target. In 1822 the group set its sights on the main prize. Bodl. Lib. MS Eng. Lett. d. 134 (f. 16), 22 February 1814.

17. *QR* Letter 61, Murray to Ellis, 2 October 1810. Article #407. *Some Unpublished Letters of Sir Walter Scott from the Collection in the Brotherton Library*, ed. J. A. Symington (Oxford: n.p., 1932), 10 January 1817. Scott wrote to Lady Abercorn upon Byron's death, 'He was generous, humane, and noble-minded ... The worst I ever saw about him was that he rather liked indifferent company ...' (*Familiar Letters*, vol. 2, pp. 205 ff). Further research is required to establish more firmly who these many persons were.

18. On the mood among conservatives in the 1820s, see Hilton, *The Age of Atonement*. On Romantic Conservatism's social agenda, see C. De Paolo, *Coleridge's Philosophy of Social Reform* (New York: Peter Lang, 1987).

19. Reiman, *The Romantics Reviewed*, vol. 5, p. 195. Reiman, 'Keats and the Third Generation', in R. M. Ryan and A. R. Sharp (eds), *The Persistence of Poetry, Bicentennial Essays on Keats* (Amherst: Univ. of Massachusetts Press, 1998), pp. 109–19.

20. JM MS, Southey to Murray, 1 November 1822, published in *NL*, vol. 2, pp. 238–9. Like his university friend Thomas Arnold, John Coleridge's politics were liberal conservative. The Philadelphia *Port Folio*, which had the benefit of a well-connected British literary informant, rumoured that 'Mr. Coleridge has succeeded Mr. Gifford .... This gentleman was formerly a republican in his political sentiments, but as he has been some time in training in an office under the government, we presume he has qualified himself for this new station' (*Port Folio*, 17 (January–June 1824), pp. 250–1). JM MS, Sir William Drummond to 'the Editor of the *Quarterly Review*', 28 February 1812. Paulding, *A Sketch of Old England*, vol. 2, p. 118. Article #456. JM MS, Southey to Murray, 9 April 1818. A few months later, Coleridge reviewed Hunt's *Foliage*, in No. 36 (article #456). In Number 28, Southey refers to Croker's review of Leigh Hunt's *Rimini* (article #374).

21. JM MSS, JM to Southey, 13 November 1822 (copy); Coleridge to JM, 12 November 1822 NLS MS 42552, Southey to Murray, 18 November 1822.

22. In part because he was uncomfortable with aspects of 'Tory' conservatism, Coleridge expressed a concern government would tie his hands by requiring a specific pledge to support the Cabinet's policies. Southey assured him, 'Government "interferes" in such things less than for its own interest, and the interest of the country it ought to do'. BL Add. MS 47533 (f. 26), 5 November 1822.

23. Bodl. Lib. MS Eng. Lett. d.130 (ff. 62–3). On 6 May 1823, Coleridge, having heard of Gifford's renewed intention to retire, reminded Murray of his willingness to take up the editorship. Murray told him that Gifford was well and 'vigorous in intellect' and that 'during his life no change [was] likely to take place'. *QR* Letters 248, 249. JM MSS: Gifford to Coleridge, 9 December 1822; same, 18 February 1823. NLS MS 3896 (ff. 44–5), Gifford to Scott, 13 February 1823.

24. Coleridge certainly conveyed his doubts in person. They are also recorded in JM MS, Coleridge to Murray, 29 January 1823.

25. Quoted in W. Thomas, 'Religion and Politics in the *Quarterly Review*, 1809–1853', in Stefan Collini, et al. (eds), *History, Religion, and Culture: British Intellectual History 1750–1950* (Cambridge: Cambridge University Press, 2000), pp. 136–55.

26. Referring to a children's game, in his *Rationale of Reward* (1825) Bentham famously stated that 'Quantity of pleasure being equal, push-pin is as good as poetry'.

27. Shattock, in *Politics and Reviewers* and Thomas in *The Quarrel of Macaulay and Croker* supply information about Croker's association with Murray, but during Lockhart's, not Gifford's, editorship.

28. *QR* Letter 251.

29. JM MS, Blomfield to Gifford, 20 May 1823.

30. *QR* Letters 237, 248.

31. See entries for Nos. 56 through 61 in the *Quarterly Review Archive* <rc.umd.edu.org>.

32. JM MSS: Gifford to Murray, 22 July 1823; Gifford to Coleridge, 29 July 1823. Barrow's loyalty to Murray and the *QR* had its limits. In the last decade of his life he deserted the *Quarterly* for its rival, the *Edinburgh*, when Lockhart declined to publish a review Barrow wrote of his own son's book of travels. He had been tempted earlier to write for other journals. When in July 1829 Macvey Napier invited him to become an *Edinburgh* reviewer, he explained his reasons for not wishing to do so: 'I was thoroughly pressed by my friend [Nassau] Senior to assist him in Blanco White's [*London*] Review, but I declined for two reasons 1st: Because I had promised Gifford that while the Quarterly existed and was conducted on [the] principles with which it started, my trifling offerings should be confined to it and secondly that I really did not feel myself at all competent to the labor of writing Articles for Reviews after the daily labor of the office' (BL Add. MS 34614, ff. 110–11, 8 July 1829). JM MS, Barrow to Murray, 26 July 1824.

33. *QR* Letter 251.

34. Indeed, in 1823 Murray had more than one opportunity to renew his interest in these two men but he declined to do so. Coleridge contacted him in May to remind him that he was still interested in the position. Senior's name came up again, in November, but again Murray declined even to consider him. See *QR* Letters 246, 247, 251, 253.

35. *QR* Letters 248, 254.

36. *QR* Letters 257, 246.

37. West Yorkshire Archive Service, Leeds, Canning papers, Liverpool to Canning, 26 April 1824.

38. *QR* Letter 259. JM MS, Gifford to Coleridge, 23, 24 September 1825.

39. Smiles, *Memoir*, vol. 2, p. 162. *Familiar Letters*, vol. 2, pp. 419–21, Murray to Lockhart, 24 November 1825.

40. *Familiar Letters*, vol. 2, pp. 419–21, Murray to Lockhart, 24 November 1825.

41. Smiles, *Memoir*, vol. 2, p. 164–5, Murray to Coleridge, 9 December 1824.

42. Smiles, *Memoir*, vol. 2, p. 165, Coleridge to Murray, 10 December 1824.

43. Smiles, *Memoir*, vol. 2, p. 168, Murray to Southey, 12 December 1824. BL Add. MS 47553 (f. 42), Southey to Coleridge, 24 December 1824.

44. *Familiar Letters*, vol. 2, pp. 419–21, Murray to Lockhart, 24 November 1825.

45. The Devonshire quarter sessions, held at Exeter, ran from mid-January to mid-April and from mid-July to mid-October. *Royal Kalendar* (London: William Stockdale, 1817), p. 32.

46. JM MS, *c*. 29 March 1825.

47. It also did not help that in June, July, and September Coleridge was laid up by bouts of rheumatism. JM MSS: Coleridge to Murray, 18 July; 11 Sept 1825. Cf. same, 19 October and 3 November 1825.

48. JM MSS: Coleridge to Field, 22 June 1825; Coleridge to Murray, 8 July 1815.

49. Because of Gooch's article, a proposal was quashed to remove plague from the quarantine laws. See Robert Southey, *The Doctor*, 7 vols (London: Longman et al., 1847), vol. 6, p. 199.

50. *SL*, vol. 10, p. 55, Scott to Sophia Lockhart, [9 June 1826]. *Blackwood's Magazine* 17 (January–June 1824), p. 475. JM MS, Coleridge to Murray, March 1825.

51. Smiles, *Memoir*, vol. 2, p. 199, Murray to Scott, 13 October 1825.

52. Ibid.

53. That in after hours Murray imbibed to excess was common knowledge.

54. Smiles, *Memoir*, vol. 2, p. 196. *SL*, vol. 6, p. 170, Scott to Lockhart, 6 April 1817. Smiles, *Memoir*, vol. 2, p. 192.

55. When Lockhart took over the *Quarterly*, concern was also raised that, as a Scotsman, he would weaken the journal's support for the constitutional prerogatives of the Church of England. Cf. J. H. Monk to H. H. Norris, 2 December 1825, Deanery, Peterborough:

    though I greatly regret that there is a danger of the Quarterly Review changing its principles along with its conductor, yet I agree with you in thinking that the crisis is most favourable to the British Critic; which ought by all means to be brought forward with the same fort which was lately held by the Quarterly, in the defence of our Establishments in Church and State (Lambeth Palace MS 3120/8–0; reference supplied by C. A. Stray).

    A devout High Churchman, as editor of the *Quarterly*, Lockhart gave, if anything, even stronger support to Monk and Norris's High Church views than did Gifford.

56. Heber to Charlotte Dod, quoted in Smith, *Bishop Heber*, p. 100.

57. *Familiar Letters*, vol. 2, p. 194, Scott to Lady Abercorn, 4 March 1824. JM MSS: Mitchell to Murray, 11 February 1821; same, 9 May 1822.

58. Smiles, *Memoir*, vol. 2, p. 194, Disraeli to Murray, 29 September 1825.

59. Barrow told Murray he did not 'think it prudent to enquire of the father-in-law as to the character of the son' (JM MS, 22 November 1825). When in May 1826 Murray publicly blamed Benjamin Disraeli for the *Representative* fiasco, Maria D'Israeli in a letter to the publisher expressed what Scott must have thought in October 1825, that 'were this story told truly it would not be believed that the experienced publisher of Albemarle Street could be deceived by the plans of a boy of twenty ...' (JM MS, Maria D'Israeli to Murray, 21 May 1826).

60. Smiles, *Memoir*, vol. 2, pp. 190–2, Disraeli to Murray, 25 September 1825.

61. Smiles, *Memoir*, vol. 2, p. 196.

62. *SL*, vol. 9, pp. 249–50. Misdated to 12 October in Smiles, *Memoir*, vol. 2, pp. 196–7.

63. Emphasis added.
64. *Familiar Letters*, vol. 2, p. 374.
65. An English law lord, Lord Gifford, related this information to Scott. See *SL*, vol. 9, pp. 253, 310.
66. Smiles, *Memoir*, vol. 2, pp. 198–9, Murray to Scott, 13 October 1825.
67. Shattock, *Politics and Reviewers*, p. 51. *SL*, vol. 9, p. 335, Scott to Morritt.
68. *SL*, vol. 10, p. 470, Scott to Lockhart, 15 July 1828. By 'humorous' Scott intends 'capricious'. BL Add. MS 47553 (f. 123), Southey to Coleridge, 11 December 1825. *Familiar Letters*, vol. 2, p. 420, Murray to Lockhart, 24 November 1825. Emphasis added.
69. JM MS, Coleridge to Murray, 10 November 1825. *QR* Letter 262. BL Add. MS 47553 (ff. 119–21), copy in Edith May's hand; published in W. Brakeman, 'Letters by Robert Southey to Sir John Taylor Coleridge', *Studia Germanica Gandensia* 6 (1964), pp. 103–230. BL Add. MS 47553 (f. 123), Southey to Coleridge, 11 December 1825. Bodl. Lib. MS Eng. Lett. d. 134 (f. 180), Keble to Coleridge, 29 January 1826.
70. *QR* Letter 262.
71. JM MS, Coleridge to Murray, 14 December 1825, 'After what you have told me, you can scarcely expect *real* services from Mr Croker ...'.
72. Years later, Murray wrote to William Johnstone that 'people never dream that the Quarterly Review is a *property* upon the cultivation of which I have expended more that *One Hundred Thousand Pounds!!!*' JM MS, letterbook, 3 November 1837.
73. *QR* Letter 41.
74. *QR* Letter 216.

Appendix A: List of Articles and Identification of Contributors

1. *M. Ch.*, 20 February 1809, 'This present month will be published ... the / First Number of / The Quarterly Review. ... Gentlemen desirous of receiving the First Number of this Journal, as soon as published, are requested to give in their names immediately to their respective Booksellers or Newsmen, either in town or country.' *M. Ch.*, 27 February 1809, 'On Wednesday next will be published ... the / First Number of the Quarterly Review.' *Courier*, 29 February 1809: 'Tomorrow, the first of March, will be published, in 8vo. / price 5s, the First Number of the Quarterly Review by John Murray, 32, Fleet-street, Hatchard, Piccadilly, and Richardson, Cornhill, London; John Ballantyne and Co. No.48, North Hanover-street, Edinburgh'. *M. Ch.*,1 March 1809, 'This Day is published the first Number of the Quarterly Review ....' J. Savage, *Librarian* (1809), p. 192: '*Books published in March*, 1809 ... The Quarterly Review No. 1'. JM printed 3,000: JM MS, accounts book. W. B. Todd and A. Bowden, *Sir Walter Scott: A Bibliographical History 1796–1832* (New Castle, DE: Oak Knoll Press, 1998), citing the *Edinburgh Evening Courant* state that *QR* No. 1 was issued in Edinburgh on 9 March. The number, however, was available in Scotland from 6 March. By 8 March, John Ballantyne had sold his whole supply and he had orders for fifty more. See JM MSS: John Ballantyne to JM, 6 March 1809; same, 9 March 1809.
2. *Courier*, 30 May 1809. *M. Ch.*, 30 May 1809. JM MS, letterbook, JM to WG (copy), 31 May 1809, encloses payment for contributors. JM MS, list of paid contributors, dated 1 June. JM printed 3,000: JM MS, accounts book.
3. *M. Ch.*, 29 August 1809, 'this day'. JM MS list of paid contributors. JM printed 4,000: JM MS, accounts book.

4. *Courier* and *M. Ch.*, 23 December 1809, 'this day'. JM printed 4,000: JM MS, accounts book.

5. *Courier*, 26 March 1810, 'Saturday next'. *M. Ch.*, 17 March 1810, 'in a few days'; 31 March 1810, 'this day'. JM MS, accounts book, 31 March 1810. NLS 3879 (f. 50), WG to Walter Scott, 28 March 1810, the review will come out on Sat. JM printed 5,000: JM MS, accounts book; *QR* Letter 42.

6. *M. Ch.*, 20 July 1810, 'to-morrow'. *Courier*, 4 July 1810, 'in a few days', repeated 5, 7 July. *QR* Letter 53: 'We shall be out next week: I hope on Thursday'. JM MS, George Ellis to JM, 22 July (1810), the *QR* has arrived. JM printed 5,000: JM MS, accounts book; Iowa MS (f. 110), JM to John Wilson Croker, 2 April 1810.

7. *Courier*, 8 October 1810, 'in a few days'. *M. Ch.*, 27 October 1810, 'this day'. NLS 3879 (ff. 227–8), WG to WS, 27 October 1810: 'We are out at last'. JM printed 5,000: JM MS, accounts book.

8. *M. Ch.*, 29 December 1810, 'this day'. JM MS, list of paid contributors, 29 December 1810. *QR* Letter 73, the *QR* will be published on Wed. (26 December). JM printed 5,000: JM MS, accounts books. By November 1811, he still had on hand 600 copies.

9. *M. Ch.*, Mon., 1 April 1811, 'on Wednesday next'. *Courier*, Mon., 8 April 1811, 'this day'. *M. Ch.*, Wed., 10 April 1811, 'now ready'. JM MS, accounts book 1810–11, p.147, 10 April 1811. It appears that both the 1 April and the 8 April *Courier* notices were premature. JM printed 6,000: *QR* Letters 81, 108; JM MS, 1803–23 letterbook, JM to WG, 25 October 1811.

10. *QR* Letter 96: 'by Saturday' (29 June). *Courier*, 29 June 1811, on 1 July. *Courier* and *M. Ch.*, 1 July 1811, 'this day'. JM MS, paid contributors, 2 July. JM printed 6,000: JM MS, 1803–23 letterbook; *QR* Letter 108. By November 1811, he still had on hand 850 copies: JM MS, accounts book.

11. *Courier*, 2 October 1811, 'on the 1st of Oct' [*sic*]; *QR* Letter 107, late because of ill health. JM MS, Southey to JM, 14 October 1811, the *QR* is advertised for Sat. (October 18). *M.Ch.*, 21 October 1811, 'this day'. JM MS, accounts book 1810–1812, pp. 2, 21: published October 1811. JM printed 5,000: *QR* Letter 108.

12. *M. Ch.*, 1 February 1812, 'at 12 o'clock this day'. Devon MS 1149M (f. 105), WG to Copleston, 4 February 1812, appeared 'on Saturday', delayed because of negotiations with government over article #178. JM printed 5,000: JM MS, accounts book. He initially sold about 4,200 copies.

13. *M. Ch.*, Fri., 8 May 1812, 'Monday next'); 11 May 1812, 'this day', inserted by JM as a special announcement – there are no other book notices that day. JM printed 5,000. He initially sold about 4,800. At this time WG estimated the journal's total readership to be at least 50,000.

14. *M.Ch.*, 13 August 1812, 'this day'. BL Add. MS 34567 (f. 305), Octavius Gilchrist to Philip Bliss, 14 August 1812, Gilchrist received his copy that day. JM printed 5,000: JM MS, accounts book. He initially sold about 4,300.

15. *M.Ch.*, 15 December 1812, 'this day'. JM printed 5,500: JM MS, accounts book.

16. *Courier* and *M.Ch.*, 5 March 1813, 'this day. JM printed 6,000: JM MS, accounts book.

17. *M.Ch.*, Mon., 14 June 1813, 'on Wed'. JM MS, accounts book, 1810–14, p. 45, JM sent Ellis a copy on 17 June and paid the Stamp Office for six advertisements. *Courier* and *M.Ch.*, 18 June 1813, 'this day', but as neither paper published book notices on 16 or 17 June, 18 June was the first opportunity for JM's 16 June notice to appear.

18. *Courier*, 24 August 1813, 'to-morrow'; 25 August 1813, 'this day'.

19. *Courier* and *M.Ch.*, Thursday 16 December 1813, 'Saturday next'. Note that JM MS, accounts book gives 17 December and JM MS, WG to R. W. Hay, 17 December 1813, states that the Number is now published. JM printed 5,500: JM MS, accounts book.
20. *Courier*, 25 March 1814, 'on Monday' (28 March). *M.Ch.*, 1 April 1814, 'this day'. JM MS, letterbook, Mdme de Staël to JM, 2 April 1814 (copy), annotation in JM's hand: 'to me upon the Criticism on *L'Allemagne* which appeared in my review No XX published the day before'.
21. *M.Ch.*, 16 July 1814, 'this day'.
22. *M.Ch.*, 5 November 1814, 'Tuesday next'; 7 November, 'to-morrow'; 8 November, 'this day'.
23. *M.Ch.*, 4 January 1815, 'Friday next'; 5 January 1815, 'to-morrow'; 6 January 1815, 'this day'. *Courier*, 6 January 1815, 'this day'. JM printed 7,000: JM MS, accounts book; *QR* Letter 162. He sold as many as 6,000 on the first day of the sale: *Selections from the Letters of Robert Southey*, vol. 2, p. 419; JM MSS: WG to R. W. Hay, 7 January 1815; same, 23 June 1815.
24. *Courier*, 22 March 1815, 'to-morrow'. *M.Ch.*, 23 March 1815, 'this day'.
25. *Courier*, 20 June 1815, 'this day'. JM MS, accounts book, 1814–16, p.117, 28 June 1815, records presentation copy to WG of No. 25.
26. *Courier* and *M.Ch.*, 1 December 1815, 'this day'. JM printed 8,000: *QR* Letter 168.
27. *Courier*, Wed., 6 March 1816, 'Saturday next'. *Courier* and *M.Ch.*, 12 March 1816, 'this day'. JM printed 7,000: NLS MS 866 (ff. 89–90), JM to WS, 12 April 1816.
28. *Courier* and *M.Ch.*, Thurs., 16 May 1816, 'Saturday next'. *Courier*, 18 May 1816, 'this day'. *M.Ch.*, having not published book notices on Saturday 18 May, on Monday 20 May repeated the 'Saturday next' notice. On 21 May it belatedly published the 'this day' notice that should have appeared on Saturday 20 May, and then, strangely, on Saturday 21 May, it published a 'this day' notice. JM printed 8,000: NLS MS 866 (ff. 89–90), JM to WS, 12 April 1816.
29. *M.Ch.*, Mon., 5 August 1816 and *Courier*, Fri., 9 August 1816, 'Saturday next'. JM MS, WG to J. T. Coleridge, 12th August 1816, 'Our No. appeared yesterday' – WG started the letter on the 11th and posted it on the 12th. *The Times* advertised the Contents of No. 29 on 9 August 1816. JM printed 8,500: NLS MS 3888 (ff. 256–7), JM to WS, n.d. He sold 7,500 in four days: *QR* Letter 173.
30. *Courier* and *M.Ch.*, 12 November 1816, 'this day'. JM MS, WG to R. W. Hay, 12 November 1816, 'We appear today'. JM printed 8,500: NLS MS 3888 (ff. 256–7), JM to WS, n.d.
31. *Courier*, 31 January 1817 and 5 February 1817, 'in a few days'; 7 February 1817, 'on Tuesday'. *M.Ch.*, 10 February 1817, 'to-morrow'; no book notices on 11 February 1817; 12 February 1817, 'this day'. JM MS, accounts book 1814–16, 11 February 1817. *SL*, vol. 4, p. 363n states 11 Feb 1817 but does not cite his source. JM printed 10,000: NLS MS 3888 (ff. 256–7), JM to WS, n.d. JM MS, WG to J.T. Coleridge, 13 February 1817, 'Murray sold of this No. on *the first* day (Thursday last) 7587'.
32. *Courier* and *M.Ch.*, 15 May 1817, 'Saturday next'; there are no book notices in either paper on Sat., 17 May. *M.Ch.*, Mon., 19 May 1817, 'this day', the paper's first opportunity to insert JM's notice intended for Sat., 17 May 1817. JM printed 12,000: NLS MS 3888 (f. 256–7), JM to WS, n.d.
33. *Courier*, Mon., 1 September 1817, 'Thursday next'; Wed., September 3 1817, 'Saturday next'. There is no *QR* notice among the book advertisements in the *M.Ch.* for Saturday 6 September 1817. *Courier* and *M.Ch.*, Monday 8 September, 'this day', the paper's earliest

opportunity to insert JM's notice intended for 6 September. Anne Cleaver, the wife of the Bishop of St Asaph, in her copy of the *QR* often recorded the date when she received it from her bookseller (present writer's collection). Anne Cleaver, 'Received Sept 8 1817'; it usually took a day following publication for Cleaver to receive her copy and there was no Sunday delivery. JM printed 12,000: Barrow, *An Auto-Biographical Memoir*, p. 506; NLS MS 3888 (pp.256–7), JM to WS, n.d. He sold 8,500 on the first day: *QR* Letter 183.

34. *Courier* and *M.Ch.*, 19 November 1817, repeated 21, 22, 25, 28, and 29 November 1817, 'on 1st day of December'. *Courier*, 29 November, 'this day', repeated on 1 December 1817. It appears that the 29 November 1817 *Courier* notice was premature. JM printed 12,000: JM MS, WG to Robert W. Hay, 1 December 1817; Barrow, *An Auto-Biographical Memoir*, p.506.

35. *Courier* and *M.Ch.*, 19 February 1818, 'on or before 21st instant'; 20 February 1818, 'to-morrow'; 21 February 1818, 'this morning'. Anne Cleaver, '1818'. Wrapper, 'February 1818'. JM sold 10,038 on the first day: Leeds WYL250 8 66a, WG to George Canning 21 February 1818. Same letter: JM increased the remuneration from 10 to 20 guineas per sheet for articles of merit. JM MS, accounts book: 12,000 were printed.

36. *M.Ch.*, 5 June 1818, 'on Tuesday, the 9th of June'. *Courier*, 8 June, 'to-morrow'; 9 June 1818, 'this day'. Anne Cleaver, 'Rec'd June 10. 1818'. Date on wrapper, 'June 1818'. JM will print 14,000: Leeds WYL250 8 66a, WG to George Canning, 28 February 1818. Note, however, JM MS, accounts book: states that 13,000 were printed. Barrow, *An Auto-Biographical Memoir*, p. 506, states that JM sold 13,000. The *Edinburgh Review* reached this level of sales in 1811: BL Add. MS 34583 (f. 325), Peter Elmsley to Samuel Butler, 3 February 1811.

37. *M.Ch.*, 25 September 1818, 'to-morrow'; and *Courier*, 26 September 1818, 'this day'. JM printed 13,000: BL Add. MS 34612 (ff. 227–8), John Barrow to Macvey Napier, 17 October 1818; JM MS, accounts book.

38. *M.Ch.*, 28 January 1819, 'Saturday next'; 29 January 1819, 'The Publication is unavoidably postponed until Tuesday next'; and *Courier*, 2 February 1819, 'this day'. The delay was occasioned by want of the last pages of a single article. JM MS, WG to J. T. Coleridge, 7 January 1819. JM printed 13,000. By 27 February all copies were sold and JM printed a 'second edition'. *QR* Letters 207, 208.

39. *Courier*, 10 June 1820. *Courier*, 10 March 1820, announcing *QR* Number 44: 'At the same time is published No. XXXIX. being Part I (to be completed in Two Parts) of a GENERAL INDEX to the first Nineteen Volumes of the Quarterly Review – which the Subscribers are requested to order from their respective booksellers'. *Courier*, 10 June 1820, announcing *QR* Number 45: 'No XL, containing the Second and concluding Part of the Index, is also published. And complete Sets may be had of the first XX Volumes of the Quarterly Review'. The publisher's decision to date the General Index 1820 contributes to the confusion over the *QR*'s real publication dates and the dates that appear on the journal's title pages. The first part of the General Index was published in March 1820 and the second part in June of that year. As the year on the title page for Volume 19 is 1818 and that for Volume 21 is 1819, the sequence of the *QR*'s title page dates was thereby confused. Anne Cleaver, an original subscriber, recorded in her copy of the first part of the General Index that she received it on 20 March. She did not indicate when she received the second part.

40. *Courier*, 28 May 1819, 'on June 1st'; 4 June 'this day'. *M.Ch.*, no book notices on 1 June 1819; book notices on 2 June 1819 but no *QR* notice; no book notices 3–8 June; 'this

day' notice on 9 June 1819 can be safely ignored. Wrapper, 'May 1819'. JM printed 13,000: JM MS, accounts book.

41. *M.Ch.*, 6 September 1819, 'on Friday'; and *Courier*, 10 September 1819, 'this day'. Wrapper, 'September 1819'.

42. *M.Ch.*, 10 December 1819, 'to-morrow'; and *Courier*, 11 December 1819, 'this day'. Anne Cleaver, 'December 11', which is unusual as she generally received her copy one day after JM's London sale. Wrapper, 'November 1819'. JM's book list inside the front wrapper is dated 'December 1819'. Title page gives the date as 'November'. JM sold 12,071: JM MS, WG to R. W. Hay, 18 March 1820.

43. *M.Ch.*, 4 March 1820, 'nearly ready'; repeated 9 March 1820. *Courier*, 16 March 1820, 'to-morrow'. *Courier* and *M.Ch.*, 17 March 1820, 'this day'. Anne Cleaver, '20 March 1820'. Wrapper, 'March 1820'. Title page for Vol. 22, 'March'.

44. *M.Ch.*, Fri., 19 May 1820, 'Saturday next'; no book notices appear on 20 May; 23 May 1820, 'Saturday next', Friday, 26 May 1820, 'this day', but as no book notices appear in the *M.Ch.* on Sat., evidently the editor inserted JM's notice a day early. *Courier*, 24 May 1820, 'Saturday next'; 27 May 1820, 'this day'. JM printed 13,000: JM MS, accounts book.

45. JM MS, JM to John Wilson Croker, 1 September 1820, 'Now we shall publish this Number of the Review in about a fortnight'. *M.Ch.*, 4 October 1820, 'to-morrow'; and *Courier*, 5 October 1820, 'this day'. W. L. Bowles, *A Reply to the Charges Brought by the Reviewer of Spence's Anecdotes in the Quarterly Review from October 1820 against the Last Editor of Pope's Works* (London: *Pamphleteer*, 1820). JM printed 13,000: JM MS, accounts book.

46. *Courier* and *M.Ch.*, 19 December 1820, 'this day'. *London Magazine* (January 1821), p. 71, 'published about the middle of December'. JM printed 13,000: JM MS, accounts book.

47. On 12 or 19 April or perhaps as early as 3 April; the evidence is unclear. *Courier*, 18 March 1821 states that No. 48 will be published on Thurs., 5 April 1821. No book notices appear on that day. *Courier*, 6 April 1821 gives Contents of No. 48 as published. *M.Ch.*, book notices appear on 5, 6, 9, 11, and 12 April 1821, but not for *QR*; 19 April 1821, 'this day'. JM MS, Mitchell to JM, 13 April 1821, Mitchell received his copy on the 12th. JM MS, James Glassford to JM, 19 April 1821, states that he does not see his article in this Number. JM MS, accounts book, states '3 April 1821'. JM printed 12,500: JM MS, accounts book.

48. *M.Ch.*, 25 June 1821, 'on Thursday.' *Courier*, 28 June 1821, 'this day'. Anne Cleaver, 'June 29 – 1821'. JM MS, accounts book, '28 June 1821'. JM printed 12,500: JM MS, accounts book.

49. *Courier* and *M.Ch.*, 16 October 1821, 'to-morrow'; 17 October, 'this day'. JM MS, accounts book, '18 October 1821'. JM printed 12,500: JM MS, accounts book.

50. *Courier* and *M. Ch.*, 21 December 1821, 'to-morrow'; 22 December 1821, 'this day'. JM MS, accounts book, '22 December 1821'. JM printed 12,000: Croker to JM, 22 December 1821, quoted in Smiles, *Memoir*, vol. 2, p. 54.

51. *Courier*, Mon., 25 March 1822, repeated 27 and 28 March 1822, 'Saturday next'. *Courier* and *M. Ch.*, 30 March 1822, 'will be published to-day'. JM MS, Bills: 28 March 1822. Wrapper, 'Published in March, 1822'. JM MS, accounts book, 12,500 copies printed 'March 1822'; cheques cut on '1 April 1822'.

52. Wrapper for No. 52, 'No. LIII Will be Published in May'. *Courier*, 3 July 1822, 'to-morrow'; 4 July 1822, 'this day'. JM MS, Bills: 4 July 1822. Anne Cleaver, 'July 5 1822'. JM

MS, accounts book, cheques cut on '26 June 1822'. JM printed 12,500: JM MS, accounts book.

53. *Courier*, 22 October 1822, 'to-morrow'; no book notices on 23 October 1822. *M.Ch.*, no book notices on or about 23 October 1822. Anne Cleaver, 'Recd October 24 1822', as usual, one day following publication. JM MS, accounts book, 1821–4, p.186: 'Quarterly Review No 54 12,000. / 25 October 1822'.

54. *Courier*, 14 January 1823, 'The Quarterly Review, which the ill health of the editor has delayed, is nearly ready for publication'; repeated frequently throughout January; 11 February 1823, 'Saturday next', repeated each day that week; 14 February 1823, 'to-mor-row'; 15 February 1823, 'this day'. NLS MS, 3896 (f.44), WG to Scott, 13 February 1823, the *QR* will be published the next day. PRO J 76 / 7 / 1 (f. 28), Notes of Gideon Gorrequer, 'On Saturday 15th Feby the Quarterly Review was published'. JM MS, Bills: 15 February 1823. Anne Cleaver, '15 February 1823'. Bodleian Lib MS Eng. Lett. c.1 (f. 114), Southey to J. T. Coleridge, 17 February 1823, the *QR* came today.

55. *Courier* 4 July 1823, 'Tuesday next'. *M.Ch.*, 9 July 1823, 'was published yesterday'. JM MS, bills, 9 July 1823. Wrapper, 'July 1823'. JM MS, accounts book, cheques cut on 8 July 1823. JM printed 12,500: JM MS, accounts book.

56. *Courier*, 16 September 1823, 'in the course of the present month'; 23 September 1823, 'Saturday next'; 26 September 1823, 'to-morrow'. *M.Ch.*, 27 September 1823, 'this day'. JM MS, Ledger B, p.34, 27 September 1823. Anne Cleaver, 'Sept 28th 1823'. JM MS, bills: 29 September 1823. Wrapper, 'September, 1823'. JM MS, accounts book, cheques cut on 29 September 1823. JM printed 12,000: JM MS, accounts book.

57. Wrapper for No. 57, 'No. LVIII. / Will be Published in / December'. WG to George Canning, 13 December 1823, quoted in Smiles, *Memoir*, vol. 2, p. 157, '... the 58th is now nearly finished'. *M.Ch.*, 25 December 1823, 'Tuesday next'; 29 December, 'to-mor-row'; and *Courier*, 30 December 1823, 'this day'. Anne Cleaver 'December 30 1823'. Wrapper, 'December 1823'. JM MS, accounts book, cheques cut on 31 December 1823. JM printed 12,500: JM MS, accounts book.

58. *Courier* and *M.Ch.*, 12 April 1824, 'Saturday next'; 17 April 1824, 'this day'. JM MS, Bills: 19 April 1824. Anne Cleaver, 'April 19. 1824'. Wrapper, 'April 1824'. JM MS, accounts book, cheques cut on 19 April 1824. JM printed 12,250: JM MS, accounts book.

59. *M.Ch.*, 25 August 1824, 'Saturday next'; 27 August, 'to-morrow'; and *Courier*, 28 August 1824, 'this day'. Anne Cleaver, 'August 30. 1824'. JM MS, accounts book, cheques cut on 1 September 1824. JM printed 12,250: JM MS, accounts book.

60. *M.Ch.*, 29 December 1824, 'to-morrow'; no book notices on 30 December; 31 Decem-ber 1824, 'this day', the first opportunity the paper had to insert JM's notice intended for 30 December. *Courier*, 30 December 1824, 'this day'. Vol. 31 title page, 'Published in December, 1824'. Anne Cleaver, 'Jan 1st 1825'. JM MS, accounts book, cheques cut on 30 December 1825.

61. *M.Ch.*, 10 March 1825, 'to-morrow'; and *Courier*, 11 March 1825, 'this day'. *Courier*, 12 March 1825, 'yesterday'. JM MS, J. T. Coleridge to JM, 13 March 1825, the *QR* is out. Vol. 31 title page, 'Published in ... March, 1825'.

62. JM MS, J. T. Coleridge to JM, 21 May 1825, *QR* will be ready the middle of the follow-ing week. *Courier*, Sat., 4 June 1825, 'Saturday next'; Tue., 14 June 1825, 'was published on Saturday'.

63. *Courier*, 19 October 1825, 'on Tuesday next, the 25th instant', repeated 21 October 1825; Mon., 24 October 1825, 'to-morrow'; 25 October 1825, 'to-day'; and *M.Ch.*, 26 October 1825, 'yesterday'.

64. *Courier*, 23 December 1825, 'on the 29th instant', repeated, 26 December 1825; 28
     December 1825, 'to-morrow'; 29 December 1825, 'this day'. *M.Ch.*, 30 December 1825,
     'yesterday'. *Courier*, 31 December 1825 and *M.Ch.*, 3 January 1826, 'was published on
     Thursday'.

Appendix B: Publication Statistics

1. On 29 March he told Constable that because he was so poor he could take on no more
    projects. JM MS, March 1803 to September 1823 letterbook, p. 317. 'Meanwhile Mr.
    Murray was becoming hard pressed for money'. Smiles, *Memoir*, vol. 1, p. 185.
2. Smiles, *Memoir*, vol. 1, p. 179.
3. JM MS, undated copy of a note in the third person in John Murray II's hand, at one time
    appended to a copy of an October 1811 letter to Robert Southey; cf. *QR* Letters 61, 108.
    Smiles, *Memoir*, vol. 1, p. 188.
4. *QR* Letter 47. JM MS, 8 July 1809.
5. Based on 51,000 copies and assuming an average cost of £200 per thousand.
6. These 'editions' were for the most part reprintings, though Gifford did permit his con-
    tributors to make a few substantive changes.
7. In April 1811, buyers could purchase new editions of each number of the *Quarterly*, price
    6 shillings, or four volumes in boards at £2.10. In October 1811, five-volume sets were
    available at £3.2.6. According to the accounts books, by then most of the original print-
    ings had sold out; Murray's warehouse was filled with 9,780 copies of second and third
    editions. In addition to this expensive inventory, 720 copies were still unsold in Edin-
    burgh and Dublin. Murray's speculation was risky and expensive. On 21 March 1811,
    he printed 1,000 copies of No, 4 at a cost of £130. By November 1811 he had sold 200
    copies. On 21 June 1811, he printed 1,250 copies of No. 3; cost, £158; sales by Novem-
    ber, fifty copies. On 6 May 1811, he printed 1,000 copies of a third edition of No. 1; cost,
    £126; sales by November, 200 copies.
8. JM MS, March 1803 to September 1823 letterbook, p. 319, Murray to Ballantyne, 29
    March 1811.
9. Smiles, *Memoir*, vol. 1, pp. 185–7.
10. His recorded expense for 'extras' in Nos. 1–8 and No. 11 is £175. I have estimated extra
    costs for Nos. 9 and 10 at £15 each.
11. A ream consisted of 20 quires, 24 sheets a quire, 480 sheets. As the *Quarterly* was printed
    in octavo, one sheet yielded eight leaves or sixteen pages. Each ream could therefore
    make about 3,800 leaves. Murray purchased paper from Christopher Magnay and Sons,
    College Hill, Upper Thames Street, stationers and rag merchants. *Gentleman's Magazine*,
    new ser., 2 (1829), p. 186. *British Book Trade Index* <bbti.bham.ac.uk>.
12. *QR* Letter 23.
13. JM MS, Coleridge to Murray, 11 October 1825.
14. A version of Table B.4 in Appendix B and of this introductory note was first published
    in the *Quarterly Review Archive* <rc.umd.edu>. The evidence for each publication date in
    Appendix A is given in the notes. In determining publication dates, I traced announce-
    ments in the *Courier*, the *Morning Chronicle* and the *Monthly Literary Advertiser*,
    references in unpublished manuscripts, and notations in Anne Cleaver's copies. The wife
    of the Bishop of St Asaph, Cleaver was a friend of the poet Felicia Hemans and Hemans's
    brother, Sir Thomas Henry Browne, to whom in her old age she presented her copies of
    the journal. Through newspaper advertisements, Murray gave booksellers notice of when

they could expect the journal to go on sale. The publisher became so frustrated at his inability to motivate his editor that he appears to have resorted to using these advertisements as a way of putting pressure on him. Consequently, many of the advertisements are misleading. Ellis asked plaintively, 'Why say that No 8 will be published in November when we know that this cannot be? Why not say fairly that No 8 will appear early in Decr. and that future Numbers will appear regularly every quarter?'

15. The *Quarterly's* irregular publication is a frequent subject in the correspondence. *QR* Letters 41, 43, 47, 57, 60, 61, 64, 65, 66, 69, 73, 75, 76, 77, 94, 96, 106, 109, 118, 119, 124, 127, 134, 141, 152, 161, 166, 171, 180, 181, 182, 225, 237, and 251.

16. See Appendix B.

Appendix C: John Murray's 1808 Lists of Prospective Contributors

1. Bedford forwarded Southey a 'hypothetical list' of potential contributors. He understood it had been drawn up by Scott, Murray, and Gifford. Bodl. Lib. MS Eng. Lett. d.51 (ff. 15–16), 21 November 1808.

2. For the principals' awareness of political and ideological nuance, see for example *QR* Letters 3, 32, 70, 121, 126, 127, 140 and 168.

WORKS CITED

Manuscript Sources

Beinecke Library, Osborne Collection, Yale University, New Haven, CT

George Canning

Bodleian Library, Oxford University

Thomas Arnold, Grosvenor Bedford, James Bland-Burges, John Taylor Coleridge, Edward Copleston, John Davison, Francis Douce, Robert Grant, George Grey, Robert Hay, Reginald Heber, Richard Heber, Robert Southey, Henry Taylor, John William Ward, William Wilberforce

British Library, London

John Barrow, Philip Bliss, Charles James Blomfield, Henry Boase, Henry Brougham, Samuel Butler, Lord Byron, Thomas Cadell, George Canning, Stratford Canning, John Clare, Edward Daniel Clarke, John Taylor Coleridge, Samuel Taylor Coleridge, John Wilson Croker, John Davison, George Ellis, Peter Elmsley, Thomas Falconer, John Hookham Frere, William Gifford, Octavius Gilchrist, Lord Grenville, William Hazlitt, William Huskisson, John Herman Merivale, James Mill, Thomas Moore, John Murray, Macvey Napier, Arthur Paget, Samuel Parr, Henry Phillpotts, John Rickman, William Roscoe, William Stewart Rose, Walter Scott, John Scott-Waring, Percy Bysshe Shelley, William Sotheby, Robert Southey, George Staunton, Sharon Turner, Nicholas Vansittart, Richard Whately, Christopher Wordsworth, William Wordsworth

Christopher Edwards, Bookseller, New York

William Gifford

Clements Library, University of Michigan, Ann Arbor, MI

George Canning, John Wilson Croker, John Gibson Lockhart, John Murray

Derbyshire Record Office, Matlock

Robert Wilmot-Horton collection

Devon Public Record Office, Exeter

William Gifford

Dudley Archives and Local History Service, Coseley

Edward Copleston, John William Ward

Duke University, Durham, NC, Perkins Library, Rare Book, Manuscript, and Special Collections Library

William Gifford

Houghton Library, Harvard University, Cambridge, MA

Walter Scott

India Office Library, London

Robert Grant

John Murray Archive, London (now at the National Library of Scotland, Edinburgh)

James Ballantyne, Eaton Stannard Barrett, John Barrow, Edward Berens, William Blackwood, James Bland, Charles James Blomfield, John James Blunt, Thomas Bowdler, Thomas Browne, Thomas Cadell, Thomas Campbell, Stratford Canning, Richard Chenevix, Francis Cohen, John Taylor Coleridge, Samuel Taylor Coleridge, John Josias Conybeare, Robert Cooke, Edward Copleston, John Wilson Croker, John Davison, Isaac D'Israeli, Donald Douglas, George D'Oyly, Nathan Drake, Joseph Duncan, Richard Duppa, George Ellis, Peter Elmsley, William Erskine, Thomas Falconer, James Forbes, Ugo Foscolo, John Hookham Frere, William Gifford, Octavius Gilchrist, George Gleig, Richard Gooch, George Gray, Olinthus Gregory, Henry Hallam, Alexander Hamilton, William Hamilton, George Hammond, Robert Hay, William Haygarth, Reginald Heber, Richard Heber, John Hoppner, William Huskisson, John Ireland, William Jerdan, John Kidd, Charles Lamb, John Gibson Lockhart, Edmund Lodge, William Rowe Lyall, Thomas Robert Malthus, Herbert Marsh, William Matthews, Charles Robert Maturin, John Herman Merivale, William Van Mildert, William Miller, Henry Milman, Thomas Mitchell, John Mitford, James Henry Monk, John Murray II, John Murray III, Macvey Napier, Joseph Parker, John Penrose, Henry Phillpotts, James Pillans, Joseph Planta, George Procter, David Ricardo, John Richardson, John Rickman, Barré Charles Roberts, Henry Salt, Walter Scott, Nassau William Senior, Robert Southey, George Staunton, James Stephen, John Stoddart, John Bird Sumner, John Symmons, Thomas Thomson, Henry Thornton, Sharon Turner, Edward Upham, David Uwins, John Valpy, Robert Walpole, Richard Wellesley, Richard Whately, Thomas Dunham Whitaker, Henry Downing Whittington, Robert Wilmot-Horton, Thomas Young

Also, bills payable ledger, cash day books, letterbooks, book loans register, warehouse inventory, unlabelled accounts books, John Murray II's 1808 planning notes, article proofs, John Murray II's *QR* office copy, *QR* subscription list, John Murray III's notes on author identifications

John Rylands Library, University of Manchester

Reginald Heber

Keble College, Oxford University

John Taylor Coleridge, John Davison, John Keble

Lambeth Palace Library, London

Edward Copleston, James Henry Monk

Linnean Society, London

James Edward Smith

National Archives, Public Record Office, Kew

Foreign Office papers; Wills

National Library of Scotland, Edinburgh

James Ballantyne, John Ballantyne, George Canning, John Wilson Croker, George Ellis, William Erskine, William Gifford, Octavius Gilchrist, James Glassford, Robert Hay, Reginald Heber, Richard Heber, Lord Liverpool, John Gibson Lockhart, William Rowe Lyall, Zachary Macaulay, John Miller, John Bacon Sawrey Morritt, John Murray, William Stewart Rose, Walter Scott, Robert Southey, James Stephen, John William Ward

National Library of Wales, Llyfrgell Genedlaethol Cymru, Aberystwyth

Edward Copleston, William Gifford, Robert Grant, Reginald Heber,

National Maritime Museum, Greenwich

John Barrow letter books

Northumberland Record Office, Society of Antiquaries of Newcastle upon Tyne deposit

William Gifford

Oriel College, Oxford University

Edward Copleston

Pierpont Morgan Library, New York

William Gifford, John Murray, Walter Scott

Southampton University Library, Southampton

Duke of Wellington

Trinity College, Cambridge University, Monk-Sanford Papers

James Henry Monk

University of Florida Libraries, Howe Society, Gainesville, FL

John Wilson Croker

University of Iowa Libraries, Iowa City, Iowa, Special Collections

John Wilson Croker, John Murray

Wellcome Library for the Understanding of Medicine, London, Autograph Letters, Archives and Manuscripts

William Gifford

West Yorkshire Archives, Leeds, Canning Papers, Earl and Countess of Harewood and Trustees of the Harewood House Trust

George Canning, George Ellis, William Gifford, Richard Heber, Lord Liverpool, Zachary Macaulay, John Miller, Walter Scott, Robert Southey, James Stephen

Westminster School Library, Westminster School, London

Peter Elmsley

Newspapers and Periodicals

Annual Register

Anti-Jacobin; or, Weekly Examiner

Antijacobin Review

Blackwood's Edinburgh Magazine

British Critic

British Review

Citizen: A Monthly Journal of Politics, Literature, and Art

Courier

Edinburgh Evening Courant

Edinburgh Review

Examiner

Gentleman's Magazine

John Bull

London Magazine

London Review

Monthly Literary Advertiser

Morning Chronicle

New Monthly Magazine

North American Review

Panoplist, and Missionary Magazine, for the Year 1816

Port Folio

Quarterly Review

Satirist

The Times

Westminster Review

Primary Sources

[Anon.], *Sketches of Eminent Medical Men* (London: Religious Tract Society, n.d.).

—, 'Proceedings in the Present Session of Parliament, *Gentleman's Magazine,* 69:2 (1819), p. 552.

—, 'The Quarterly Review', *London Magazine,* 3 (1821), p. 72.

—, 'Rhapsodies in a Punch Bowel, No. 1', *Blackwood's Edinburgh Magazine,* 11 (1822), pp. 344–8.

—, 'Note on the Quarterly Reviewers', *Blackwood's Edinburgh Magazine*, 15 (January 1824), p. 84.

—, 'Our Relations with Great Britain', *North American Review*, 27 (1828), pp. 481ff.

—, 'Edinburgh Critics and Quarterly Reviewers', *Athenaeum*, 2473 (20 March 1875), pp. 393–5.

Bagot, J. (ed.), *Canning and His Friends*, 2 vols (London: John Murray, 1909).

Barrow, J., *An Auto-Biographical Memoir of Sir John Barrow* (London: John Murray, 1847).

Blomfield, A. (ed.), *A Memoir of Charles James Blomfield, with Selections from His Correspondence*, 2 vols (London: John Murray, 1863).

Boswell, J., *The Life of Samuel Johnson, LL. D.: Including a Journal of a Tour to the Hebrides*, ed. J. W. Croker, 2 vols (New York: George Dearborn, 1833–4).

Bowles, W. L., *A Reply to the Charges Brought by the Reviewer of Spence's Anecdotes in the Quarterly Review from October 1820 against the Last Editor of Pope's Works* (London: Pamphleteer, 1820).

Bramston, Clarissa Sandford Trant, *The Journal of Clarissa Trant, 1800–1832*, ed. C. G. Luard (London: J. Lane, Bodley Head, [1925]).

[Byron, Lord], *English Bards and Scotch Reviewers. A Satire* (London: Cawthorne, 1809).

—, *Byron's Letters and Journals*, ed. L. A. Marchand, 12 vols (London: John Murray 1973–82).

Carmichael, A., *A Memoir of the Life and Philosophy of Spurzheim* (Boston, MA: Marsh, Capen, and Lyon, 1833).

Conder, J., *Reviewers Reviewed* (Oxford: J. Bartlett, 1811).

Constable, T., *Archibald Constable and His Literary Correspondents* (Edinburgh: Edmonston and Douglas, 1873).

Copleston, W. J., *Memoir of Edward Copleston, Bishop of Llandaff, with Selections from His Diary and Correspondence* (London: Parker, 1851).

Croker, J. W., *The Correspondence and Diaries of the Right Honourable John Wilson Croker, LL.D., F.R.S., Secretary to the Admiralty from 1809 to 1830*, ed. L. J. Jennings, 3 vols (London: John Murray, 1884).

Davison, J., *Remains and Occasional Publications* (Oxford: J. H. Parker; London: J. G. F. & J. Rivington, 1841).

DeQuincey, T., *The English Mail Coach* (Boston, MA: Ticknor, et al., 1851).

Douglas, S. *The Diaries of Sylvester Douglas*, ed. F. Bickley (London: Constable, 1928).

D'Oyly, G., *Sermons, With a Memoir by His Son* (London: Rivington, 1847).

Dudley, John William Ward, Earl of, *Letters of the Earl of Dudley to the Bishop of Llandaff*, ed. E. Copleston (London: John Murray, 1840).

—, *Letters to 'Ivy' from the First Earl of Dudley*, ed. S. Romilly (London: Longmans, Green, 1905).

Duncan, G., *Memoir of the Rev. Henry Duncan* (Edinburgh: Oliphant, 1848).

Farington, J., *The Diary of Joseph Farington*, ed. K. Garlick and A. Macintyre, 17 vols (New Haven, CT: Yale University Press, 1978–98).

Foster, J., *Life and Correspondence of John Foster*, ed. J. E. Ryland, 2 vols (New York: Wiley and Putnam, 1848).

Gamer, M., *Romanticism and the Gothic: Genre, Reception, and Canon Formation* (Cambridge: Cambridge University Press, 2000).

Gregory, O., et al (eds), *Pantologia. A New Cabinet Cyclopædia*, 12 vols (London: G. Kearsley, et al., 1808–13).

[Gurney, H.], *Memoir of the Life of Thomas Young* (London: John & Arthur Arch, 1831).

Hall, J. (ed.), *Trial of Abraham Thornton* (Edinburgh; London: W. Hodge, 1926).

Hazlitt, W., *A Letter to William Gifford, Esq*, *The Collected Works*, ed. A. R. Waller and A. Glover, 12 vols (London: J. M. Dent, 1902–6), vol. 1.

[Heber, A. S.], *The Life of Reginald Heber, D. D., Lord Bishop of Calcutta*, 2 vols (London: John Murray, 1830).

Heber, R., *The Heber Letters, 1783–1832*, ed. R. H. Cholmondley (London: Batchworth Press, 1950).

Hobhouse, J. C., *Recollections of a Long Life*, 6 vols (London: John Murray, 1909).

Horner, F., *Memoirs and Correspondence of Francis Horner*, ed. L. Horner, 2 vols (London: John Murray, 1843).

Jerdan, W., *The Autobiography of William Jerdan*, 3 vols (London: Hall, Virtue, 1852–3).

Keble, J., *Occasional Papers and Reviews* (Oxford: J. Parker, 1887).

Keightley, T.. *The Fairy Mythology* (London: n.p., 1850).

Knight, C., *Passages of a Working Life during Half a Century*, 3 vols (London: Bradbury and Evans, 1864).

Lamb, C., and M. A. Lamb, *Letters of Charles and Mary Anne Lamb*, ed. E. W. Marrs, 3 vols (Ithaca, NY: Cornell University Press, 1976–9).

Lane-Poole, S., *The Life of the Right Honourable Stratford Canning*, 2 vols (London: Longmans, Green, 1888).

Lockhart, J. G., *Memoirs of the Life of Sir Walter Scott, Bart*, 7 vols (Edinburgh: Constable, 1837–8).

Malthus, T. R., *Five Papers on Political Economy*, ed. C. Renwick (Sydney: University of Sydney, Reprints of Economics and Economic History, No. 3, 1953).

Merivale, A. W., *Family Memorials* (Exeter: For private circulation, 1884).

Mill, James, 'Periodical Literature: The Edinburgh Review, Vol. 1, 2, &c', *Westminster Review*, 1 (January 1824), pp. 206–49.

—, 'Periodical Literature: The Quarterly Review', *Westminster Review*, 2 (October 1824), pp. 463–503

Morgan, S., *Lady Morgan's Memoirs: Autobiography, Diaries and Correspondence*, 2 vols (London: William H. Allen, 1868).

Murray, J., *The Letters of John Murray to Lord Byron*, ed. A. Nicholson (Liverpool: Liverpool University Press, 2007).

Napier, M., *Selections from the Correspondence of Macvey Napier*, ed. M. Napier (London: Macmillan, 1879).

Nichols, J. G., 'Biographical Memoirs of Thomas Dunham Whitaker' in *An History of the Original Parish of Whalley and Honor of Clitheroe*, 2 vols, 4th edn (London: n.p., 1876).

Paulding, J. K., *A Sketch of Old England*, 2 vols (New York: Wiley, 1822).

Pettigrew, T. J., *Biographical Memoirs of the Most Celebrated Physicians, Surgeons, etc., etc.* (London: Fisher, Son and Co., 1840).

[Potter, J. P.], *Essays on the Lives of Newton, Cowper, and Heber* (London: B. Fellowes, 1830).

Redding, C., *Personal Reminiscences of Eminent Men*, 3 vols (London: n.p., 1867).

Ricardo, D., *The Works and Correspondence of David Ricardo*, ed. P. Sraffa, 10 vols (Cambridge: Cambridge University Press for the Royal Economic Society, 1951–5).

Robinson, H. C., *Henry Crabb Robinson on Books and Their Writers*, ed. E. J. Morley (London: J. M. Dent, 1938).

Romilly, S., *Memoirs of the Life of Samuel Romilly*, 2 vols (London: John Murray, 1841).

Ross, J., *Voyage of Discovery made under the Orders of the Admiralty* (London: John Murray, 1819).

Salt, H., *The Life and Correspondence of Henry Salt*, 2 vols (London: H. Bentley, 1834).

Savage, James, Librarian, Being an Account of Scarce, Valuable, and Useful English Books, Manuscript Libraries (London: William Savage, 1809).

Scott, W., *The Journal of Sir Walter Scott: from the Original Manuscript at Abbotsford* (Edinburgh: D. Douglas, 1891).

—, *Familiar Letters of Sir Walter Scott*, ed. D. Douglas, 2 vols (Edinburgh: Douglas, 1894).

—, *Some Unpublished Letters of Sir Walter Scott from the Collection in the Brotherton Library*, ed. J. A. Symington (Oxford: n.p., 1932).

—, *The Letters of Sir Walter Scott*, ed. H. Grierson (ed.), 12 vols (London: Constable, 1932–7).

Senior, N. W., *Biographical Sketches* (London: Longman, Green, Longman, Roberts & Green, 1863).

—, *Essays on Fiction* (London: Longman, Green, Longman, Roberts & Green, 1864).

Shelley, P. B., *The Letters of Percy Bysshe Shelley*, ed. F. L. Jones, 2 vols (Oxford: Clarendon Press, 1964).

Simond, Louis, *Journal of a Tour and Residence in Great Britain* (Edinburgh: Constable, 1817).

Smiles, S., *A Publisher and His Friends: Memoir and Correspondence of the Late John Murray*, 2nd edn, 2 vols (London: John Murray, 1891).

Smith, G., *Bishop Heber: Poet and Chief Missionary to the East, Second Lord Bishop of Calcutta, 1783–1826* (London: John Murray, 1895).

Smith, S., *Selected Letters of Sydney Smith* (Oxford: Oxford University Press, 1981).

Southey, R., *Life and Correspondence of Robert Southey*, ed. C. C. Southey, 6 vols (London: Longman, et al., 1849–50).

—, *Selections from the Letters of Robert Southey*, ed. J. W. Warter, 4 vols (London: Longman, et al., 1856).

—, *The Doctor*, 7 vols (London: Longman et al., 1847).

—, *The Correspondence of Robert Southey with Caroline Bowles*, ed. E. Dowden (Dublin: Hodges, Figgis, & Co., 1881).

—, Some Unpublished Letters of Robert Southey', *Blackwood's Edinburgh Magazine*, 164 (August 1898), pp. 167–85

—, *New Letters of Robert Southey*, ed. K. Curry, 2 vols (New York: Columbia University Press, 1965).

—, *The Letters of Robert Southey to John May 1797 to 1838*, ed. C. Ramos (Austin, TX: Jenkins, 1976).

Stanley, A. P., *The Life and Correspondence of Thomas Arnold, D.D.* , 2 vols. (New York: D. Appleton & Co., 1846).

Stapylton, H. E. C., *Two Under-Secretaries* (London: William Clowes and Sons, *c.* 1891).

Sumner, J. B., *A Treatise on the Records of the Creation, and on the Moral Attributes of the Creator*, 2 vols (London: J. Hatchard, 1816).

Sutherland, J., *The Life of Walter Scott* (London: Blackwell, 1995).

Symington, J. A. (ed.), *Some Unpublished Letters of Sir Walter Scott* (Oxford: Basil Blackwell, 1932).

Taylor, G., *Memoir of Robert Surtees* (Durham: Surtees Society [1852]).

Taylor, H., *Autobiography, 1800–1875*, 2 vols (London: John Murray, 1885).

Walker, W. S., *The Poetical Remains of W.S.W., Edited, with a Memoir by J. Moultrie* (London: n.p., 1852).

Whately, R., *Miscellaneous Lectures and Reviews* (London: Parker, Son and Bourn, 1861).

Secondary Sources

Ades, J. I., 'Lamb on Wordsworth's Excursion', *Review of Arts and Letters*, 3 (1969), pp. 1–9.

Altick, R. D., *The English Common Reader: A Social History of the Mass Reading Public 1800–1900* (Chicago, IL: University of Chicago Press, 1957).

Ben-Israel, H., *English Historians on the French Revolution* (Cambridge: Cambridge University Press, 2002).

Brakeman, W., 'Letters by Robert Southey to Sir John Taylor Coleridge', *Studia Germanica Gandensia*, 6 (1964), pp. 103–230.

Brightfield, M. F., *John Wilson Croker* (Berkeley: University of California Press, 1940).

Cameron, J. M. R., 'John Barrow, the *Quarterly*'s Imperial Reviewer', in J. Cutmore (ed.), *Conservatism and the Quarterly Review: A Critical Analysis* (London: Pickering and Chatto, 2007), pp. 133–50.

Carnall, G., *Robert Southey and His Age: The Development of a Conservative Mind* (Oxford: Oxford University Press, 1960).

Chandler, J., *England in 1819: The Politics of Literary Culture and the Case of Romantic Historicism* (Chicago, IL: University of Chicago Press, 1998).

Clark, R. B., *William Gifford: Tory Satirist* (New York: Columbia University Press, 1930).

Clive, J., *Scotch Reviewers: The Edinburgh Review, 1802–1815* (London: Faber and Faber, 1957).

Colley, L., *Britons: Forging the Nation 1707–1837* (New Haven, CT: Yale University Press, 1992).

Corson, J. C., *Notes and Index to Sir Herbert Grierson's Edition of the Letters of Sir Walter Scott* (Oxford: Clarendon Press, 1979).

Curry, K., *Sir Walter Scott's Edinburgh Annual Register* (Knoxville: University of Tennessee Press, 1977).

Curry, K., and R. Dedmon, 'Southey's Contributions to the *Quarterly Review*', *Wordsworth Circle*, 6 (1974), pp. 261–72

Cutmore, J., 'The *Quarterly Review* under Gifford: Some New Attributions,' *Victorian Periodicals Review*, 24:3 (1991), pp. 137–42.

—, 'The Early *Quarterly Review* 1809–24: New Attributions and Sources,' *Victorian Periodicals Review*, 27:4 (1994), pp. 308–18.

—, 'The Early *Quarterly Review*: New Attributions of Authorship,' *Victorian Periodicals Review*, 28:4 (1995), pp. 305–25.

—, 'A Plurality of Voices in the *Quarterly Review*', in J. Cutmore (ed.), *Conservatism and the Quarterly Review: A Critical Analysis* (London: Pickering and Chatto, 2007), pp. 61–85.

— (ed.), *Conservatism and the Quarterly Review: A Critical Analysis* (London: Pickering and Chatto, 2007).

De Paolo, C., *Coleridge's Philosophy of Social Reform* (New York: Peter Lang, 1987).

Dewey, C., *The Passing of Barchester* (London: Hambledon Press, 1991).

Dibdin, T. F., *The Library Companion; or, The Young Man's Guide, and the Old Man's Comfort, in the Choice of a Library*, 2 vols (London: Harding, et al., 1824).

Dire, G., *British Satire and the Politics of Style, 1789–1832* (Cambridge: Cambridge University Press, 1997).

Eastwood, D., 'Patriotism Personified: Robert Southey's *Life of Nelson* Reconsidered', *Mariner's Mirror*, 77.2 (May 1991), pp. 143–9.

Flynn, P., *Francis Jeffrey* (Newark: University of Delaware Press, 1978).

Furbank, P. N., and W. R. Owens, *Defoe De-Attributions: A Critique of J. R. Moore's Checklist* (London: Hambledon Continuum, 2003).

Gilmartin, K., *Writing Against Revolution: Literary Conservatism in Britain, 1790–1832* (Cambridge: Cambridge University Press, 2007).

Graham, W., *Tory Criticism in the* Quarterly Review, *1809–1853* (New York: Colombia University Press, 1921).

Griffin, J. R., 'John Keble and the *Quarterly Review*', *Review of English Studies*, 29 (November 1978), pp. 454–5.

—, *John Keble, Saint of Anglicanism* (Macon, GA: Mercer University Press, 1987).

Hayden, J. O., *The Romantic Reviewers: 1809–1824* (Chicago, IL: Chicago University Press, 1968).

Hilton, Boyd, *The Age of Atonement: The Influence of Evangelicalism on Social and Economic Thought, 1785–1865* (Oxford: Oxford University Press, 1988).

—, *A Mad, Bad, And Dangerous People?: England 1783–1846* (Oxford: Oxford University Press, 2006).

—, '"Sardonic Grins" and "Paranoid Politics": Religion, Economics, and Public Policy in the *Quarterly Review*' in Cutmore (ed.), *Conservatism and the Quarterly Review* (London: Pickering and Chatto, 2007), pp. 41–60.

Houghton, W. E. (ed.), *The Wellesley Index to Victorian Periodicals 1824–1900*, 5 vols (Toronto: University of Toronto Press, 1966–87).

Johnson, E., *Sir Walter Scott: The Great Unknown*, 2 vols (London: Hamish Hamilton, 1970).

Kaderly, N. L., 'Southey and the *Quarterly Review*', (London: Pickering & Chatto, 2007) *Modern Language Notes*, 70:4 (April, 1955), pp. 261–3.

Kramnick, J. B., *Making the English Canon: Print-Capitalism and the Cultural Past, 1700–1770* (Cambridge: Cambridge University Press, 1998).

Levy, S. L., [and F. W. Fetter], *Nassau W. Senior: The Prophet of Modern Capitalism* (Boston, MA: Bruce Humphries, 1943).

Lipking, L., *Ordering of the Arts in Eighteenth-Century England* (Princeton, NJ: Princeton University Press, 1970).

Martin, C., 'William Scoresby Jr. (1789–1857) and the Open Polar Sea – Myth and Reality', *Arctic*, 41 (1988), pp. 39–47.

Matthew, H. C. G., and B. Harrison (eds.), *Oxford Dictionary of National Biography* (Oxford: Oxford University Press, 2004); online edn, ed. Lawrence Goldman.

Meacham, S., *Henry Thornton of Clapham, 1760–1815* (Cambridge, MA: Harvard University Press, 1964).

Millgate, J. (ed.), *The Millgate Union Catalogue of Walter Scott Correspondence* – National Library of Scotland <www.nls.uk> (accessed 8 November 2007).

Newman, G., *The Rise of English Nationalism: A Cultural History 1740–1830* (London: Weidenfeld and Nicolson, 1987).

Peacock, G., *Life of Thomas Young* (London: John Murray, 1855).

Pratt L., 'Hung, Drawn and Quarterlyed: Robert Southey, Poetry, Poets, and the *Quarterly Review*', in J. Cutmore (ed.), *Conservatism and the Quarterly Review: A Critical Analysis* (London: Pickering and Chatto, 2007), pp. 151–64.

Ragaz, S., 'Walter Scott and the *Quarterly Review*', in J. Cutmore (ed.), *Conservatism and the Quarterly Review: A Critical Analysis* (London: Pickering and Chatto, 2007), pp. 107–32.

Ragussis, M., *Figures of Conversion: "The Jewish Question" and English National Identity* (Durham, NC: Duke University Press, 1995).

Reiman, D. H., *The Romantics Reviewed: Contemporary Reviews of British Romantic Writers*, 5 vols (New York: Garland, 1972).

Roper, D., *Reviewing Before the Edinburgh, 1788–1802* (Cranbury, NJ: University of Delaware Press, 1978).

Ryan, R. M., and A. R. Sharp, *The Persistence of Poetry, Bicentennial Essays on Keats* (Amherst: University of Massachusetts Press, 1998).

Sack, J. J., *From Jacobite to Conservative: Reaction and Orthodoxy in Britain, c. 1760–1832* (Cambridge: Cambridge University Press, 1993).

Saglia, D., *Poetic Castles in Spain: British Romanticism and Figurations of Iberia* (Atlanta, GA: Rodopi, 1999).

Shattock, J., *Politics and Reviewers: The Edinburgh and the Quarterly in the Early Victorian Age* (Leicester: Leicester University Press, 1989).

Shine, H., and H. C. Shine, *The Quarterly Review Under Gifford: Identification of Contributors* (Chapel Hill, NC: University of North Carolina Press, 1949).

Sorenson, J., *The Grammar of Empire* (Cambridge: Cambridge University Press, 2000).

Speck, B., 'Robert Southey's Contribution to the *Quarterly Review*', in J. Cutmore (ed.), *Conservatism and the Quarterly Review: A Critical Analysis* (London: Pickering and Chatto, 2007), pp. 165–77.

Stray, C. A., 'Politics, Culture, and Scholarship: Classics in the *Quarterly Review*', in J. Cutmore (ed.), *Conservatism and the Quarterly Review: A Critical Analysis* (London: Pickering and Chatto, 2007), pp. 87–106.

Sutherland, J., *The Life of Walter Scott* (London: Blackwell, 1995).

Thomas, W., *The Quarrel of Macaulay and Croker: Politics and History in the Age of Reform* (Oxford: Oxford University Press, 2000).

—, 'Religion and Politics in the *Quarterly Review*, 1809–1853', in Stefan Collini, et al. (eds), *History, Religion, and Culture: British Intellectual History 1750–1950* (Cambridge: Cambridge University Press, 2000), pp. 136–55.

Thompson, E. P., *The Making of the English Working Class* (New York: Vintage, 1963).

Thorne, R. G. (ed.), *The History of the House of Commons 1790–1820 (The History of Parliament)*, 5 vols (London: Secker and Warburg, 1986).

Todd, W. B., and A. Bowden, *Sir Walter Scott: A Bibliographical History 1796–1832* (New Castle, DE: Oak Knoll Press, 1998).

Trumpener, K., *Bardic Nationalism: Romantic Novel and the British Empire* (Princeton, NJ: Princeton University Press, 1997).

Tunnicliffe, S., 'A Newly Discovered Source for the Early Life of William Gifford', *Review of English Studies*, n.s. 16 and 61 (1965), pp. 25–34.

Wechselblatt, M., 'The Canonical Ossian', in Greg Clingham (ed.), *Making History: Textuality and the Forms of Eighteenth Century Culture* (Lewisburg, PA: Bucknell University Press, 1998), pp. 19–34.

Wheatley, K., 'Plotting the Success of the *Quarterly Review*', in J. Cutmore (ed.), *Conservatism and the Quarterly Review: A Critical Analysis* (London: Pickering and Chatto, 2007), pp. 19–39.

Williams, O., *Lamb's Friend the Census-Taker: Life and Letters of John Rickman* (London: Constable, 1911).

INDEX OF AUTHORSHIP ATTRIBUTIONS

The index is keyed to article serial numbers assigned in Appendix A.

GENERAL INDEX

This General Index excludes Appendix A, for which see the Index to Authorship Attributions.